W9-CFO-267

Palestine

A Twice-Promised Land?

VOLUME 1

Palestine
A Twice-Promised Land?

The British, the Arabs & Zionism
1915–1920

Isaiah Friedman

Transaction Publishers
New Brunswick (U.S.A.) and London (U.K.)

Copyright © 2000 by Transaction Publishers, New Brunswick, New Jersey 08903.

All rights reserved under International and Pan-American Copyright Conventions. No part of this book may be reproduced or transmitted in any form or by any means, electronic or mechanical, including photocopy, recording, or any information storage and retrieval system, without prior permission in writing from the publisher. All inquiries should be addressed to Transaction Publishers, Rutgers—The State University, 35 Berrue Circle, Piscataway, New Jersey 08854-8042.

This book is printed on acid-free paper that meets the American National Standard for Permanence of Paper for Printed Library Materials.

Library of Congress Catalog Number: 99-30396
ISBN: 1-56000-391-X
Printed in the United States of America

Library of Congress Cataloging-in-Publication Data

Friedman, Isaiah
    Palestine, a twice-promised land? / Isaiah Friedman.
        p. cm.
    Includes bibliographical references and index.
    Contents: v. 1. The British, the Arabs, and Zionism,
    ISBN 1-56000-391-X (alk. paper)
    1. Palestine—History—1917–1948. 2. Palestine—Politics and government—1917–1948. 3. Jewish–Arab relations—History—1917–1948.
4. Great Britian—Foreign relations—Middle East. 5. Middle East—Foreign relations—Great Britain. I. Title.
    DS126.F76 1999
    327.41056' 09' 041—dc21   99-30396
                                                                                    CIP

In memory of my parents,

to whom I owe more than I can possibly convey.

Contents

Acknowledgments

As in my previous publications, I humbly acknowledge the wisdom of my Alma Mater's motto: *Rerum Cognoscere Causas*. It was there that I first acquired the craftsmanship of a historian, the respect for detail and for a detached presentation. I cherish the memory of the late Professor W. N. Medlicott, Stevenson Professor of International History at the London School of Economics and Political Science, and of his successor, the late Professor James Joll. During and after my post-graduate studies at the School they gave me unstintingly of their time and knowledge whenever I turned to them for advice. I was particularly touched by Professor Medlicott's warmth and friendship. Shortly before he died I was permitted to visit him in Richmond, Surrey. I assured him that my study would vindicate the British Government of the day and show that their hands were clean. He greeted my statement with a mixture of disbelief and delight. His comments and good wishes have imprinted themselves deeply in my memory. I was extremely fortunate to have the goodwill of the late Professor Sir Isaiah Berlin, O.M. His interest and faith in my work over thirty-six years were a constant source of encouragement and have left an indelible impression on me. I am sorry that none of the three mentioned have survived to see this work completed.

I am grateful to Professor Michael Leifer, then Chairman of the Steering Committee of the Centre for International Studies at LSE for inviting me to join the Centre as a visiting Fellow during the years 1989-1991. I had numerous useful conversations with him and benefited from his scholarly advice. I have had the great privilege of Lord Beloff closely reading my chapters. I am greatly indebted to him for his many vital insights and giving me generously of his time.

Mrs. Catherine Logan has been more than a typist. I have learned to appreciate her prudent and expert advice. I should like to express my warm thanks. I am also greatly indebted to Mr. Pieter Loupin, the cartographer of the Department of Geography, Ben-Gurion University of the Negev, for scanning so skillfully the appendices and the material for the preamble, and for his expert scanning and preparation of the maps for publication. I am sure that my appreciation of his labor will be shared by the readers of my book.

My article on the "McMahon-Hussein Correspondence" and the ensuing dialogue with Professor Arnold J. Toynbee, which appears in the "Preamble," are republished with the permission of Professor Walter Laqueur, the Editor of the *Journal of Contemporary History*. I gladly acknowledge his generous assistance in this, as well as in other matters in the past.

I should also like to record my indebtedness to the staff of many libraries and archives: the British Library of the London School of Economics and Political Science, the London University Library, the British Museum, the National Library of the Hebrew University, the Aranne Library of the University of Ben-Gurion in the Negev, the Central Zionist Archives, as well as the Israel State Archives, Jerusalem, the Ha'aganah Archives, Tel-Aviv, the Weizmann Archives, Rehovot, the Wingate Archives at the School of Oriental Studies, Durham, and particularly to the Public Records Office, London. My study would not have been possible without the wealth of documents which have become available there. Transcripts and quotations of Crown Copyright material appear by permission of the Controller of H. M. Stationary Office.

My debt to my wife, Barbara, remains the greatest of all. She has read my manuscript, and her advice and encouragement have been invaluable.

I do not believe that it is customary for a author to thank his publishers, but in this particular case I feel it would be appropriate to express my appreciation to Professor Irving L. Horowitz, Editorial Chairman of Transaction Publishers, as well as to Mrs. Mary E. Curtis, President and Publisher, for their patience and forbearance with the long delay in my completion of the manuscript of this book. Inevitably, my study expanded much beyond its originally planned scope. I hope that, like the readers, they will feel rewarded by having two volumes, instead of one.

Finally, I am grateful to Ben-Gurion University of the Negev for a generous grant to cover expenses incurred in compiling the index and for the preparation of the camera-ready copy of my manuscript.

Isaiah Friedman
Ben-Gurion University of the Negev, Israel
March 1999

Introduction

The notion that during World War I the British Government made conflicting commitments to Arabs, to the French, and to the Jews has become almost a cliché. This belief had serious political and moral implications; it impinged on Britain's standing and good faith. The French were resentful of the systematic attempts made by British military officers to undermine their position in Syria. The Muslims in India and elsewhere were incensed at the destruction of the Ottoman Empire and the encouragement given by Britain to Hussein, the Sharif of Mecca, to rebel against the Caliph. The Arabs regarded themselves to have been cheated. They maintained that, when an agreement had been negotiated with Sharif Hussein to grant the Arabs independence, the Allies, without telling Hussein, had divided the Ottoman Asiatic provinces among themselves as future spoils of the war. They condemned the Sykes-Picot Agreement as "a product of greed and a startling piece of double-dealing."

Palestine, in particular, was a controversial issue engendering passionate debate: the Zionists were aggrieved by the gradual whittling down of the Balfour Declaration and the failure of the British Government to live up to its commitments according to the terms of the Mandate, while the Palestine Arabs pointed to the Balfour Declaration as the root of all their troubles. The latter maintained that, in his letter of 24 October 1915, Sir Henry McMahon, the High Commissioner in Egypt, promised the Arabs independence. However, the "pledge," they insisted, was violated. It was this letter of 24 October 1915 that was at the center of the controversy and the subject of hair-splitting exegesis.

In spite of persistent official disclaimers, the idea that the British Government had made conflicting commitments did not go away. It was embraced by some well-meaning and sincere, albeit misguided, British intellectuals. Thus, characteristically, on 26 October 1930, Beatrice Webb noted in her *Diaries*: "The man on the spot gave promises to the Arabs; the British Cabinet gave promises to the Jews."[1] In the late thirties, Arnold Toynbee propagated these arguments on numerous occasions, infecting British intellectuals with feelings of guilt and shame. The appearance of George Antonius's book, *The Arab Awakening* (1938), spread the idea that the British had defrauded the Arabs. This book came to be regarded as the most authoritative guide to Anglo-Arab relations during World War I. Foreign Office officials admired his work to the total neglect of searching in their own records. It imbued them with a corrosive feeling of embarrassment and eroded their conviction in the justice of the British case. It had a demoralizing effect on British Middle Eastern policy-makers.

Geoffery Furlonge, a former Head of the Eastern Department, in a biography of Musa al-Alami, a Palestinian notable, subscribed unreservedly to Antonius's thesis.[2] J. R. Colville, who served as secretary of the British representatives on the committee set up to investigate the McMahon-Hussein Correspondence during the London Conference in 1939, confirmed in his book that the Balfour Declaration "promised the Jews a home," but in the same breath stated that Sir Henry McMahon, in his correspondence with the King of the Hedjaz, "had assured the Arabs . . . that when they were liberated from the rule of the Turkish Sultan, all Arabia, including Palestine, should be theirs to inhabit and govern."[3] Such a statement is all the more remarkable, since the same committee, headed by Lord Maugham, Lord Chancellor, had concluded just the opposite, and Colville had had a hand in drafting the Committee's report.[4]

Misperceptions plagued British officials. To quote yet another glaring example, Sir Hugh Foot (later Lord Caradon), who served officially in Palestine and the Middle East for about fifteen years, declared in his memoirs:

> The failure of British administration in Palestine was inevitable. The double sin had been committed of raising false hopes both with the Arabs and with Jews. The hopes were false be-

cause they were conflicting. The Arabs who fought with Great Britain in the first world war to throw off the yoke of the Turkish Empire were led to believe that they were fighting for their freedom ... the main responsibility was ours ... by prevarication and procrastination and basically by the fundamental dishonesty of our original double dealing we had made disaster certain. ... In 1915 we supported King Feisal's desert rising. In 1917 we signed the Balfour Declaration.[5]

Breast-beating was contagious. It was practiced in the press and in some of the history books. Thus, Elizabeth Monroe, wrote in her book: "Measured by British interests alone [the Balfour Declaration] was one of the greatest mistakes in our imperial history."[6]

It was therefore in the late 1960s, when the British records for the period of 1914-1922 were opened to the public for inspection at the Public Record Office, London, that I immersed myself enthusiastically in the official files in order to find out what had really happened. I was fortunate to be the first scholar to do so. In my book, *The Question of Palestine 1914-1918*,[7] I challenged the view current among British historians, that the Balfour Declaration was the result of miscalculation, a product of sentiment rather than of considered interests of the state, and showed that there was no incompatibility between the Sykes-Picot Agreement and the Correspondence with the Sharif of Mecca—that Sir Henry McMahon had definitely excluded Palestine and so it was understood by Hussein at that time. The idea that Palestine was a "twice-promised land" was without foundation.

A chapter of *The Question of Palestine*, "The McMahon-Hussein Correspondence and the Question of Palestine," was published in the *Journal of Contemporary History* (April 1970) and a dialogue between Professor Arnold Toynbee and myself appeared thereafter in the same journal. For the readers' convenience, these are republished in the preamble to this volume.

In due course I found to my amazement that, during World War I and thereafter, Toynbee had been a convinced Zionist—not only out of narrow British interests, but also ideologically. On the other hand, he was not at all sympathetic toward the Arabs. I also discovered how his ill-conceived notion of the "twice-promised land" originated. (See Chapters 3 and 4). His much quoted "Memorandum on British Commitments to King Hussein" (October/November 1918), which was widely circulated in print, misled a great number of British statesmen, officials, and, consequently, also historians. Armed with this newly found data, I approached Toynbee, asking him for some clarifications. To my regret he remained silent.

To probe into such a complicated subject, I felt that a more comprehensive study of British Middle Eastern policy was called for. The documentary material was immense. It was not until the years 1989-1991, when I was a visiting Fellow at the Centre for International Studies at LSE, that I was able to devote all of my time to research at the Public Record Office and elsewhere.

I think I have showed in the present study that McMahon's letter of 24 October 1915 was not a legal letter, as it had been treated heretofore, but a political and nonbinding document. It was a part of a series of letters that were inconclusive and left in abeyance until the Peace Conference. Moreover, the letter did not bear a *unilateral* nature, as it has been misrepresented; the "pledge" for Arab independence was conditioned on the general Arab uprising in the whole area of the Fertile Crescent. The British, as well as the Allies, committed themselves merely to recognize and uphold Arab independence in the area liberated by the Arabs themselves. From all that we now know, only the tribes in the Hedjaz, and thereafter those in the territory east of the River Jordan, rebelled against the Turks; the Arabs in Palestine, Syria, and Mesopotamia fought shoulder to shoulder with the Ottoman troops against the British. If any party remained in debt toward the other, it was rather the Arabs to the British than vice versa.

Gallons of ink have been spilled on the meaning of the phrase "district of Damascus." I was fortunate to discover at the Public Records Office the Arabic version of McMahon's letter of 24 October 1915—which was thought to have been lost—as well as its retranslation into English made at the British Residency in Cairo in November 1919. Of the latter document, neither the Foreign Office, nor any historian, was aware. By juxtaposing these two documents and comparing them to McMahon's original letter of 24 October 1915, it becomes crystal clear that the Arab term *wilāya*, the Ottoman vilayet, and the English "district" were identical in meaning, and so it was understood at the time by the contemporary *dramatis personae*, both British and Arab. The "district of Damascus" covered the whole area, which later became Trans-Jordan, down to Ma'an and Akaba.

Although this startling discovery may well lay the long drawn-out controversy finally to rest, I thought it expedient not to limit myself to the analysis of the Correspondence and its implications, but also to describe the surrounding circumstances, to trace the genesis of the policy, and to examine whether it paid off. I tried to re-examine the rationale behind the Inter-Allied Agreement (May 1916), commonly known as the Sykes-Picot Agreement—whether it was compatible with the arrangement with King Hussein and whether there was any substance in later accusations that this Agreement had been deliberately concealed from King Hussein.

In view of French complaints in the aftermath of the war that the British did not play fair with them in Syria, I tried to investigate how Damascus had been captured in October 1918, and particularly to examine the conduct of British officers, first and foremost, as to whether their activities conformed with official policy.

During the interwar period and after, the Palestinian delegations buttressed their case on McMahon's letter of 24 October 1915, jealously regarding it as their title-deed to Palestine. It was therefore of prime importance to find out what Hussein's understanding of the Correspondence with the High Commissioner was, and what was his response to the British Jewish National Home policy. Investigation into Emir Feisal's motives for concluding an agreement with Chaim Weizmann and into the reasons for its failure also provided some interesting insights.

In the second volume of this study, subtitled *The Creation of the Historical Myth: 1920-1939* (forthcoming), I have described the role of Herbert Samuel, the High Commissioner, in shaping the Palestinian policy and have tried to show how Winston Churchill, the Colonial Secretary, did carry out British commitments to the Arabs during the conferences in Cairo and Jerusalem in March 1921. At this juncture it was necessary also to demonstrate how Churchill, as well as succeeding British Governments, viewed their obligations toward the Jews, as embodied in the Balfour Declaration and the Mandate.

Confrontation between the Palestinian leadership and the British is the central theme of volume two. Particularly intriguing is the question of how the loophole in McMahon's much-quoted letter was discovered, consequently opening the floodgates to endless controversy. George Antonius and his *Arab Awakening* will be the subject of special scrutiny, and, in the concluding chapter, there will appear a critical review of bibliography.

Perhaps the greatest delight for an historian is when he is able to revise stereotyped versions and demythologize deeply ingrained theories. A subject of this nature, laden with emotion and mired with distortions, is a veritable challenge to any student of history. I, for one, have endeavored to treat the subject matter as a purely academic issue. Intellectual curiosity alone propelled my research and examination of a huge mass of documentation. If I were to be asked what is the ultimate criterion for judging an historian, I would summarize in one word: honesty. I sincerely hope that in this study too, I have lived up to the very generous compliment that Arnold Toynbee paid me in his "Comments."

Preamble

The McMahon-Hussein Correspondence and the Question of Palestine*

The controversy over this question is half a century old. Today it has no more than an academic interest, but in the past the keenest brains in Middle East politics were pitted against each other to prove their respective cases, only to demonstrate the gulf that separated them. Despite statements made by the high-ranking British officers directly involved in negotiations with the Arab leaders, passions did not subside. To those who could see only duplicity in the conduct of the British government of the time, the slogan of the "twice-promised land" became almost an article of faith. It infected some well-meaning and sincere, albeit misguided, British intellectuals.

Publication of the relevant records could have dispelled much of the misunderstanding, but, though this was urged in both Houses of Parliament since 1921, successive British governments objected on the ground that publication would be "detrimental to the public interest."[1] The refusal to allow publication was due not to the weakness of the British government's case, as its critics suspected, but to considerations entirely unconnected with Palestine. The chief reason for official secrecy, as we are now able to learn, was that the correspondence contained encouragement to the Sherif of Mecca (given both by Lord Kitchener and his successor as High Commissioner in Egypt, Sir Henry McMahon) to rebel against the Sultan-Caliph in Constantinople and seek the Caliphate for himself with British assistance. Publication of this fact, it was feared, would have precipitated a storm of indignation in the Moslem world, particularly in India, with most embarrassing consequences. The Foreign Office held the view that it would not be possible to publish part of the correspondence, omitting the allusions to the Caliphate, that partial publication would almost certainly lead to complete publication, and, still worse, would have involved raking up the detailed history of serious disagreements between the British and French governments respecting the Near East in the latter part of the first world war and the earlier armistice period.[2]

Whatever the merits of these considerations, official records now available for research provide us with the long-awaited opportunity to re-examine this complex problem.[3] But before venturing to investigate whether or not Palestine was included in McMahon's pledge to Sherif Hussein, it is pertinent first to appraise the nature of the British commitments to the Arabs, to ask whether they bore a *unilateral* character — heretofore the accepted criterion by which Anglo-Sherifian relations were judged — or whether the other party, the Arabs, were equally under certain obligations, the discharge of which conditioned the validity of the understanding. Textual examination of the correspondence alone will not lead us far. The task of interpretation requires a reconstruction of what went on behind the official façade and a scrutiny of the motives and expectations of the chief *dramatis personae*.

The dominant theme in the correspondence is "Arab independence." This loosely used phrase caused much misunderstanding. What did it mean? A note written by Sir Edward Grey, the Foreign Secretary, to Sir James Rodd, the ambassador in Rome, on 21 September 1916, is illuminating:

> The Shereef of Mecca had communicated to the [Anglo-]Egyptian authorities his desire to make himself independent but had insisted upon knowing whether we were prepared to recognize an independent Arab State. We were, of course, prepared to do that if he succeeded in establishing his independence; for all we were pledged to was that the Moslem holy places should remain in independent Moslem hands.[4]

This tallies with Grey's earlier communication. On 14 April he had authorized Sir Reginald Wingate, Sirdar of the Sudan, to inform the Sherif of Mecca that the British government "will make it an essential condition, in any terms of peace, that the Arabian Peninsula and its Mohammedan Holy Places should remain in the hands of an independent Sovereign Moslem State." The message was apparently passed on to Hussein by Seyyid Sir Ali Morghani, Grand Kadi of the Sudan, who was in close contact with Wingate. By the end of June, its substance was embodied in a proclamation which was distributed in the form of a leaflet in Arabia, and on 29 July 1916, following the Sherifian revolt against Turkey, an official communiqué to the same effect was made public.[5]

Hence it would be fair to deduce that, apart from the Holy Places, Britain (as well as the Allied governments) was not pledged to the establishment of an independent Arab state or confederation of states. It was up to the Arabs themselves to make good their aspirations to independence. But as there was no likelihood of their being able to stand on their own feet, it was natural for the British and French governments to fill the vacuum and assume the role of "protectors."[6] Absence of a protective shield would have inevitably invited "foreign [i.e., Turkish] aggression," nipping the scheme of an Arab state or confederation of states in the bud. It was to make the creation of an Arab entity possible, as well as to harmonize it with their own legitimate interests in that region, that the British and French governments concluded the Sykes-Picot Agreement. Although this document became notorious in ensuing years, there was nothing in it that was inconsistent with McMahon's pledge.

It is evident that, at that time, neither the Arabs nor the British took the meaning of "independence" in its literal sense. The Arabs, Sir Mark Sykes disclosed to the War Committee after his return from the East, "must ask for theoretical independence, otherwise, if they ask for an obvious European tutelage, the Committee of Union and Progress will take the reactionary party over on their side."[7] Despite his grandiose claim, Hussein was well aware of his own limitations. Hence his request for "assistance" in order to ensure "the stability of Arab independence." Not only was he apprehensive of "constant provocations . . . and utmost vengeance" from the Turks during the war should Britain leave him alone, but even after its termination.[8] McMahon indeed reassured the Sherif that Britain would not conclude "any peace . . . of which the freedom of the Arab peoples and their liberation from the German and Turkish domination do not form an essential condition"[9]; and it is only in this context that the meaning of Arab "independence" should be understood: liberation from their adversaries, not necessarily independence. Neither to Sherif Hussein nor to any other Arab leader did the British "ever explicitly guarantee or even promise anything beyond liberation from the Turk."[10] This was the testimony of David G. Hogarth, formerly Director of the Arab Bureau in Cairo, a scholar of repute who had intimate knowledge of Anglo-Arab relations.

Least of all did the sponsors of the Arab movement themselves take the word "independence" at its face value. What McMahon had in mind was, as he told Grey, recognition of "the principle of Arab independence," but no more. When read together with the text of a subsequent cable, we may well deduce that the term was merely a convenient substitute for autonomy: "I have endeavoured in my statement to Sherif Hussein [of 24 October, 1915] to make any such future Arab state (within the British sphere) subject to our creation, direction and control." The term "independent Sovereign State," Grey had been told six months earlier, "has been interpreted in a generic sense because idea of an Arabian unity under one ruler, recognized as supreme by other Arab chiefs, is as yet inconceivable to [the] Arab mind."[11] Lt-Col., later General Sir Gilbert Clayton, Director of Military Intelligence in Cairo and one of McMahon's chief advisers, denied that it was his intention to promote "the establishment of a powerful Arab Kingdom . . . all we want is to keep the friendship and, if possible, the active assistance of the various Arab chiefs . . . while at the same time, working towards maintenance of the *status quo ante bellum,* and merely eliminating Turkish domination from Arabia." Five weeks later he confided to another friend:

> to set up a great Arab State . . . was never my idea. . . . The conditions throughout Arabia, Syria and Mesopotamia did not allow of such a scheme being practical, even if anyone were so foolish as to attempt it. . . . The object we have to aim at is, I

consider, to work to preserve all the various elements in the Arab territories very much in the same position as they were before the war, but minus the Turks. In this way we shall have an open field to work in.[12]

The underlying assumption was that the Arabs for some time to come were bound to need European assistance and protection. This situation, as Clayton saw it, offered an opportunity for the British to step in. The term "independence" was merely a euphemism for supersession of Turkish rule by British and French in their respective spheres of interest. Looked at from this point of view, the concessions made to Sherif Hussein were not so far-reaching as they appeared, and it explains why McMahon, in his celebrated letter of 24 October 1915 to the Sherif of Mecca, granted them so lightly, though this is not the whole explanation.

When, in mid-August, Hussein's note of 14 July 1915 arrived in Cairo to open the long-drawn-out correspondence, it was received at the British Residency with astonishment. "It was at the time and still is my opinion," commented Ronald Storrs, its Oriental Secretary, "that the Sharif opened his mouth and the British Government their purse a good deal too wide. . . . We could not conceal from ourselves (and with difficulty from him) that his pretensions bordered upon the tragicomic,"[13] These related to the comprehensive demand for recognition of the independence of the Arab countries bounded on the north by the line Mersina-Adana to parallel 37°N, to include the whole of the Arabian peninsula (except Aden), Mesopotamia, Syria, what was later Transjordan, and Palestine. Hussein's messenger, Muhammed Ibn Arif, who brought this letter to Cairo, assured Storrs on his master's behalf that the Arabs were "ready and well prepared"; "our word," Abdullah, Hussein's son, asked him to tell Storrs, "is a word of honour and we will carry it out even at the cost of our lives; we are not under the order of the Turks but the Turks are under our orders." Arab officers in the Ottoman army, Ibn Arif went on, had sworn allegiance to the Sherif and were prepared to fight under his banner. Many had deserted already and consequently Hussein's prestige had become so paramount that even the Sultan had proclaimed him Chief Governor and Administrator of Hedjaz, with the Wali "under his orders." But Storrs was not deceived. "It may be regarded as certain," he noted, "that [Hussein] has received no sort of mandate from other [Arab] potentates." As to the territorial desideratum, "he knows he is demanding, possibly as a basis for negotiations, far more than he has the right, the hope, or the power to expect. Like his co-religionists elsewhere, he will modify his tone later."[14] To McMahon, Hussein's profession of "sincere friendship" was welcome, as was the idea of "reversion of the caliphate to a true Arab"; but as to the question of frontiers and boundaries, so long as the war was in progress and the Turks' occupation of their Asiatic provinces effective, negotiations were "premature and waste of time."[15]

McMahon's negative response was fully in line with the attitude adopted by Grey, who was reluctant to commit himself to delimitation of territory of the projected Arab state, particularly in the north.[16] The predicament confronting him emerges clearly from a note quoted earlier (above, note 4):

> We had no difficulty in agreeing to any boundaries which the Shereef wanted on the south [i.e., in the Arabian Peninsula] but on the north the Shereef came up against Syria, where we had always admitted French interest and the French would not make concessions to the Shereef of places like Damascus without knowing what the limits of their sphere were to be.

But McMahon had additional grounds for pouring cold water on Arab territorial desiderata: Syrian Arabs, instead of aiding the British, "have lent their assistance to the Germans and the Turks," he reminded the Sherif on 30 August 1915. What then made McMahon change his mind two months later and yield so generously to Hussein's demands, as is apparent from his letter of 24 October 1915?

It was the arrival of Muhammad Sherif al-Faruqi in Cairo that constituted the decisive turning point. Al-Faruqi[17] was an Arab staff officer in the Ottoman army and a prominent member of a Young Arab secret society called al-'Ahd, an off-shoot of the civilian al-Fatat. On some pretext, he managed to make his way to the English lines in Gallipoli, whence he was taken to Cairo. Under interrogation, he revealed to Colonel Clayton that Young Arab secret societies in Syria and Mesopotamia had decided to cooperate with England in return for British support for Arab independence. Learning of Sherif Hussein's communication with the British High Commissioner in Cairo, and realizing how far-reaching the consequences might be, they hastened to stake their claim to the northern boundary of the Arab Empire. This would follow the Mersina-Diarbekir line. Direct contact was established thereafter with Jedda. Al-Faruqi claimed that the Young Arab party wielded great influence in Syria and Mesopotamia and that Turkey and Germany, alive to this fact, had approached their leaders and promised to meet their demands "in full." The Young Arabs, however, trusted England and preferred a deal with her, but unless they received a favorable reply within a few weeks, the Young Arabs would throw in their lot with Turkey and Germany in order to secure the best terms they could.[18]

We learn from Antonius that, early in the war, the *al-Fatat* committee passed a resolution "to work on the side of Turkey in order to resist foreign penetration of whatever kind or form," but shortly after Emir Feisal's arrival in Damascus on 26 March 1915, they switched their allegiance and decided on cooperation with Britain against Turkey; their so-called "Damascus Protocol"[19] served later as a blueprint for Hussein, in his letter to McMahon of 14 July 1915, to outline the boundaries for Arab independence. But al-Faruqi's statement on a rival proposition by Turkey and Germany is puzzling. Antonius is silent about it. Moreover, no evidence of such an offer can be traced in the German Foreign Ministry files. If anything, it is rather to the contrary. The Young Turk government, with its strong centralist disposition, was in no mood to grant the Arabs autonomy, let alone independence, and with Djemal Pasha's autocratic rule in Syria and Palestine, this was a practical impossibility. As for the Germans, though not slow to criticize Turkish short-sightedness, any negotiation with an Arab secret society behind the back of their ally was out of the question.

German records belie al-Faruqi's testimony on Young Arab influence and the revolutionary fervor among the population. "The anti-Turk movement . . . aiming at Arab autonomy," Dr. Prüffer, the Consul-General in Damascus, reported early in December 1915, "appears much to be weakened. Among the wealthier middle classes, reformism has scarcely any suppor-

ters, and among the small land-owners, merchants and wor-
kers, who constitute the bulk of the population, the cause of the
Ottoman Government is quite popular. . . . The brilliant succes-
ses of the Ottoman army strengthened the confidence of the
people in the future of the Empire." The anti-Turkish elements
enjoyed little support and, with the population riven by
dissent, an uprising had little chance of success. Prüffer's successor, Dr. Loytved-Hardegg, by no means an anti-Arab,
assured Berlin five months later that "no rebellion need be
feared in Syria. The Syrians are shopkeepers but no warriors.
They are little gifted for the profession of revolutionaries."[20]
Djemal Pasha had only praise for the loyalty of the Arab regiments in his army. He could find no better proof of his conviction that "the Arab would not revolt and turn traitor."[21]

In view of this evidence, al-Faruqi's report about Turco-
German overtures to the *al-'Ahd* and *al-Fatat* societies, and the
latter's ability to foment a revolt against the Ottoman government, merits little credence. Moreover, it would be reasonable
to assume that this tale was deliberately fabricated in order to
strengthen the Arabs' bargaining position vis-à-vis the British,
as in fact it did. How successful al-Faruqi was can be gauged
from the impression he made on his interrogator, Colonel Clayton, who thought his proposals "very grave and of urgent
importance," and that the rebellious position adopted by the
Sherif reflected that "of the majority of the Arab peoples."
Should the British prove accommodating, the Young Arab Committee would embark "at once" on their operations in Syria,
Palestine, Baghdad, and Mosul, where their influence was
great. On the other hand, rejection, or even evasion, of the
proposals, Clayton feared, would "throw the Young Arab
party definitely into the arms of the enemy. Their machinery
will at once be employed against us throughout the Arab
countries, and the various Arab chiefs, who are almost to a
man members of, or connected with, the Young Arab party, will
be undoubtedly won over . . . the *Jehad*, so far a failure, may
become a very grim reality, the effect of which . . . might well be
disastrous."[22]

Clayton was a shrewd and down-to-earth man. Few could
rival his experience with the native Arabic-speaking people;
and his "balanced advice," as Storrs put it, could not be

hustled by a sudden crisis.[23] His acceptance of al-Faruqi's account is, therefore difficult to comprehend. Was it because of faulty intelligence and inadequate information on the true state of affairs behind the Turkish lines,[24] or because, following the setback at the Dardanelles, the fear of a *jehad* was so all-pervading that British officers in Egypt were apt to grasp at every floating straw to relieve them of their growing feeling of isolation. Whatever the reason, it was on the basis of these findings that General Sir John Maxwell, Officer Commanding in Egypt, urged Lord Kitchener, then Secretary of State for War, that it was imperative to meet Hussein's wishes:

> A powerful organization . . . of the Young Arab Committee . . . with considerable influence in the [Ottoman] army and among Arab chiefs . . . appears to have made up its mind that the moment for action has arrived. The Turks and Germans are already in negotiations with them and spending money to win their support. The Arab Party is, however, strongly inclined towards England. . . . If their overtures are rejected, or a reply is delayed . . . the Arab party will go over to the enemy and work with them. . . . On the other hand, their active assistance . . . in return for our support, would be of the greatest value in Arabia, Mesopotamia, Syria and Palestine.[25]

Kitchener replied promptly: "The Government is most-desirous of dealing with the Arab question in a manner satisfactory to the Arabs. You must do your best to prevent any alienation of the Arabs' traditional loyalty to England." McMahon too pressed the Foreign Office to win over the Arabs through a speedy settlement of the boundaries, but only "in so far as England is free to act without detriment to the interests of her present Allies." This was urgent, because the Arab party in Syria was "ready to revolt . . . they are on the point of parting of their ways." The Sherif of Mecca was in communication with Imam Yehhia of Yemen and endeavored to dissuade him from aiding the Turks. It was therefore imperative, McMahon urged, to deal without delay.[26]

Grey, no less than Kitchener, appreciated the urgency of the matter and was favorably disposed. But suspecting (as it turned out quite correctly) some ulterior motives for the undue haste, he warned the High Commissioner to avoid giving the impression that the British supported Arab interests in Syria merely in order to establish their own at the expense of the French. However, McMahon, without further consultation, dispatched his crucial letter of 24 October 1915 to Sherif Hussein. Two days later he cabled that the matter brooked "no delay" and he had, therefore, to act "without further reference."[27] The Rubicon was crossed. The Arabs won their Magna Carta and Great Britain a standing embarrassment. The responsibility was solely that of McMahon.[28]

The India Office was aghast. Since Britain's declaration of war against Turkey, Moslem loyalty in India had been strained. The position was still more complicated because Hussein was highly unpopular among the pilgrims to Mecca for his high-handed methods. His rebellion against the Sultan, openly encouraged by the British, might have had an incalculable effect on Moslem opinion. Lord Hardinge, the Viceroy, bitterly complained that he had not been consulted before "a pledge of such vital importance was given to the Arabs." He thought that London should not have committed itself to such a policy at all. "We have always regarded with much [?diffidence] creation of strong Arab state lying astride our interests in the East and in the [Persian] Gulf as not unlikely source of ultimate trouble, and we doubt either military or political advantage likely to accrue from it."[29] Austen Chamberlain, Secretary of State for India, was also disturbed by McMahon's letter. According to his information, the Grand Sherif of Mecca was "a non-entity without power to carry out his proposals," the Arabs were "without unity and with no possibility of uniting" their followers. Chamberlain doubted the reality, and certainly the efficacy of the suggested Arab revolt in the Ottoman army and elsewhere. He pointed out that al-Idrissi, the Imam of Asir, and Ibn Saud, the Amir of Najd, friends of the British, were hostile to the Sherif, whereas the latter's friends, Imam Yehhia of Yemen, and Ibn Rashid, ruler of Hayil, were pro-Turk. Until therefore both the Sherif and Faruqi proved themselves able to carry out their promises, it was imprudent for the British Government to undertake any commitment. "The next step should be to make clear to them that promises made by McMahon are dependent on immediate action by them in sense of their offers and will not be binding on us unless they do their part at once."[30]

Lord Crewe, Chamberlain's immediate predecessor, now deputizing for Grey, also criticized McMahon for negotiating, as he put it, "without great wisdom."[31] Sir Arthur Hirtzel, head of the Political Department of the India Office, subscribed to the Chamberlain-Crewe appraisal. However, should it be considered expedient to pursue the negotiations with the Sherif, he noted, any commitments in future should be "as vague as possible" and made subject to the extent and success of Arab co-operation.[32]

McMahon disagreed with the India Office. He regarded the Sherif as a leader of importance, both by descent and personality, and the only rallying point for the Arab cause.[33] Yet, as his policy had been censured and Hussein remained elusive about the proposed revolt, McMahon adopted a tougher line. He urged Hussein in unequivocal terms:

> It is most essential that you spare no effort to attach all the Arab peoples to our united cause and urge them to afford no assistance to our enemies. It is on the success of these efforts and on the more active measures which the Arabs may thereafter take in support of our cause, when the time for action comes, that the permanence and strength of our agreement must depend.

Hussein thereupon assured McMahon that he fully "understood the contents" of his note.[34] There was thus no unilateral commitment. The Arabs were equally under definite obligations to fulfill their part, and it was on the nature and quality of their performance that the "permanence and strength" of the agreement depended.[35] That recognition of the "independence of the Arabs," in specified areas "south of latitude 37° was conditional on an Arab revolt," was testified also by T. E. Lawrence (in a letter to *The Times*, 11 September 1919), and confirmed by Lloyd George.[36]

During the winter and early spring of 1916, there seemed no reason for McMahon to question his trust in the Arabs. According to Brigadier-General W. M. Walton, British Political Resident in Aden, the Sherif of Mecca undertook to organize a "general rising" of Arabs against the Turks both in the Hedjaz and Syria. Simultaneously Idrissi and Imam Yehhia were to raise the standard of revolt in Asir and the Yemen. The Sherif estimated that he could raise a force of 250,000 men and measure up to the Turks.[37] Some of these good tidings McMahon learned directly from Hussein, who revealed in his letter of 18 February 1916 that his son Emir Feisal, at that time in Syria, was planning to attack the Turkish troops from the rear should the latter advance on the Suez Canal. Feisal was awaiting the arrival of troops from Aleppo and Mosul, 100,000 strong, the majority of whom were Arab. Thereafter Abdullah would deploy sufficient forces to buttress Feisal's rebellion and, should circumstances permit, would occupy the Hedjaz railway. This would mark "the beginning of the principal movement," entirely different from what the Turks expected.[38]

The news that Feisal would enlist the support of the native Arab element in the Ottoman army was very encouraging. However, as the Turco-German advance towards Egypt did not seem to be imminent, McMahon suggested that the Sherif employ the Arab tribes in the north to demolish the Baghdad railway instead. To prepare the ground, al-Faruqi and al-Masri were to infiltrate the Turkish lines. So elated was Sir Mark Sykes (at that time in Cairo) that, assuming that the Arab movement would lead to a successful rebellion in Syria and Hedjaz and that Arab troops would defect, he hoped that an "avenue [would be] open to liquidating Mesopotamian expedition and doing away with [this] theatre of war."[39]

However, these expectations proved misplaced. The British military authorities in Basra were sceptical as to the advisability of the al-Faruqi/al-Masri mission to Mesopotamia. Experience with Arab officers who had defected from the Ottoman army had been discouraging, and Turkish vigilance remained unabated. As time wore on and the much vaunted rising did not materialize, London became impatient. Grey warned McMahon not to go beyond assurances already given to the Sherif: "We are giving arms and money and the sole question is whether the Arabs will do their part." A week later, McMahon received the bad news from Hussein that "owing to dispersal of chiefs," the Syrians could neither engineer a revolution nor seize the Hedjaz railway. Instead, he asked the British to help the Anaizah tribes (on the eastern side of the river Jordan)

financially and blockade the coast of Yemen.[40] Its Imam remained loyal to Turkey and was reluctant to join forces with Hussein (see note 37). Colonel Clayton had now to admit that "a certain rapprochement" between the Arab decentralization party and the Turks had evidently taken place. A general Arab uprising seemed to be a mirage and Arab unity practically non-existent. The newly established Arab Bureau in Cairo arrived at the inescapable conclusion that the British had been misled. The Sherif had always posed as spokesman of the Arab nation, but in fact no such entity or organization existed; "nor, given the history, economic environment and character of the Arabs, can it be expected to exist."[41]

But the most crippling blow for McMahon was the revelation contained in Feisal's confidential message to his father. From its contents McMahon learned, much to his surprise, that Feisal wrote "as an upholder of Islam against Christian encroachment" and seemed to imply that, had the Turks been "strong enough to keep Moslem frontiers intact . . . he would have backed" them rather than the British. McMahon had to concede the bitter truth that the Hedjaz Arabs were "unlikely to act efficiently in Syria . . . or to cut the Baghdad Railway." He advised the Sherif to confine his action to Arabia proper and to recall Feisal. "We can safely trust Sherif but we have no guarantee of Feisal's attitude."[42]

Such a contraction of the original plan of the Arab revolt undermined much of the validity of the McMahon understanding with Hussein, but it did not make the High Commissioner draw the logical conclusions. Was it because he attached so little importance to his pledge[43] that he thought modification of the agreement with the Sherif superfluous? Or because such a suggestion would have *ipso facto* implied an admission of error in his policy and it was better to gloss over the issue altogether? Whatever the reason, McMahon continued the pretense that it was safe to back the Hedjaz revolt. At any rate, a public demonstration to the Moslem world that the Sherif was against the Turks was still a creditable achievement. Yet, however commendable, this was not why McMahon had agreed to meet such extravagant claims to recognize Arab independence in regions lying north of the Arabian peninsula.

Sir Arthur Nicolson was indignant. "As regards . . . the Sherif, I think we have gone quite far enough . . . we should wait for some action on his part. Hitherto, we had plenty of promises from him — but nothing more — while we have given him, beyond assurances, arms and money."[44] "The Arabs," as General Walton commented, "are waiting for our victories in other fields."[45] But it was not before the autumn of that year that the bubble exploded. Soon after Hussein had rebelled against the Turks on 6 June 1916, his forces were on the point of collapse. Wingate, much perturbed, cabled from Sudan: "unless supposed Syrian revolt interferes with . . . Turkish reinforcements . . . Sherif is faced with possible recapture of Medina and an advance on Mecca. . . . He will have to choose then between accepting offer by us to dispatch a military expedition and almost certain defeat." McMahon, who had been responsible for inflating the Arabs' military importance, now claimed that the revolt had been undertaken with "inadequate preparations in ignorance of modern warfare," whereas four months later Wingate reported that the Arabs, even if adequately equipped and organized, were incapable of acting on the defensive. Both Wingate and McMahon bombarded London with requests for military assistance to cut off the Turks and "prevent early collapse of Sherif's movement." This movement not only did not snowball, but was widely condemned by Mohammedan opinion in India and elsewhere, and produced a bad effect in Syria. Hussein was blamed for ingratitude towards the Turks and his revolt commanded little or no sympathy. McMahon and his entourage in Cairo were alarmed. "We are morally committed to support the Sherif and shall certainly be held in a large measure responsible for his failure." So hopeless seemed the position that, in contravention of Moslem custom prohibiting the presence of non Moslems in the Hedjaz, Hussein himself requested British military assistance in troops, which, he claimed, "is a condition of our alliance."[46]

The General Staff was indignant. The Sherif had undertaken to expel the Turks from the Arab area and asked in return for British assistance in the shape of arms and money, which had been given. Before the revolt, Hussein had estimated that he could raise a force of 250,000 men and gave the impression of commanding sufficient resources to overcome the Turks. His predicament was as unexpected as it was embarrassing. It was

he who had pledged military assistance to the British and not
vice versa. Technically, the military argument went on, the British government was under no obligation to come to his rescue.
Yet, as prestige was involved, the General Staff was prepared
to overlook that it had not been consulted during the correspondence with Hussein, and suggested a speed-up of the
operations in Sinai in order to capture El-Arish and Aqaba, a
move that would simultaneously relieve Turkish pressure on the
Sherif and encourage the Syrian Arabs to revolt.[47] The War
Council doubted whether an offensive in Sinai would rescue
Hussein in time. On the other hand, a landing of Christian
troops in the Hedjaz posed a serious problem. Not only would
they run a grave risk of offending Mohammedan opinion, but
various reports indicated that the native troops would disperse
rather than be supported by Europeans. In addition, the General Staff strongly objected to mounting another expedition with
unforeseen consequences. Overtaxed on the Western front and
short of transport and manpower, they feared that the deploy-
ment of 15,000 men to save Rabeqh would impair the El-Arish
operation.[48] For nearly six months an awkward dilemma confronted the British government. The difficulty was eventually
resolved because the much feared Turkish assault on Rabeqh
and Mecca did not materialize.

During this episode, the British drew some comfort from the
prospect that, should succor be brought in time to the Sherif,
and when the British invaded Palestine, the Arabs in the north,
"discontented with the Turkish rule," would rise. "A very
favourable turn might [then] be given to events in the whole of
Syria and Palestine besides putting the Sherif out of all danger."[49] Sykes placed so much hope in such a development that
he expected Turkish authority to crumble and their military
operations to be hindered.[50] This, however, proved an illusion.
At the turn of 1916, an Arab Legion was organized by the
British to prop up the Sherifian forces and to serve as a rallying
point for discontented elements in Syria and Mesopotamia, but
this came to nothing. "I must honestly confess," Clayton told
Sykes, "that, viewed as a symbol of Arab nationalism, the
Legion has been a failure. It has not been received with any
enthusiasm by the local Arabs, in spite of much propaganda.
. . . I cannot say that it is worth either the money or the time of

skilled officers which has to be expended upon it."[51] Had it not been for the steady flow of gold from the British Treasury and guidance provided by the British officers, the Northern Arab Army (composed of the Legion, as a regular force, and the Sherifian tribesmen) would have been crushed by the Turks or have disintegrated from within.[52] The capture of Aqaba on 6 July 1917 was a bold military maneuver, but it failed to become the rallying point for a movement on which the British Residency in Cairo pinned their hopes. Philip Graves had some words of praise for the Arabs of the Hedjaz and their Bedouin allies, but those of Syria and Palestine "remained passive or aided the Turks."[53] C. S. Jarvis, formerly Governor of Sinai, expressed himself in less complimentary terms: "The Syrians as a people did nothing whatsoever towards assisting the Arab cause . . . beyond hold secret meetings and talk. The inhabitants of Palestine did rather less."[54] Lloyd George recalled ironically that "the Arabs of Palestine, who might have been helpful in many ways, were quiescent and cowering. Right through the War and up to the end, there were masses of Arab soldiers from Mesopotamia, Syria and Palestine in the Turkish Armies fighting against the liberation of their own rule . . . the Palestinian Arabs were fighting against us."[55] Despite much encouragement, when the British troops were already firmly entrenched in Jerusalem, the results of recruiting for the Sherifian forces were disappointing; no more than 150 Arabs were recruited.[56] The verdict of the Palestine Royal Commission was clear: "It was the Sherif's own people . . . who bore the brunt of the actual fighting. The Arabs of Palestine did not rise against the Turks."[57]

But in this context Palestine was of marginal importance. The big plum was Damascus, and it was primarily with an eye on the Syrian hinterland that the Declaration to the Seven was issued in June 1918. It pledged that those territories conquered by the Arabs would remain Arab. Yet the response was negligible. With no substantial rising in sight when Allenby's forces were converging on Damascus towards the end of September 1918, the only way out, for those who engineered it, was to stage a victory by the Sherifian troops, to give the impression that the Arabs had taken the city from the Turk. Even so, the Sherifians found the city in a state of turmoil,[58] not of rejoicing, thus giving the lie to the belief that the Syrians craved nothing better than liberation from Turkish rule. Testifying before the Palestine Royal Commission in 1937, Amin al-Husseini, the Mufti of Jerusalem, denied that the Arabs were ever "under the yoke of the Turks" or that they expected to be relieved from such a yoke. For centuries they had been fully integrated within the Ottoman Empire and enjoyed equality of rights.[59] During the Committee of Union and Progress regime, they might have nourished some grievances against Constantinople, but fundamentally they "would prefer to remain under Turkish domination, with all its mis-government, tyranny and oppression . . . rather than . . . fall under the Christian yoke."[60] Arab troops in the Ottoman army remained essentially loyal and would not aid the destruction of a Moslem power.[61] Throughout the war, the Sherifian rebellion remained an isolated phenomenon. As Wingate, one of its chief protagonists, admitted in September 1918: "The Moslems in general have hitherto regarded the Hedjaz revolt, and our share in it, with suspicion and dislike."[62] A distinguished British historian, and a close observer of Middle East politics, attested that "a *general* Arab insurrection was planned [but] it never took place . . . [It was] mainly the soldiers of Britain, the Commonwealth and India, who played a part in the overthrow of Ottoman rule."[63] Ronald Storrs, judging retrospectively, doubted whether the deal with the Sherif was after all worthwhile. It "imposed upon us the real obligation of raising and maintaining his prestige to the limit of the possible, so that for this and other reasons we were in the end committed far more deeply in bullion, in munitions of war and in promises very hard to fulfil, than most of us had dreamed of in September 1914."[64]

This did not mean that Hussein's revolt, though limited in scope, was devoid of advantages. Politically, it set one Moslem against another,[65] and militarily, it harassed Ottoman troops and occasionally disrupted communications along the Hedjaz railway. But between the original expectations, on which the deal between the British and Hussein was based, and the actual performance, there was a considerable gap. There was no general uprising against the Turk. The Arab revolt, as Lawrence succinctly concluded, bore a distinctly *"local* nature."[66] If any party remained in debt towards the other, it was rather the

Arab to the British than vice versa.

It remains now to examine the question whether Palestine
was in fact included or excluded from the promises made to
Hussein, and why McMahon's wording was so vague as to give
rise in subsequent years to such acrimonious controversy.

The point of view advanced during the twenties and thirties
by the Arabs was that, since Palestine was not specifically
mentioned in the reservations made by McMahon in his letter of
24 October 1915, it followed that it was *ipso facto* included in
the territory in which Great Britain was to recognize Arab independence.[67] In contrast, the British government maintained that
McMahon's reservation applied to "those portions of Syria
lying to the west of the district of Damascus," reading the term
"district" as equivalent to "vilayet"; and since the vilayet of
Damascus comprised *inter alia* also the sanjaks of Hauran and
Maan, which became known as Transjordan, it followed that
the vilayet of Beirut and the independent sanjak of Jerusalem,
were covered by the reservations, to the effect that "the whole
of Palestine, west of the Jordan, was thus excluded from Sir H.
McMahon's pledge."[68] The Arabs rejected the equation of "district" with "vilayet" and remained adamant in their position.
Yet a succession of British officials, notably McMahon, Clayton, and William Ormsby-Gore, then Colonial Secretary, testified that it was never their intention that Palestine "should be
included in the general pledge given to the Sherif."[69] Clayton,
according to his own testimony, was "in daily touch with Sir
Henry McMahon throughout the negotiations with King Hussein, and made the preliminary drafts of all the letters," whilst
Ormsby-Gore served in 1916 in the Arab Bureau in Cairo and
on McMahon's staff. In spring 1939, in connection with the
Palestine Round Table Conferences in London, a joint committee of British and Arab representatives was set up to examine
the McMahon correspondence, but failed to reach agreement on
matters of interpretation. The British representatives agreed
that the language used to indicate the exclusion of Palestine
was "not so specific and unmistakable as it was thought to be
at the time," and that "Arab contentions regarding the meaning
of the disputed phrase [district] have greater force than has
appeared hitherto," but maintained that "on proper construc-

tion of the Correspondence Palestine was in fact excluded."
Lord Maugham, Lord Chancellor and spokesman for the British
representatives, confidently reiterated that: "The Correspondence as a whole, and particularly the reservation in respect of
French interests in Sir Henry McMahon's letter of the 24th
October, 1915, not only did exclude Palestine but should have
been understood to do so."[70] Official Foreign Office records,
now available at the Public Record Office, fully confirm this
conclusion. It is however a matter of surprise that the Committee, though said to have examined microscopically the wording
of the actual correspondence, did overlook much other material
related to its background which tends to support the British
case.

   It may be recalled that Hussein, in his letter of 14 July 1915,
when outlining the boundaries of territory to fall within the
sphere of Arab independence, was acting under the inspiration
of the Arab secret societies in Syria. Hussein himself declared
that these boundaries represented not the suggestion of one
individual, but the "demands of our people" in the regions concerned.[71] Although excessive, they were not taken at the British
Residency in Cairo at their face value, but regarded merely as a
basis for negotiations, an assumption which statements made
by al-Faruqi in October-November of that year fully endorsed.
Al-Faruqi conveyed the impression that the aims of the al-'Ahd
and al-Fatat societies were moderate. They fully realized that
the establishment of an Arab Empire, as they visualized it, was
entirely outside the realm of practical politics; in al-Faruqi's
own words: "our scheme embraces all the Arab countries, including Syria and Mesopotamia, but if we cannot have all, we
want as much as we can get." They appreciated that, in the
regions in question, England was bound by obligations to her
Allies and they would recognize the French position in Syria.
The point on which the Young Arabs would not budge was the
inclusion of Damascus, Aleppo, Hama, and Homs in the Arab
Confederation. Otherwise, Clayton noted, the leaders of the
Arab societies were "open to reason and ready to accept a considerably less ambitious scheme than that which they formulated" earlier.[72]

   That the inclusion of Aleppo, Homs, Hama, and Damascus
within the Arab state was the Syrian nationalist leaders' pri-

mary concern is evident also from General Maxwell's cable to
Lord Kitchener, as well as from McMahon's private communication to Sir Edward Grey of 18 October: "The occupation by
France of the purely Arab districts of Aleppo, Hama, Homs
and Damascus, would be opposed by the Arabs by force of
arms, but with this exception, they would accept some modifications of the northwestern boundaries proposed by the Sherif
of Mecca."

On the same day, McMahon assured the Foreign Office that
the Arabs "have not included the places inhabited by a foreign
race in the territories which they demand."[73] What then was
the nature of the modifications of the northwestern boundaries
and conversely the extent of the territories excluded from the
sphere of Arab independence? The answer can be gauged from
al-Faruqi's statement to Sykes on 20 November 1915, during
the latter's stay in Cairo. Sykes, anticipating difficulties with
France, pressed Faruqi to be specific. The latter responded:
"Arabs would agree to convention with France, granting her
monopoly of all concessionary enterprise in Syria and Palestine"; the area to be bounded by the Euphrates in the north running south to Deir Zor, and to Dera'a and along the Hedjaz
Railway to Maan. Furthermore, "the Arabs would . . . agree to
employment of none but Frenchmen as advisers and European
employees in this area. . . [and] to all French educational establishments having special recognition in this area." An identical
convention would be concluded with Britain with regard to
Irak, Jazirah, and Northern Mesopotamia, Basra and its
enclave to the south would be recognized as British territory.[74]

If Sykes' cryptic language conveyed al-Faruqi's thoughts
faithfully and if the terms "monopoly of all concessionary
enterprise" and "employment of advisers" were substitutes for
sphere of influence, which in the given context was most likely,
then we can visualize two lines demarcating the French sphere
from that designated for an independent Arab state. One was
to run in a crescent from Adana to the Euphrates, and from
there along the river as far as Der-es-Zor, taking in the district
of Aleppo. The second line was to run from the center of the
crescent southwards towards Dera'a and along the Hedjaz
railway to Maan, leaving out the four towns of the Syrian hinterland. Thus the Arab state or confederation of states was to

cover the districts of Aleppo, Hama, Homs, and Damascus, then southwards the territory which later became known as Transjordan and the Arabian peninsula, except Aden and the sheikdoms adjacent to the Persian Gulf. The bulk of Mesopotamia east of the Euphrates was to fall within the British sphere of interest, and the districts of Mersina and Alexandretta, the Lebanon and the whole of Palestine extending eastwards as far as the Hedjaz railway and southwards to the Egyptian border, under the French sphere of influence. The desiderata of *al-'Ahd* and *al-Fatat* covered only Aleppo, Hama, Homs, and Damascus. Inclusion of these districts was regarded as *conditio sine qua non* for initiating a revolt against Turkey. Palestine and the Syrian littoral were left out. Both because of the long-standing French interests there and because these regions could hardly be termed "purely Arab districts," the two societies did not see fit to claim them. As Lloyd George put it: "The Arabs' special concern was for Irak and Syria. . . . Palestine did not seem to give them much anxiety. For reasons which were obvious to them they realized that there were genuine international interests in Palestine, which placed it in a totally different category."[75]

Al-Faruqi was operating at a high level. His statements, McMahon understood, conveyed "the purpose" of the Sherif's letter of 14 July 1915, which outlined the boundaries of Arab independence. But Faruqi was more than an interpreter or even a representative of Hussein in Cairo. "Your honour will have realized," Hussein briefed McMahon on 1 January 1916, "that after arrival of Mohammed [Faruqi] . . . all our procedure up to the present, was of no personal inclination or the like . . . but that everything was the result of the decisions and desires of our peoples . . . we are but transmitters and executants." McMahon had therefore reason to take al-Faruqi's word as reflecting, if not binding upon, that of his fellow Arabs. Being under the firm impression that Palestine was excluded from Arab desiderata, there was no compelling necessity for him to specify its exclusion, all the more as he understood that the Arabs "have not included the places inhabited by a foreign race in the territories which they demand."[76] This limitation applied with particular force to Palestine where, according to British Consular reports, there were before the war about 100,000

Jews.[77]

This, however, does not dispose of the enigma of Mc-
Mahon's ambiguous wording in his fatal letter of 24 October
1915, which left a loophole for future assertions that the British
pledge extended also to Palestine. Was the failure a mere accident caused by undue haste in despatching the note which
admitted "no delay," or a deliberately calculated risk? Philip
Graves was the first, in a book published in 1923,[78] to throw
some light on this question. We are now in a position to confirm
that Graves' statement was, in fact, a repetition of McMahon's
confidential letter to Sir John Shuckburgh at the Colonial Office
dated 12 March 1922. With the controversy unfolding, Mc-
Mahon wished it to be put on record that in his letter of 24
October 1915 it was his intention to exclude Palestine from the
Arab state. He thought that he had so worded his letter as to
make this "sufficiently clear for all purposes." He elucidated:

> My reasons for restricting myself to specific mention of Damascus,
> Homs, Hama and Aleppo in that connexion in my letter were: (1)
> that these were places to which the Arabs attached vital im-
> portance and (2) that there was no place I could think of at the
> time of sufficient importance for purposes of definition further
> south of the above.
>
> It was as fully my intention to exclude Palestine as it was to
> exclude the more northern coastal tracts of Syria.
>
> I did not make use of the Jordan to define the limits of the
> southern area, because I thought it might be considered desirable
> at some later stage of negotiations to endeavour to find some more
> suitable frontier line east of the Jordan and between that river
> and the Hejaz Railways. At that moment, moreover, very de-
> tailed definitions did not seem called for.
>
> I may mention that I have no recollection of ever having any-
> thing from the Sherif of Mecca, by letter or message, to make me
> suppose that he did not also understand Palestine to be excluded
> from independent Arabia.[79]

McMahon's predicament is understandable. Neither the river
Jordan nor the eastern limit of the French sphere, as sketched
out by al-Faruqi — running from Der-es-Zor to Dera'a and
along the Hedjaz railway to Maan — seemed to him to offer a
practical border between Palestine and the projected Arab

state, and since the matter at that time was only of academic import, McMahon did not think it necessary to spell out a precise delimitation. But Palestine's exclusion was embodied also in the phrase "the regions . . . in which Great Britain is [not] free to act without detriment to the interests of her ally France." In this case, we are fortunate to have McMahon's contemporary explanation. On 26 October 1915, he told Grey:

> I have been definite in stating that Great Britain will recognize the principle of Arab independence in purely Arab territory, this being the main point on which agreement depends, but have been equally definite in excluding Mersina, Alexandretta and those districts on the northern coast of Syria, which cannot be said to be Arab and where I understand that French interests have been recognized.

However, with regard to the portions lying south of the vilayet of Beirut, he had no option but to be vague:

> I am not aware of the extent of French claims in Syria, nor of how far His Majesty's Government have agreed to recognize them. Hence . . . I have endeavoured to provide for possible French pretensions to those places by a general modification to the effect that His Majesty's Government can only give assurances in regard to those territories 'in which she can act without detriment to the interests of her ally France'.[80]

The territory about which McMahon was dubious as to the extent of French claims being recognized by the British was Palestine, or, more precisely, the sanjak of Jerusalem. Four months earlier, a specially appointed Committee on Asiatic Turkey, under the chairmanship of Sir Maurice de Bunsen, Assistant Under-Secretary of State in the Foreign Office, had submitted a report on British desiderata in Turkey-in-Asia. The committee rejected the French claim to Palestine but considered that, for similar reasons, it was futile for the British to demand it.[81] Such an imprecise formulation of policy could provide no guidance for McMahon in phrasing the relevant passage of his letter. But as France's standing in the Holy Land was a matter of common knowledge in the Levant, it seemed expedient to resort to the ambiguous but also elastic phrase of not being "free to act without detriment to the interests of her ally France" in order to meet all possible contingencies. This was particularly the case since Grey had specifically warned McMahon to take heed of French susceptibilities in that area and agreed that the general reservation, especially with regard to the northwest boundaries [i.e., Syrian littoral and Palestine], was "most necessary."[82]

The recommendations of the de Bunsen committee, it should be noted, pointed to the internationalization of Palestine and not to placing it under a single power. Although aware of this, McMahon thought it inadvisable to warn Hussein about it. "It will be observed," he wrote to Grey in the above mentioned letter, "that I have definitely specified France as the only Ally concerned. The use of the term 'Allies' would, I understand, inevitably have aroused the suspicion of the Arabs, who would have conjured up visions of all our Allies putting forward claims in various parts of the Arab territories." The reference to France was no indication that McMahon and his aides in Cairo unreservedly accepted the French claim to Palestine. He was well aware of its strategic importance, both as an eastern outpost for Egypt and a link with Mesopotamia. This may explain his interest in Edgar Suarès's scheme for Jewish settlement in Palestine under British protection, which could have usefully tipped the scales in Britain's favor. That McMahon detected no contradiction between Suarès's scheme and the promises made to Hussein only reinforces the case that Palestine was not meant to be given to the Arabs. Neither Grey nor his staff at the Foreign Office discerned any such inconsistency.[83] A marginal annotation on a translated copy of Hussein's letter of 14 July 1915 indicates how London understood the limits of Arab independence. "It includes vilayets of Basra, Baghdad, Mosul, Aleppo and Damascus."[84] In other words, in the opinion of the Foreign Office officials, Hussein's desiderata did not include the Syrian littoral and Palestine. If O'Beirne feared that the scheme of Jewish colonization in Palestine "with the possible prospect of eventual Jewish self-government . . . might have a very chilling effect on the Arab leaders,"[85] it was not because he thought it conflicted with the McMahon-Hussein correspondence, but because it might entail displacement of a "large proportion of the 6-700,000 [native] Arabs," although he believed this could be avoided.[86]

In 1922, Sir Vivian Gabriel testified that Lord Kitchener, when Secretary of State for War, "would certainly not have admitted the exclusion of Palestine" from the Arab state.[87] Careful examination of both Foreign Office files and the Kitchener Papers[88] shows that there is no foundation for such a contention. Kitchener was indeed "most desirous," as he told General Maxwell, "of dealing with the Arab question in a manner satisfactory to the Arabs," but apart from this general statement he made no specific reference to the territorial extent of Arab independence. This was a political matter which lay within the province of the Foreign Office on which he, as Secretary of State for War, would not encroach. As far as Palestine was concerned, Kitchener adhered always to the view that it lay predominantly within the French sphere. "The French," he told the War Committee on 16 December 1915, "would leave the [Jerusalem] *enclave* [to be internationalized] but beyond that they would take everything up to the Egyptian boundary." Kitchener's favorite scheme was the acquisition of Alexandretta, linked territorially with Mesopotamia under a British protectorate. Palestine, curiously enough, he dismissed as of "no value." Should Turkey be partitioned, he reasoned, an Arab kingdom in Arabia under British auspices should be established, "bounded on the north by the. . . Tigris and Euphrates, and containing within it the chief Mohammedan Holy Places: Mecca, Medina and Kerbala."[89] The omission of Jerusalem, and even of Damascus, was not accidental; these were meant to fall within the French sphere of interest in recompense for their concession of Alexandretta. It is therefore highly improbable that Kitchener had the slightest intention of awarding Palestine to the Arabs. Such an idea never originated with any British minister or official in London or in Cairo.

Least of all would Lloyd George have entertained it. On 3 April 1917, at a conference at 10 Downing Street at which Curzon was present, Lloyd George warned Sykes before his departure on a mission to the East not to commit the British government to "any agreement with the [Arab] tribes which would be prejudicial to British interests." He impressed on Sir Mark also "the importance of not prejudicing the Zionist movement and the possibility of its development under British auspices."[90] It would have been inconceivable for the Prime Minister to issue an instruction of such fundamental importance in the knowledge that it was incompatible with earlier promises made to Arab leaders.

"I was a party to the Balfour Declaration," Lord Milner declared in the House of Lords on 29 June 1923. "I do not believe that the Balfour Declaration is inconsistent with any pledges which have been given to King Hussein or to anybody else. . . . When all the documents are published it will be clearly established that in the promises which we made to King Hussein a distinct reservation was made of [Palestine]."

This was the consensus of opinion within the British government both before the Balfour Declaration was made public and after. A notable exception was Dr. Arnold J. Toynbee, at that time attached to the Political Intelligence Department of the Foreign Office. In a *Memorandum on British Commitments to King Hussein,* he stated: "With regard to Palestine, His Majesty's Government are committed by Sir H. McMahon's letter to the Sherif on the 24th October 1915, to its inclusion in the boundaries of Arab independence." And in the same breath, he added: "But they have stated their policy regarding the Palestinian Holy Places and Zionist colonization in their message to him of the 4th January, 1918 — the well-known Hogarth message. In a second memorandum, dated 21 November 1918, in the item dealing with Palestine, he wrote: "We are pledged to King Hussein that this territory [i.e., west of Jordan] shall be 'Arab' and 'independent'."[91]

This is rather a matter for surprise. Had Toynbee consulted McMahon's letter of 26 October 1915 to Grey, in which the High Commissioner explained why he had phrased his reservation covering the territory of Palestine as he did, Toynbee would have presumably arrived at a different conclusion. But even more puzzling is his failure to detect the relation between al-Faruqi's desiderata, which he gives in full, and McMahon's letter to Hussein of 24 October 1915. It was, it may be remembered, al-Faruqi's exclusion of the Syrian littoral, running from Alexandretta down to the Egyptian border near Rafah, from the projected Arab state, which was the cornerstone of McMahon's crucial letter to Hussein. Nor was Toynbee struck by the inconsistency between Hussein's acceptance of the formula conveyed to him by Hogarth and his own conclusion that the British Government had pledged that Palestine should be "Arab" and "independent." Had this been the case, Hussein would not have been slow to protest against such an unwarranted intrusion.

What grounds did Professor Toynbee have for reaching his conclusion? He has been good enough to say that, in the autumn of 1918, when considering the question, much depended on the meaning of the word "vilayet of Damascus." In Ottoman administrative usage, it was applicable in a wider sense, covering Cis-Jordanian Palestine, whereas in Arabic, wilayah meant "environs," "banlieux." Professor Toynbee thinks that McMahon could not have used the Ottoman terminology in his letter of 24 October 1915, in which case Palestine was meant to be included.[92] This is, however, a hypothesis which, though cogently argued,[93] cannot hold good when juxtaposed with McMahon's contemporary testimony. Moreover, in correspondence on political matters, it is most unlikely that a High Commissioner would have resorted to ambiguous wording in the Arab vernacular in preference to accepted terminology in which both Hussein and his son Abdullah were well versed.

Nearer the mark would be the explanation offered by W. J. Childs of the Foreign Office in a paper dated 24 October 1930.[94] Childs pointed out, quite correctly, that Dr. Toynbee, when preparing his memorandum, used a copy of the Arab Bureau's *History of the Hedjaz Rising*,[95] as his various references showed. The *History*, in Childs's view, perverted McMahon's pledge. It was "in no way authoritative and should not be taken at face value." It read the phrase "districts of Damascus" as meaning its immediate neighborhood, thus gratuitously including Palestine in the Arab area; a most peculiar interpretation, since subsequent statements, private and public, made by prominent members of the Arab Bureau contradicted it.[96] At any rate, Childs goes on to explain, when Toynbee was preparing his memorandum, he felt that he was on "safe ground, being conclusively supported by the views of the Arab Bureau," a fact which accounted for his failure to make any serious attempt "to examine the pledge critically." Toynbee did not trace the connection between al-Faruqi's declaration and McMahon's wording which was "construed in the wide sense intended by El-Faroki [sic]; that the 'district of Damascus' extended to the Gulf of Akaba," thus, by implication, excluding Palestine from the Arab area.[97]

Curzon was the only Minister who thought that the British government had made conflicting promises to Arabs and Jews. On 5 December 1918, at a meeting of the Eastern Committee, of which he was chairman, he made a statement which practically amounted to a verbal repetition of that produced by Toynbee.[98] Curzon did not however persist in his mistake for long. On 15 October 1919, in his letter to Emir Feisal, he made no mention of Jerusalem (or of any other city in Palestine) being included in the area where the British government was bound to recognize the establishment of "an independent Arab State."[99] Several weeks later the whole question was re-examined by Major Hubert Young, an Arabist who had participated in Arab military operations east of the Jordan under Emir Feisal and T. E. Lawrence. In 1920, when serving in the Eastern Department of the Foreign Office, he read the Arabic text of McMahon's letter of 24 October 1915 and found that the meaning in Arabic of the words "district of Damascus" was equivalent to the Ottoman "vilayet," which extended southwards to the Gulf of Akaba, with Damascus as its capital. It followed that the area of Palestine to the west of the vilayet's boundary (running along the river Jordan and the medial line of the Dead Sea), was excluded. The British government adopted Young's interpretation and, in the ensuing years, followed it consistently. It was not without good reason that Lloyd George, in his memoirs, when reproducing Curzon's statement in the Eastern Committee almost in its entirety, pointedly omitted the passage that "the British Government pledged itself that [Palestine] should be Arab and independent in the future."[100]

McMahon's statement that the fact that Palestine was not included in his pledge "was well understood . . . at the time . . . by King Hussein,"[101] is fully borne out by contemporary evidence. Although Hussein must have been aware that Sir Henry's letter of 24 October 1915 was nearly a replica of al-Faruqi's scheme, Wingate was not satisfied and, through Seyyid Ali Morghani, hastened to reiterate the "reservations which we [the British] have made in Syria, Palestine and Mesopotamia."[102] Two months later (letter dated 1 January 1916) the Sherif reminded the High Commissioner that after the conclusion of the war he would claim "Beirut and its coastal regions,"[103] but made no mention of the sanjak of Jerusalem. The following year, Fuad Khetib, Hussein's Under Secretary for Foreign Affairs, was reported to have said that he anticipated "no difficulty with the Jews . . . 'now we understand each other.'"[104] Even more indicative of Hussein's attitude was his deliberate silence following the publication of the Balfour Declaration. He categorically refused to add his voice to protests against this document, though urged to do so by the Syrian notables in Cairo. On the contrary; we learn from Antonius that Hussein "ordered his sons . . . to allay the apprehensions caused by the Balfour Declaration among their followers [and] dispatched an emissary to Feisal at Aqaba with similar instructions."[105] When Hogarth called on the King, 4 January 1918, the latter seemed quite prepared to accept the formula that "no obstacle should be put in the way of the realization of [the Zionist] ideal . . . and agreed enthusiastically, saying that he welcomed Jews to all Arab lands."[106] About three months later, Antonius tells us, Hussein caused an article to be published in *al-Qibla* (23 March 1918), his official mouthpiece. Palestine, the article attested, was "a sacred and beloved homeland . . . [of] its original sons (*abna'ihil-l-asliyim*)" — the Jews. "The resources of the country are still virgin soil" which could not provide a livelihood for the Palestinian native. But the Jewish immigrants would develop the country. "Experience has proved their capacity to succeed in their energies and their labours. . . . The return of these exiles (*jaliya*) to their homeland will prove materially and spiritually an experimental school for their [Arab] brethren . . . in the fields, factories and trades."[107]

In 1920, Colonel C. E. Vickery, an accomplished Arabist, was sent on an official mission from Cairo to Jedda to examine the original Arabic text of the correspondence and found that Palestine was not included in the proposals to Hussein. But it was not before 1939 that Vickery published his impressions:

> I can say most definitely that the whole of the King's demands were centred around Syria, and only around Syria. Time after

time he referred to the vineyard, to the exclusion of any other claim or interest. He stated most emphatically that he did not concern himself at all with Palestine and had no desire to have suzerainty over it for himself or his successors.[108]

As for Feisal, he seemed first to have fallen under the spell of the Syrians in Cairo and was "inclined the other way," but Clayton endeavored to persuade him, through Lawrence, that his sphere stretched east of the Jordan and not to Palestine, which lay "outside the real Arab policy." But it was only following Feisal's meeting with Weizmann in Aqaba on 4 June 1918 that Clayton was able to tell Miss Gertrude Bell: "There is little doubt that the main ambition of the Sherifian Arab lies (at any rate, of Sherif Feisal) in Syria. His eyes are fixed on Damascus and Aleppo and nothing else seems to matter to him. . . . It is this that leads him to welcome Jewish co-operation, as he is quite prepared to leave Palestine alone provided he can secure what he wants in Syria."[109] Guided by his mentor Lawrence, Feisal proved so zealous in forcing his way into Syria that he soon overplayed his hand. He was urgently summoned by General Allenby, who, reminding him of the terms of the Sykes-Picot Agreement, told him that he would "have the Administration of Syria (less Palestine and the Lebanon Province) [but] under French guidance and financial backing, [and] that the Arab sphere would include the hinterland of Syria only." Feisal, according to General Chauvel's note, "objected very strongly" and pretended to have no knowledge about arrangements with France; he understood from Lawrence that the Arabs were to have "the whole of Syria including the Lebanon but excluding Palestine."[110]

Four months later, when asking the Supreme Council at the Versailles Conference for recognition of Arab independence, he specifically excluded the Lebanon and Palestine. "Palestine, for its universal character," according to D. H. Miller, "be left on one side for the mutual consideration of all parties concerned."[111] Feisal's agreement with Weizmann on 3 January 1919[112] shows that, in principle, he was prepared to give the Zionists a free hand in Palestine and renounce any claims to it provided, as the inserted postscript in Arabic indicates, the

Arabs achieved independence in Syria. This was also implicit in Feisal's positive response to William Yale's solution setting Palestine apart under British mandate and permitting the Zionists to carry out their plan.[113] Not before 1921 were accusations of betrayal and double dealing hurled against Britain. This is understandable. With Feisal's eviction from Damascus, Palestine provided a convenient outlet for the Arabs' mounting frustration, but the charges were unfounded. As Professor Temperley put it: "Had . . . the Emir not been ejected from Syria by the French, much less might have been heard of his father's claim to Palestine."[114]

Feisal made the first challenge on 20 January 1921 in an interview at the Foreign Office with R. C. Lindsay, representing Curzon, the Foreign Secretary. Feisal claimed that "nothing in the original correspondence stated that Palestine should be excluded from the Arab boundaries." To this Lindsay pointed out that Palestine had been "expressly reserved" from these boundaries and the relevant passage from McMahon's letter of 24 October 1915 was read aloud to the Emir in Arabic. After an exchange of views, Feisal conceded that it had been the original intention of the British government to exclude Palestine. This concession, however, he qualified by the contention that, "as the Arabic stood, it would clearly be interpreted by any Arab, and had been so interpreted by King Hussein, to refer to the four towns and their immediate surroundings [and as] Palestine did not lie to the west of the four towns [it] was therefore . . . included in the area for which His Majesty's Government had given pledges to his father."[115]

Childs, who cited Feisal's statement in his memorandum, commented that, in 1915, it suited Sherif Hussein and his advisers to give the word "district" the widest possible interpretation, whereas in 1920, "the narrowest interpretation promised them the greater advantage." He found Feisal's arguments "deliberately disingenuous." That Feisal persistently substituted the word "town" (not prefixed in McMahon's letter) for "districts" suggested that he was fully alive to the weakness of his case. The native Arab populace might have had a local usage of the word vilayet, as meaning vicinity or immediate surroundings, but this argument, Childs remarked, was beside the point. He was convinced that the British government's interpretation of the contested passage had been adopted on "adequate grounds, and in good faith."

The dispute which bedeviled Middle East politics during the twenties and thirties can now be comfortably resolved: the exclusion of Palestine from promises made by McMahon to Hussein was covered both in the phrase "the regions . . . in which Great Britain is [not] free to act without detriment to the interests of her ally France," and in that "portion of Syria lying to the west of the districts of Damascus." That advantage would be taken of its ambiguity to interpret "districts" in the narrower sense of "neighborhood" could not be foreseen. Moreover, examination of Foreign Office records shows how shaky, on all counts, was the basis of the McMahon-Hussein understanding. It was extracted from the British by the unwarranted assertion that German-Turkish recognition of Arab independence was imminent. McMahon thereupon made a hasty decision, misjudging its far-reaching implications. He made a pledge on behalf of the British government, yet did little to consult London. The correspondence, although protracted, remained inconclusive.[116] However, the deal was not a unilateral one. Its permanence and strength depended on how the Arabs fulfilled their part; and, as our evidence suggests, it was they who remained in debt, not the British. Hussein contributed his share and for this he was amply rewarded in the Hedjaz.[117] But when the general Arab uprising in the regions of the Fertile Crescent failed to materialize, the corresponding part of the understanding, pledging the recognition of Arab independence east of the Jordan and in the Syrian hinterland, lapsed. All in all, the correspondence was not a foundation on which sound Anglo-Arab relations could be built; its imperfections were pinpointed by Dr. Toynbee:

> Our commitments to King Hussein are not embodied in any agreement or treaty signed or even acknowledged by both parties. In this way they differ from those to Russia, France, Italy [the 1916 Asia Minor Agreement] and certain independent Arab rulers such as the Idrisi and Bin Saud. They can only be analysed by summarizing the history of our dealings with the King during the War, under different heads. And the position is complicated by the King's habit of ignoring or refusing to take note of conditions laid down by us to which he objects and then carrying

on as if the particular question had been settled between us according to his own desires.[118]

Significantly, Emir Feisal made no reference to his father's correspondence when presenting the Arab case to the Peace Conference in Paris. Neither Britain's Allies, signatories to the Asia Minor Agreement, nor the League of Nations, endorsed it. From the point of view of international law, the Mc-Mahon-Hussein correspondence had no validity.

Preamble

The McMahon-Hussein Correspondence: Comments by Arnold Toynbee

Mr. Friedman's article in the *Journal* on this subject is by far the best of the discussions of it, known to me, that have been published so far. He has made a very comprehensive and careful study of the information now accessible. He has not only studied the official papers, now on view in the Public Record Office, which are the most important part of the evidence; he has also taken into account other sources of information, both published and unpublished. Moreover, Mr. Friedman has been non-polemical in his treatment of a subject that has become controversial, and he has dealt courteously and considerately with the people, living and dead, who were personally concerned.

In writing the following notes on Mr. Friedman's article, my purpose is not to enter into controversy with him, but to supplement what he has written from my own knowledge and to put some questions which arise, I think, out of Mr. Friedman's paper, but which are not fully answered there. Very likely, Mr. Friedman knows what the answers are, since it is clear that he has made himself a master of the subject.

The reasons why there are memoranda, written by me, among the relevant official documents, now in the Public Record Office, are as follows. In 1918, I was a temporary Foreign Office clerk in the FO's Political Intelligence Department. About six weeks before the Armistice of 11 November 1918, I was told to get from the FO Registry all files dealing with HMG's existing commitments in the Middle East (including still valid pre-war commitments; e.g., the international agreements of the eighteen-sixties about the Lebanon) and to submit memoranda setting out what these commitments were and stating whether, in my judgment, they were or were not all compatible with each other. The FO Registry is efficient, and I do not think that any relevant FO files failed to reach my desk. I quickly noticed one blank. The files concerned with the St. Jean de Maurienne Agreement (which assigned zones to Italy in Anatolia) did not include the record of the actual agreement. On inquiry, I was told that, at the crucial stage in the negotiations, Lloyd George had taken these out of the FO's hands and had eventually presented the FO with a fait accompli. However, the St. Jean de Maurienne Agreement is not relevant to Palestine. I am sure that I had before me every relevant file that was in the Foreign Office. I certainly had all those, of dates earlier than the end of 1918, that are mentioned by Mr. Friedman in his article.

One of my memoranda was the paper on *British Commitments to King Hussein*.[1] I submitted this and my other memoranda to Crowe, who was then Permanent Under-Secretary, and I went through them with him personally. He ordered them to be put into the FO Print, and to be included in the FO's dossier of papers for the Peace Conference. This was done. Immediately after our arrival in Paris, I was sent for by Smuts and was told by him to boil down my memoranda to something that the statesmen who were going to take the decisions would have time to read. I then produced the second paper to which Mr. Friedman refers.[2]

The following points are, I think, undisputed:

i.   It was the arrival of Muhammad Sherif al-Faruqi in Cairo that constituted the decisive turning-point[3] in the British negotiations with Hussein. Al-Faruqi's formula seemed to the British authorities to give an opening to her satisfying the Ottoman Arabs without falling foul of the French.

ii. According to al-Faruqi, "the point on which the Young Arabs would not budge, was the inclusion of Damascus, Aleppo, Hama and Homs in the Arab Confederation."[4]

iii. McMahon, in writing his letter of 24 October 1915 to Hussein, took his cue from al-Faruqi's hint in the name of the Ottoman Arab organizations, on whose behalf al-Faruqi claimed to be speaking, that the Ottoman Arabs might acquiesce in territorial concessions to France that did not extend to the four towns that al-Faruqi had named.

McMahon, in his letter to Hussein of 24 October 1915, named "the wilayahs of Damascus, Homs, Hama, and Aleppo" as being the Ottoman territories in, and to the east of which, but not to the west of which, HMG was prepared to recognize and uphold Arab independence. Why was McMahon's use, in this letter, of the word "wilayahs" apparently interpreted on 29 November 1916, by the author of the Arab Bureau's *History of the Hedjaz Rising*,[5] and certainly interpreted by me in my two memoranda and by the Arab Delegation to London in 1922, as meaning, not "vilayets," in the Ottoman official meaning of the word, but "environs" or "banlieux," which was the unofficial usage of the word in Arabic? When I was writing my first memorandum (my second was merely an abridgment of the whole of my set of memoranda), I had before me the English version of McMahon's letter of 24 October 1915, as well as the Arab Bureau's *History*. Why did I interpret McMahon's "wilayahs" in the sense in which the author of the *History* appears to have interpreted it? And why did the Arab Delegation put forward the same interpretation in 1922?

The identical interpretation was made independently by three different people at three different dates. In 1918, I did not have the time or the opportunity to compare notes with the author of the Arab Bureau's *History* (I still do not know who he was). In 1922, the Arab Delegation cannot have had access to my papers, and I never met any of the members of the Delegation or had any correspondence with any of them. (I had ceased to be a temporary Foreign Office clerk in the spring of 1919, and in any case I should not have been entitled to give the Arab Delegation any information.) Of course, by 1922, the Arab Delegation had an obvious political motive for interpreting McMahon's "wilayahs" as meaning "environs," not "provinces." But the author of the Arab Bureau's *History* in 1916, and I in 1918, had no political ax to grind. We were concerned solely to make out, if we could, what HMG's commitments actually were. Nor would the Arab Delegation in 1922 have felt it worth while to interpret McMahon's "wilayahs" as we had done if there had not been a convincing reason for interpreting the word in this context in this way.

Mr. Friedman is quite right in saying (pp. xlv) that the most natural interpretation of the words "the wilayah of Damascus" would have been "the Ottoman province of Damascus," not "the environs of Damascus." However, McMahon did not write "the wilayah of Damascus," he wrote "the wilayahs (in the plural) of Damascus, Homs, Hama, and Aleppo," and this is why his word "wilayahs" was interpreted three times, independently, as meaning not "provinces," but "environs."

There were no Ottoman vilayets of Homs and Hama. In the vilayet of Damascus there was a sanjaq of Hama consisting of four kazas, two of which were the kazas of Hama and Homs. There was a vilayet of Aleppo, but this vilayet extended westwards to the coast. Its sanjaq of Aleppo included, among its kazas, the three coastal kazas of Iskanderun, Beilan, and Antaqiyeh. It is quite certain that McMahon was not intending to include these three kazas in the area within which HMG undertook to recognize and uphold Arab independence. In his letter of 26 October 1915, to Grey, McMahon says "I have been definite in excluding Mersina, Alexandretta (i.e., Iskanderun) and those districts on the northern coast of Syria which cannot be said to be Arab and where I understand that French interests have been recognized."

If McMahon was intending (as certainly was to be expected) to write in terms of Ottoman official administrative areas, what he ought to have written was "the vilayet of Damascus and the portion of the vilayet of Aleppo that lies to the east of a line running northward from. . ." — and here he would have had to describe a line running northwards, from the north-east corner of the Ladiqiyeh sanjaq of the vilayet of Beirut through the vilayet of Aleppo to this vilayet's northern boundary.

Subject to Mr. Friedman's opinion of this point, I guess that this was why the author of the Arab Bureau's *History* substituted the word "line" for McMahon's word "districts." I think that he must have been trying, as I was trying, simply to make out what McMahon had meant.

The consequences of interpreting McMahon's "wilayahs" as

meaning "Ottoman provinces" are so disconcerting that it was
— and, to my mind, still is — difficult to believe that McMahon
was intending to use the word in this sense in his letter. This
interpretation would force on us a choice between the two following alternative conclusions:

i. First alternative: McMahon was completely ignorant of Ot-
    toman administrative geography. He did not know that the
    Ottoman vilayet of Aleppo extended westward to the
    coast, and he did not know that there were no Ottoman
    vilayets of Homs and Hama. It seems to me incredible that
    McMahon can have been as ill-informed as this, and that he
    would not have taken care to inform himself correctly when
    he was writing a letter in which he was making very serious
    commitments on HMG's account.
ii. Second alternative: McMahon was properly acquainted with
    Ottoman administrative geography, and was using the word
    "wilayahs" equivocally. Apropos of Damascus, he was
    using it to mean "Ottoman provinces"; apropos of Homs
    and Hama, and Aleppo, he was using it to mean "envi-
    rons." This equivocation would have been disingenuous, im-
    politic, and pointless. I could not, and still cannot, believe
    that McMahon behaved so irresponsibly.

I do not know when, in the discussion between al-Faruqi
and the British, and in the correspondence between McMahon
and Hussein, the word "wilayahs" was first introduced in
association with the names of the four towns that had been
designated by al-Faruqi. Was this done by McMahon himself,
or by his draftsman, or by the translator into Arabic of the letter that McMahon or his draftsman had composed for dispatch
on 24 October 1915? It seems to me most improbable that
McMahon got the word "wilayahs," as well as the four
place-names, from al-Faruqi. Al-Faruqi was an Arab Ottoman
officer. I shall not be convinced that al-Faruqi ever wrote or
said "the wilayahs of Damascus, Homs, Hama, and Aleppo"
unless and until these words appear in a document written or
dictated in Arabic by al-Faruqi himself. Mr. Friedman does not
quote any documents of al-Faruqi's own, and I do not know of
any. The only information that I know of about al-Faruqi's

statements is contained in reports, at second hand, of British officials who had talked to him. There can be no doubt that he mentioned the four place-names, and he must have had in mind, not just the four towns but a continuous belt of territory linking them together. But is there any evidence of the extent of the area that he had in mind, and of the words in which he described it?

The areas that al-Faruqi outlined to Sykes on 20 November 1915[6] were those in which the Ottoman Arabs would be willing to give a monopoly of concessions, foreign advisers and employees, and foreign educational work, to France and Britain, respectively. In this conversation — and, I believe, throughout — al-Faruqi took care to avoid defining the area which the Arabs would recognize as being French territory, though he did commit himself to Sykes, on this occasion, to recognizing an area round Basra as British territory. Al-Faruqi included not only the territory to the west of Damascus, Homs, Hama, and Aleppo in his proposed French sphere of influence; he also included in it the four towns, and, since he carried the eastern boundary of the suggested French sphere of influence as far south as Maan, he was proposing to include in this sphere not only Damascus itself but also the whole of the Ottoman vilayet of Damascus. Mr. Friedman infers (p. xliv) that al-Faruqi was implying that all the territory between the western boundary of the Ottoman vilayet of Damascus, "down to the Egyptian border near Rafah," was to be French territory. But this is only an inference. As I read al-Faruqi's proposal according to Sykes' report of it, al-Faruqi was deliberately limiting himself to defining the future French sphere of influence, and was taking care to avoid specifying, within this sphere, a boundary between French territory and Arab territory.

As long as I was in temporary government service I was never challenged on my interpretation of McMahon's word "wilayahs": not by Crowe, who was both well-informed and precise; not by Smuts (but Smuts was concerned only for brevity); and, most surprising of all, not by McMahon himself.

When the Western Powers decided to send an international commission of inquiry to Syria and Palestine, McMahon was appointed head of the British section, and I was appointed secretary. I came from Paris to London, met McMahon in

London for the first time, and worked there with McMahon every day, for several weeks, on making preparations for our intended expedition to the Middle East. I then fell sick, and, a week or two later, Britain and France withdrew from the commission and the United States carried out the inquiry alone. (It resulted in the King-Crane Report.)

During those weeks that I was in daily contact with Mc-Mahon, he never raised with me the question of the interpretation of his letter to Hussein of 24 October 1915. Of course, I did not raise it on my side; this was not my business, and also I was not aware that McMahon's interpretation of his letter was different from mine. Yet my memoranda must have been in Mc-Mahon's hands long since, and I was now going to be his aide. If, in the spring of 1919, McMahon was convinced that he had excluded Palestine from the area of Arab independence, it is incomprehensible to me that he did not take me up on this point — a point of great personal importance to him, as well as of public importance for the Commission — as soon as I arrived in London and reported to him. Yet McMahon never said a word to me about this. Nor had he previously taken up with the Arab Bureau its substitution of the word "line" for his word "wilayahs." The substitution had been made already in a prototype of the Arab Bureau's *History* which McMahon himself had forwarded to Grey on 19 April 1916.[7] He forwarded this interpretation of his own letter without demur.

The first challenge to the Arab Bureau's interpretation and my interpretation that I had was from Major Hubert Young. He told me that he had been looking into the meaning of Mc-Mahon's letter of 24 October 1915 and had concluded that, apropos of Damascus, McMahon's "wilayahs" meant "the Ottoman vilayet of Damascus" — which would mean, of course, that in this letter McMahon had excluded Palestine from the area of Arab independence. The date at which Major Young told me this must have been about the time when he was writing his memorandum of 29 November 1920.

I have pointed out that, by 1922, the Arab Delegation to London had a political motive for interpreting McMahon's word "wilayahs" as meaning "environs." I must now also point out that, as soon as HMG was sure that it was going to get the mandate for Palestine, it had a political motive for interpreting

McMahon's word "wilayahs" as meaning, apropos of Damascus, "Ottoman vilayets." The acquisition of the mandate for Palestine carried with it, for Britain, the obligation to implement the Balfour Declaration, and HMG would have found it embarrassing to do this in the teeth of Palestinian Arab protests if it had not now maintained that Palestine was excluded from the area within which McMahon had pledged HMG to recognize and uphold Arab independence. The documents written by British officials, contesting the interpretation of McMahon's word "wilayahs" that was made by me and, before me, by the author of the Arab Bureau's *History*, all date from after the time at which HMG had become sure that Britain had Palestine in her pocket. The date on which the Principal Allied Powers assigned the mandate for Palestine to Britain is 24 April 1920. The date of Major Young's memorandum is 29 November 1920[8]; the date of McMahon's confidential letter to Sir John Shuckburgh is 12 March 1922[9]; the date of Childs's memorandum is 24 October 1930.[10]

It can be, and has been, argued that, even if the interpretation of McMahon's "wilayahs" as meaning "environs," not "Ottoman vilayets," is correct, McMahon's letter still excludes Palestine from the area of Arab independence by the reservation, included in the letter, that HMG could give assurances to the Arabs only in regard to those territories "in which she [*sic*] can act without detriment to the interests of her ally France." In making this reservation, McMahon was giving HMG carte blanche to revoke the undertakings that McMahon himself was making to the Arabs on HMG's behalf; but this reservation was a contingent one. It would come into effect only in so far as France claimed to have interests and pressed her claims.

In October 1915, McMahon did not know, because HMG did not know, what the extent of the French claims was going to be or how hard France was going to press them. On 24 April 1920, the Principal Allied Powers, of whom France was of course one, assigned the mandate for Palestine to Britain, and thus France implicitly renounced any interest in Palestine that she may previously have claimed. On the same date, however, the Principal Allied Powers, of whom Britain also was one, assigned the mandates for the Lebanon and Syria to France, so, on that date, the contingent reservation in France's favor that

McMahon had included in his letter of 24 October 1915 was liquidated in respect of Palestine but simultaneously came into force in respect of Damascus, Homs, Hama, and Aleppo — the very places that McMahon had explicitly included (subject to this reservation) in the area within which he pledged HMG to recognize and uphold Arab independence. Accordingly, HMG made no move to uphold Arab independence there when, in July 1920, France pressed her claim to the four towns in the interior of Syria by conquering them by force of arms.

In any case, the McMahon-Hussein correspondence, of which McMahon's letter of 24 October 1915 to Hussein was a part, did not result in the conclusion of any agreement or treaty. I "pinpointed" this, as Mr. Friedman says (p. l), in my memorandum on British Commitments to King Hussein. Thus the commitments in this letter of McMahon's had no juridical validity. Yet an undertaking may be morally valid, even if it does not have the force of law. McMahon's letter of 24 October 1915 was not, and is not, a dead letter, and the attempts to ascertain the true meaning of this letter have not been wasted labor. I do not agree with Mr. Friedman's judgment (p. xix) that today, the controversy over this question has no more than an academic interest. McMahon's letter of 24 October 1915 struck some of the sparks that have set ablaze the present conflagration in the Middle East.

I do not think that Young's or Childs's or Mr. Friedman's interpretation of McMahon's use of the word "wilayahs" is tenable. After studying Mr. Friedman's paper and writing these notes, I am inclined to think that the drafting of this letter was not disingenuous, but hopelessly muddle-headed. Incompetence is not excusable in transacting serious and responsible public business. If the draftsman had been Crowe or Hirtzel (I did some work for both of them, and have first-hand knowledge of their carefulness and precision), I think it is improbable that this important letter would have been as ambiguous as, unfortunately, it has proved to be.

lsaiah Friedman replies

I am grateful for Professor Toynbee's comments and for the opportunity to elucidate a few points. (Figures in parentheses refer to the pages of my article.)

I agree that, unlike the Arab Delegation, Toynbee in 1918 had no political ax to grind. If anything rather the reverse, for, in his memorandum dated 21 November 1918,[1] he recommended, consistently with Whitehall's desideratum, that Britain should administer Palestine and advised that the British Government should ensure "reasonable facilities" for Jewish colonization, without giving offense to Arab or general Moslem opinion. On this point he made an important contribution:

> The problem of Palestine cannot be solved entirely on the principles of self-determination and free choice of assistance. As in Armenia, there will be a mixed population, and there will be one element in that population, in this case the Jewish colonists, which, for special reasons, will be entitled to a position more than mathematically proportionate to its numbers at the start.
>
> Moreover, in Palestine there are international religious interests so important and so difficult to reconcile that they almost overshadow the internal problems of the native inhabitants.

However, his dilemma with regard to what appeared to him contradictory commitments made to Sherif Hussein (24 October 1915) and the Zionists (2 November 1917) remained unresolved, and his doubt has persisted for over half a century.

1.   On what grounds did Dr. Toynbee reach his conclusion? At the time this question was only marginal, and I am inclined to think that W. J. Childs, in his paper dated 24 October 1930, was correct in assuming that, when Toynbee was preparing his memorandum, he used a copy of the Arab Bureau's *History of the Hedjaz Rising*, as his various references show (pp. xliv-xlv). Since writing my article, I have ascertained that the author of this work was Ormsby-Gore, then on the staff of the Arab Bureau.[2] It is not a "History," certainly not an interpretative one, nor even a summary, but merely a collection of cables and dispatches set out in chronological order about the Hedjaz rising and negotiations with the French representative in London

leading to the Sykes-Picot Agreement. The document in question, on which Toynbee based his conclusion, is dated 16 April 1916. I recently traced its paternity to David Hogarth.[3] Noting that the correspondence with Sherif Hussein remained inconclusive, Hogarth attempted to establish what was and what was not agreed. He wrote:

> We for our part have not agreed to:
>
> A) Recognize Arab independence in Syria west of the line [sic] Aleppo-Hama-Homs-Damascus, or in any portion of the Arab area in which we are not free to act without detriment to our ally, France . . .
>
> What has been agreed to, therefore, on behalf of Great Britain is:
>
> A) To recognize the independence of those portions of the Arab speaking area in which we are free to act without detriment to the interests of France. Subject to these undefined reservations, the said area is understood to be bounded north by about latitude 37°. East by the Persian frontier. South by the Persian Gulf and Indian Ocean. West by the Red Sea and the Mediterranean up to about latitude 33° and beyond by an indefinite line [sic] drawn west of Damascus, Hama, Homs and Aleppo; all that lies within this last line and the Mediterranean [i.e., the Syrian littoral] being, in any case, reserved absolutely for future arrangements between the French and the Arabs.

Hogarth joined the newly established Arab Bureau in mid-March 1916 and, beyond the correspondence, had no first-hand knowledge of relations with Sherif Hussein. Even a cursory examination of his note shows that:

1. He considered Hussein's letter of 14 July 1915, in which the latter outlined the boundaries of the Arab Empire bounded on the north by the line Mersina-Adana to parallel 37°N to include the whole of the Arabian peninsula (except Aden), Mesopotamia, Syria and what was later Transjordan and Palestine, as the ultimate embodiment of Arab desiderata. This was obviously not the case, since this letter served merely as a *basis* for negotiations (pp. xxiii-xxv);

2. He was completely unaware of what had passed since al-

Faruqi's appearance on the scene — a fatal gap, since it was the statements made by Faruqi that formed the cornerstone of McMahon's crucial letter of 24 October 1915 and his reservations set out therein;

3. He overlooked the correspondence between Cairo and London, for had he seen it, he would have realized from McMahon's cable to Grey of 26 October 1915 (p. xli) that "the area in which we are not free to act without detriment to the interests of our ally, France," was Palestine.

Moreover, Hogarth erroneously substituted the word "line" for the word "districts" used by McMahon, compounding this lapse by another mistake. By inventing a second line "up to about latitude 33° and beyond an indefinite line drawn inland west of Damascus . . . and the Mediterranean," he gratuitously included Palestine within the area of Arab "independence," contrary to McMahon's intention. When he reserved it "absolutely for future arrangement between the French and the Arabs," he tacitly admitted that Palestine fell within the French sphere of interest; the term "independence" was not used in its literal sense but was synonymous with liberation from the Turk.[4]

Hogarth's blunder stands out even more conspicuously when set against another section of his note where, discussing the Sykes-Picot Agreement, he wrote: "Palestine, west of Jordan, to be internationalized. Acre and Haifa to be British . . . Independent Arab State to consist of remaining area [i.e., east of Jordan and the Syrian hinterland], but to be divided into two spheres of influence . . . French and British." This inconsistency apparently accounts for McMahon's failure to notice Hogarth's error when forwarding a copy of his note (undated and unsigned) to London.[5]

However much Hogarth might have disliked the system of an international regime, particularly so close to the eastern Egyptian border, he saw one advantage in it: "Palestine under International Control was perhaps the best solution, especially in view of the aspirations of the Jews to the area in which they may enjoy some sort of proprietorship." This statement, written only two weeks after his note of 16 April 1916, is interesting, since he thought that the Lebanon, unlike Palestine, should have been included in the area of Arab independence.[6]

Hogarth's mistake, although unfortunate, was soon obliterated from his memory. Henceforth he regarded British-oriented Zionism as a useful tool with which to undermine the French position accorded by the May 1916 Asia Minor Agreement.[7] On 4 January 1918, when delivering his (now famous) message to King Hussein, Hogarth could detect no contradiction between the terms of the Balfour Declaration and McMahon's pledge. Nor did his host, who referred to Palestine as "a sacred and beloved homeland . . . [of] its original sons (*abna'ihill-asliyim*)" — the Jews (p. xlvii). Hogarth was one of the high-ranking British officers who gave his unequivocal support to Yale's solution during the Peace Conference (p. xlix). In a paper read on 27 January 1925, he assured his audience that the British Government was "guiltless . . . of any betrayal of King Hussein. The sole condition of his active alliance . . . that he be freed from his Ottoman overlords and recognized as an independent sovereign — has been fulfilled."[8] In the discussion that followed, Col. Jacob, Ormsby-Gore, Sir Percy Cox, and Sir Arnold Wilson participated. None of them disputed Hogarth's contention.

All signs show that Ormsby-Gore was unaware of the error that Hogarth made in his note of 16 April 1916, when he incorporated it into his voluminous collection entitled "Summary of Historical Documents . . .," on 29 November 1916. Early in 1917, Ormsby-Gore moved from Cairo to London to join the War Secretariat. He advised Lord Milner in drafting the Balfour Declaration, and like Sir Mark Sykes was considered an expert on Arab and Zionist affairs. In 1918, he accompanied the Zionist Commission to Palestine, and in 1919 assisted the British delegation to the Peace Conference. In none of his numerous memoranda, minutes, or dispatches is there the slightest hint that he saw any inconsistency between the British commitment to the Zionists and that made to Hussein. On 21 July 1937, then Colonial Secretary, he assured the House of Commons that "it was never in the mind of anyone on that staff [i.e., Arab Bureau] that Palestine west of the Jordan was in the area within which the British Government then undertook to further the cause of Arab independence . . . the whole sequel proves the case."

2. That McMahon made no comment on Toynbee's statement in 1919 does not prove that he agreed with it. It constituted a small part of Toynbee's memorandum and McMahon might have overlooked it (if he saw it at all). More telling is that McMahon fully endorsed Yale's solution on Palestine and the Middle East at the Peace Conference. Other distinguished British officers like Cmdr. Hogarth, General Allenby, Col. Lawrence, Col. Cornwallis, Col. Stirling, as well as Lord Robert Cecil, Emir Feisal, Rustum Haidar Bey, and Nuri Said, also approved Yale's plan. Yale, as his reports show, was well-informed about the nature of British commitments to Hussein and was in a position to judge whether or not they conflicted with those made to the Zionists.

Sir Eyre Crowe was undoubtedly a competent man, but in 1915-16 did not deal with the Arab question, and in 1919 also probably relied on other Middle East experts. How could he have suspected a "breach" if Emir Feisal, representing his father, publicly left Palestine aside and entered into an agreement with Dr. Weizmann? The late Sir Charles Webster (during the war, in Military Intelligence), who also assisted the British Delegation to Paris, in a personal interview with myself, categorically rejected any idea of contradictory promises to Arabs and Jews.

3. Not until January 1921, when Feisal made his first challenge, did the Foreign Office examine the whole question thoroughly. The "Summary of Historical Documents . . ." (on which Toynbee relied) was traced and printed with the explicit purpose of showing "without any possibility of doubt" what McMahon meant by the relevant passage of his letter of 24 October 1915.[9] Professor Toynbee had by then left the Foreign Office and subsequently it was shown (see Childs's paper dated 24 October 1930) how he had been misled.

4. As to the meaning of the word "districts,"[10] it would certainly have been much tidier had McMahon phrased the passage as Professor Toynbee suggests. But the fault was not McMahon's. As Childs had shown, this phrase originated with al-Faruqi. McMahon referred to it in his dispatch to Grey on 18 October 1915 (p. xxxviii) six days before making his territorial

pledges to Hussein. Since then it had become a cliché in both Cairo and London. Al-Faruqi certainly did not intend a narrow interpretation of the "immediate neighbourhood," since this would have been fatal to the whole concept of an Arab state stretching from the Syrian hinterland southwards through what later became Transjordan to Hedjaz. Moreover, we have McMahon's own interpretation given to Sir John Shuckburgh on 12 March 1922 (p. xxxix-xl), which I have no reason to question. The Arab Bureau staff were of course quite familiar with the administrative division of Syria and Palestine. Thus Ormsby-Gore specifically referred to the region east of the Jordan as "part of the Vilayet of Damascus."[11]

5. Al-Faruqi specifically mentioned Palestine by name when excluding it, as well as the Syrian littoral, from the area destined to become an Arab state. Palestine was also covered in al-Faruqi's phrase "the places inhabited by a foreign race"; his statement conveyed the purpose of the Sherif's letter of 14 July 1915 outlining the boundaries of Arab independence. This is not my inference, as Professor Toynbee suggests; it was so understood at the time by McMahon, Clayton, Sykes, Sir Arthur Nicolson, and Grey (as their respective dispatches and notes show), and it was on the basis of this understanding that the Sykes-Picot Agreement was subsequently outlined. Moreover, al-Faruqi's reservations tally with Hussein's admission in his letter to his friend, Seyyid Ali Morghani: 'We have no reason for discussing the question of the frontier other than a preliminary measure.' Professor Toynbee overlooked all the evidence adduced in my article to this effect (pp. xxxvii-xxxix, xlvi-xlvii).

6. France's standing in the East was a matter of common knowledge. Following her claim to Syria and Palestine in March 1915 (on the heels of Russia's claim to Constantinople), the British Government was in no position to assign any part of these provinces to the Arabs without French consent. Paris insisted that Syria was a purely French possession and by Syria meant the region bounded by the Taurus ridges on the north and the Egyptian frontier near Rafah on the south. This was what Picot stated officially to Nicolson during their

meeting in London on 23 November 1915.

With the Arab desiderata centered on the Syrian hinterland and their four towns, the future of Palestine was left exclusively to France and Britain and their allies. It is therefore immaterial to argue that, on 24 April 1920, when France renounced her interest in Palestine in favor of a British mandate, the force of the reservation made by McMahon in his letter of 24 October 1915 lapsed, and that, by the same token, the British Government was free to give Palestinian Arabs their independence. This argument is not new. It was advanced by successive Arab delegations to London (1922-39) and by Antonius. Lord Maugham, Lord Chancellor, dismissed it as "irrelevant"; Mr. Leonard Stein termed it "irrational" and "cynical" whilst Childs maintained that French interest remained. The official French position, was that the Jewish National Home policy should be implemented; the award of Palestine to the Arabs would have violated the French pledge given to the Zionists in June 1917 and February 1918, to say nothing of a similar pledge given by the Italian Government and the subsequent arrangement made by the League of Nations in 1922.[12]

I do not excuse the conduct of the French in Syria in July 1920, but it is worth bearing in mind: a) that British advice to Feisal in 1919/20 to come to terms with the French Government, as set out in the Asia-Minor [Sykes-Picot] Agreement, remained unheeded; b) that the nature of Arab "independence" in the Syrian interior was conditional on the extent of the Arab rising against the Turk, which did not take place; and, c) that the British position in regard to Palestine and the pledge to the Zionists, were unrelated to Franco-Arab relations in Syria.

7. I agree that, if the draftsman had been Crowe or Hirtzel, the important letter to Hussein would have been written differently. I presume that the readers of my article did not fail to take note of the attitude of Sir Arthur Hirtzel and the India Office to the whole affair (p. xxix).

8. I cannot accept Professor Toynbee's contention that, though devoid of any juridical validity, the undertaking to Sherif Hussein is still "morally valid." This undertaking, as I hope was

shown in my paper, was not of a *unilateral* nature, and, if any party remained in debt, it was rather the Arabs toward the British than vice versa; the method employed by al-Faruqi to extract far-reaching obligations from the British could not be termed moral. Nor can I accept Toynbee's assertion that, because of the British Government's interest in retaining the mandate over Palestine, statements and memoranda produced by British officials after April 1920 are not reliable. The charge that high-ranking officers and Ministers consistently and deliberately perjured themselves is to my mind inadmissible. Nor can I understand how Professor Toynbee overlooked a considerable body of evidence relating to the pre-1920 period (adduced in my article) that belies his conclusion. It would be legitimate to ask at this point why, in his 1918 memoranda, Toynbee recommended that Britain assume the role of trustee of the Jewish National Home, rather than hand Palestine to the Arabs, if he thought that it was included in the boundaries of Arab independence?

Whether or not the subject has any political bearing, is not for me to say. For me it was and remains an academic issue and I hope I treated it in that spirit. On the basis of my study, I do not hesitate to state that the record of the British Government in this matter is clean. It was not McMahon's letter of 24 October 1915, unfortunate though its phrasing was, that complicated Anglo-Arab-Jewish relations, but the myth that was built up around it. If to reveal historical truth helps to create a better climate of international understanding, the labor was not in vain.

Maps

Map 1 - reproduction of original
Ottoman administrative division of vilayets (districts) covering the territory of Syria, Lebanon, and Palestine.

Reproduced in Palestine Royal Commission Report, July 1937 (Peel Commission), Cmd 5479 (London 1937), facing page.

Map 2 - schematic & reproduction of original
Ottoman administrative division of vilayets (districts), in Arabic terminology, *wilāya*. The *wilāya* of Esh SHAM covers the territory of the Syrian hinterland and east of the River Jordan down to Akaba. Esh SHAM (Damascus) is the capital of this *wilāya*, vilayet in the Ottoman terminology.

Map 3 - schematic & reproduction of original
Map sketched by Lawrence (end of November 1918?). The line that separates Palestine from the territory to be allotted to the Arab State under Feisal runs 10 miles approximately east of the River Jordan and the Dead Sea.

Map 4 - schematic & reproduction of original
A map sketched by Toynbee on 8 October 1918. The eastern border of Palestine runs 10 miles approximately east of the River Jordan and the Dead Sea.

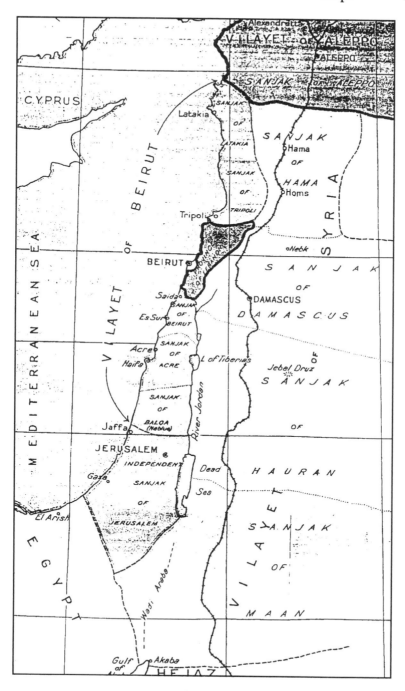

Map 1

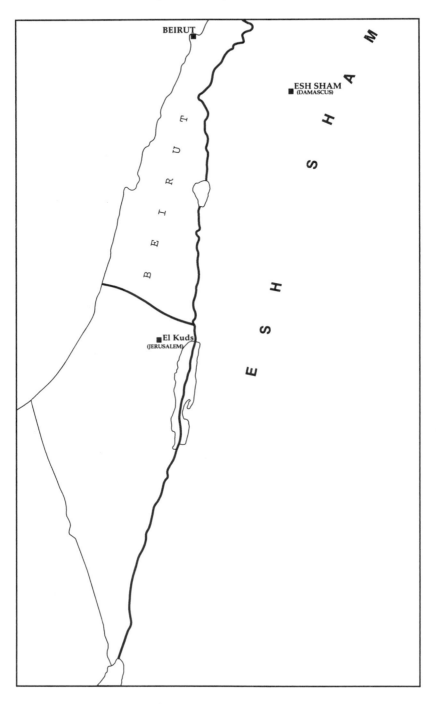

Map 2

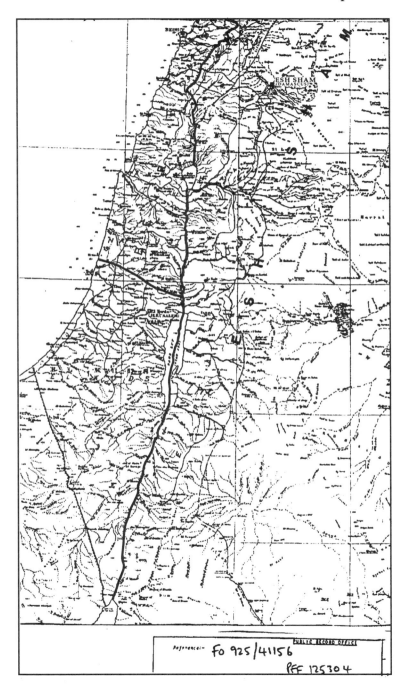

Map 2

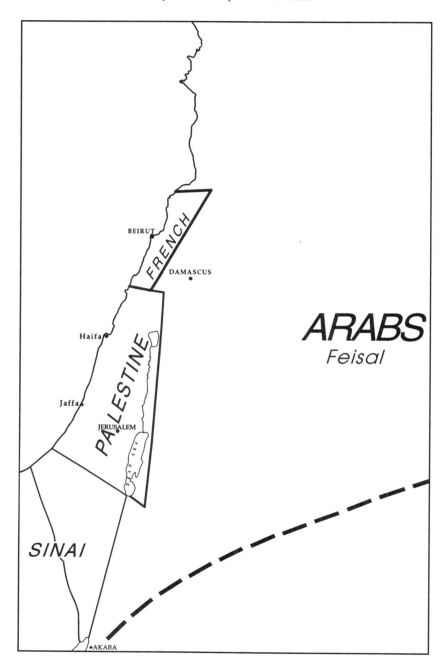

Map 3

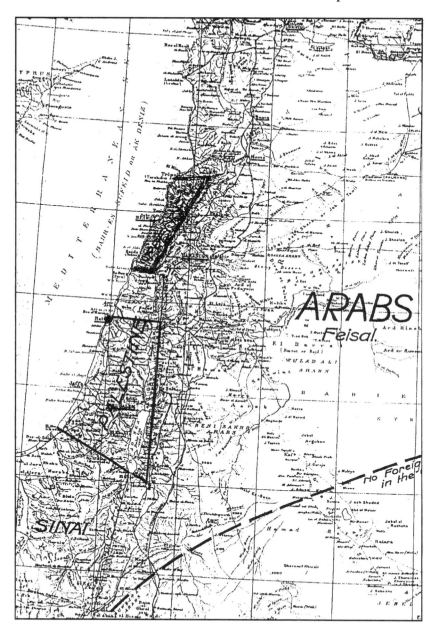

Map 3

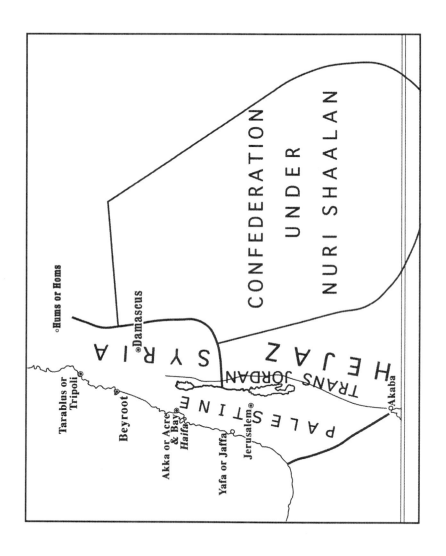

Map 4

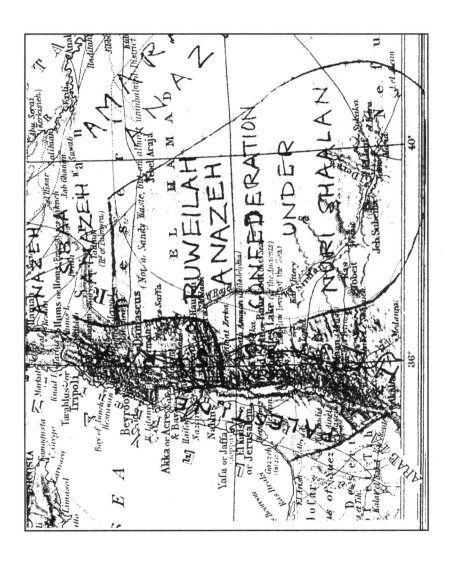

Map 4

1

A Follow-up to the Dialogue
with Arnold J. Toynbee

Replying to the criticism made by Professor Trevor-Roper, Professor Toynbee wrote:

> I agree that my claim cannot be sustained if I have not tried to test my theories and hypotheses by the facts, or if I have tried but have not done the job properly or successfully. For, while it is true that theories and hypotheses can never be deduced from facts, it is also true that they can be validated only if they are confronted with the relevant facts and are confirmed by them.[1]

Toynbee's self-proclaimed credo was: "I have greater respect for the historical evidence than I have for a particular hypothesis that I happen to have picked out of my tool-bag."[2] The author of the present study had therefore expected that Toynbee would be willing to continue our discussion and clarify certain points that remained unresolved. Regretfully, my further correspondence elicited no reply, and on 22 October 1975 he died.

In 1969, Toynbee told this author that, when considering the question in the autumn of 1918, much depended on the meaning of the phrase "Vilayet of Damascus." In Ottoman administrative usage, vilayet was used in a wider sense, covering Cis-Jordanian Palestine, whereas, in Arabic, *wilāya* meant "environs" or "banlieux." He further stated that McMahon could not have used the Ottoman terminology in his letter of 24 October 1915, in which case Palestine was meant to be included.[3]

However, there is no scintilla of evidence that this was what

Toynbee thought when preparing his "Memorandum" on British Commitments to King Hussein" (October/November 1918). His reason for concluding that the British Government was pledged that Palestine "shall be 'Arab' and 'independent'" was quite different.[4] Moreover, it is most unlikely that the word *wilāya* was considered by him at any time. Toynbee did not know Arabic and the term in this particular sense does not exist.

In vain can one search for *wilāya* among British, French, or German official records. Nor does it appear in the vast literature of travelers, among whom Seetzen[5] and Volney[6] are prominent. The latter, noted for his acuteness of mind, was familiar with Arabic and, during his lengthy sojourn in Syria, learned to appreciate the customs and character of the native people. His book was translated into five languages including Arabic. The term does not appear in Baedeker's authoritative handbook either,[7] or in any other guidebooks of the time. Nor is it mentioned in any of the letters of Gertrude Bell or T. E. Lawrence. In her memorandum of 23 June 1917, Miss Bell gave a vivid description of Damascus and its environs, but nowhere does she use the term *wilāya*.[8] This is important, since Syria, by her own admission, was the province with which she was "most familiar."[9] In his comprehensive memorandum on Syria, Lawrence used the familiar Arab word *Shám* for Damascus.[10] Had *wilāya* been in current use, he would have undoubtedly mentioned it as well when describing its neighborhood.

Major Hubert Young served on the staff of Emir Feisal's army in 1918 and took part in operations in the Dera'a-Damascus region. He spoke Arabic fluently. Nonetheless, he never, as far as evidence goes, came across the word *wilāya* used in the sense indicated by Toynbee.

Even more telling is its absolute absence from the classic study of Vital Cuinet, *Syrie, Liban et Palestine. Geographie Administrative* (Paris, 1896), whose thoroughness and erudition is noticeable on every page. His map of the administrative division of the region during the Ottoman period was published in the *Palestine Royal Commission Report* (the Peel Report) of 1937, and later in countless modern Middle East histories and textbooks. Similarly, the word does not appear in the specialized studies of Gibb and Bowen,[11] Rafeq,[12] Barbir,[13] Maoz,[14] and others.

Ironic as it may seem, the Palestine Delegation to London in 1922 did not mention the word *wilāya* at all when they challenged the British for equating the term "district" with the Ottoman "vilayet." They argued that the name of the area in question was not the Vilayet of Damascus, but the Vilayet of Syria and, since Homs were "districts" within the Vilayet of Syria, the district of Damascus could only have meant a smaller administrative unit. "Palestine," they concluded, "thus comes within the scope of the promise."[15] Antonius repeated this argument in his book *The Arab Awakening* (pp. 177-178), which appeared first in November 1938.

It was not until the Round Table Conference in London early in 1939 that the word *wilāya* was aired for the first time. The person who brought it out was the same Antonius, then Delegate and Secretary-General to the Arab Delegation. He claimed that the Arabic *wilāya* did not correspond to the Turkish vilayet and that, in the given context of the 1915-1916 Correspondence, the word *wilāya* was "without any reference to administrative boundaries."[16] This interpretation, as we shall see later was palpably not true and was meant merely to confuse his British opposite numbers. Sir Michael McDonnell, the Legal Adviser to the Arab Delegation, reiterated this argument, insisting that the Arabic word *wilāya* "does not necessarily impart an Ottoman *vilayet*, which was a determined administrative unit," and that "the Sharif was using the Arab term *wilāya* . . . in the sense of the *environs* of the towns named."[17]

It was from these statements in 1939, that Toynbee learned that *wilāya* could mean "environs" or "banlieux," but not before that time. In 1967, when writing to the present author, and thereafter in his "Comments," he quite erroneously attributed this interpretation to himself when he prepared his "Memorandum on British Commitments to King Hussein" in 1918.

Since the meaning of the terms vilayet/*wilāya*/district was so hotly disputed — still remains controversial — a more detailed examination is called for.

The word *wilāya* is derived from the Koran (Sura IV, 62) and in constitutional law means the sovereign power (e.g., sultan), or the power delegated by the sovereign, the office of a governor, a *wāli*. In time it came to be applied to the area governed by a *wāli*. In Turkish, it was pronounced vilayet, and, from the sixteenth century (when it was called also *eyalet*), the term was applied to the largest administrative units.[18] *The Shorter Encyclopedia of Islam*[19] also states that the term means the appointment and certificate of appointment of an official, and, in later times, an administrative district.

Professor Bernard Lewis, in his *Handbook*, equates *wilāya* with vilayet, or state.[20] Professor Philip Khoury put it thus: "*wilāya*(A); vilayet(T) = Ottoman administrative unit or province."[21] Dr. Welga Rebhan, in her authoritative history of Arabic political terms during the nineteenth century, states that *wilāya* means *Herrschergewalt*, which stands for sovereign power.[22] According to the Arabic-English dictionary of J. G. Hava (a Jesuit priest), which appeared in Beirut in 1915, *wilāya* means: government, supremacy, dominion, management of a province, state, vilayet; while the most authoritative and relatively recent dictionary of Hans Wehr[23] terms it similarly: sovereign power, rule, government, administrative district, headed by a *wāli*, vilayet, province, state. In this respect, there is no material difference between the colloquial and literary Arabic. *Wilāya* is essentially associated with a governmental, not geographical, concept and is invariably related to a large administrative unit, not to a town and its environs.[24] Arab scholars at the University of Haifa have confirmed this deduction.[25] The Arab scholar Rafiq Tamimi entitled his book (in Arabic) that dealt with the Vilayet of Beirut, *Wilāya Bairut* (Beirut, 1331/1913).[26] The substantive body of all this learned opinion belies the Antonius/McDonnell contention.

Contemporary records show that British officials considered the terms *wilāya*, vilayet, and district, as well as province, to be synonymous in meaning. Thus, in a cable to Grey, Cheetham referred to "districts of Mesopotamia."[27] On the other hand, General Barrow used the Arabic term "Basra *wilayat*,"[28] while Lord Crewe, Secretary of State for India, stated during the meeting of the War Council on 19 March 1915 that "Basra Vilayet must be part of the British Empire."[29] Holderness, Admiral Jackson, Major-General Calwell, Sir Mark Sykes, and other members of the de Bunsen Committee used the terms "province, vilayet" interchangeably during their meetings with regard to the districts of Mosul, Baghdad, and Basra.[30] In his important telegram of 20 October 1915 to McMahon, Grey used the word "Vilayet" with regard to Basra, but "province" for Baghdad, although they had an identical administrative status. On the other hand, the Viceroy of India (4 November 1915) called Basra a "Vilayet" but used the Arabic word *wilāya* for Baghdad. The following day McMahon applied "vilayets" to both Baghdad and Basra, while Sykes, in his cable from Cairo to the Director of Military Operations on 21 November 1915, wrote "Baghdad and Basra provinces."[31] On 2 November 1918, in a note to the India Office, the Foreign Office referred to Mosul as "district," while the Political Officer in Baghdad (Wilson) on 27 November 1918 preferred to use the Ottoman term "vilayet."[32]

Hedjaz was a vilayet, but Lt. General Sir Edwin Locke Elliot, in a conversation with Sir Afsur Bahadur of Hyderabad, chose the English term "district" of Hedjaz.[33] The British Consul in Aleppo followed a similar pattern when reporting to Sir Louis Mallet, the British Ambassador in Constantinople: "Syrians in this district [of Aleppo]."[34] Sir Reginald Wingate urged the necessity of holding on to the Aleppo and Beirut Provinces and, in the same breath, insisted on retention of Baghdad and Basra Vilayets.[35]

It is even more illuminating to juxtapose the English and Arabic versions of the Correspondence,[36] in which *wilāya* is invariably translated as district, province, or vilayet. Thus, Sharif Hussein, in his letter of 5 November 1915, used the word *wilāyātain*, which is the dual of *wilāya*, with regard to Aleppo and Beirut; at the British Residency it was translated into "provinces of . . ." In the second paragraph of the same letter, where the English translation reads "since the provinces of Iraq . . . ," the Arabic original is *wilāyāt*, the dual number of *wilāya*. Vilayets of Aleppo and Beirut in McMahon's letter of 14 December 1915 were translated as *wilāyat* (plural); whereas "Vilayet of Baghdad," in the same letter of McMahon, as well as in his subsequent one of 30 January 1916, was translated as *wilāya* (singular). These examples remove any doubt about the identity of meaning of the English, Turkish, and Arabic terms. Parenthetically, it should be added that *wilāya* is even stronger in meaning than its English equivalent, since it denotes rule and authority; the territory that it covered was always governed by a high-ranking official called a *Vali* (in Arabic, *wāli*). The Ottoman vilayet was merely a linguistic derivation of the Arabic word. Professor Geoffrey Lewis, the distinguished philologist in Turkish at St. Antony's College, Oxford, thinks that "*vilayet* is simply the Turkish pronunciation of the Arabic *wilāya*."[37]

There was, however, an exception. In his much quoted letter of 24 October 1915, McMahon referred to the districts of Mersina and Alexandretta (translated in Arabic to *wilāyāt*) — obviously a lacuna in his knowledge, since neither Mersina nor Alexandretta were vilayets, the first laying in the Vilayet of Adana and the second in that of Aleppo. But the error was seized on by those who rejected the British equating district with vilayet as additional proof to fortify their case. Their deduction, however, is fallacious, if not mischievous, for, had this been so, the vilayets of Aleppo and Beirut, as well as those of Mosul, Baghdad, and Basra, would have to be downgraded in their respective administrative status, which is absurd.

At this juncture it would be of interest to point out that, in his reply of 5 November 1915, Sharif Hussein committed a similar mistake. The relevant sentence translated literally to English reads:

> We renounce our insistence on the inclusion of the *vilayets* of Mersina and Adana in the Arab Kingdom. But the two *vilayets* of Aleppo and Beirut and their sea coasts . . .[38]

Was Hussein as ignorant as the High Commissioner in this particular case, or was he merely repeating his correspondent's error? The only explanation for this peculiar confusion is that, before the introduction of the Law of Vilayets in 1864, the boundaries separating provinces from each other were arbitrary and subject to many changes. They were fixed for military, fiscal, and administrative convenience and altered at will. Moreover, irrespective of official delimitation, the local population had their own notions of local boundaries, often determined by agricultural requirements or ancient custom.[39] Barbir, who relied on Gibb and Bowen's study,[40] concluded:

> The problem of provincial boundaries in the Ottoman Empire has been taken too seriously by modern observers. They tend to assume that boundaries were literally fixed and provinces clearly defined. This often reflects a desire to project the limits of

modern states back into the past.[41]

But the main bone of contention, which generated so much heat, related to "the districts of Damascus, Homs, Hama and Aleppo." Gallons of ink have been spilt on it, only to demonstrate the gap between the disputants. The controversy was fraught with emotion; it had serious political implications and impinged on Britain's good faith. It would therefore be useful to examine the matter more carefully.

In official Ottoman parlance, the district of Damascus was called Vilayet of Syria. It extended from the Vilayet of Aleppo in the north to the Vilayet of Hedjaz in the south. On the east, it reached the *mutesarriflik* of Zor and the desert of Syria, and in the west — a border which is most relevant in our case — ran conterminously with the eastern border of the Vilayet of Beirut and the Sanjak of Jerusalem, bisecting the Sea of Galilee, the Jordan River, and the Dead Sea. From its lower end, it took a southwesterly course to the Egyptian border about seventy miles northwest of the Gulf of Akaba (see Map 1).[42] To comply with the laws of Vilayets 1864 it was divided into four sanjaks: those of Hama, Damascus, Hauran, and Ma'an, which were each subdivided into kazas, and the kazas into *nāhiyes* and villages. Damascus was the seat of the Vali, a governor with extensive authority. One of his tasks was to ensure the safety of the pilgrimage to the holy places in Mecca and Medina, an appointment that acquired religious prestige, coupled with financial benefits.[43] For Moslems through the centuries, the link between Damascus and the Hedjaz has been essential.

A distinction should be drawn between the Vilayet of Syria and Syria (in Turkish *sûristân*), which, in contrast to the former, did not have administrative significance, being merely a geographical expression. The area that Syria covered extended from the Taurus Mountains in the north to el-Arish in the south, and from the Mediterranean in the west to the Euphrates in the east.[44] With the exception of Aleppo, the Vilayet of Syria covered the whole of geographical Syria until the mid-nineteenth century; hence its name. But, following the separation of the Sanjak of Jerusalem in 1872 and the reconstruction of the Vilayet of Beirut in 1888, the Vilayet of Syria in 1888 became confined strictly to the eastern part of geographical Syria.

The name Syria is an abridgment of Assyria and took root when the country became the western province of the Assyrian Empire. The Greeks thereafter transmitted the name to the European languages, but the Arabs, who did not adopt the Greek names, were ignorant of it and called Syria Barr-ush-Shám or ush-Shám. *Shám* signified the country of the left, whereas all the territory of the south (named by the Romans Arabia Felix), which covered the Arabian Peninsula, was called Yamin, which meant country of the right.

Ush-Shám was also the name of Damascus; the native inhabitants were delighted to name their capital after the country. Damascus had yet another name — Dimashq-ush-Shám — which is derived from the Hebrew *Dammeseq* (2/Kings, viii, 5, 6), corresponding to the *Aram Dammeseq* of the Bible.[45] Literally it meant "Damascus of Syria." The city itself was called *Madinat Dimashq.*[46] The Arabic equivalent of the Ottoman Vilayet of Syria was wilāya ush-Shám, while geographical Syria, which also embraced Palestine, was often referred to by a more specific name — Bilad ush-Shám — *bilad* meaning country, or, in modern political vocabulary, translated as Greater Syria.[47] It is essential to bear all these details in mind when we examine the Arabic translation of McMahon's much-disputed letter of 24 October 1915.[48]

The British, too, refrained (at least during the period under discussion) from using the term Vilayet of Syria, both in literature and in official dispatches, albeit for entirely different reasons than the Arabs. They tried either to avoid confusion with the geographical Syria and/or, for the sake of convenience, to conform with the vilayets. A number of examples illustrate the point. Thus, a Foreign Office official lumped together the "Vilayets of Basra, Baghdad, Mosul, Aleppo and Damascus."[49] Likewise, Sir Mark Sykes, in his cable from Cairo to the D.M.O., wrote, "vilayets of Aleppo, Beirut and Damascus."[50] And a week later, when writing to Cox, he referred to the "vilayets of Damascus, Beirut, Aleppo, Mosul [and] Baghdad," as well as to "Mosul, Baghdad and Basra Provinces."[51] He used the terms interchangeably with regard to identical locations. T. E. Lawrence wrote the following: "[The Vilayet of] Syria in Turkish (the word exists not in Arabic) is the province of Damascus,"[52] whereas McMahon, in a "Note on Possible Terms of Peace with

Turkey," pointed to the "Vilayets of Damascus and Aleppo."[53]

Father Janssen, a noted geographer serving in British Naval Intelligence, wrote in a joint memorandum with M. Savignac his French counterpart, about Trans-Jordan: "Administratively, all the region forms part of the Vilayet of Damascus . . . whose southern boundary passes between El Ala and Medain Saleh" in the Sanjak of Ma'an.[54] In like manner, Ormsby-Gore referred to the region east of the Jordan as "part of the Vilayet of Damascus,"[55] while Hogarth preferred to use the word "district."[56] During his last visit to the East, Sykes reported that "Damascus and district [are] pro-Feisal but anti-Sherifian."[57] By "district," he meant all the territory south toward Akaba, Feisal's headquarters during the summer of 1918. Moreover, Toynbee, when working on the terms of an armistice or peace with Turkey early in October 1918, sketched out the boundaries of "Six Vilayets," one of which was that of Damascus.[58] That he did not use "Vilayet of Syria" on this or on any other occasion was not accidental, since nowhere does the term appear in the "History of the Hedjaz Rising" (29 November 1916) or in any other document that Toynbee had consulted.

For similar reasons, the Germans and the French preferred the Vilayet of Damascus to the Vilayet of Syria. Thus, Loytved-Hardegg, the German Consul in Damascus, reported on the "Angliederung des . . . Deschofgebietes als Kasa an das Wilayet Damascus."[59] On 21 December 1915, during a meeting at the Foreign Office, Picot referred to the Vilayet of Damascus; he specifically emphasized that "the whole of the Damascus vilayet . . . as defined by the Turks" must be included in the French sphere.[60] Likewise, the French Apostolic Missionary, in his highly valued *Guide to the Holy Land*, stated that Syria was composed of the Vilayet of Aleppo, the Vilayet of Beirut, and the Vilayet of Damascus.[61]

Shortly before drafting his letter of 24 October 1915, McMahon consulted the Report of the de Bunsen Committee. In paragraph 36, the Report delineated the boundary between "Arabia proper and those Arabs who belong to the districts of Damascus and Mesopotamia." Accordingly, the boundary ran "from Akaba . . . thence to Ma'an, on the Hedjaz Railway, then eastwards in a northerly course to the limits of Kuwait."[62] In other words, the district of Damascus covered the whole area of what later became Trans-Jordan. As a newcomer to the area, McMahon did not know the exact position of Mersina and Alexandretta, but he was fully apprised of the status, as well as the scope, of the district of Damascus. There is also no reason to suspect him of inadequate command of his native tongue, since, in English, district is understood to mean not a geographical, but a well-defined administrative unit.

This, however, does not dispel the confusion caused by the linkage between "districts" and the four cities. It was argued that, since there were no districts of Homs and Hama — the former being a sanjak in the Vilayet of Syria, and the latter a kaza in the Sanjak of Homs — McMahon's phrase could only make sense if "districts" was taken to mean the regions adjacent to the four cities. This point was made first by Feisal during his meeting at the Foreign Office with R. C. Lindsay on 20 January 1921, and repeated over and over again by the Arab Delegations in 1922-1939, as well as by Toynbee in his "Comments."[63] However, the argument is a red herring, since, whatever the incongruity, neither on logical nor on factual grounds could the status of Homs and Hama affect that of Damascus or Aleppo.

The phrase originated with Muhammad Sharif al-Faruqi[64] and, as Childs cogently showed, al-Faruqi certainly did not intend a narrow interpretation of the immediate neighborhood, since this would have been fatal to the whole concept of an Arab state stretching from the Syrian hinterland southward through what later became Trans-Jordan to Hedjaz. The minimum for which "the Arabs would fight" was a continuous stretch of territory to ensure the control of the Hedjaz Railway and unimpeded traffic of the pilgrims to Mecca.[65] A narrow interpretation would have been self-defeating, since it would have left the four cities as isolated islands within French territory.

Al-Faruqi might have had a special reason for lumping the four cities together, but this was not an extraordinary case. Thus, in 1848, Colonel Rose, the British Consul in Beirut, complained about the state of insecurity of "the great towns [of] Aleppo, Hama, Homs [and] Damascus."[66] Early in 1915, Lawrence wrote: "Damascus, Homs, Hama, and Aleppo are the four ancient cities in which Syria takes pride. They are stretched like a chain along the fertile valleys of the interior . . ."[67] And in September 1919, William Yale, a member of the American Delegation to the Peace Conference in Versailles and an expert on Syria, presented a memorandum in which he referred to the four towns at least three times, almost as a cliché.[68]

There was apparently a good reason for this habit. During the sixteenth century, Hama and Homs were removed from the control of Damascus; the former became attached to the newly created Vilayet of Aleppo, and the latter to that of Tripoli, although they still continued to pay taxes to the Valis of Damascus in their capacity as commanders of the pilgrimage. This disposition lasted throughout the eighteenth century.[69] Geographically, the arrangement makes little sense, but was perfectly in line with the Ottoman system of government under which administrative units were frequently shifted from one vilayet to another.[70] For someone like al-Faruqi, who was keen to ensure the territorial integrity of the Syrian hinterland, specifying the four cities was not only natural, but even essential. Hence, it is reasonable to assume that what both he and McMahon had in mind were the districts that *contained* the four cities of Damascus, Homs, Hama, and Aleppo; the word "contained" was probably omitted for brevity's sake, or because it was self-evident. This was, in a way, a variant of the formulae given in McMahon's preceding cables to London, in which al-Faruqi was quoted as pressing for the inclusion of the four cities within the Arab Confederation or Arab sphere. However, the meaning, as well as the purpose, of all the formulae was identical: to secure for the inhabitants of the Syrian hinterland a territorial contact with Arabia.

If this was the case, why, it could be asked, was not McMahon more specific in delineating the boundary of the district of Damascus, particularly in the south, where it was contiguous with that of the Hedjaz? We are fortunate to have McMahon's own explanation in this matter in his letter to Sir John Shuckburgh, dated 12 March 1922.[71] The reason for restricting himself to specific mention of the four cities in the Syrian hinterland, he explained, was because: (a) "these were places to which the Arabs attached vital importance"; and, (b) because there was no place he could think of at the time "of sufficient importance for purposes of definition further south of the above." (Places like Dera'a, Salt, Ma'an and Akaba were at that time no more than large villages.) It may be recalled that the Ottoman boundary separating Galilee (in the southern part of the Vilayet of Beirut), as well as the Sanjak of Jerusalem, from the Vilayet of Syria bisected the Sea of Galilee, the River Jordan, and the Dead Sea, but McMahon refrained from making use of it either, because, he continued,

> I thought it might be considered desirable at some later stage of negotiations to endeavour to find some more suitable frontier line east of the Jordan and between that river and the Hedjaz Railway. At that moment, moreover, very detailed definitions did not seem called for.

As George A. Smith, the author of the *Historical Geography of the Holy Land*, told Herbert Samuel, the River Jordan never constituted a boundary of Palestine.[72] Nor did it make much sense economically and militarily. A natural strategic boundary runs several miles eastward along the ridges of the adjacent plateau, which dominates the Jordan Valley. This was recognized by some British officials toward the end of World War I and during the Peace Conference in Paris. Ormsby-Gore, a member of the British Delegation to the Conference, suggested that "a line drawn a few (not exceeding 10) miles east of the main stream of the Jordan should form the eastern boundary" separating Palestine from the Arab State.[73] Ormsby-Gore was following the footsteps of two other Britons deeply involved in Middle Eastern affairs: one was Lawrence, the other — Toynbee.[74]

In this respect, McMahon revealed remarkable prescience. However, when drafting his hapless letter of 24 October 1915, he was in a dilemma. According to the map for the Ottoman Devolutionary Scheme (Course IV), provided by the de Bunsen Committee, the Ayalet of Palestine, which was to be internationalized, extended deep into the territory east of the River Jordan.[75] This clashed with the desiderata of the Arab nationalists; but, since Palestine was not an issue at that time, McMahon thought it prudent to postpone the exact definition of the southwestern boundary of the projected Arab State. He thereby unwittingly left a loophole in an already badly phrased document, unable to envisage that advantage would be taken of the ambiguity.

In his "Comments,"[76] Toynbee was unduly dismissive of McMahon's explanation given on 12 March 1922. He suggested that McMahon had ulterior motives. But Shuckburgh thought otherwise. He interviewed McMahon and thereafter invited him to put his words on record. "You will see," Shuckburgh told Forbes Adam, "that he is quite clear on the point that the intention was to exclude Palestine. I hope that the question will not become a practical one, but it is just as well that we should have all the evidence possible at our disposal in case we are definitely challenged on the subject." Forbes Adam agreed that McMahon's statement was "important and will be most useful if and when the matter is raised again."[77]

Philip Graves, the noted Near East correspondent of *The Times* and a member of the Arab Bureau Staff from 1916 to 1918, also trusted McMahon and, after interviewing him, deemed it important that his statement to the Colonial Office be published in order to counter the misleading propaganda launched by the *Daily Mail* at that time.[78]

When preparing his "Memorandum on British Commitments to King Hussein," Toynbee ignored a sizable body of documentation showing that, in October 1915, Britain was in no position to award Palestine to the Arabs without the prior agreement of the Quai d'Orsay. Nor did he take much notice of the work being done at that time by the Historical Section of the Foreign Office on French interests in the East,[79] which, by common knowledge, were of long standing. Dating from the Crusader period, these interests had made an indelible impression on the French psyche. During the sixteenth and seventeenth centuries, France had secured from the Sublime Porte exceptional privileges, known as Capitulations.[80] On the strength of these, the Porte recognized France as Protector of the Christians, not only in Palestine and Syria, but throughout the Ottoman Empire. Henceforth, French monarchs interested themselves in projects for occupying and annexing Egypt, Palestine, and Syria. This ambition was almost realized during Napoleon's campaign in 1799 and subsequently under France's protégé Mehemet Ali (1831-1840). Although these efforts were frustrated, France remained jealous of her rights. In 1853, friction between the Latin monks and their rivals, the Greek Orthodox Church, over the right of custody of the Holy Places in Palestine led to the Crimea (1854-1856). France scored a diplomatic victory during the Congress of Berlin, 1878,[81] when her rights were expressly recognized; and, following the Cyprus Convention, which was signed on 4 June 1878, the British Government assured the French that its occupation of Cyprus would in no way jeopardize the privileged position France enjoyed in Syria. In a separate dispatch, Lord Salisbury, the Foreign Secretary, confirmed that "the interests of France as a great Catholic Power in the Lebanon and in the Holy Places of Palestine have always been scrupulously respected."

The Anglo-French Agreement of 1904 opened a new page. In return for French withdrawal from Egypt, Britain gave her unqualified approval for consolidation of the French position in North Africa and Syria. And in 1912, Raymond Poincaré, reassured by Grey, made it clear, after coming to office, that France had no intention of renouncing her "traditional mission" in the East. The determination and vigor with which this mission was pursued did not escape the notice of Toynbee himself. In 1915 he wrote: "The French railways and missions succeeded in transforming Syria into a dependency of France."[82] And two years later he added:

> All over Syria there are French clerical, secular, and Judaic schools. Beirut and Damascus, Christian and Moslem . . . are equally under the spell of French civilisation; and France is the chief economic power in the land . . .[83]

On the eve of World War I, France formalized her position still further, initialing an agreement with Germany 15 February 1914, and two months later with Turkey.[84] By this agreement, France gained a free hand in Central and Southern Syria, including Palestine. In return for receiving a substantial loan, the Porte granted France liberal concessions to construct ports in Haifa and Jaffa, as well as in Tripoli, and to further develop the Syrian railway system, including its southward extension to a point on the French-owned railway running from Jaffa to Jerusalem. It was therefore quite reasonable for the French to point out their newly "acquired rights" when negotiating with the

British on the future of Turkey in Asia.[85]

In October 1914, a month before Turkey entered the War, M. Lèygues, the Chairman of the Foreign Affairs Committee of the Chamber, asserted the French claims to Syria in language that showed that, by Syria, he meant Greater Syria including Palestine:

> The Mediterranean will not be free for us . . . unless Syria remains in our sphere of influence. By Syria must be understood, not a Syria mutilated and discrowned, but Syria in its entirety, that extends from El Arish to the Taurus.[86]

Le Matin of 30 December 1914 went so far as to propose the merger of Syria with Palestine under one name, *La France du Levant*; and in the following year, Paul Cambon told Grey most seriously that France regarded Syria as a "dependency."[87] On 4 March 1915, in consequence of Russia claiming Constantinople, France made a counter-claim to Cilicia and Syria, which included Palestine. These desiderata were aired two weeks later in London. Thereafter, it became obvious in Whitehall that Britain was "not free to act" in any northern or southern region of Syria. For Lord Crewe, then Secretary of State for India, it was a foregone conclusion that France regarded Palestine and Syria as her "inheritance."[88]

It is true that St. Petersburg objected to the inclusion of Palestine within the exclusive French sphere and that the de Bunsen Committee recommended its internationalization: "Palestine must be recognised as a country whose destiny must be the subject of special negotiations, in which both belligerent and neutrals are alike interested."[89] But, if anything, recognition that Palestine was *sui generis* and a country that had a universal appeal circumscribed to an ever greater degree Britain's freedom as to its future disposition. To assign it unilaterally during the War to Arabs, or for that matter to Jews,[90] without prior consultation with the Allies, was unthinkable. Any decision on the future status of Palestine could certainly not be effected without French concurrence. Throughout 1915 — in fact, almost until the end of December of that year — the French were in no mood to forego their pre-eminent position in Palestine lightly. Any doubts that might have lingered on this count were dispelled on 23 November, when Picot met Sir Arthur Nicolson and his colleagues at the Foreign Office. Picot insisted that Syria was a purely French possession, and, by Syria, he meant the region bounded by the Taurus ridges in the north, Diabekir, Mosul, Kerkuk, and Deir al-Zor (on the Euphrates) in the east, and the Egyptian border in the south. No French Government that surrendered this claim, he maintained, would survive a day.[91]

Grey displayed great sensitivity toward French sensibilities. "I am well aware of French feeling toward Syria and we have no intention of disregarding it," he told Bertie.[92] This was why he rejected so brusquely the Alexandretta scheme advocated by Cairo. "You should do all you can," he instructed McMahon on 17 February, "to discourage any movement of the kind . . . as regards Alexandretta or places near Syria [such as Haifa or Gaza]."[93]

He felt so strongly on this matter that, three weeks later, he repeated his warning in a private telegram, which he drafted himself. He emphasized that a claim to Syria by England, or even one made for Egypt, which in the given circumstances would be tantamount to a claim for England herself, would inevitably bring a break with France.[94] On the same day, Ronald Storrs advised Fitzgerald, Kitchener's Secretary that

> H. E. [McMahon] has just received a private wire from Sir E. G[rey] stating that any Syrian aspirations for ourselves or [for] Egypt would mean a break with France and are therefore unthinkable.[95]

Even more indicative is Grey's minute, dated 27 November 1915: "I made it clear to Picot that we have no designs in Syria and [will] promise nothing about it to anyone [i.e., the Arabs] unless the French agree."[96] This minute was drafted two days after Picot's meeting with Arthur Nicolson and a month after the dispatch of McMahon's letter of 24 October 1915.

If Grey showed such deference to French interests, it was not only because of his innate decency and unquestionable loyalty to an ally, but primarily because of highest strategic considerations. This transpires clearly from his memorandum that he circulated to the War Committee. Germany, he revealed, was making persistent overtures to both Russia and France, who "could have peace tomorrow on comparatively favourable terms" — an option which was not open to Britain, whose very survival hinged on the outcome of the war.

> We are therefore dependent upon the Allies for our safety to a greater extent than they are upon us. My conclusion is [he continued] that we must therefore efface ourselves in the councils of the Allies . . . [and] if we cannot make ourselves prevail by argument and influence, we must be very careful not to proceed to threats or pressure that might alienate our Allies.[97]

This was why, in March 1915, he conceded to Russia Constantinople and the Straits — the "richest prize of the entire war."[98] It also explains why, until the fall of Asquith's government, he cared so scrupulously for France's interest, as well as the kind of predicament that confronted him when he received a copy of Hussein's letter of 14 July 1915. As he later revealed to Sir James Rennell Rodd, the British Ambassador to Rome,

> We had no difficulty in agreeing to any boundaries which the Shereef wanted on the south [i.e., in the Arabian Peninsula], but in the north the Shereef came up against Syria, where we had always admitted French interest and the French would not make concessions to the Shereef of places like Damascus without knowing what the limits of their sphere were to be.[99]

McMahon too was nonplused. He found Hussein's pretensions with regard to the boundaries of the Arab state "in every way exaggerated, no doubt beyond his hope of acceptance," while Chamberlain, then Secretary of State for India, dismissed them forthrightly as "unacceptable. . . . [They] appear to be dictated by extreme Pan-Arab aspirations."[100] McMahon was all the more taken aback by the Sharif's overweening territorial ambitions because, three months earlier, he had received a reassuring letter on this question from Sir Reginald Wingate:

> In my talks with the Arab leaders here, I think they now admit that we must stick to Mesopotamia and I am inclined to think that they realise that parts of Syria and Palestine cannot — in all the circumstances of the case—be incorporated in their future utopian sovereign state. On the whole they are becoming more reasonable . . .[101]

Wingate was referring to Sir Sayyid Ali al-Mirghani, the Chief

Cadi of the Sudan, through whom he was conducting parallel negotiations with Jeddah. So, the question that inescapably comes to mind is what made Hussein change his demands so drastically in such a short time?

On 23 May, practically on the same day that McMahon received Wingate's letter, Feisal, on his return journey from Constantinople, met for the second time the leaders of *al-Ahd* and *al-Fatat* societies and received from them their so-called "Damascus Protocol." It will be recalled that this protocol demanded recognition by Great Britain of the independence of Arab countries bound by the line Mersina-Adana to parallel 37°N; the Indian Ocean (with the exclusion of Aden) in the south; the Persian frontier in the east; and, the Red Sea and the Mediterranean Sea in the west.[102] It was also during this meeting that the leaders of the societies endeavored to impress upon Feisal the following they enjoyed and their readiness to take action against the Turks. Yasin al-Hashimi, Chief of Staff of the 12th Ottoman Division, which was then stationed in Syria, and who acted as spokesman for the "Young Arabs," declared rather bombastically for Sharif Hussein's consumption: "We ask for nothing. . . . you only have to lead us and to march in the vanguard."[103] Hussein, disappointed with the Young Turks' lukewarm response to his overtures,[104] embraced the *al-Ahd* and *al-Fatat* plan *in toto* and incorporated it into his letter of 14 July 1915 to McMahon. (This letter was written on his behalf by his son Abdullah.) But such extreme claims led nowhere.

It was Muhammad Sharif al-Faruqi who broke the impasse. Al-Faruqi was an aide-de-camp of Fakhri Pasha, the Turkish Commander of the 12th Ottoman Division and Djemal Pasha's deputy. As a descendant of Omar Ibn El Faruq, the second Khalifa of El Islam, al-Faruqi claimed to be of noble lineage and, despite his youth — he was then twenty-four years old — had reached a leading position within the ranks of the Arab secret societies. On his initiative, *al-Ahd* forged closer links with *al-Fatat*, its civilian counterpart, and when Yasin al-Hashimi assumed the overall leadership of the societies, al-Faruqi became his deputy. On 23 May 1915, he was a member of the delegation that met Feisal on his return from Constantinople. Later, at the height of Djemal Pasha's repressive measures against Arab nationalists, al-Faruqi was arrested, but, as there was no incriminating evidence against him, he was deported to Constantinople together with Yasin al-Hashimi, Amin Lufty Bey, and Abd al-Qādir. There they conceived a plan to defect to the British in order to win them over. The idea, to which al-Faruqi was made privy, originated with Yasin al-Hashimi. The headquarters of the societies in Damascus were also informed. Al-Hashimi's aim, and that of the other conspirators, was to create an identity of Arab and British interests and convey a message of friendship: "We must be friends," they asserted. Those who could manage to cross the lines to the British should impress upon them "the strength of the Arab movement and the sincere loyalty and attachment" of the Young Arabs to Sharif Hussein's cause.[105]

Al-Faruqi arrived in Cairo on 10 September 1915, where, in the home of Na'um Shuqair, a Syrian Christian notable employed by British Intelligence, he met some of the leaders of the Syrian colony in Cairo. Present were Rashid Ridā, Rafiq al-Azm, Hakki al-Azm, Jamil al-Rifai, and Aziz Bey Ali al-Misri.[106] It was to the last-named that al-Faruqi confided the purpose of his mission, for al-Misri, as Lawrence described him, was "an idol of the Arab officers,"[107] the founder of *al-Ahd*, and Yasin al-Hashimi's predecessor. Thereafter, when negotiating with McMahon, al-Faruqi's name was linked inseparably with that of al-Misri.

Al-Faruqi was not the only Young Arab who defected to the British. Habib Lutfallah, a Staff Officer in the Ottoman Army who had participated in the Young Turk Revolution, made his way to Cairo via Athens, but General Maxwell distrusted him:

> He is a . . . vain type of a Syrian with no bottom, full of schemes. I allowed him to return to Syria to bring me, or send me, information; he did neither, but allowed himself to get mixed up with the Turks and took office with them.[108]

In contrast, al-Faruqi was singularly successful in his mission. Having interrogated him thoroughly, Clayton deduced that,

The influential leaders [of the Arab party] appear open to reason and ready to accept a considerably less ambitious scheme than that which they have [originally] formulated, which the more enlightened [ones] allow to be beyond their hopes at present.

Moreover,

They realise that to carry out the idea of an Arab Empire in its entirety is probably outside the region of practical politics at present, and [al-Faruqi] at any rate appreciates the fact that England is bound by obligations to her Allies in this war. The more experienced probably are aware that England could hardly be expected to regard with equanimity the establishment of a powerful and united Arab Empire, marching with Egypt and on the flank of the highway to India. But they do ask that England should promise to assist them to obtain a reasonable measure of independence and autonomous Government in those Arab countries where England can fairly claim that her interests are greater than those of her Allies. . . . Syria is of course included their programme but they must realize that France has aspirations in this region.

Although initially al-Faruqi made a bold statement that "French occupation of Syria would be strenuously resisted by the Mohammedan population," he eventually scaled down his claim to "the inclusion of Damascus, Aleppo, Hama, and Homs in the Arab Confederation." In his own words: "our scheme embraces all the Arab countries including Syria and Mesopotamia, but if we cannot have all, we want as much as we can get."[109]

Delighted, Clayton broke the good news to Wingate:

I have had some extremely interesting discussions with an Arab officer [al-Faruqi] . . . a leading spirit in the Pan-Arab party . . . their aims are . . . very much more moderate and practical [than Rashid Ridā's] and do not appear to be tinged to the same extent by Moslem fanatics. [Their leaders] are not carried away by the dream of an Arab Empire but appear to be reasonable men, quite prepared to give and take and fully aware of the fact that the elements of such an Empire do not exist among the Arabs . . .[110]

On the basis of Clayton's report, General Maxwell reported to Kitchener:

We have reason to believe that in negotiations with Great Britain [the Arab party] would accept considerable modification. ... [They] will, I think, insist on Aleppo, Homs, Hama and Damascus being in their sphere.

[Hence] if we can make the French realize that we are up against a big question of the future of Islam, they may be more inclined to agree to a settlement.[111]

At the Foreign Office, Sir George Clerk noted with satisfaction that the Arabs had recognized the impossibility of totally excluding France — and this was a good omen.[112]

Thus, al-Faruqi's statement gave the British an opening to negotiate with the Arabs without giving undue offense to the French. But what attracted the British officers in Cairo in particular was the prospect of a wholesale defection of Arab troops from the Ottoman Army coupled by an ensuing uprising of the native population in the whole territory of the Fertile Crescent down to the Arabian Peninsula. Such an outcome would have altered the course of the war in the Eastern theater — no mean feat, especially after the traumatic debâcle of the Allies in the Gallipoli campaign and the setbacks that the British sustained in Kut and elsewhere.

Al-Faruqi assured Clayton that the Arab party was "a power which cannot be disregarded"; that ninety percent of Arab officers in the Turkish Army and some of the Kurdish officers were members of his society; that these officers formed the backbone of the military administration of the Aleppo, Damascus, and Beirut provinces; that in April 1915, two battalions of Arabs and Kurds of the 36th Division of the 12th Ottoman Army in Hama caused disturbances and "were able to raise in revolt." As proof that the Young Arab party wielded "very great power," he quoted the fact that neither the Turks nor the Germans dared to suppress it, although they were fully aware of the Arabs' active sympathy toward the Allies, especially toward Great Britain. He claimed that Turkey and Germany had already approached the leaders of the Young Arab Committee and promised to concede to their demands "in full." The German Consul at Aleppo was particularly active in this matter. However, he went on, the Committee "are strongly inclined toward England, the Power on whom they can rely. We would sooner have a promise of half from England than of the whole from Turkey and Germany." Should Britain view Arab aspirations favorably, "the Committee would at once begin to work actively and their operations, begun in the Hedjaz . . . would soon extend to Syria and Palestine . . . [as well as] to Baghdad and Mosul, where the Committee's influence is perhaps the greatest."

Al-Faruqi maintained that he was "accredited by the Committee" to represent it vis-à-vis the British, an assurance that he qualified subsequently, stating in rather obscure and labyrinthine language:

> I am not authorised to discuss with you officially our political programme, but . . . I can, for the sake of shortening negotiations . . . give answers to any questions you wish to make re the agreement and if necessary make modifications in its articles including Mersina-Diarbekr line; modifications which I promise to try my utmost to convince most of them to go by my agreement.

In spite of these equivocations, Clayton felt confident that he was confronting "a leading spirit in the Pan-Arab party." This was particularly so since al-Faruqi assured him at the same time that "if we come to the arrangement I guarantee to go to Mesopotamia and bring over a great number of officers and men, especially from the 35th Division of El Mosul, who all know me." The matter was pressing, since his Committee would no longer remain neutral and, unless they received a favorable reply from England within a few weeks, would throw in their lot with Turkey and Germany to secure the best possible terms.

Faced with such an ultimatum, Clayton considered the matter to be of "very grave and urgent importance." He warned that

> to reject the Arab proposals entirely, or even to seek to evade the issue, will be to throw the Young Arab party definitely into the arms of the enemy. Their machinery will at once be employed against us throughout the Arab countries, and the various Arab chiefs, who are almost to a man members or connected with the Young Arab party, will be undoubtedly won over. Moreover, the religious element will come into play and the Jehad, so far a failure, may become a very grim reality, the effects of which would certainly be far-reaching and at the present crisis might

well be disastrous.[113]

McMahon reached an identical conclusion. After further conversation with al-Faruqi, he cabled London,

> it appears evident that [the] Arab party are at a parting of the ways and, unless we can give them immediate assurance of nature to satisfy them, they will throw themselves into the hands of Germany who, he says, has furnished them fulfilment of all their demands. On the one [hand] they seem ready to work actively with us which will greatly influence the course of Mesopotamia[n] and Syrian campaigns, while on the other [hand] the Arabs will throw in their lot against us and we may have all Islam in the East united against the Allies.[114]

The matter was considered "urgent." General Maxwell also thought that al-Faruqi's idea of arranging desertions of Syrian troops would be helpful to the British plan of operations and should therefore be encouraged.[115]

At that time, Aubrey Herbert, M.P., the younger son of the Earl of Pembroke, arrived in Cairo from Gallipoli. Before joining the Gallipoli campaign. he had served a few months as Intelligence Officer under Clayton. He therefore had easy access to senior officers in Cairo and to confidential information. Soon after his arrival, he met General Maxwell, Clayton, Cheetham, and the High Commissioner. They all agreed that it was of the utmost importance to win the Arabs over and that the opportunity would be lost if this was not done soon.

Herbert interviewed al-Misri who impressed him as "a man of striking personality." The latter revealed that the Germans had some "dazzling gifts to offer" and that the Arabs had reached a crossroads. Should England offer an unambiguous alliance, Arab officers would switch their allegiance away from the CUP (the Committee of Union and Progress of the Young Turks). Herbert was certain that such a move would greatly facilitate the Mesopotamian campaign and reduce the chance of another attack on the Suez Canal.[116]

This was the atmosphere that prevailed in Cairo. Little wonder that Grey's earlier instruction was totally ignored: that Cairo should be exceedingly careful not to commit the British Government in negotiations with deserters or emissaries from the Ottoman army without London's prior approval.[117] Ignored also was the opinion of Lord Hardinge, then Viceroy of India, who dismissed the idea of an Arab rebellion in Mesopotamia as unrealistic. "I regard [the] scheme as unlikely to materialise, both owing to [poor] quality of leaders and because tribes and sheiks concerned are too backward to pay attention to Young Arab propaganda."[118] Likewise little notice was taken of the report of the British Consul in Aleppo, who characterized the native inhabitants of his district as "deficient in any strong feelings unconnected with money-making or intrigue."[119] More amazing is the fact that even Lawrence's note was overlooked. From the beginning of the war, Lawrence had worked in the Intelligence Department under Clayton. Early in 1915, he prepared a memorandum[120] in which he gave a penetrating analysis of the geographical and socio-political conditions in Syria based on his personal knowledge of the country and on the vast amount of information amassed in the Department. The memorandum was not circulated at that time, but its contents must have been known to his superiors. He wrote:

> . . . a review of the present components of Syria proves it as vividly coloured a racial and religious mosaic today as it has notoriously been in the past . . . .
>
> Between town and town, village and village, family and family, creed and creed, exist intimate jealousies, sedulously fostered by the Turks to render a spontaneous union impossible . . . .
>
> Hamah and Homs are towns which dislike one another . . . An Aleppine always calls himself an Aleppine, a Beyrouti a Beyrouti, and so down to the smallest villages.
>
> This verbal poverty indicates a political condition. There is no national feeling . . . .

This description tallies with that given by Gertrude Bell in her book entitled *Syria* (p. 228) which appeared first in 1907 and was reprinted in 1919.

As already shown,[121] there was no shred of truth in al-Faruqi's report about Turco-German overtures to the al-Ahd and al-Fatat societies and the latter's ability to foment a revolt against the Ottoman Government. All the evidence adduced from the German Foreign Office files points the other way. Moreover, al-Faruqi's own testimony belies his claim. In his letter of 7 December 1915 to Sharif Hussein (already quoted), he bitterly complained that the aim of the Turks was "to kill us, our people, and our sacred aspirations."[122] When interrogated by Na'um Shuqair in Cairo, he submitted a list of members, both civilian and military, who had been executed, and made a passionate plea: "now that I have escaped from the hands of the Turks, I consider it is my first duty to try and help my companions to escape from their hands as well."[123] In 1919, the Arab Bureau confirmed that, early in 1915, the al-Ahd Committee became so harassed and disorganized by Djemal Pasha that they were "almost a negligible quantity and of no importance."[124] In September 1915, when al-Faruqi, as well as Habib Lutfallah, defected to the British, the Young Arabs had already been cowed and scattered. Far from being courted by the Turks and their German allies, many had been executed, others were languishing in prisons, and the remainder were fleeing for their lives.

Nor was there much truth in al-Faruqi's claim of the Societies' widespread network and influence. As Professor Dawn ascertained, only 126 men were known to have been public advocates of Arab nationalist societies before October 1914. Even this number, according to the Arab sources on which he based his estimate, is too large, since only thirty of the men could without any doubt be regarded as "active Arab nationalists before 1914." How many of the convicted nationalists were actually engaged in anti-Ottoman activities during 1914-1915 is, in his view, impossible to determine.[125] Professor Khoury also concluded that Arabism was not translated from an idea into a viable political instrument, and, though it was spreading, it nevertheless "remained a humble minority position in Damascus and elsewhere, unable to erode the loyalty of the dominant faction of the local political elite in Syria to Ottomanism. . . . The political leadership in the Syrian towns either continued to identify with the ideology of Ottomanism and thus with [the] Empire, or they opted not to take a stand until the outcome of the War was known."[126]

Not only was there no political will to rebel against the Ottoman regime but even a rudimentary infrastructure, as well as the indispensable machinery to carry out such a move, was lacking. Gertrude Bell, with her unerring sense of observation, pointed to the "fatal lack of cohesion in a society which has never succeeded in obliterating its tribal origins," a state that militated against any idea of "any national union. At best there was little more than what may be described as municipal patriotism, a unity which extended no further than the limits of the big townships. Comprehensive organization was non-existent . . ."[127]

Gerhard Mutius, the scholarly German Consul in Beirut, discounted any likelihood of a popular uprising. He conceded that, politically, the local population was "unreliable." Nonetheless, "they do not dare even to think about a revolt. They have neither the leaders nor the means to resist the Turkish troops."[128]

In fact, contrary to al-Faruqi's protestations, the leaders of the societies did not seriously contemplate such a daring move. Under the Young Turk regime before World War I, the societies had continued to be solidly loyal to the Ottoman Empire. No separatist tendencies whatsoever were in evidence; the sole aspiration of Arab nationalists was to achieve administrative decentralization of the Arab provinces and a certain degree of local autonomy coupled with the recognition of Arabic on a par with Turkish. In 1913, an Arab Congress was convened in Paris. It reiterated the need for decentralization and the recognition of Arabic; but, in deference to more extreme members of the secret societies, it demanded, for the first time, recognition of "political rights" to be exercised through actual participation in the administration of the empire. The only individuals who aimed at "ultimate Arab independence" were the al-Fatat, formed by some half a dozen students in Paris, as well as al-Ahd. "But neither the few army officers nor the handful of students in Paris were the unchallenged representatives of general Syrian, still less of Muslim, public opinion. . . . More experienced and thoughtful Syrians were still striving for a basis of collaboration with the Turks."[129]

This was particularly true of Aziz Bey Ali al-Misri. Born in Egypt of Circassian extraction, he was a devout Moslem and loyal to the Ottoman Caliphate. In Constantinople, to which he moved in 1891, he became an outspoken opponent of British occupation of Egypt and, during his studies in the Ottoman Military Staff College, developed unbounded admiration for his German tutors. He also struck up friendships with his Turkish

classmates and, after the 1908 Revolution, became an influential member within the CUP ranks. However, disturbed by their
subsequent policy of Turkification, he became convinced that
the only way to resolve a potential Turco-Arab conflict and ensure the territorial integrity of the Empire was decentralization.
This was his overriding motive when founding the *al-Ahd* society. Its program was in the nature of a broad federal scheme,
modeled after the Austro-Hungarian *Ausgleich*, in which all nationalities would be given autonomous status. It was only after
the Porte rejected the demands set out by the Congress in Paris
in 1913 that the objectives of *al-Ahd* became radicalized.[130]

The outbreak of World War I put an end to this trend. Otto-
manization prevailed. "All nationalist and pro-Entente propaganda ceased . . . [and] the former ardent agitators became
ultra-patriots."[131] Members of the secret societies resolved "to
work on the side of Turkey in order to resist foreign penetration
of whatever kind or form." A few months later, on 16 March
1915, when Feisal met the leading members of the *al-Fatat* and
al-Ahd societies (he was then on his way to Constantinople), he
too made it known that he favored cooperation with the
Turks.[132]

Djemal Pasha, however, rightly or wrongly, suspected the Arab
nationalists of treason and dealt with them severely. Only then
did their leaders decide to throw in their lot with England. Even
so, just six members are known to have embarked on anti-
Turkish activities; of these, two were in Egypt.[133] Professor
Dawn does not list their names, but even the uninitiated reader
will have no difficulty in identifying at least three members.
They were Yasin al-Hashimi, al-Faruqi, and al-Misri.

Their alleged friendship toward England proved, however,
to be skin deep and motivated by opportunism. Yasin al-
Hashimi, with whom the idea of Anglo-Arab cooperation originated, decided to follow Lutfallah's example after all and
rejoined the Ottoman Army. During the summer of 1918, Feisal,
then in Akaba, offered him the post of a Commander-in-Chief
of the Arab Army, but he rejected the invitation and preferred
the command of an Ottoman division instead. He fought the
British until the fall of Damascus, when suddenly he switched
allegiance and became Feisal's Chief of Staff, though only to

assert himself soon after as "one of the extreme exponents of Arab independence, as against a French mandate or any other form of foreign control." His pro-Turkish sentiment remained undiminished, and, when it was discovered that he was in league with the CUP, as well as with Mustafa Kamal,[134] working against British interests, he was arrested on General Allenby's orders on 22 November 1919.[135]

Al-Faruqi, al-Hashimi's deputy and the societies' emissary, was found, several months after his arrival in Cairo, to be unreliable[136] and intriguing against the British. Ruhi, who watched his activities while in Jeddah, thought that he was "a rascal [and] entirely Anglophobe."[137]

Al-Misri nourished similar sentiments. Following Hussein's uprising in June 1916, he was, at the suggestion of the British, asked to take over command of the Arab revolt as Minister of War; but at his meeting with the Sharif in Jeddah, al-Misri told Hussein that he still adhered to his original aim of an Arab autonomy within the framework of the Ottoman realm, as embodied in the *al-Ahd* program. An acrimonious quarrel between the two broke out, which subsequently led to al-Misri's stormy resignation. During an interview with Professor Khadduri, he revealed that his purpose was to conclude a separate peace with Turkey as opposed to Hussein's policy. Like other Egyptian nationalists, he regarded the Arab revolt as a blow to Ottoman unity and thought that his own participation in the war on Germany's side would influence the German Government to bring pressure to bear on the Sultan to reorganize the Empire on a decentralized basis. With this in mind, he tried to make his way to Germany through neutral Spain. However, on learning of Germany's defeat, he felt "so depressed that he contemplated suicide." Nevertheless, he proceeded to Germany and stayed there until the proclamation of Egypt's independence in 1922.[138]

It gradually dawned on British officials in Cairo that they had miscalculated badly. First came the report of Sir Mark Sykes. As he had anticipated, he found during his visit to Mesopotamia that the country was riven by deep ethnic and religious schisms, that the idea of a Sharifian Caliphate had no following, and that there was hardly any evidence of Arab nationalism.[139] More shattering was the letter that General

Maxwell received from Lord Hardinge. Perturbed by Cairo's policy, Hardinge told the General,

> I fail to see why we should make any sacrifice to the Arabs . . . in view of the fact that they have been fighting against us the whole time and have no claim whatever upon us. I cannot tell you how strongly I feel upon this point.

Moreover, from a purely practical point of view, he added,

> it will be quite useless to endeavour to form an enormous Arab State which would be entirely lacking in cohesion and would be torn by intrigues. If the Sherif of Mecca is capable of forming an Arab State embracing part of Syria and the littoral of the Red Sea, well and good. I think even then it will be more than any Arab could possibly manage, and that he would soon have very serious difficulties to contend with in Syria and in the interior of Arabia.[140]

To a Commander-in-Chief who had claimed all along that a "powerful" Arab organization existed and was "ready to act" and assist the British in their Mesopotamian campaign, the Viceroy's stark assessment made bitter reading. Al-Faruqi and al-Misri were therefore dispatched to Mesopotamia to try and foment the much-promised Arab uprising behind the Turkish lines. British military authorities in Basra, however, dismissed the idea as unrealistic; experience with Arab officers who had defected from the Ottoman army had been discouraging.[141] Rebuffed, Cairo sent Lawrence instead. Terse and sarcastic in tone, his report was an eye-opener for his superiors:

> I have been looking . . . for Pan-Arab party at Basra. It is about 12 strong. Formerly consisted of Sayed Taleb and some jackals. The other Basra people are . . . peasants who are interested in date palms. . . . There is no Arab sentiment and for us the place is negligible.[142]

But the most serious blow for the Cairo officials was the news from Hussein. On 18 February 1916, he had reassured McMahon that his son Feisal, at that time in Syria, was planning to attack the Turks from the rear and was only awaiting the arrival of troops from Aleppo and Mosul, 100,000 strong, the majority of whom were Arabs. This would mark "the beginning of the principal movement." However, six weeks later he had to concede the bitter truth that "owing to dispersal of chiefs," the Syrians could neither engineer a revolution, nor seize the Hedjaz railway.[143] Ali, Hussein's elder son, told his father on Feisal's behalf that there was no hope that the Syrians would start any "movement . . . because the notables and the leaders of the party and those who steer the movement have all departed." With regard to the Anazah tribe in the Syrian desert, "we shall send them as much money as we can, in accordance with their request, as money is the only axis on which everything revolves."[144]

The much vaunted Arab revolt was a mirage. Clayton, in total despair, vented his frustration to Wingate, his former master and mentor:

> The Sherif allows that Syria is useless for revolutionary purposes. Can we expect that the Hedjaz Arabs, with their proverbial lack of organisation, and far from their base, can do more than waste our money and supplies in a series of aimless and indecisive raids in a country which they are too uncivilised even to rule as it should be ruled?[145]

A year later he mentioned, though only in passing, that, soon after the outbreak of the war, the Arab party had been systematically dissipated and broken up by the Turkish Government.[146] He never admitted that he had been deceived.

In contrast, David Hogarth, the newly appointed Director of the Arab Bureau (February 1916), had no hand in negotiating with the Arab leaders and was therefore in a position to draw some far-reaching conclusions. He was a man of high integrity and sound judgment, and questioned the very premise on which the British Residency had built its policy. The Sharif, he observed, had always written as a spokesman of the Arab nation, but all factual evidence disproved his claim; he was not supported by any Arab organization. "No such organisation exists . . . nor given the history, economic environment and character of Arabs, can be expected to exist."[147]

A more devastating criticism came from Sir Arthur Nicolson, the Permanent Under-Secretary of State for Foreign Affairs. Sceptical of Cairo's policy from its very inception, he made no secret of his displeasure:

> People talk of Arabs as if they were some cohesive body, well armed and equipped [he wrote to Lord Hardinge], instead of a heap of scattered tribes with no cohesion and no organisation. I think myself that we are trying to treat with a shadow, and it would be a delusion to imagine that we should be able to detach a really powerful Arab force from Turkey.[148]

Written a month before Hussein confessed his impotence, Nicolson's letter proved remarkably prescient. His prognostication was confirmed later by Gertrude Bell's penetrating analysis. Looking retrospectively, she maintained that the Arab societies, so loosely organized, with a "shadowy, if not fictitious" framework, failed to translate their theories into political reality. In Syria, where Arab nationalism was born, great efforts were made to create a genuine movement regardless of social differences, but it came to nothing. When it was put to the test during the first year of the war, "it broke down without an effort at self-preservation. . . The Turks crushed it out of existence . . . without difficulty." But if in Syria the Arab national movement proved ineffective, elsewhere it was simply valueless. In Basra, Sayyid Talib's opposition to the Ottoman Government was motivated solely by personal ambition. In Baghdad, the Arab party was even less coordinated than in Basra; whereas, in Mosul (al-Faruqi's native town), the movement was practically non-existent. *In sum toto,*

> Political union is a conception unfamiliar to a society which is still highly coloured by its tribal origins and maintains in its midst so many strongly disruptive elements of tribal organisation. The Pan-Arab leaders have not succeeded in calling the scattered bones to life.[149]

Clayton and McMahon had greatly overestimated the Arabs' ability to assist the Allied cause. They committed one of the gravest mistakes in British Middle Eastern policy. Clayton, in particular, seems excessively credulous. He took al-Faruqi's statements at face value without investigating their veracity, as is customarily done in intelligence agencies. Nor, it appears, did he ask, when interrogating al-Faruqi, two pertinent questions of critical importance: (a) how did the Arab party propose to engineer the rebellion, and, (b) how did he reconcile the alleged

Turco-German offer to the Arab societies with the merciless Turkish oppression of the same societies? It seems odd that these glaring contradictions were overlooked.

When McMahon was preparing his letter of 24 October 1915, he was unaware that he had been duped. Nor could he have imagined that al-Faruqi's reasonableness and moderation was largely due to the fact that he had nothing to lose. He also took too seriously his threat that the Arab party was "at the parting of the ways" and that, unless Britain gave them "immediate assurances" to their satisfaction, "they will throw themselves in the hands of Germany," who, he said, had offered "fulfilment of all their demands." If the Young Arabs came to an agreement with the Germans, McMahon warned Grey, "we may have all Islam in the East against the Allies. Matter therefore urgent."[150]

More than McMahon's talents were needed to call al-Faruqi's bluff. His story seemed all the more credible since Hussein, too, assured McMahon that

> all Arabs, even those obeying Turco-German orders, are only waiting for the result of the present negotiations. This result depends on our refusal or acceptance of their territorial proposals and our declaration to safeguard their religion and their rights.[151]

Although perturbed, McMahon was not thrown off balance completely. He explained to al-Faruqi that, owing to obligations to France, Britain did not have "a free hand as regards all Arabia. . . . This the Arab representatives here fully understood and admitted."[152] As a result, al-Faruqi finally stated that the Arab party would accept an assurance on the following lines:

> England will recognize inviolability of Holy Places and guarantee them against [external] aggression. With regard to North Western boundaries proposed by Sherif of Mecca, al-Faruqi thinks Arabs would accept modification leaving in Arabia purely Arab districts of Aleppo, Damascus, Hama and Homs, whose occupation by the French they would oppose by force of arms. He also accepts the fact that British interests necessitate special measures of British control in Basra Vilayet.

McMahon asked Grey what assurances he should give to the

Sharif and the Arab party through al-Faruqi.[153]

Here is the genesis of the formula used by McMahon in his controversial letter of 24 October 1915. The word "district" appears for the first time. It was al-Faruqi who introduced it. Considering what his ideal desideratum was — "our scheme embraces all the Arab countries, including Syria and Mesopotamia, but if we cannot have all, we want as much as we can get" — al-Faruqi could not possibly have referred to "districts" in the narrow sense of "immediate surroundings," since this would have allowed France unhindered occupation of the territory south of Damascus astride the pilgrims route to Medina and Mecca. Such an outcome would have been fatal to Arab national aspirations, as well as offensive to Moslem feelings. On the contrary, al-Faruqi clearly intended to convey a broad definition of the Syrian hinterland, as distinct from the Mediterranean littoral; by districts, he meant the territory stretching from Aleppo to the Gulf of Akaba linked with the Arabian Peninsula. How important this link was for the secret societies was revealed by al-Faruqi when interrogated by British Intelligence:

> We also found out that the Sherif of Mecca was in communication with the High Commissioner in Egypt and . . . that the English have given their consent to the Sherif establishing an Arab Empire, but the limits of this Empire were not defined. It was mentioned that the dominions of the Sherif shall include "the Sherif and those who follow him." When this phrase reached Damascus, it was suggested that the northern line of limit of Sherif's Empire should be [the] "Mersina-Diarbekr" line.[154]

The Arab nationalists intended to incorporate the four cities into the Sharifian state in order to benefit from the British promises of supplies of arms and money and support for Arab independence.

Note should be taken also of the order in which the four cities were grouped: "districts of Aleppo, Damascus, Hama and Homs." "Districts of Aleppo and Damascus" would have sufficiently indicated his intention, but, wishing apparently to emphasize the territorial continuity of the Syrian hinterland, he listed Hama and Homs as well. This was vital to Arab interests, and its occupation by France, as he had warned, would be resisted by force of arms. At no time did he mention that the Arabs would fight for Beirut and Jerusalem as well. Lebanon and Palestine, on account of long-standing French and international interests, were out of bounds.

From the above quotations, it is clear that the introduction of the word "districts" was unconnected with Palestine at all. It applied exclusively to the Syrian hinterland. The phrase "purely Arab" prefixed to "districts" is additional indication of his thinking. This formula, taken together with Hussein's earlier assurance (letter dated 9 September 1915) that "within these limits they have not included places inhabited by a foreign race," left McMahon in no doubt as to the nature of modifications made by the Arab leaders. "They have not included places inhabited by a foreign race in the territories which they demand," he reassured the Foreign Office.[155] This reservation applied with particular force to Palestine, where, according to official British and German, as well as Zionist, sources, there were about 100,000 Jews before World War II.[156] They formed a sixth of the whole population, but in Jerusalem they had an overwhelming majority.[157] To the Christians, by any standard, the Holy Land could not have been regarded as a "purely Arab district."

Grey now had a pretty clear idea of the Arab leaders' territorial exclusions, but, acutely sensitive to French interests, he forewarned the High Commissioner: "the general reserve you propose is however necessary more especially for North Western Boundaries." These related to all geographical Syria, which included Palestine. The sphere of British control, he added, ought to be extended from Basra Vilayet to Baghdad province:

> But, the important thing is to give assurances that will prevent Arabs from being alienated, and must leave you discretion in the matter as it is urgent and there is not time to discuss our exact formula. . . . You should keep Wingate informed.[158]

McMahon was thus given wide latitude qualified by a suggestion that Wingate should be taken into his confidence, for, unlike the High Commissioner, Wingate was an old hand in the region, more adept at dealing with the intricacies of Middle Eastern politics. When the idea of the creation of "a Great Mos-

lem [Arab] Power" was first broached by al-Mirghani, he
reacted with caution: "Of course, we must make no promises
that we cannot redeem."[159] At the same time, Wingate prevailed upon Arab leaders that Mesopotamia, Syria, and Palestine "cannot . . . be incorporated in their future Utopian Sovereign State."[160] And on 25 August, taking a cue from the de
Bunsen Committee's report, he opined: "I presume we should
take as far North as Haifa, the Persian Gulf zone and Mesopotamia, [while] Palestine might be the subject of a special
arrangement in which Russia would participate, and the rest of
Syria presumably would fall to the French."[161] When he learned
that the High Commissioner was negotiating with al-Faruqi, he
hastened to remind his colleagues in Cairo of the British obligations to France and urged that, in order to create a favorable
basis for negotiations, the Sharif should be apprised by a competent emissary of both the French claims in Syria and those of
Britain in Mesopotamia. He appended a formula which read as
follows:

> H.B.M.'s Government will recognise and support the principle of
> Arabian independence . . . without prejudice to the claims of
> Great Britain and her allies to exercise such local measures of
> protection and control over certain districts as may be neces-
> sary . . . and will exercise her good offices with her allies to
> this end . . .[162]

Such a formula would have been of great use to McMahon,
since it eschewed territorial precision and fully conformed with
Grey's instruction to the High Commissioner in his cable of 20
October, where he wrote:

> The simplest plan would be to give an assurance of Arab indepen-
> dence saying that we will proceed at once to discuss boundaries if
> they send representatives for that purpose . . .[163]

Grey's purpose was to prevent Arabs from being alienated and
leave definition of boundaries to further negotiations, presumably jointly with France. However, McMahon made a hasty
decision and dispatched his crucial letter of 24 October 1915 to
Sharif Hussein without consulting the Foreign Secretary or even
his closest advisors. The only person with whom he was in con-

tact was al-Faruqi. It was he who created the atmosphere of panic and it was he who directly or indirectly caused McMahon to formulate his letter to Hussein as he did. "The matter appeared to me to admit no delay," McMahon wrote to Grey two days later, to which he added,

> The composition of a reply which would be acceptable to the Arab party and which would at the same time leave as free a hand as possible to His Majesty's Government in the future has been a difficult task.[164]

As difficult as the task might have been, it was not skillfully discharged. The product of McMahon's labor was a vague and obscure formula which subsequently gave rise to misinterpretations and provided fertile ground for disputes and recriminations. Nonetheless, at that time there was no apparent reason for any misunderstanding of its meaning. The nature of the accord reached with al-Faruqi that formed the basis of the 24 October 1915 letter may be derived from McMahon's dispatch to Grey of 26 October, as well as from his subsequent cable to the Foreign Office, dated 7 November 1915. To Grey he explained,

> . . . while recognizing the towns of Damascus, Hama, Homs and Aleppo as being within the circle of Arab countries I have endeavoured to provide for possible French pretensions to those places by a general modification to the effect that His Majesty's Government can only give assurances in regard to those territories "in which she can act without detriment to the interests of her ally France." I venture to emphasize the fact that the eventual arrangement [with the Arabs] would be very greatly facilitated if France would consent to forgo any territorial claims she may have to purely Arab territories, such as Damascus, Hama, Homs and Aleppo. The inclusion of such districts in Arabia will be insisted on by the Arabs . . .

And on 7 November he cabled to the Foreign Office:

> Arabs attach very great importance to inclusion of Damascus, Hama, Homs and Aleppo in Arab boundaries and have, in fact, repeatedly expressed the determination to fight for those territories if necessary.

Here followed a paragraph which has already been quoted:

> It was explained to them that owing to our obligations to our ally France, we had not a free hand as regards all Arabia and therefore the above mentioned provision applies, as is clearly stated in the preamble of our assurances, to those portions only of Arab territory wherein Great Britain is free to act without detriment to the interests of our ally, France. This the Arab representatives fully understood and admitted . . .
>
> There is nothing in my assurances to prevent some similar understanding between France and the Arabs regarding the hinterland of Syria, i.e., Aleppo, etc. [as was made with regard to British interests in Mesopotamia].165

The above quotations reaffirm McMahon's earlier statement made in his private telegram to Grey of 18 October 1915, which included the following points:

1. The Arab desideratum centered exclusively on the Syrian hinterland and its inclusion in the projected Arab state. The phrases: "towns of Damascus . . . being within the circle of Arab countries" (dispatch, 26 October 1915), as well as "purely Arab territories such as Damascus. . . . The inclusion of such districts in Arabia . . ." (telegram, 7 November 1915), convey an identical meaning and throw light on the ambiguous phrase in the letter to Hussein of 24 October 1915.

2. The Syrian littoral, as well as Palestine, were excluded by the Arabs themselves; Palestine specifically was not even mentioned.

3. That it was made sufficiently clear to the Arab representatives that Britain was unable to dispose of any territory in Syria, including the Syrian hinterland, without French concurrence; that they fully realized it; and that it was up to the Arabs to make similar arrangements with France as they did with the British with regard to Mesopotamia.

Al-Faruqi's influence on the decision-making process in Cairo, as well as on McMahon's letter to Hussein of 24 October 1915 was profound. Although clumsily and inexpertly drafted, Mc-Mahon adopted al-Faruqi's own phrase in order to assign the Arabs the territory for which, they declared, they were pre-pared to fight. Moreover, McMahon used the phrase in the same comprehensive sense that al-Faruqi meant: the area that covered the Syrian hinterland southwards to the Gulf of Akaba. There was no disagreement between the Arabs and the British as to the interpretation of McMahon's letter. On 26 October, McMahon cabled to the Foreign Office: "I now propose to com-municate the above terms in definite form to Faroki [sic] and Aziz el al-Misri and facilitate their commencement of propa-ganda."[166] Four days later, Clayton confidently advised Sir William Tyrrell that al-Faruqi had seen the conditions laid down there and in the main agreed with them, and that al-Misri also agreed.[167] Gleefully, Maxwell also asserted that "Faruqi and others of his party here, including Aziz Bey El al-Misri, have accepted the proposals and are ready to act."[168]

Grey therefore had no reason to be dissatisfied with the provisos regarding French interests; the scathing criticism that was leveled against the High Commissioner, in particular by the India Office, related to his Arab policy in general.[169] Early in November, Grey received from Aubrey Herbert, M.P., who had just returned from Cairo, first-hand information on the thinking prevalent at the British Residency. Herbert suggested that, in order to compensate the French for the loss of Damascus "and those territories," the British should declare "a policy of disin-terestedness in Palestine in favor of France."[170]

The French, however, were in no mood for a deal of this kind. On 10 November, Grey proposed to Cambon another deal: Britain would forego her claim to Baghdad and Basra in return for a French concession of "certain places" in Syria to be promised to the Arabs. Cambon curtly rebuffed the proposal; Mesopotamia and Syria were not on the same footing; "the con-nection of France with Syria was very ancient and France really regarded [it] as a dependency."[171] Picot, during his meeting on 23 November 1915 with his British counterparts, was also uncompromising. He maintained that, with the exception of Jerusalem and Bethlehem, which might be formed into a sepa-rate enclave under an International regime, the whole of Syria and Palestine must be treated as French.[172] In these circumstances, to allege, as Toynbee did in his memorandum of 21 November 1918, that Britain intended and indeed was committed to award Palestine to the Arabs, was to demonstrate a very imperfect understanding of the political realities of the day.

But how did Hussein understand McMahon's letter? In 1937, the Palestine Royal Commission, the Peel Commission, expressed the view that "it was in the highest degree unfortunate that, in the exigencies of war, the British Government was unable to make their intention clear to the Sherif."[173] This judgment weakened the British case during the Round Table Conference in 1939 and impressed a great number of historians. However, on this particular point, the Peel Commission was at fault. We have been fortunate to unearth the Arabic translation of the 24th of October letter, from which it is clear beyond any doubt that Hussein could not have understood it in any way other than had been intended by McMahon. The Arabic translation is far more specific than its English original and is free of any ambiguity. The credit for it must go to Hussein Ruhi, an Arabic-speaking Persian and a member of the Baha'i sect, who served as Storrs's Arabic secretary and agent. Storrs described him as "a fair though not profound Arabist, and a better agent than scholar."[174] This was not necessarily a disadvantage, for, as an intelligence agent, he was able to familiarize himself with the workings of the Arab mind and render some valuable services. In 1916, he exposed al-Faruqi's unreliability, and in May 1917, was transferred to Jeddah as Arabic Secretary to Colonel C. E. Wilson and assisted him in negotiating with King Hussein.[175] Although there is no hard evidence to prove it, it would not be too farfetched to assume that, in October 1915, he helped McMahon during his encounters with al-Faruqi. The latter did not speak English, while the former was a complete stranger to Arabic. Ruhi was therefore well-placed to appreciate what was at stake and to convey faithfully McMahon's thinking when translating his letters. Ruhi's prose was not the most scholarly, but it was incomparably more intelligible than the English original.[176]

The phrase on which the controversy revolved reads:

> The two districts of Mersina and Alexandretta and portions of Syria lying to the west of the districts of Damascus, Homs, Hama and Aleppo cannot be said to be purely Arab, and should be excluded from the limits demanded.

Ruhi translated the word "Syria" to Bilad ush-Shám, which means the country of Shám. Shám, it will be recalled, was the Arabic name for geographical Syria, which extended from the Taurus Mountains in the north to el-Arish in the south and from the Mediterranean in the West to the Euphrates and the Syrian desert in the east.

But Shám was also the name of the city of Damascus. So, in order to avoid confusion about which "portion of Syria" was meant to be excluded, Ruhi used another Arabic name of Damascus, Dimashq ush-Shám, preceded by *wilāyats* (plural). For any Arab there was only one meaning of *wilāya* — a large administrative district, equivalent to the Turkish vilayet. And there was no *wilāya* of Dimashq other than that which covered what later became Trans-Jordan down to the Gulf of Akaba. If McMahon had in mind "environs," or "banlieux," as argued by Toynbee, Ruhi would have used the word sanjak, which was the smaller administrative unit, or still better *muqata* or *nāhiya*. Nor, significantly, did he use *mudum* (the plural of *madina*), the Arabic equivalent of "towns of . . ."

The conjunction of Homs and Hama with Damascus and Aleppo caused much confusion and provided fertile ground for biased speculation, for, unlike the latter two cities, the former were never vilayets. But, as suggested already,[177] what both al-Faruqi and McMahon had in mind was the districts that *contained* the four cities; the word "contained" was omitted either for brevity's sake or because of negligence. Any other explanation is implausible and bound to lead to self-contradictory absurdities.

Ruhi rendered also quite satisfactorily into Arabic the so-called "general" reservation with regard to France. The English text reads:

> As for those regions lying within those frontiers [claimed by Hussein in his letter of 14 July 1915] wherein Great Britain is free to act without detriment to the interests of her ally France, I am empowered . . .

Ruhı's translation literally reads:

> But with regard to those regions embraced by those boundaries where Great Britain [is] free to act without encroaching on the interests of her ally France, I am authorised . . .

The style is cumbersome and not the one that an Arab scholar would have chosen. Nonetheless, the contents are perfectly intelligible, and Hussein's response to it on 5 November 1915 bears this out. Moreover, Antonius, in his *Arab Awakening*, as well as the Palestine Arab Delegations (1921-1939), who made so much heavy weather of the word "district," were silent with regard to this particular clause.

Examination of the translated version shows that Ruhi was perfectly familiar with the High Commissioner's thinking. He specifically segregated the sentence from the preceding one by a full stop — rather an unusual practice among Arab writers who are careless of punctuation marks or omit them altogether. Even more significant is the translation of the English word "wherein" as "*haithu,*" not preceded by a comma. This is of extreme importance, for, had he used a variant of it equivalent to "whereas" preceded by a comma, the whole meaning of the reservation would have been altered. It would have implied that, within the area reserved for France (the Syrian littoral and Palestine), the British Government was free to act without reference to the French Government.

It was necessary to probe into the matter, because this was exactly what happened during the encounter between Feisal and Major Young late in December 1920, when Feisal challenged the British interpretation of McMahon's letter for the first time, Young was in a weak bargaining position, since the Arabic text prepared by Ruhi had disappeared from the files of the Arab Bureau — this was the second time that the same document was mislaid — and Young had to rely on the copy produced by Feisal. This, as we shall see later, was not authentic, and, upon reading it in Feisal's presence, Young was shocked to discover how "badly" the phrase had been translated. "The effect of this careless translation," he noted in dismay, was "that Hussein and Feisal have always thought that Great Britain was free to act in the whole of the restricted area . . ."[178]

But if Ruhi's translation was less than scholarly, though not inaccurate, Hussein's language was hardly intelligible; his terminology was often faulty. Sir Laurence Grafftey-Smith, Acting Consul-General in Alexandria, and, from December 1920, Vice-Consul in Jeddah, recalled that Hussein's mental processes were Turkish rather than Arab. His spoken Arabic was "of almost kitchen-simplicity," but his written style was "a translation of Turkish complexities, which favor immense Proust-like gerundial clauses and leave [open] the question whether a thing is, or is not . . ." Grafftey-Smith would plough through Hussein's prose with the assistance of a qualified translator, but neither of them was ever sure what the King was trying to say.[179]

These shortcomings are very much in evidence in his Correspondence with McMahon. Thus, in his letter, dated 5 November 1915, he referred to Mersina, Adana, Aleppo, and Beirut as *wilāyat* (plural), although only the latter two cities were vilayets (districts). He was also inaccurate when using the plural and dual Arabic numbers. When translating the words "and their sea coasts" (after "Aleppo and Beirut"), he used *sawāhil* (pl. of *sahil'*), which stands for "the shore," but, curiously, failed to specify where the coasts began or ended, although it clearly was not to his advantage to be vague. The second paragraph of the same letter is so involved that it defies translation. The argument relates to the presence in Mesopotamia of British troops, which Hussein wished to be placed on a temporary footing ("those districts now occupied by British troops," in English translation). The Arabic word used to translate "districts" was not *wilāyat*, as it should logically have been, but *jihāt*, meaning "side" or "direction" — a vague and undefined term. So, Ruhi, by improving a faulty text, unwittingly rendered Hussein a useful, though unsolicited, service.

Wingate received only the English copy of McMahon's letter to Hussein of 24 October 1915, not its Arabic translation. Suspecting, quite correctly, that the phrase "districts of . . ." might lead to misunderstandings in the future, he urged al-Mirghani to explain to Hussein the nature of "the reservations which [the British] have made in Syria, Palestine and Mesopotamia."[180]

Wingate's message and Ruhi's Arabic version were very pointed and left Hussein in no doubt as to the meaning of McMahon's letter. Replying (5 November 1915), the Sharif made some comments with regard to the Iraqi vilayets, as well as to those of Aleppo and Beirut, but avoided any reference to Palestine. On 4 January 1918, he approved Hogarth's formula and three months later in *al-Qibla* enthusiastically welcomed the return of the Jews to their "sacred and beloved homeland." In October 1919, he declared most emphatically to Colonel Charles E. Vickery, the newly appointed Agent in Jeddah, that he did not concern himself at all with Palestine and had no desire to have suzerainty over it, for himself or his successors.[181]

This declaration was all the more remarkable, since in the meantime Hussein had reverted to his earlier claim, accusing Britain of not fulfilling her promises. Cairo officials were in an awkward position, since the Arabic version of McMahon's letter had disappeared and Hussein jealously guarded the Correspondence, not allowing anyone to inspect it. It was therefore "essential," Grafftey-Smith recalled, "to disabuse Hussein urgently of any genuine misconceptions . . . [for] although we knew what Storrs and his Baha'i translator Ruhi had meant to write, we could not be certain that their Arabic pen had not slipped. The King's pretensions became yearly more personal and fantastic; we could never get a peep at the precious Arabic document he held."[182]

It fell upon Colonel Vickery to call Hussein's bluff. Like Major H. G. Garland, the Acting Director of the Arab Bureau, Vickery had served in Feisal's army and was familiar with Arab affairs. Knowing the Arabs, he was more forthright with the King than his predecessor and sometimes even brutal. Forcefully and adroitly he provoked him into showing his treasured possession; Vickery was the first British official to see the Arabic version of McMahon's letters since their dispatch from Cairo. On 3 October 1919, he cabled to Garland:

> Have now practically complete copies which will be forwarded first mail. Do not think that they commit us to much. King has exaggerated idea of their importance with very little justification.[183]

Transcribed and checked word for word with the originals by Vickery personally and certified as "absolutely correct," the much coveted documents were dispatched to Cairo.[184] This extraordinary coup prompted A. Keown-Boyd, who in 1918 succeeded Storrs as Oriental Secretary, to make yet another search for the missing copy of Ruhi's version of McMahon's letter of 24 October. Soon afterwards he found it caught in the back of a drawer in Storrs's desk.[185]

Keown-Boyd arrived in Khartoum in September 1907 and was appointed Deputy Inspector of the Sudan Government.[186] Thereafter he served as Wingate's private secretary, and in October 1916, when Wingate succeeded McMahon as High Commissioner in Cairo, 1916, Keown-Boyd followed him. Unlike the controversial and erratic Storrs, Keown-Boyd was solid and reliable. The skill, experience and the "esoteric mysteries" he acquired during his service in the Sudan made him "a first-class Oriental Secretary" and qualified him in a later period for higher positions in Egyptian administration.[187] He was intimately acquainted with the Anglo-Sharifian relations, and, both on account of his superb command of Arabic and in his capacity as Oriental Secretary, it could be taken almost for granted that the Arabic transcripts provided by Vickery were retranslated into English by him. He rendered the so-called "specific reservation" thus:

> The two "Vilayets" of Mersina and Alexandretta and parts of the country of "Esh-Sham" (Damascus) situated in the Western directions of the "Vilayets" of Damascus, Homs, Hamah and Aleppo cannot be said to be purely Arab. Therefore they must be excluded from the claimed boundaries [by the Sharif].

The "general reservation" was translated in this way:

> As for the districts which are included within those boundaries [claimed by Hussein], where Great Britain [has] freedom of duties without touching the interests of her Ally, France, I am authorized . . .[188]

It will be recalled that Ruhi translated the word "districts" to *wilāyat*, which, in turn, Keown-Boyd retranslated to "Vilayets." The identicality in meaning among these terms in the English, Arabic, and Ottoman usage can no longer be doubted, and so it was understood at the time of the contemporary *dramatis personae*, both British and Arab. The long, drawn-out controversy in this matter can be finally laid to rest.

The "general reservation" is also crystal clear. In some respects it is even stronger than the English text. McMahon wrote: "As for the regions lying within these frontiers [claimed by the Sharif]," whereas Ruhi's text reads: "As for the districts (*wilāyats*) which are included in these boundaries." Clearly, in the given context, the term "districts"/*wilāyats* is much more meaningful than McMahon's "regions"; the "districts"/*wilāyats* that Hussein claimed related to those of Damascus and Aleppo, which, logically included the four towns of the Syrian hinterland.

Soon after the Arabic text came to light, and following its re-translation, Laurence Grafftey-Smith concluded that "it confirmed our own and not the King's interpretation."[189] The King, however, as we shall see later, based his interpretation on an entirely different letter,[190] and not on that of the 24 October 1915 — which bears out our point that, in 1915-1916 and thereafter, Hussein fully understood its meaning.

2

The "Pledge" to Hussein and the Sykes-Picot Agreement

Following T. E. Lawrence's accidental death on 18 May 1935, Toynbee wrote an essay dedicated to his memory. In it he referred to the Sykes-Picot Agreement as "the Anglo-French deception. . . . The Arabs had come out empty handed." He suspected that Lawrence's conscience reproached him for having promised to the Arabs, in the name of the British Government, an independence that, in the event, was withheld from them. Lawrence felt guilty, Toynbee surmised, for being instrumental, albeit unconsciously, "in the perpetration of the Anglo-French fraud at the Arabs' expense."[1] This portrayal was fanciful. It reflected Toynbee's self-inflicted feelings of guilt rather than Lawrence's state of mind. For, in his famous letter to *The Times* (11 September 1919), Lawrence categorically stated that he saw "no inconsistencies or incompatibilities in these four documents, and I know nobody who does." The four documents were:

1. The British promise to King Hussein, dated 24 October 1915, which undertook, conditional on an Arab revolt, to recognize the "independence of the Arabs" south of latitude 37 degrees, except in the provinces of Baghdad and Basra, and except where Great Britain was not "free to act without detriment to the interests of France."

2. The Sykes-Picot Agreement of May 1916.

3. The British statement to the seven Syrians in Cairo, dated 11 June 1917.

4. The Anglo-French Declaration of 8 November 1918.[2]

A month later, during the Peace Conference, Lawrence approved wholeheartedly of Yale's proposed solution for the postwar settlement of the Middle East, saying that "it gave the Arabs more than he had dared to hope to secure for them." He urged Yale to see Lord Allenby and Lloyd George. Sir Henry McMahon declared that Yale's proposals "were in accordance with the agreements he had made with King Hussein" in 1915-1916, while Nuri al-Said, as well as Rustum Haidar Bey, members of the Hedjazi Delegation to the Peace Conference, agreed, on Emir Feisal's behalf, that they would accept Yale's solution.

William Yale (later Professor) was an expert on Syria. During World War I, he served as an American intelligence officer in Cairo and thereafter joined the America Delegation to the Peace Conference. To break the deadlock among the Allied Powers on the one hand and the Arabs on the other, he proposed the following solution:

1. *Palestine* to be placed under the mandate of Great Britain and the Zionists to be allowed to carry out their plan.

2. *Mount Lebanon* to become a separate political unit under the mandate of France.

3. *Syria*, from Ma'an and Akaba in the south to Aleppo in the north, together with the ports of Tripoli and Latakia, to be constituted as a "provisional" independent Arab state under the mandate of France.

4. *Mesopotamia* to be divided into two areas, the northern one embracing the former Ottoman vilayets of Mosul and Baghdad; and the southern one that of Basra and the Emirate of Mohammerah. The northern area to become a "provisional" independent Arab state and the southern one to be granted self-government. Both areas were to be placed under a British mandate.[3]

As soon as Lawrence learned that the British War Cabinet had adopted Yale's plan, he wrote to Lloyd George:

I must confess to you that in my heart I always believed that in difficult to know how to thank you. It concerns me personally, because I assured them during the campaigns that our promises held their face value, and backed them with my word, for what it was worth. Now in your Agreement over Syria you have kept all our promises to them, and given them more than perhaps they ever deserved, and my relief at getting out of the affair with clean hands is very great.[4]

Toynbee might have been unaware of Yale's plan, since by that time he had left the Foreign Office, but it is inconceivable that he did not see Lawrence's letter to *The Times*. He must have forgotten that, on 25 February 1919, in a joint memorandum with Ormsby-Gore, he had stated categorically that the Sykes-Picot Agreement "did not conflict with [British] undertakings to King Hussein," and that Palestine "was specially excepted from Syria." In a subsequent minute, Toynbee asserted that the principle of self-determination annulled the validity of both the claims of King Hussein and those of France.[5] This statement must have also escaped his memory.

If Toynbee's statements with regard to the Sykes-Picot Agreement were the result of his highly selective memory and unmethodical way of thinking,[6] for the Arabs it served as proof of the Allies' iniquitous conduct toward themselves. The notion that they had been deceived had a lasting emotional impact. It became almost an article of faith and turned into a source of perennial grievance. George Antonius denounced it as

> . . . a shocking document. It is not only the product of greed at its worst, that is to say, of greed allied to suspicion and so leading to stupidity: it also stands out as a startling piece of double-dealing.

Moreover, he continued, it was

> . . . the breach of faith. The Agreement had been negotiated and concluded without the knowledge of the Sharif Hussein, and it contained provisions which were in direct conflict with the terms of Sir Henry McMahon's compact with him. . . . [It] was dishonestly concealed from him because it was realised that, were he to have been appraised of it, he would have unhesitatingly denounced his alliance with Great Britain.[7]

The Anglo-Sharifian "compact" was allegedly embodied in McMahon's letter of 24 October 1915. Antonius described it as "by far the most important [letter] in the whole correspondence . . . perhaps the most important international document in the history of the Arab national movement. It contains the pledges which brought the Arabs openly into the war on the side of the Allies." In the years that followed World War I, he went on, it became "an outstanding bone of contention" and was invoked as "the main piece of evidence on which the Arabs accuse Great Britain of having broken faith with them." He rejected the British equation of "districts" with "vilayets" and assiduously referred to the 24 October letter as the Arabs' title deed to Palestine; it was a contract and a "pledge" — a pledge, which he claimed, was violated.[8]

The Arabs consistently accused the British Government of duplicity and perfidy; Palestine was sold twice, or rather three times: first to the Arabs, thereafter to the French, and finally to the Zionists. Subsequently Arnold Toynbee made these arguments his own and propagated them on numerous occasions, infecting British intellectuals and public men with feelings of guilt and shame.

The contention is based on fallacious premises and is untenable. The claim that "district" meant "vicinity" or "neighbourhood" was a bogus claim. McMahon's letter of 24 October 1915 was not a legal, but a political, document, and considering the way it had been extracted, was devoid of a moral base essential to any contract, private or public. At any rate, the loose and often unintelligible language employed by Hussein[9] would hardly have lent itself to the construction of an agreement befitting accepted norms.

The letter was composed in haste and dispatched without the State Secretary's prior approval. It made the Foreign Office unhappy; the India Office was furious; while the Viceroy of India and the General Staff were highly critical of not being consulted. Kitchener's silence is louder than words. It was not brought before the Cabinet for a debate at all. So, when McMahon told Hussein: "I am empowered in the name of the Government of Great Britain to give the following assurances . . . ," he was in fact committing his Government to something that the Cabinet did not endorse. For this he had to suffer the penalty. In the following year, when Hussein's rebellion was on the point of collapsing and the British Government was faced with the unsavory task of saving him from certain defeat, Sir Edward Grey consulted the Prime Minister and thereafter dismissed McMahon unceremoniously; Sir Reginald Wingate was appointed to succeed him.[10]

The Arabs singled out the letter of 24 October as a privileged document which embodied a definite commitment. This was false, for it was only one of a series of letters that remained inconclusive. These letters contained a number of disagreements of cardinal importance, the resolution of which was left in abeyance by common consent until after the war. McMahon's letter of 24 October 1915, therefore, could not be regarded as a "compact" or an agreement. It was merely an expression of intent and goodwill. It was a provisional preliminary to a final settlement to be ironed out after termination of hostilities. Hussein himself, in his letter of 9 September 1915 to the High Commissioner, confirmed: "As to the limits and boundaries demanded...we should discuss them after the war is over..." And in his letter of 1 January 1916, he restated that "at the first opportunity after this war is finished, we shall ask you (what we avert our eyes from today) for what we now leave to France in Beirut and its coasts." And as if to emphasize his point, he attached a copy of his letter to Sayyid Ali al-Mirghani (28 December 1915), in which he wrote: "We have no reason for discussing the question of the frontier other than as a preliminary measure."[11] Hussein's letter of 1 January 1916 terminated all the discussions on the question of boundaries.

For the British, too, the matter was not final and was contingent on the approval of the Allies. On 2 February 1916, Sir Arthur Nicolson told Grey despondently that it was next to impossible to discuss the northern limits of the future Arab state until French desiderata in Syria had been examined first, since Picot adamantly refused to separate the two questions.[12] Moreover, Russian consent also had to be solicited. Several days later, Buchanan was requested to reassure Petrograd that nothing would be concluded between the British and the French "until the consent of the Russian Government is obtained."[13] At this juncture, Nicolson briefed McMahon:

> We have submitted the agreement to which we and France have
> come to in principle . . . to Petrograd, and we are waiting for the
> views of the Russian Government on the subject. . . . We then
> have to consider the question as to the manner in which to
> approach the Sherif on the subject of boundaries and other
> matters.[14]

The differences were finally overcome and by mid-March
1916 an Inter-Allied agreement was concluded, termed officially
the Turkey-in-Asia Agreement. On his return to London, Sykes
asked Clayton to send al-Faruqi and Aziz Bey Ali al-Misri to
Picot and himself for discussion "about the boundaries of the
Arab state in the framework of the [Turkey-in-Asia] Agreement."[15] It was only within this framework that it was possible
to recognize the boundaries of the future Arab state. The idea
that Britain could act single-handedly and conclude a separate
agreement with the Arabs with regard to the northern boundaries of their future state was an illusion.

The Inter-Allied Agreement legitimized these boundaries,
since the McMahon-Hussein Correspondence on its own had no
legal validity. There was no incompatibility between these two
sets of documents. None of those directly involved in the negotiations in London, such as Nicolson or Sykes, noted any inconsistency. Nor did McMahon and other British officials in Cairo
think that it conflicted with assurances given to the Sherif. The
Sykes-Picot Agreement was specifically designed to fit in with
the modified territorial Arab desiderata. In a letter to Sykes on
3 May 1916, Clayton confirmed that

> The present arrangement seems the best possible. It does not clash
> with any engagements which have been given to the Sherif and
> has the advantage of clearly defining our position vis-à-vis
> other parties.[16]

And, on the following day, McMahon re-echoed this assessment: "There is nothing in arrangement agreed between France
and Russia and ourselves . . . that conflicts with any agreements
made by ourselves or assurances given to Sherif and other Arab
parties . . ."[17]

The Sykes-Picot Agreement was the direct consequence of
negotiations with the Arab leaders. Its true progenitor was not

the March 1915 Constantinople Agreement, as has been generally assumed, but the McMahon-Hussein Correspondence.
There was no double-dealing. The overriding aim was to make
the Arab rising possible and this hinged on French concessions
in the Syrian hinterland. Nor could military operations on the
eastern front take place without French concurrence. As Sir
Arthur Hirtzel summed up tersely three years later:

> French consent was therefore doubly necessary . . . and *the Sykes-Picot Agreement was the price we had to pay for it.* Without the
> British offensive there could have been no Arab revolt; and
> without the Sykes-Picot there would have been no British
> offensive.[18]

The Sykes-Picot Agreement was a compromise among all
the parties concerned: the British, the French, and the Arabs.
The groundwork was laid by Sir Arthur Nicolson, but the credit
for the compromise must go to Sir Mark Sykes. David G.
Hogarth, no friend of the Inter-Allied Agreement, had some
words of praise for his skillful diplomacy:

> Sir Mark Sykes no doubt achieved the utmost in persuading M.
> Picot to resign the eastern part of Syria with the chain of impor-
> tant inland cities to independent Arab government, to leave
> Haifa to us, and to accept the internationalization of Palestine.
> That Sir Mark Sykes should have brought [it about] . . . is
> remarkable and that the accord should be such as it is, attests
> emphatically [to] his powers of persuasive persistence.[19]

In order to reconcile the overlapping territorial desiderata,
Sykes first prevailed on al-Faruqi to accept the French interests
in Syria. This he achieved during their meetings in Cairo. On 21
November 1915, he cabled to the Director of Military Operations:

> With regard to France and Arabs our task is to get Arabs to
> concede as much as possible to French. . . . Thus we smooth the
> way for France with Syrians and in the matter where France has
> a traditional interest, deal directly with her.

And on the previous day he reported:

> Arabs would agree to convention with France granting her mono-

poly of all concessionary enterprise in Syria and Palestine, Syria being defined as bounded by Euphrates as far south as Deir Zor and from there to Deraa and along Hedjaz Railway to Maan.

. . . Arabs would agree to identical convention with Great Britain with regard to remainder of greater Arabia viz. Irak and Jazirah and Northern Mesopotamia.[20]

Al-Faruqi's statement to Sykes was appended to Nicolson's note "The Arab Question" to Grey, dated 2 February 1916 (quoted already), as an indication that the Arab leaders' claim was confined to the Syrian hinterland. On 16 December 1915, Sykes reported to the War Committee in a similar vein.[21] "Monopoly of enterprise" was taken to mean "sphere of interest," and this was how Nicolson understood it. When meeting Picot on 23 November 1915, he reassured him that the Arabs were willing to concede to the French a monopoly of concessions, grant security to their educational and other establishments, and admit French advisers. In these circumstances, in a short time, he emphasized, Syria would become in fact a French protectorate. Picot was not impressed, but when Sykes managed finally to persuade him, Nicolson noted triumphantly that the "four towns of Homs, Hama, Aleppo and Damascus will be included in the Arab State or Confederation of States."[22]

Both the British and the French Governments undertook not only to recognize the boundaries of the future Arab State, but also to protect it. "To recognize and uphold an independent Arab State or a Confederation of Arab States in the area . . . (A) and (B),"[23] was no mean achievement for the Arabs. This was more than they had or hoped to obtain from the Turks. The very phrase "independent Arab State" was anathema to the latter. As Lloyd George aptly put it, "the first promise of national liberation given by the Allies was the Sykes-Picot Agreement of May 1916. It guaranteed freedom to the Arabs from the shores of the Red Sea to Damascus."[24]

It was in response to the Arab demands, and as the consequence of the prevailing conditions in the region, that the Allied Powers were willing to provide their benevolent protection. As early as August 1914, al-Misri invited Britain to assume the "tutelage and control of foreign affairs . . . of a united Arabian state independent of Turkey."[25] In his letters, dated 14 July and

5 November 1915, Hussein requested "assistance" in order to ensure "the stability of Arab independence," and not to be left alone even after the conclusion of the war. And in his letter to Sayyid Ali al-Mirghani of 28 December 1915, he admitted that, for some time to come, Arabs would need British protection:

> I say this [not only] from a purely economic point of view, but [particularly] from the military point of view [that] none of us [can] ignore the certainty that we shall stand in great need of the power of Great Britain to extinguish any trouble that is liable to break out in the interior of the country . . . because our friends will not hesitate by all possible means to incite their own partisans against us . . . [26]

Following his visit to Basra, Sir Mark Sykes concluded that the vilayets of Baghdad and Basra were "incapable of self-government and a new and weak state could not administer them owing to Shiah and Sunni dissension."[27] A few days later, during a meeting with al-Faruqi, he indicated that the Arabs would be prepared to make a treaty with the Entente Powers provided they guaranteed to protect Arab independence.[28] Both Dr. Faris Nimr, the editor of *Mokattam*, and Said Shuckair Pasha thought that, in the foreseeable future, Syria would not be able to exist as an independent state "even for a day," and that therefore some form of European control was indispensable.[29] More emphatic was Chekri Ganem, who was an influential Syrian Christian from Beirut domiciled in Paris and the editor of the Arabic newspaper *Al-Mustakbal* [The Future]. Ganem deprecated the precipitate claim for Syria's "complete independence." In his opinion, only the ignorant, motivated by personal ambition, could indulge in such wild dreams. Any sane-minded person could visualize that it would bring about "a complete anarchy and the ruin of the country." The Arabs were not prepared and not educated for self-government, he pointed out. For centuries they had been ruled by the Turks. Premature independence would invite a worse disaster than Turkish rule:

> We need protection and advice [of] England and France. We know that under their guidance our country will thrive and prosper. If in time to come the protecting Powers will see that we are ripe

for self-government, only then [will] they withdraw their protectorship and leave us to rule our country.[30]

This assessment was characteristic of an educated Francophile Arab, and Grey duly took note of it.

The presence of the Powers in the region in the aftermath of Turkey's demise was essential, not only in order to protect their own legitimate interests, but also to ensure good government and provide an umbrella under which Arab independence could gradually mature. The alternative was chaos or, still worse, the return of the Turks — an outcome that filled Hussein with the utmost trepidation. The Agreement was an act of responsibility, an attempt to provide authority in a turbulent and unstable part of the world from which the Arabs were to benefit. However, it was up to the Arabs themselves to make good their aspirations to independence. The Allied Powers undertook only "to recognise and uphold it," but this undertaking was made on the clear condition that the Arabs rebelled to a man against their Turkish overlords and sided with the Allies.

Such reasoning was fully in line with common practice in any political or commercial intercourse. Nor was it novel. The principle of *do ut des* with regard to the Arabs was laid down by the de Bunsen Committee in their report of 30 June 1915. Referring to negotiations with Arab Chiefs in the Arabian Peninsula (paras. 91-92), they remarked that any guarantee for the independence of the Arabs should be given only in return for their "effective [and] successful support in the war against Turkey"; to which the Committee added ironically, "it still remains to be seen . . . whether the Chiefs will fulfil their part of the bargain."

On 4 February 1916, an interdepartmental committee met in which — in addition to Grey, Crewe, and Nicolson — Kitchener, Bonar Law, Holderness, and Hirtzel also participated. The relevant section of their decision reads:

. . . provided that the co-operation of the Arabs is secured, and that the Arabs fulfil the condition and obtain the towns of Homs, Hama, Damascus and Aleppo, the British Government would not object to the arrangement [made between Sykes and Picot].[31]

In an outline of the Agreement, Nicolson made it clear that

It is understood that the putting into effect of the proposals is contingent on the successful assistance of the Arabs and their leaders in the establishment of an Arab State or Confederation of Arab States under the protection of France and Great Britain; and on their active co-operation with the Allies.[32]

Lord Curzon was none too happy with the draft Agreement, but Grey assured him that it would become effective only if and when the Arabs threw in their lot with the Allies, a condition that had been expressly stipulated in the arrangement.[33] And to Bertie, Grey wrote:

> The French Ambassador pressed me earnestly to sign a note of agreement about Asia Minor. I again referred to the point of its being conditional upon action taken by the Arabs. M. Cambon said that it was well understood that it was dependent upon an agreement with the Sherif of Mecca and this provisional character was already in writing.[34]

Five days later, he confirmed to Cambon: "Provided that the co-operation of the Arabs is secured, and that the Arabs fulfil the conditions and obtain the towns of Homs, Hama, Damascus and Aleppo, His Majesty's Government . . . are ready to accept the arrangement" arrived at in London and Petrograd.[35] From all these statements it is evident that the Inter-Allied Agreement and all that it entailed was contingent on the Arabs doing their part in the struggle for their own liberation. Failing that, as Nicolson made crystal clear, "all the proposals fall to the ground,"[36] the inescapable corollary being that the British position was to revert to the *status quo ante*; that is, to the courses originally proposed by the de Bunsen Committee in which no account of Arab aspirations was to be taken. Like the McMahon-Hussein Correspondence, the Turkey-in-Asia Agreement bore a provisional nature, and all the arrangements were left in abeyance until the future Peace Conference. This goes a long way toward explaining Grey's reluctance in the early summer of 1916 to divulge its terms to Hussein.

It will be recalled that it was Austen Chamberlain, Secretary of State for India, who was the first to alert Grey to the fatal flaw in McMahon's letter of 24 October 1915 in making a unilateral promise to the Sharif. Chamberlain doubted the reality of the suggested Arab revolt in the Ottoman army and elsewhere. He thought that it was imprudent for the British Government to undertake any commitment until both the Sharif and al-Faruqi proved themselves able to carry out their promises:

> The next step should be to make clear to them that promises made by McMahon are dependent on immediate action by them in sense of their offers and will not be binding on us unless they do their part at once.[37]

Grey fully agreed with Chamberlain and instructed the High Commissioner: "If Arabs do their part we will fulfil promises made through you, but in next communication . . . you should state that they should act at once."[38] On the same day, the Viceroy of India insisted:

> We are still in dark as to actual quid pro quo to be given by Arabs in return for those sweeping assurances, but trust it may be of sufficiently definite character to enable us, if Arabs fail to perform their part, to repudiate those assurances — at any rate as far as Mesopotamia is concerned.[39]

On 14 December 1915, McMahon therefore told Hussein in no unequivocal terms:

> . . . It is most essential that you spare no efforts to attach all the Arab peoples to our united cause and urge them to afford no assistance to our enemies.
>
> It is on the success of these efforts and on the more active measures which the Arabs may thereafter take in support of our cause, when the time for action comes, that the permanence and strength of our agreement must depend.

On 1 January 1916, Hussein assured McMahon that he fully "understood the contents" of his note.

The Syrian nationalist societies had sworn allegiance to Hussein and he was confident that the revolt was imminent. On 1 March 1916, McMahon triumphantly told the Foreign Office that the Sharif considered negotiations to be "complete and that time for action on his part has arrived."[40] However, a few weeks later Hussein had to admit that "owing to dispersal of chiefs," the Syrians could neither engineer a revolution nor seize the Hedjaz railway.[41] A general Arab uprising seemed unlikely and Arab unity was practically nonexistent. Under these circumstances it was neither timely nor politic to disclose the terms of the Turkey-in-Asia Agreement. How irritated Grey was is evident from his minute dated 3 May 1916: "We have gone far enough with promises to the Sherif and he has as yet done nothing." Grey insisted that until Hussein restored his credibility, negotiations should not be continued. Nicolson fully concurred: "We should wait for some action on his part. Hitherto we have had plenty of promises from him — but nothing more — while we have given him beyond assurances, arms and money."[42] To recognize a nonexistent Arab State and offer it Allied support and protection at a time when the Arabs themselves were so demonstratively elusive was premature and hardly justifiable.

· It was not until May 1917 that Hussein was briefed by Sykes and Picot, when in Jeddah, of the terms of the Agreement, although he might have heard about it earlier from the Sultan of Egypt, who was personally appraised of it by Hogarth.[43] Whatever Hussein's response to the Agreement was at that time, he could not claim ignorance of the conditions laid down in McMahon's letter of 14 December 1915, which was the other side of the bargain.

British assurances with regard to Arab "independence" were predicated on a general Arab uprising and on a large-scale desertion from the Ottoman army. The letters of 24 October and that of 14 December 1915 must be read together. There was no unilateral British commitment. To claim the contrary — namely, that there was only a British "pledge" and that the Arabs were the injured party — is to fly in the face of all documentary evidence and to distort the nature of the deal between the British High Commissioner and the Sharif of Mecca.

3

Toynbee *versus* Toynbee

Toynbee's errors originate in his much-quoted "Memorandum on British Commitments to King Hussein,"[1] as well as in the subsequent "Memorandum Respecting the Settlement of Turkey and the Arabian Peninsula" of 21 November 1918.[2] The first is undated, but from the relevant minutes, it can safely be assumed that it appeared in print at the very end of October 1918. The list of distribution (105 copies) was provided by Toynbee himself and approved by Sir Eyre Crowe, then Permanent Under-Secretary of State. It was composed in response to Hussein's letter of 28 August 1918 to Wingate, then the High Commissioner in Egypt.

It will be recalled that the Correspondence with the Sharif in 1915-1916 remained inconclusive, and that negotiations about the future boundaries of the Arab state were left in abeyance until the termination of the war. But Hussein's ambitions never abated. He had alluded to his ultimate goal on a number of occasions during 1917 and 1918, but his letter of 28 August 1918 came as a bombshell to the Residency. This was the first time that he stated his position so bluntly. He declared that his fundamental purpose was to preserve the integrity of the Islamic State which, with the imminent collapse of the Ottoman Empire, was threatened with dissolution; only the fulfillment of his claims would justify his revolt. British policy would therefore have to be modified and pre-empt any deliberations at the future Peace Conference. Failure to comply with his demands would expose him to accusations that he had disrupted the status quo of a Moslem entity and intrigued with the British in

61

opposition to the fundamental principles of the Rising. It would blacken his record and would destroy the Arabs' trust in Great Britain because she had gone back on her agreements that had been solemnly given to him both verbally and in writing. He would feel "defrauded . . . deceived . . . as well as deprived of any personal benefit," in which case he would resign.

Hussein appended a document entitled "The Agreement [concluded] with the British Government Regarding the Rising and its Foundation." It contained five clauses:

1. "Great Britain agrees to the formation of an Independent Arab Government in every meaning of the word 'independence' [both] internally and externally, the boundaries of the said Government being . . ." — here the delimitation followed the pattern set in Hussein's first letter of July 1915, except that, on the east, it stretched beyond and reached to the river Euphrates and its junction with the Tigris. In the south, the boundary took in all the Arabian Peninsula, emphasizing that any Arab or Emir who happened to be within these boundaries would submit to the suzerainty of the Arab Government, which would supersede the British Government as a guarantor of their respective rights.

2. "Great Britain undertakes to shield the said Government and protect it against any interference or encroachment of any kind or form whatever . . . and even, in the case of an internal rising, caused by enemy intrigues or the jealousy of the Emirs, the British Government will give the Arab Government moral and material help in putting down the rising..."

3. Basra will remain under temporary British occupation until the formation of an Arab Government is completed. A sum of money will be allotted to it as a gift in return for the right of the said occupation.

4. Great Britain undertakes to supply her "foster daughter," the Arab Government, with all its [requirements] in arms, war materials and money in the form of a subsidy for the duration of the war.

5. Great Britain will undertake to cut the railway line at Mersin, or any other convenient spot in that area.

Such an "Agreement" did not exist. It was the product of Hussein's own imagination. He had reverted to his original claim, made in July 1915, which had been rejected, and went far beyond it. His pretense that the British Government had obligated itself to make him suzerain over his Arab neighbors in the Peninsula was new, as was the clause with regard to Basra and the other clauses. He seemed to be unaware that "independence . . . in every meaning of the word" and the alleged British undertaking to protect him, both externally and internally, were contradictory and that no ruler who was subsidized in arms and money to such an extent could be considered independent. Hussein failed also to appreciate that, by reverting to his original claim, he was unwittingly undermining the validity (or whatever validity was left) of McMahon's "pledge" in his letter of 24 October 1915. What strikes the reader even more is the absence of any Arab obligations to Britain as a *quid* pro *quo*. His veiled threat that failure to comply with the Agreement would bring Britain into disrepute amounted to blackmail and presaged the long-standing Arab accusations against the British of breach of faith and betrayal.

Reaction in Cairo was muted. Major Kinahan Cornwallis, who replaced Hogarth as Director of the Arab Bureau, had the unenviable task of translating Hussein's "Agreement," since its style was very involved and scarcely contained any full stops. Having examined its clauses meticulously, he stated categorically that none of them was acceptable; the King had reiterated his original claims and ignored all the reservations contained in McMahon's replies. With regard to Palestine, although Hussein did not mention it specifically, Cornwallis felt obliged to quote in his note Hogarth's Message of January 1918, with which the King had agreed: "It is with the Arabian Peninsula that [he] is primarily concerned and in which he hopes to secure his future."

Clayton opined that the settlement of Syria and Mesopotamia should await the Peace Conference, but refrained from warning Hussein that he was under a misapprehension. The only officer who thought that such a warning was imperative was Colonel C. E. Wilson, who, on 15 September 1918, urged Colonel Symes, Wingate's Secretary, to make it unmistakably clear to Hussein that his demands were inadmissible. Failure to do so would only confirm the King's belief that the so-called "Agreement" was valid and this would lead to further mis-understandings with adverse consequences in the future.

Wilson was the most reverential and protective of the British officers who had dealings with King Hussein, but, during his sojourn in Jeddah, he had learned Hussein's mind and his assessment proved correct. His advice, however, was not taken. Wingate had other considerations, and, rather than confront the King firmly and unambiguously, he skirted the issue and referred it to Balfour. Although admitting that Hussein's claims were "unacceptable," Wingate wondered whether, in view of Hussein's disturbed state of mind, it would be advisable for the British Government to reconsider its policy. Hussein was suspicious of British intentions and, unless reassured, was likely to carry out his threat:

> [His] withdrawal would entail consequences little short of disastrous. It would remove the only commanding figure and reduce Arab military participation to spasmodic tribal activity against the Turks. Further disintegration would ensue, leading, in all probability, to a conflagration in Central Arabia of which our enemies would take full advantage, and which would seriously affect our military operations.

Wingate strongly recommended that Hussein be verbally assured of his pre-eminent position in the Arabian Peninsula and that in the north the appellation "Arab Kingdom" be extended, though in a nominal form, to those areas which were restricted in McMahon's letter of 24 October 1915 to Hussein.[3]

Some of these ideas had been propounded earlier by Clayton and Cornwallis in their respective notes. That Wingate, who was intimately involved in negotiations between his predecessor and the Sharif in 1915, should have endorsed them in an official dispatch is a matter of surprise, although this was not the first time that he hammered them home. They manifested the long-cherished desire of the Cairo officials to use the Sharifians as a cloak in order to establish British predominance in the East at the expense of the French. Wingate's statement in his dispatch — "I am unaware to what extent the terms of the Sykes-Picot agreement are still considered binding" — coupled with his urgings that a French disclaimer of annexation in Syria was necessary, is indicative of much.

Wingate took Hussein's threat to resign too seriously. When General Allenby was knocking at the gates of Damascus and the Turks were on the run, it was ludicrous to suggest that "the withdrawal of King Hussein . . . would seriously affect our military operations." Nor was there any foundation for his warning that Hussein's abdication would cause "a conflagration in Central Arabia." The opposite was true. An attempt to impose him on his neighbors was more likely to produce an upheaval.

Wingate had exceeded his brief. Rather than acting as an adviser, he assumed the role of an advocate for a policy which was at variance with that pursued by his own government. No wonder his suggestion was not taken up. Sir Eyre Crowe pointed out that the matter could not be dealt with until Turkey was decisively defeated, and that it would be essential to consult the Allies, as well as the United States, on the future of the Asiatic provinces. Lord Robert Cecil endorsed Crowe's judgment.[4] In the meantime, an in-depth examination of British commitments to King Hussein was called for.

Initially, a committee composed of Sir Mark Sykes, Ormsby-Gore, and Toynbee was supposed to deal with the matter, but, as Sykes was about to depart for the East and Ormsby-Gore was busy electioneering, the task fell to Toynbee. Early in the War, he had served in the Propaganda Department of the Ministry of Information. At the beginning of 1918, the Department was transferred to the Foreign Office and became the Political Intelligence Department (P.I.D.). Its task was to gather and collate dispatches and telegrams and evaluate the trends and events in foreign countries. When Toynbee joined this Department on 28 March 1918,[5] he had scant knowledge of Anglo-Arab relations and even less of the McMahon-Hussein Correspondence. He had, however, an extraordinary capacity for gathering and digesting vast amounts of disparate information and for rapid composition,[6] although, as we shall see later, this talent was largely at the expense of comprehension of the material consulted and the depth of analysis. Hussein's letter of 28 August irritated him:

> It is a most important document — and most disquieting [he minuted on 23 October], since it gives a foretaste of the penalty

we shall have to pay for having no precise document, signed by both parties, recording the agreements between us and the King, as we have in the case of the Idrisi and bin Saud . . .

He went on,

On the other hand, our original method of negotiating with him — namely, by an interchange of letters in which reservations were constantly made by one party and ignored by the other . . . gives every encouragement to the Oriental instinct to be imprecise on such matters.

And five days later he remarked sternly:

I submit that it is essential that we should not allow to pass unchallenged the King's new letter and memorandum of Aug. 28th.

The document of which the King's memorandum purports to be a translation does not exist, and the conditions set out by him differ fundamentally from those actually agreed upon.

We ought to give the King no opportunity of assuming that we accept his memorandum as a true statement of the position.

I therefore submit that the King should be told courteously but clearly that his memorandum differs in many respects from our view of our agreements with him, but that we are giving it close consideration, and are disposed to discuss the question *au fond* later — at a suitable moment.[7]

Toynbee had just completed his "Memorandum on British Commitments to King Hussein," which appeared in print at the end of October. As his references show, Toynbee relied heavily on the "Summary of Historical Documents from the outbreak of the War . . . 1914, to the outbreak of the Revolt of the Sherif of Mecca in June, 1916," dated 29 November 1916. This is a collection of cables and dispatches set out in chronological order and interspersed with brief comments and analyses. The first part deals with the McMahon-Hussein Correspondence and negotiations with the French representative in London leading to the Sykes-Picot Agreement. Its author was Ormsby-Gore, then on the staff of the Arab Bureau in Cairo.[8] The copy consulted by Toynbee was unsigned and he was unaware of its paternity. In the Preamble to his "Memorandum," Toynbee declared:

> Our commitments to King Hussein are not embodied in any agreement or treaty signed, or even acknowledged by both parties. In this way they differ from those to Russia, France, Italy, and certain independent Arab rulers such as the Idrissi and ibn Saud. They can only be analysed by summarising the history of our dealings with the King during the war, under different heads. And the position is complicated by the King's habit of ignoring or refusing to take note of conditions laid down by us to which he objects and then carrying on as if the particular question had been settled between us according to his own desires.

Toynbee reiterated these observations in another short memorandum, dated 5 November, adding that

> The version of these commitments set out by the King's memorandum in no way corresponds to the actual facts, but is simply a repetition . . . of the demands originally made by the King when he opened negotiations in July 1915. Some of these demands were accepted, and others rejected by His Majesty's Government in the course of the negotiations.

Toynbee did not suggest that, in presenting his case, the King was "acting in bad faith. Oriental diplomacy is seldom precise unless compelled to be so." Nonetheless, his claims were inadmissible.[9]

Two distinct features of the above-quoted statements stand out. First, in Toynbee's opinion, the Inter-Allied Agreements were superior in status to the Correspondence with the Sharif of Mecca, and, unlike the latter, the former were contractually binding. In this respect, Toynbee clearly and unequivocally dissociated himself from the views advocated by Wingate and his colleagues in Cairo. Second, British commitments to Hussein rested on shaky foundations, and, in view of his erratic behavior, the British Government had to guard against his fanciful and unpredictable interpretations.

Throughout October and November, Toynbee's attitude toward the Turkey-in-Asia Agreement remained fixed and determined. On 9 October, a critical article on this subject appeared in the *Manchester Guardian*. It castigated the Inter-Allied

Agreement as "a characteristic example of the old unredeemed diplomacy," which, since the entry of the United States into World War I and its repudiation by Russia, had lapsed both morally and legally. *Palestine* (12 October 1918), the organ of the British Palestine Committee, echoed similar sentiments. Toynbee deprecated these articles as "inopportune." In his view, renunciation by Russia did not "legally invalidate the quite independent earlier agreement between Great Britain and France"; that is, the Sykes-Picot Agreement. The Wilsonian principles did create a new climate in the political situation, but, instead of repudiating the Agreement, the Allies should revise it "with the concurrence of the other party to it." Sir Eyre Crowe concurred and took up Toynbee's point with the editor of the *Manchester Guardian*.[10]

Even more telling was Toynbee's attitude toward the impending clash between Feisal and the French. Concerned lest the Emir resist French interference in Damascus, he advised that "it may be argued that Syria was not, in effect, liberated by Arab but by British arms."[11] In view of subsequent Arab claims to the contrary, this was a remarkable statement.

Five weeks later, Toynbee produced yet another memorandum,[12] in which he attempted to reexamine British Inter-Allied commitments in the altered political circumstances. In the very first sentence, he stated categorically that "changes in the situation cannot juridically affect the validity of signed agreements, unless these are specifically contingent upon factors which can be shown to have changed, or contain a general *'rebus sic stantibus'* clause." He traced the origin of the Sykes-Picot Agreement and admitted that it began

> as an incidental corollary to the Arab revolt — the intention being to admit the widest claims of the Arabs consistent with the interests of our Allies. It was begun as part of a plan which was to encourage the Arabs to act and so contribute largely to Turkey's military defeat — in fact, as a political adjunct to a military undertaking.

Toynbee went on to say that, when the Anglo-Franco-Russian Agreements were concluded, the Arabs

> had not yet moved [but] have since "made good" in the Hedjaz, [and] co-operated with us east of Jordan . . . Their failure to

effect a revolt in Syria unaided was disappointing, but it is only fair to take into consideration the fact that this has been due as much to the general military situation as to the ineffectiveness of the Arabs themselves.

This statement of Toynbee, that the Inter-Allied Agreement was a "corollary to the Arab revolt" and that it was meant to encourage them to act and thereby contribute to Turkey's military defeat, was noteworthy. What he did not appreciate was the effect the Arabs' failure to do their part during the war would have on the Allied commitment to "recognise and uphold an independent Arab state."

The lapse in his "Memorandum on French and Arab Claims in the Middle East in Relation to British Interests,"[13] composed a month later, is even more conspicuous. In its first part, entitled "The Value of the Sherifian Arab Movement for British Policy," he wrote:

> Our commitments to King Husein look formidable on the map; they limit, at least in appearance, our freedom of action in Mesopotamia and Palestine, and in Syria cause difficulties with the French. It is easy to point out that the Arabs have given us little military help in return for all this, and it is a legitimate and necessary question to ask, why we should look upon the Arab movement with favour, or at least why, in cases where our commitments to King Husein clash with those to France or other Arab rulers, we should not let the latter take precedence?
>
> The answer is that the permanent political advantages of the Arab movement for British policy outweigh its comparative military ineffectiveness and the diplomatic embarrassment which it may cause.

Toynbee thereby obliquely admitted that the help obtained from the Arabs in defeating Turkey was marginal and their performance was ineffective. If, nonetheless, he thought that they should be rewarded, it was not because of their military contribution during the War, but for their supposed "permanent political advantages . . . for British policy" that outweighed any diplomatic embarrassment with France.

What, then, were these advantages? Toynbee explained in para. (a) of his "Memorandum":

If we support the Arab movement, we shall destroy Turkey with much less risk of arousing against us the permanent antagonism of Islam, we shall knit up our Empire by establishing a link between Egypt and India, without being compelled to take France into partnership, and placing her in a position to break our newly-won territorial continuity. On the other hand, if we allow the Arab movement to fail, and Syria to pass from Turkish to French domination, we shall be playing into the hands of the Pro-Turkish faction among our Moslem subjects; we shall incur the resentment of the Arabs, who will consider that we have broken the spirit, if not the letter, of our engagements, and we shall place ourselves and France in a position in which our traditional rivalry in the East, which has been removed only with great difficulty, will be bound to arise again in an aggravated form.

Moreover, he maintained, (paras. 2 & 4):

. . . the rise of the Arab movement has been a fortunate develop-ment for the British Empire at a crucial period of its history, and that it offers for our Moslem policy and our Middle Eastern policy a way out of serious dilemmas which were created by the situation before the war and have been accentuated by the war itself . . .

King Husein's attitude toward ourselves and Islam fits in admirably with our interests. He needs our financial and politi-cal support because he has broken with the Turks and cannot be self-sufficing; he will therefore look to us, and will let us have what we want in Mesopotamia, in return for an annuity out of the Mesopotamian revenues. On the other hand, he is bound to draw a veil over his relationship with us in order to justify himself in the eyes of the Moslem world, and must, therefore, keep up an appearance of independence, both for the Hedjaz and for all Moslem territories detached from the Turks as a result of the war. In this his interests coincide with ours . . .

And, since there was such a remarkable identity of interests between Britain and the Sharifians, and since the latter viewed France with undisguised hostility, it followed that any contin-ued association with France would be detrimental to Britain's standing in the East:

Great Britain, with her millions of Moslem subjects, could not afford to be a consenting party to an arrangement under which a

Moslem people, liberated by British arms from a Government which, though oppressive, was also Moslem, would be abandoned to foreign conquest again, and this time by a Christian Power.

To embark on a joint operation with France to suppress "the whole Islamic world" would be not only at variance with British traditional policy in India and elsewhere, but would definitely be beyond her strength. Moreover, such an "impossible undertaking" will incur a grave "strategic danger"; it would impel Britain to concede to France

> a foothold in areas where we least want to see her . . . Damascus is the key, not only to Area "A" but to territory in Area "B," extending to a point south-east of the oasis of Jof, in the heart of the Arabian tribal country. The tribes down to this point buy and sell at Damascus and are economically dependent upon the Power in control there. Whatever the 1916 agreement may provide, the French, if they establish themselves at Damascus, will make their influence felt over a great part of the Arabian peninsula. It is no exaggeration to say that the presence of the French here would be at least as detrimental to British interests as the presence of the Russians was in the zone of Persia which they held before the war . . .

Such an outcome would inevitably engender competition and would have a "disastrous effect" upon Anglo-French relations. Here he quoted General Clayton's memorandum of 18 October 1918, wherein the General strongly advocated the amalgamation of Areas "A" and "B" into one single unit. Partition of the Arab State, as provided by the Sykes-Picot Agreement would, in Clayton's view, result in "confusion and inefficiency" and, still worse, would sow "the seeds of future friction between France and Great Britain in a region where the policies of the two countries have been in opposition for many years." Toynbee went on:

> It may be argued, indeed, that all considerations in favour of the Arab movement are illusory, because the Moslem world looks toward the Caliph at Constantinople and not toward the Sherif at Mecca; but this is surely an anachronistic view which ignores the changes produced by the war.

Toynbee marshaled an array of arguments to prove "The Untenability of the Anglo-French Agreements of 1916" and denounced Cambon's insistence (on 18 November 1918) on the validity of the Agreement, which in any case was incompatible with the joint Anglo-French Declaration of 8 November 1918. The French, he implied, were adopting double standards: of claiming, on one hand, that the Agreement was immutable, and, on the other, of employing the principle of self-determination with regard to the projected Independent Armenian State only in order to secure "priority of political assistance for themselves in . . . large territories . . ." Such a position was "monstrous."

This was not the kind of memorandum that the Foreign Office expected. By his own admission, Toynbee had been asked to examine whether in his judgment "HMG's existing commitments in the Middle East . . . were compatible with each other."[14] In his Preamble to the "Memorandum on British Commitments," he had maintained that, in contrast to the Correspondence with Hussein, the Inter-Allied Agreements were valid; but what he claimed now was the opposite. Expected to deal primarily with the legal aspects of the various international agreements, Toynbee had instead drifted into the uncharted waters of high policy. By virtue of his brief, he was supposed to assemble and collate documentary material and present an orderly digest of it to his superiors for their consideration. But, instead, Toynbee had become an advocate of a particular policy, using whatever arguments seemed likely to convince his superiors.

Like his colleagues in the Political Intelligence Department, nicknamed "Ministry of All the Talents," Toynbee was youthful (then thirty years old), assertive and held few doubts about his own ability to forecast the future. He was delighted to be so near to the seat of power and was eager to exert his personal influence on the decision-making process. However, as his biographer attested, his advice was "usually rejected, and often not even listened to."[15] This was particularly true with regard to the memoranda under our consideration, perhaps not surprisingly, since they ran counter to official British policy.

Whatever Anglo-French relations had been in the past, from 1904 *entente cordiale* was the order of the day in London and Paris. During the War, the French, either out of deliberate calculation or because of lack of choice, found it more prudent to follow British policy in the East in tandem. This applied equally toward Zionism as toward the Arabs. They supported, albeit half-heartedly, the Arab Revolt and, like the British, nailed to their mast the principle of self-determination, under the assumption that the least they would be able to salvage for themselves at the end of World War I was a status of parity with the British. Their territorial desiderata were limited to Syria, encompassing northern Palestine, in the south, and Cilicia and Armenia, in the north. The idea that the French entertained expansionist ambitions toward the Arabian Peninsula through Area "B" was false.

After the War, France emerged a weak, tired nation. In these circumstances, to consider her as "a strategic danger" to the British position in the East was as unreal as it was dishonest. Such a concept of manifest disloyalty to an ally was alien to the Foreign Office, as well as to Lloyd George. On 1 December 1918, he struck a deal with Clemenceau during the latter's visit to London. Against a concession that Palestine would pass into British control and Mosul attached to Mesopotamia, Lloyd George promised his support for a French mandate of Syria, which included not only the "blue zone" in the littoral, but also the four towns in the Syrian hinterland (Area "A").[16] The agreement survived the subsequent squabbles during the Paris Peace Conference and served as a model for the arrangement at the San Remo Conference. A few weeks after submitting this 19 December memorandum, Toynbee was able to witness for himself Lloyd George's personal predilections. He recorded:

> One day I had to hand some papers to Lloyd George just after the close of some meeting on Middle Eastern affairs. I had frequently seen Lloyd George and heard him speak, but this was the only occasion on which I had ever met him, and this encounter of mine with him had lasted for no longer than a minute or two, but it had been unexpectedly revealing; for, when he had taken the papers and started to scan them, Lloyd George, to my delight, had forgotten my presence and had begun to think aloud. 'Mesopotamia . . . yes . . . oil . . . irrigation . . . we must have Mesopotamia; Palestine . . . yes . . . the Holy Land . . . Zionism . . . we must have Palestine; Syria . . . h'm . . . what is there in Syria? Let the French have that.'[17]

As a rule Lloyd George relied on his own instincts and was disdainful of experts. Nor did he pay much attention to advice emanating from the Foreign Office. As his biographer notes, "Toynbee's wisdom and knowledge were therefore wasted."[18] In this particular case, Toynbee's exposé clearly collided with the Prime Minister's policy. Toynbee did not record what Lloyd George's reaction to his ideas was, but, judging from the fact that, in the spring of 1919, his appointment came to an abrupt end in the middle of the Peace Conference, it may be deduced that it could not have been favorable. Toynbee thereafter "carried with him a fierce, intensely personal grudge against Lloyd George and . . . lent a willing hand to postwar newspaper campaigns against the Prime Minister's Near Eastern policies."[19]

Thus, more than hurting the French, Toynbee undermined his own standing. But what must have made such distasteful reading to his superiors was the suggestion that Great Britain "could not afford to be a consenting party to an arrangement under which a Moslem people, liberated by British arms . . . would be abandoned to foreign conquest again, and this time by a Christian Power," such as France. Toynbee must have conveniently overlooked that he too came from Christian stock and ignored the fact that Arab population in Syria and Mesopotamia did not see the British troops as their "liberators." Nor was there any truth in his assertion that realization of the agreement would be tantamount to breaking "the spirit, if not the letter," of the engagement with Hussein.

Toynbee's primary consideration was not for the Arabs, but for British imperial interests as he saw them. He thought that the creation of a Sharifian Arab State could neutralize Moslem resentment caused by Turkey's demise and could simultaneously serve as a cloak behind which the British could exert control over a vast territory. However, such a concept was illusory. Ambitious and highly sensitive, Hussein was unlikely to have become a voluntary tool of British imperial interests. For the Guardian of Moslem Holy Places to submit, even symbolically, to a Christian Power was an anathema; it would have removed the last vestige of his credibility in the eyes of his co-religionists. His insistence on independence "in every meaning of that word . . . internally and externally" was not accidental. His ultimate goal was not the one Toynbee wished it to be. As his numerous utterances show, he hoped to take advantage of British support to impose his rule over his fellow Arabs. In this respect there was no real identity of interests between him and the British.

Toynbee's ideas were not original. "I am working a lot with Laurence [sic] — the man who cut the Hedjaz railway and marched round through the desert to Damascus," he wrote to his mother.[20] Lawrence made a strong impression on him,[21] and Toynbee, like many of his contemporaries, fell under his spell. Robert Cecil, in a critical comment on one of Toynbee's proposals, had no difficulty in identifying its paternity: "the views [are] of Colonel Lawrence and his school."[22]

After his return to England, Lawrence endeavored to win friends in Whitehall over to the Arab cause and to undermine the French position. When he saw Cecil on 28 October 1918, he denounced the Sykes-Picot Agreement in unmeasured terms as "folly" and referred to the boundaries as "entirely absurd and unworkable. . . . He was violently anti-French and suggested that, if there were to be fresh conversations, it would be well to have both Arab and Zionist representatives present, as well as Americans and Italians."[23] That same day, Lawrence called on General Macdonogh at the War Office and on the following day appeared before the Eastern Committee. Thereafter he submitted a comprehensive memorandum setting out his proposal.[24] But here his diplomatic sortie ground to a halt. Sir Arthur Hirtzel of the India Office delivered a devastating counterattack. More realistic and sagacious, Hirtzel struck at the heart of the matter:

> We are not pledged to King Husain to prevent the French from establishing a protectorate: our pledges relate only to those areas in which we can act without detriment to French interests, and we ought to take our stand firmly on that ground, and not allow ourselves to be used by the Arabs to secure their interests in Syria at the expense of the French. That, however, is what we are doing at present; and in doing it we risk losing the fruits of the Mesopotamian campaign for the *beaux yeux* of King Husain and his scheming sons . . .

Hirtzel went on:

> It is submitted . . . that Colonel Lawrence's scheme has nothing to commend it so far as Mesopotamia and Iraq are concerned, conven-

ient as it may be as a means of providing for the embarrassing
ambitions of King Husain's other two sons, when Ali has been
installed at Mecca and Feisal at Damascus . . .

I cannot see that we are bound by honour or interest to defend
the Arabs against the French. That the French will allow
themselves to be eliminated from Syria by any local option under
the [Anglo-French] declaration — or that, if they do, they will
allow us to take their place, as some imagine — is surely incredible. Syria is too deeply graven on the heart of France for that. If
we support the Arabs in this matter, we incur the ill-will of
France; and we have to live and work with France all over the
world. We have no interests of our own in Syria at all commen-
surate with those in Mesopotamia; and if we had, and could
eliminate the French in our own favour, could we possibly undertake the control of Syrian politics and administration in addition to our responsibilities in Mesopotamia and the Arabian
peninsula?

And if we cannot eliminate the French from Syria, neither can
we weaken their hold there without, *pro tanto*, weakening our
hold over Mesopotamia. But if Mesopotamia is to be developed,
our control of the administration must be complete, for only so (to
put it at its lowest) will the capital necessary for its development be forthcoming.

The future of the region would have to be decided at the Peace
Conference, but "in the meantime we dare not gamble away our
responsibility for the sake of anyone's dreams in Syria."[25]
Members of the Committee were impressed. Subsequently
Toynbee himself realized that he was mistaken and, in a joint
memorandum with Ormsby-Gore dated 25 February, reverted
to his previous position.[26] In fact, the Arabs wanted neither
French nor British tutelage. The King-Crane Commission, con-
firmed this during their investigation in the Middle East.
Toynbee was present during their testimony to the Council of
Ten at the Peace Conference. He recalled:

King and Crane correctly reported that the Syrian and
Palestinian Arabs wanted independence without any strings.
They had just been relieved of a Turkish domination that had
been weighing upon them for the last four hundred years; they
did not want to see one obnoxious foreign regime replaced by
others . . . King and Crane's finding was that this proposal was

unacceptable to the Arabs, whoever the mandatory power or powers imposed on them might be. The least objectionable mandatory power, from the Arabs' point of view, would be the United States. The Arabs were totally unwilling to be mandated either to Britain or to France.

Toynbee's impression was that all three observers on the Commission were "honest and disinterested: all three were telling the truth."[27]

Toynbee's investigation into British Commitments to Hussein is even more bizarre. In this case, it was not Lawrence who misled him. The fault was his own. It will be recalled how critical he was of King Hussein's version of the "Agreement," and showed how shaky was the legal basis of the correspondence as compared to the Inter-Allied Agreement.[28] And yet, throughout the twenty printed pages of his "Memorandum," he conveyed the distinct impression that the British Government was committed to Arab "independence" in the whole area claimed by Hussein in July 1915, ignoring all the reservations and conditions which had been set out in McMahon's letters. This is peculiar, since internal correspondence between British officials reproduced in the "Summary of Historical Documents" also prove the opposite. Suffice to quote just a few of them. Thus, on 22 May 1916, Clayton wrote to Wingate: "Luckily we have been very careful indeed to commit ourselves to nothing whatever," and, on 19 April, McMahon assured Grey that

> no guarantees which could give rise to embarrassment in the future between ourselves and the Allies, or ourselves and the Arabs have been given by us to any of the Arab parties. . . . We have made every attempt to avoid definite commitments for the future . . .

Hogarth, in a note dated 3 May 1916, elucidated:

> The Sherif . . . has dropped all decisions of geographical limits since the beginning of the current year, and has promised Arab action at an early date without making our agreement about his claims in any way a condition preliminary. Therefore, as regards him at any rate, it has become our policy to remain uncommitted in the matter of boundaries and to give him no cause to think [to the contrary].

Moreover, on 29 May 1917, Toynbee himself, noting the Sharif's "unlimited" ambitions, confirmed that

> the British Government has been careful not to commit itself to anything beyond his sovereignty and independence of the Hedjaz itself.[29]

Like Hussein, in his letter of 28 August 1918, Toynbee took the meaning of the word "independence" in its literal sense. This was not the case. As shown above, both in Cairo and in London, the word was understood in its generic sense, since the Arabs, at least at this stage, were not yet capable of maintaining an independent state. Toynbee read al-Faruqi's statements both to Clayton (11 October 1915) and to Sykes (20 November 1915) requesting that the Entente Powers guarantee "to protect independence of the Arabs"; and reproduced Hussein's letter to Sayyid Ali al-Mirghani of 28 December 1915. In this letter, Hussein admitted that for some time to come the Arabs would need British protection. In the given circumstances, "independence" could have had only one connotation — Arab autonomy under a British umbrella.

Toynbee ignored his own conclusions and implied that the British pledge toward the Arabs was unilateral and irrevocable. This was fallacious, for the Correspondence in its entirety was preliminary in nature and the British Government could not make any commitment without the prior approval of her allies. In May 1916, when the Allies, prodded by the British, did undertake a commitment toward the Arabs, they worded it specifically "to recognise and uphold an independent Arab State ...," but not necessarily to bring that state about; and, here again, on the clear understanding that the Arabs fulfilled their part in overthrowing the Turks and established their own independence. Hogarth explained the issue thus:

> In the [Inter-Allied] Agreement ... the three governments engaged mutually to support and recognize an Arab National State in the interior of Syria with probable centre at Damascus, whenever established by the Arabs themselves.

Moreover,

> Thus our recognition [of Arab independence], was to depend, of

course, on abstention by the Arabs from helping the enemy's side and on their positive co-operation with ours . . .[30]

What makes the reader even more bewildered is Toynbee's failure to take any notice of McMahon's letter of 14 December 1915. In this letter, it will be recalled, the High Commissioner stipulated that the permanence and strength of the agreement would depend on the nature and quality of Arab performance. In his reply of 1 January 1916, Hussein assured McMahon that he fully understood the contents of his note, but Toynbee seemed blind to this exchange and failed to understand that British commitment was contingent on Arab performance. In his "Memorandum on French and Arab Claims," he made it unmistakably clear that "the Arabs have given us little military help," and in his "Memorandum on Changes in the General International Situation," he was even more specific.

> It was expected [he wrote] that the Arab revolt might make an end of Turkish control in the whole country south of Taurus. But this possibility, though more promising than it afterwards became, was not . . . even partially realised. . . . Their failure to effect a revolt in Syria unaided was disappointing . . .

This was particularly so in view of the reverses sustained by the British, both in Gallipoli and in Kut. In the final analysis, Toynbee observed, it was the Russian army that "saved the military situation in Turkey for the Allies by their operations in Western Persia at the end of 1915, and by the capture of Erzerum in February 1916. . . . More than half the Turkish divisions were being engaged by the Russians in Armenia" alone.

What were the reasons for the Arabs' inaction? On this point Toynbee had written two years earlier:

> The Syrians . . . have not, as the Turks and Germans allege, been disloyal to Turkey in her hour of danger. The Arab . . . conscripts have fought dutifully [on Turkey's side] in the present conflict.

To which he added:

> Their leaders are too prudent and the people too peaceable, their stake is too great . . . to allow them for a moment to contemplate rising in arms.[31]

The confirmation that the Arabs in Syria, as well as in Palestine and Mesopotamia, sided, for this reason or another, with the enemy should have made Toynbee consider whether, in these circumstances, Britain was still under any obligation toward the Arabs in these particular territories. However, such an idea, it seems, did not cross his mind.

His uncritical reading of al-Faruqi's statements is another instance of his glaringly defective analysis. Clayton and McMahon committed a grave error of judgment in taking al-Faruqi at his word, though, in view of the Allies' military setbacks in 1915, their credulity is perhaps understandable. But Toynbee was not laboring under such pressure. He had the benefit of hindsight, as well as sufficient information, to enable him to expose al-Faruqi's tale. Thus, in his book, *Turkey: A Past and a Future*,[32] he showed convincingly how inimical the Young Turks were toward Arab nationalism. In a lecture to Arab officers, a leading Turkish professor at the Military College in Constantinople was quoted as saying: "You and your nation must realise that you are Turks . . . there is no such thing as Arab nationality and an Arab fatherland." The author Djelal Nouri Bey wrote: "The Arab lands . . . must become Turkish colonies and the Arabs must be Turkified." "If the Porte loses sight of this duty," Ahmed Sherif Bey warned in the *Tanin*, a leading Turkish daily, "it will be digging its [own] grave . . . for the Arabs . . . will seek to restore their ancient empire on the ruins of Ottomanism." Such a brand of Pan-Islamism, Toynbee concluded, "leaves no room for an Arab race under Ottoman rule."

This conclusion should have prompted Toynbee to question the veracity of al-Faruqi's claim that Turkey and Germany had promised the Arab party the fulfillment of "all their demands." Nor did he question whether the secret societies were capable of fomenting a general uprising. The societies were "crushed . . . their military branch [*al-Ahd*] was broken up about August 1915, while the civilian leaders [of *al-Fatat*] were mostly hanged or deported," Toynbee wrote in his "Memorandum," not noting that this had taken place several weeks before al-Faruqi's arrival in Cairo. He concluded quite correctly that, as a result of the societies' demise, Hussein's effective sovereignty had become confined solely to the Hedjaz; and that the Sharif could no longer rely on the Arabs of Syria and Jezireh, "whose allegiance had promised to make him the indispensable leader of the National Movement in the (Asiatic) Arab countries." But he did not go as far as Hogarth did in his note of 16 April 1916, that henceforth Hussein could only speak for himself.[33]

Nor did Toynbee show greater skill when examining the boundaries question. In his "Memorandum on British Commitments," he stated that the boundaries of Arab independence to which the British Government was committed by McMahon's letter of 24 October 1915 also included, among other territories, Basra (p. 6). And in his "Memorandum Respecting the Settlement of Turkey...," dated 21 November 1918, which was the final version of his labor, he declared confidently that "His Majesty's Government are pledged to King Hussein that the whole of this area [i.e., Mesopotamia (Iran and parts of Jezireh)] shall be 'independent' and 'Arab' " (p. 6).

This was a gross misreading of McMahon's letter, for in this particular case McMahon had been very specific, emphasizing that

> With regard to the vilayets of Baghdad and Basra, the Arabs will recognise that the established position and interests of Great Britain necessitate special measures of administrative control . . .

McMahon was following instructions given in Grey's important cable of 20 October:

> In view of the special interests in the Baghdad Province and area actually in our occupation, the proposed sphere of British control, namely, the Basrah vilayet, will need extension.

Both documents are quoted in Toynbee's "Memorandum" (p. 7). Quoted also is McMahon's letter of 14 December, in which he rejected Hussein's claim (5 November), as well as McMahon's last letter of 30 January 1916, which left discussion on the future of Mesopotamia in abeyance (p. 8). It would have been incomparably more useful had Toynbee prepared a gist of the "Summary of Historical Documents" instead.

In the "Summary," reproduced, among other documents, is Clayton's letter to Wingate of 15 November 1915, which illuminates the thinking in Cairo and Khartoum. Clayton maintained that the administrative and commercial control of the Baghdad and Basra vilayets "should be very specifically stated," and that the British should have "an entirely free hand as to the time limit." An exchange of cables between McMahon (30 November) and the Foreign Office (10 December 1915) shows that Clayton's suggestions were adopted. Toynbee missed this point, as well as the comment made by the author of the "Summary" (Ormsby-Gore) that Hussein, in his letter of 1 January 1916, "practically accept[ed] all the propositions set out in the High Commissioner's letter of 14 December 1915 with regard to Mesopotamia." The document which did impress Toynbee was a note (16 April 1916), which, as we now know, was written by Hogarth. Summarizing what was and what was not agreed upon with the Sharif, Hogarth stated that the British Government had not committed itself to any time limit or conditions with regard to the occupation of Mesopotamia. Toynbee repeated this statement elsewhere in his memorandum (p. 9), apparently unaware that he had thus contradicted himself.

This was not the final twist in Toynbee's thinking. In the second part of his "Memorandum Respecting the Settlement of Turkey" (21 November 1918), entitled "Desiderata," he suggested that, since the population of Iraq and Jezirah was "backward," neglected, and riven by religious and social disunity, it was necessary for a foreign Power to administer it in order to develop the country's natural resources, and that Power should be Great Britain. He urged that the British administer Mesopotamia "for an indefinite period as mandatories of the Arabs." This recommendation was fully in line with British policy but inconsistent with Toynbee's earlier statement that "Mesopotamia shall be 'independent' and 'Arab.'" Nor did he elucidate how Britain was to become a Mandatory Power — whether at the invitation of the native population, or at the behest of the victorious Powers. It took him only three months to appreciate the kind of difficulty the British were to face in Mesopotamia. Commenting on a batch of telegrams on the rise of anti-British sentiment there, he jotted despondently: "the ideal of the natives [was] to have the benefits of our presence without our presence."[34]

In December 1918, however, Toynbee was still hammering home the idea that "we have pledged ourselves to King Hussein that Mesopotamia shall be 'Arab' and 'independent,'" He upheld the idea of Pan-Arabism, which had been advocated in an anonymous article in *The Times* (written by T. E. Lawrence), and distributed his memorandum without clearing it first with Sir Eyre Crowe, his superior.

Toynbee's exposé was disputed by Sir Arthur Hirtzel. He rejected the premise on which Toynbee's memorandum was built and questioned his reading of McMahon's letters:

> I can find no evidence that we are committed to King Hussein to support the Arab nationalist movement in the sense suggested by the Foreign Office memorandum. We have undertaken that the Arab countries, within certain limits, shall be independent and free: we have not undertaken that they shall be united, still less that they shall be united under King Hussein . . .

Such an idea was novel and did not exist early in the War when the British were negotiating with the Sharif. It had only recently gained currency in the War and Foreign Offices when certain circles had "passed under the hypnotic influence of Colonel Lawrence. . . . It has never had anything to commend it in Mesopotamia, and . . . there is all the difference in the world between Hussein's ambitions and our commitments . . . " When Sir Eyre Crowe saw the exchange between Toynbee and Hirtzel, he minuted that Toynbee should have shown his memorandum to him before passing it on to the India Office. He added: "I am in agreement with much that Sir A. Hirtzel says."[35] Toynbee's position was thus seriously compromised.

Toynbee displayed even greater incompetence when dealing with Palestine. On 8 October 1918, he prepared a "Sketch Map relating to possible Armistice and Peace with Turkey." He drew it on the assumption that the Ottoman Empire would be divided into independent states that would be organized, wherever possible, on the basis of nationality and to be accorded administrative assistance by one or more Powers. Each state was marked by a different color: Hedjaz — green, Syria — blue, Iraq and Jezireh — red, and Palestine — brown. Palestine was singled out as a separate unit. Its southern border ran from Rafah toward the Gulf of Aqaba and about seventy miles northwest of it toward the southern tip of the Dead Sea. Its eastern border ran parallel about ten miles east of the Dead Sea and of the river Jordan, cutting the Bekka Valley, thence taking, in the north, a sharp turn to the west along the Litani river in the Lebanon toward the Mediterranean. These boundaries coincided with those which the Zionist Organization intended to submit to the Peace Conference and were favored in British official circles. Toynbee's sketch map commended itself to his superiors. Sir Eyre Crowe minuted: "It will be most useful in any discussion with the allies respecting the future of these regions," an opinion with which Sykes concurred. Cecil also agreed that it was "a very useful map" and asked that a copy be kept for Balfour.[36]

With such praise from his seniors, there is little wonder that Toynbee was considered sufficiently competent to examine British commitments to Hussein, first with Sykes and Ormsby-Gore, and thereafter on his own. However, Foreign Office confidence proved misplaced. It will therefore be instructive to follow step by step, his method of work and analysis.

Toynbee pointed out that al-Faruqi's statement, as quoted in McMahon's telegram to Grey of 18 October 1915, was "important," since it served as the basis for negotiations between the British Government and France, and that this "is the origin of the division between the Blue Area and Area 'A,'" which was embodied in McMahon's letter of 24 October 1915 (p. 4). On the next page he quoted Hussein's reply of 5 November 1915, and observed:

> It may be remarked that [Hussein] does not mention either the vilayet of Lebanon or the sanjak of Jerusalem — territories which were both excluded from the independent Arab state in the subsequent Anglo-French Agreement . . . he has expressly claimed Lebanon on other occasions [but not Palestine].

Toynbee's admission that the Arab leaders had not demanded Palestine, as well as a number of other documents quoted in his memorandum, should have brought him to the self-evident conclusion that Palestine was excluded. However, he appears to have been guided by a different logic. "With regard to Palestine," he declared, "His Majesty's Government are committed by Sir H. McMahon's letter to the Sherif on the 24th October 1915, to its inclusion in the boundaries of Arab independence."

This extraordinary deduction was compounded by the sentence that followed: "But they have stated their policy regarding Palestinian Holy Places and Zionist colonization in their message [the Hogarth Message] to him of the 4th January 1918" to the effect that

1. a special regime would have to be erected to deal with the Moslem, Christian and Jewish Holy Places;

2. the Mosque of Omar would not be subjected directly or indirectly to any non-Moslem authority;

3. since world Jewish opinion was in favor of a return of Jews to Palestine, and since this opinion "must remain a constant factor," and since the British Government "viewed with favour the realisation of this aspiration, His Majesty's Government are determined that, in so far as is compatible with the freedom of the existing population, both economic and political, no obstacle should be put in the way of the realisation of this ideal."

Toynbee thus implied that the British Government had made contradictory commitments: one to the Arabs and the other to the Jews. This was as downright false as it was absurd. He made no attempt to query how it was possible for a man of intellect and stature like Hogarth to become implicated in double-dealing of this nature, or how it was possible that his message did not elicit any protest from King Hussein. Quite the contrary: the King welcomed enthusiastically the return of the Jews to their "sacred and beloved homeland." Moreover, Toynbee did not ask himself why it was necessary to guarantee that the Mosque of Omar would not be subjected "directly or indirectly to non-Moslem authority" if, by his reasoning, Palestine was to become an independent Arab state. Over-confident, he thought it superfluous to consult Hogarth or McMahon, then in England, on such a complex matter.

That this judgment was not impetuous, nor the result of an oversight, is clear from his subsequent "Memorandum respecting the Settlement of Turkey" (21 November 1918),[37] which was the final version of his investigation. There he restated his view that "We are pledged to King Hussein that this country shall be 'Arab' and 'independent'" (p. 8). However, elsewhere in the same memorandum, he maintained that both Britain and France were "pledged to . . . recognise and uphold an independent Arab state or Confederation of States" in the respective Areas "A" and "B" (but not elsewhere); that France "accorded the ports of Acre and Haifa to Great Britain"; that, according to the Sykes-Picot Agreement, Palestine was to be international (Brown Area); and that the Balfour Declaration, which he quoted verbatim, was a distinct British commitment. He listed the Balfour Declaration among fourteen Middle Eastern commitments, whereas the Correspondence with Hussein he termed as an "understanding . . . not embodied in any single instrument . . ." (p. 2). In view of all these statements, most of them correct, it required an unusual degree of imagination to reach the conclusion that the British Government had "pledged" to King Hussein that Palestine "shall be 'Arab' and 'independent.'"

Of greater interest are the final parts of his memorandum, where he argued with considerable skill why strategically and politically Palestine was important to British interests. One of the reasons that he enumerated was the British Government's "desire to insure reasonable facilities . . . for Jewish colonisation." Palestine, he maintained, should be independent and administratively assisted either by America or, preferably, Great Britain (pp. 14-15). As a rule, British policy in the Middle East should be guided by the principle of self-determination, but with regard to Palestine, this criterion was inapplicable:

> The problem of Palestine cannot be solved entirely on the principles of self-determination and free choice of assistance. As in Armenia, there will be a mixed population, and there will be one element in that population, in this case the Jewish colonists, which, for special reasons, will be entitled to a position more than mathematically proportionate to its numbers at the start.
>
> Moreover, in Palestine there are international religious interests so important, and so difficult to reconcile, that they almost overshadow the internal problems of the native inhabitants.
>
> For these reasons, the desires of the inhabitants, or of the several sections of them, will have, to some extent, to take the second place. The assisting Power will be bound to act not merely as their mandatory, but as the mandatory of the world, and in cases where local and international interests conflict, the former may often have to give way (p. 22).

This was an expanded version of the minute prepared jointly with Namier on 19 December 1917,[38] and was fully in line with the British Government's policy. There is no reason to question Toynbee's sincerity in this matter. What seems to be questionable is his reasoning, for how could one reconcile in good faith encouragement of Jewish colonization in Palestine under a British mandate with a conviction that the country was to be "Arab" and "independent"?

Balfour read Toynbee's memorandum and noted that it was "a very able and useful paper," but that he could not possibly endorse it without much more discussion.[39] It was apparently on his instruction that L. Storr, of the War Cabinet Secretariat, pointed to the inconsistency in Toynbee's thinking: in his memorandum on "Commitments to King Hussein," the British Government was committed "to include Palestine in Arab territories," whereas, according to his "Synopsis on the British Obligations to her Allies," the contrary was the case.[40]

Before replying, Toynbee sent a note to Harold Nicolson:

I think our territorial commitments to King Hussein depend on his (undated) letter of July, 1915, to Sir H. McMahon, the terms of which Sir H. McMahon, acting on instructions from the Foreign Office accepted, with certain reservations, in his letter of Oct. 24, 1915 . . .

I think [therefore] that Palestine shall be 'Arab' and 'independent' . . .[41]

This minute provides a clue to the origin of Toynbee's error. He firmly believed that Hussein's letter of July 1915 committed the British unilaterally to Arab maximal demands. He was also mistaken in attributing McMahon's phraseology in his letter of 24 October to the Foreign Office. As we have seen, the matter was not as simple as that. French interests, too, were of little or no consequence to him. He ignored McMahon's subsequent correspondence with the Sharif, as well as all the surrounding circumstances. It is not at all certain whether, in his letter of 28 August 1918 to Wingate, Hussein considered Palestine to be included in the territories promised by McMahon,[42] but Toynbee, it appears, was convinced that this was the case. At this juncture, it is worth pointing out that the word *wilāya*, of which he made so much heavy weather, both in his correspondence with the author, and in his "Comments,"[43] was not even mentioned, and it is most unlikely whether he had heard of it at all at that time.

Nicolson replied tersely, "I think your version is more accurate."[44] Nicolson was not the right man to be consulted in this matter, for, unlike Sir Arthur, his distinguished father, Harold was a junior clerk at the Foreign Office and had only a hazy conception of Anglo-Sharifian relations. In July 1917, he was asked by Balfour to examine British obligations to the Arabs and to the Allies and reached the strange conclusion that Correspondence with the Sharif was superior in status to the Inter-Allied Agreement:

> We are bound to the King of the Hedjaz in a far more complex and ineludible manner than we are to our European Allies, and the position is rendered all the more delicate by the fact that our prestige in Arabia and the Middle East will stand or fall by the extent to which we are enabled to act up to our promises.

He took it for granted that Palestine was excluded from the commitment to Hussein; it was a British desideratum, but Sir Ronald Graham corrected him. In view of the Sykes-Picot Agreement, the British Government was committed to "an internationalized Palestine."[45] On 5 July 1917, Nicolson defined the Foreign Office position thus: "Our present attitude toward the Palestine question is based on a compromise between the desirability of encouraging Jewish national aspirations and the necessity of avoiding the creation of suspicion in the French Colonial party."[46] And yet, in his well-known book, *Peacemaking 1919*, first published in 1933, he wrote:

> Our pledges to the Arabs, conflicting as they did with the promises we made to France in the subsequent Sykes-Picot agreement, produced a triangular situation of great embarrassment as between the French, President Wilson and ourselves.[47]

This assertion was as incorrect as it was unfair to his father, who had taken the utmost care to ensure that British obligations to the Arabs did not conflict with those to the Allies.

It would have been more prudent for Toynbee to consult Ormsby-Gore instead, who was *au courant* with the subject, or, alternatively, Forbes-Adam, a member of his own Department.[48] Reassured by Nicolson, Toynbee replied to Storr for the War Cabinet's consumption:

> "Palestine was implicitly included in King Hussein's original demands and was not explicitly excluded in Sir H. McMahon's letter of 24.10.15. We are, therefore, presumably pledged to King Hussein by this letter that Palestine shall be 'Arab' and 'independent'.[49]

During the 1930s, this argument inspired George Antonius, both in *The Arab Awakening* and subsequently at the 1939 London Conference, to claim that, since Palestine was not specifically mentioned in the reservations, it followed that it "formed part of the territory accepted by Great Britain as the area of Arab independence."[50]

This argument was invalid. Palestine was not mentioned, first, because during the Ottoman period it did not constitute a separate administrative unit, and, second, because in 1915-1916 it was not an issue. Both Hussein and al-Faruqi realized — more precisely, were made to realize — that there were weighty international interests which placed it in a totally different category. From the documents Toynbee had consulted, he could have deduced with relative ease that al-Faruqi's main concern was to obtain independence for the four cities in the Syrian hinterland and their territorial connection with the Holy Cities, Mecca and Medina, and that the Syrian littoral and Palestine were of no inherent interest to him. Toynbee must have also forgotten that three weeks earlier he himself had implicitly excluded Palestine from the Arab State. This was occasioned by a telegram from Cairo of 31 October, 1918, reporting that the British military authorities had handed over the areas of Kerak and Salt to Ja'far al-Askari, the Commander of the Arab Army, Ormsby-Gore observed:

> This is of course the recognition of Transjordanian Palestine as an Arab country and recognizes the Jordan as the boundary of Palestine, and sooner or later will involve our telling the Zionists that the ancient territory of Reuben, Gilead and Manasseh is not to form part of the [Jewish] 'National home'.

Toynbee concurred:

> We may, then assume that Trans-Jordania will be an Arab country, and there is everything to be said in favour of this.
>
> The population is Arab, there are no Jewish agricultural colonies there yet, and there would be grave inconvenience if Palestine, the political problems of which are complicated enough already, were to be saddled with a desert frontier and all the tribal questions which that involves.
>
> The question remains: what Arab State is Trans-Jordania to belong to?

On Crowe's advice, Toynbee spoke to Lawrence and found that he regarded the country of Trans-Jordan as "an integral part of Syria."[51] It was also from him that he subsequently learned that British commitment to Hussein did not cover Palestine.

W. J. Childs, in his otherwise excellent memorandum[52] prepared for the Foreign Office in 1930, attributed Toynbee's error to his uncritical reliance on the Arab Bureau's "perverted reading" of McMahon's pledge. There is no evidence to support this belief. Toynbee's notes to Nicolson and Storr show clearly that it was his own misreading of the McMahon-Hussein Correspondence that lay at the root of his mistake. Nor was Childs correct in assuming that the Arab Bureau had some ulterior motive in misinterpreting McMahon's letter of 24 October 1915. The relevant note on which Childs built his argument is dated 16 April 1916, a section of which is reproduced in the "History of the Hedjaz Rising." Childs maintained that it erroneously substituted "line" for the word "district" (used by McMahon), and compounded this lapse by yet another mistake: it invented a second line "up to about latitude 33° N and beyond an indefinite line drawn inland west of Damascus . . . and the Mediterranean," thus gratuitously including Palestine within the area of Arab "independence," contrary to McMahon's intention. This interpretation, Childs concluded, was "in no way authoritative."[53] The matter caused considerable confusion among historians,[54] and it is worth deviating momentarily from the main topic under discussion.

When preparing my reply to Toynbee's "Comments" in 1970, I ascertained that the author of the 16 April 1916 memorandum was David Hogarth.[55] Originally I was inclined to agree with Childs, but on further examination, I concluded that, in substance, Hogarth committed no mistake whatsoever. He was fully cognizant of the Inter-Allied Agreement, as well as the Correspondence with the Sharif, and the "lines" which he had introduced were of no consequence whatsoever; they served merely as a schematic demarcation of spheres of influence. The horizontal one drawn along latitude 33° N from the Mediterranean north of Haifa to the southern edge of Damascus was, as he explained himself, "reserved absolutely for future arrangements between the French and the Arabs." In this respect, Hogarth followed the point made by McMahon in his cable to the Foreign Office dated 30 November 1915. McMahon wrote: "In these Vilayets of Beirut and Aleppo, as elsewhere in Syria, our ally France has considerable interests, to safeguard which some special arrangements will be necessary and this is a matter for the French Government [and the Arabs]."[56] The territory south of latitude 33° N, as Hogarth repeatedly stated, was to be placed under international control. The exclusion of Palestine was covered in the phrase "in any portion of the Arab area in which we are not free to act without detriment to our ally, France . . ."

It is quite inconceivable that Hogarth would have awarded Palestine to the Arabs. In a book published in 1902, he wrote:

> For some centuries Palestine has been in the evil case of having to receive from time to time broken remnants of Hamad tribes worsted in desert warfare, who must perforce take up the uncongenial status of *fellahin*. Such have no skill in agriculture and no heart. They impoverish the land and lightly abandon it to denudation and sand-drift; and it is largely due to them that Palestine, especially in the south of Judea, is the waste that it is. The Bedawin, born of the desert, becomes in turn its creator; and it remains yet to be seen whether the strangers [such as the] Jews . . . will be able to reclaim permanently for agriculture what has so long been exposed to the worst neglect of nomads.
>
> For the moment great change has been wrought . . . in Western Judea . . . and it is worth remark, that the Jewish immigration has largely restored its importance to Jerusalem.[57]

He adhered to this opinion. On 3 May 1916, he told William

Reginald Hall, "Palestine under International control was perhaps the best solution, especially in view of the aspirations of the Jews to the area in which they may enjoy some sort of proprietorship."[58]

In order to appreciate what Hogarth had in mind one should read his memorandum in its entirety; and not only the section which was reproduced in the "History" that Childs read. Surveying the Correspondence, Hogarth specifically stated that, in his letter of 24 October, the High Commissioner "definitely asked for the exclusion, not only of Mersina and Alexandretta . . . but also of portions of Syria lying West of the districts of Damascus, Homs, Hama and Aleppo." He used the word "districts" advisedly (not "line"). He added that McMahon's pledge related only to those areas "in which Great Britain is free to act without detriment to the interests of her Ally, France"; the reserved area covered the Syrian littoral and Palestine. Moreover, Hogarth pointed out that, in his letter of 14 December 1915, McMahon "deferred the further discussion of all Syrian questions in deference to France," and concluded that, "since the Sharif's reply on 1 January 1916, questions about the boundaries or the constitution of the independent Arab area ["A" and "B"] have been left wholly aside."

In a covering note, McMahon observed that

> no guarantees which could give rise to embarrassment in the future between ourselves and the Allies, or ourselves and the Arabs, have been given by us to any of the Arab parties . . . we have made every attempt to avoid definite commitments for the future . . . [59]

There was no misunderstanding at the Foreign Office end, therefore, as to what Hogarth had in mind. Sir George Clerk discussed Hogarth's paper with Sykes, and it was agreed that the latter should meet with Picot and Clayton in Paris. On the other hand, Grey, as well as Arthur Nicolson, vented their frustration on the Sharif at having done nothing in return for all the promises, arms, and money given to him by the British Government.[60]

In March 1917, Hogarth prepared a draft note on the terms of the Anglo-French-Russian Agreement to be communicated verbally to the Sultan of Egypt by the High Commissioner. In it, the word "line" drawn along latitude 33° N appears again as it did in his memorandum of 16 April 1916. It is followed by an illuminating sentence:

> The region between this last line [West of Damascus] and the Mediterranean is reserved absolutely for future arrangements with the French and the Arabs, and France is given a free hand in this respect.

Even more telling is the following paragraph:

> Palestine, west of Jordan, will be international. HAIFA and ACRE to be in British sphere with 15 miles hinterland and railway rights through international area. . . . Northern portion of Independent Arab State to be French sphere of economic (and political) interest: southern portion to be British. Division of these two spheres is by a line drawn from TIBERIAS through BOSRA and Verdi to Kol.[61]

The line "drawn from TIBERIAS" eastward corresponds approximately to the one along latitude 33° N, which bears out our point that the sole purpose of using it was to delineate the British and the French spheres of influence. It could safely be deduced that Hogarth in no way corrupted the meaning of McMahon's letter and that he well understood that Palestine had been excluded from the deal with the Sharif.

As shown already, Toynbee committed his mistake for an entirely different reason. However, the misunderstanding did not last for long. On the same day that he dispatched his note to Storr, he read General Clayton's cable of November 18th in which the latter advocated amalgamation of Areas "A" and "B" presumably under British aegis. The idea appealed strongly to Toynbee, as can be judged from his minute dated 26 November.[62] One of the points that Clayton made was that the creation of a unified Arab State comprising the Syrian hinterland and the Trans-Jordanian region would soften the opposition of the Arabs in Palestine, who were "strongly anti-Zionist and are very apprehensive of Zionist aims." Their fear was heightened by the growing conviction that "Great Britain is pledged to support the Zionist programme in its entirety." Clayton believed that the arrangement he had proposed "would

↖ greatly facilitate the settlement of the Zionist question."

> A sound administration established in Damascus would permit of
> the development of the arable country to the East of the Jordan
> and the construction of communications to enable its produce to be
> exported with profit. The districts East of the Jordan are thinly
> populated and their development would allow of considerable
> [Arab] emigration from Palestine thereby making room for Jewish
> expansion.

In a post-script, Clayton added that he had shown his proposal in a rough outline to Sir Mark Sykes, then in Palestine. In
Whitehall, Ormsby-Gore greeted it with undisguised delight:

> This is one of the most valuable telegrams we have received from
> General Clayton and these views should be carefully noted.[63]

Statements from leading officials intimately involved in shaping
Arabian policy must have made Toynbee realize that he had
been under a misapprehension as to the nature of British commitment with regard to Palestine.

Toynbee was also in close touch with Lawrence. Before the
war, Lawrence developed a sneaking admiration for the Jewish
enterprise in Palestine: "The Jewish colonies . . . are honest in
their attempts at colonization and deserve honour," he wrote
early in 1915 in his memorandum on "Syria."[64] However, he
remarked ominously, "Behind these Jews is their enemy, the
Palestine peasant, more stupid than the peasant of North Syria,
materialistic and bankrupt." By contrast, he thought that cooperation between the Sharifians and the Zionists was both
feasible and desirable. On Clayton's advice, he briefed Feisal
that Palestine was excluded from the British understanding
with his father,[65] and, during the Peace Conference, he acted as
an intermediary between the Emir and Weizmann. It would
therefore not be too far-fetched to assume that it was Lawrence
who reassured Toynbee that the British Government had given
no conflicting promises to the Jews and to the Arabs.

A map which Lawrence prepared at that time on the
disposition of the territories in the Middle East[66] reflected his
thinking. An Arab State comprising the Syrian hinterland and
Trans-Jordan are shown as separate. The northern border of

Palestine runs along the Litani river in southern Lebanon, and the eastern border ten miles east of the river Jordan. In this respect, it resembles the map that Toynbee produced on 8 October 1918[67] before he became entangled with his notorious error. The only conspicuous difference between the two maps appears on the southern border: Toynbee's encompasses the Negev, whereas Lawrence's excludes it. On 2 December 1918, Toynbee minuted:

> On the east, Trans-Jordania is bound to fall to the Syrian Arab State, and the Jordan forms a good natural frontier. Nor are there any Jewish agricultural colonies east of the river.

> It might be equitable, however, to include in Palestine that part of the Arabah and Jordan trough — between the lower end of the Sea of Galilee and the upper end of the Dead Sea — which lies east of the Jordan stream.

> The Arabah is a sub-tropical district, at present desolate, but capable of supporting a large population if irrigated and cultivated scientifically. The Zionists have as much right to this no-man's land as the Arabs, or more.

By this amendment, Toynbee demonstrated even greater generosity toward the Zionists than he had originally in his map of 8 October 1918. He insisted also that the northern border of Palestine should be extended as far as the mouth of the river Litani. Sir Louis Mallet and Lawrence read Toynbee's minute and did not demur.[68]

Late in December, Toynbee joined the British Delegation to the Peace Conference in Paris and kept in touch with the Zionist leaders. On 17 January 1919, he was present at Mallet's office when Weizmann reported on his meeting with President Wilson. From his minute, it is evident how greatly he appreciated the usefulness of the Zionists for British interests.[69] A week later, Toynbee saw Ormsby-Gore's memorandum entitled "Palestine." Ormsby-Gore hoped that the Peace Conference would ratify the Balfour Declaration and incorporate it in Palestine's constitution. The Mandatory Power would then have to carry it out and would be precluded from changing the policy without reference to the League of Nations.

> The Mandatory Power will have to provide such a Government of Palestine as will ensure . . . making Palestine a national home for

the Jewish people, and it will at the same time have to safeguard the civil and religious rights of the non-Jewish population.[70]

Toynbee was granted the privilege of attending the meetings of
the Council of Ten. On 6 February, he heard Emir Feisal's
exposé of the Arab national aspirations. "My seat," Toynbee
recorded, "gave me a good view of everyone in the room, since
the number of participants was not large."[71] During his speech,
Feisal specifically excluded the Lebanon and Palestine. "Palestine, for its universal character should be left on one side for the
mutual consideration of all parties concerned," he declared.[72]

Toynbee's earlier misconceptions were now completely
dissipated. There were few, if any, doubts in his mind when,
late in February, he was asked by Philip Kerr, on behalf of the
Prime Minister, to prepare a joint memorandum with Ormsby-
Gore. The salient points made in this document were:

1. "King Hussein never suggested, and the British Government
   never undertook, that any of the Arab provinces should be
   made subject to one another and that they should be combined against their will in a single Arab state."

2. "The British Government undertook to 'recognise and support' the independence of the Arabs within a certain area,
   without prejudice . . . to special interest[s] of . . . France."

3. The Sykes-Picot Agreement "represented a compromise between French claims and Arab aspirations. . . . This Agreement did not conflict with [British] undertakings to King
   Hussein."

4. "Palestine, owing to the many international interests there,
   including Jewish aspirations, was specially excepted from
   Syria."[73]

A week later, Toynbee declared:

In view of the adoption of President Wilson's points as the basis
for the [Peace] Conference, both the claims of King Hussein and
those of France may be regarded as having lost their validity . . .

This important statement was occasioned by Hussein's renewed plea that his demands be met as spelled out in the

"Agreement" submitted to Wingate on 28 August 1918.[74] It was a distilled version of a point made earlier by Hogarth.[75] Toynbee thus came full circle. However, his conspicuous flaws of judgment, a string of self-contradictions, and inaccuracies made his services to the Foreign Office dispensable.

Lord Curzon, Lord President of the Council, was one of the Ministers misled by Toynbee into thinking that the British Government had made conflicting promises to Arabs and Jews. On 5 December 1918, at a meeting of the Eastern Committee, of which he was Chairman, he made a statement which amounted to a verbal repetition of that produced in Toynbee's memorandum on "British Commitments.'[76] Sir Louis Mallet, the head of the Turkish section of the British Delegation to the Peace Conference and Toynbee's immediate superior, was another victim. On the basis of Toynbee's memorandum, Mallet stated that the division of the Arab countries, as had been prescribed in the Anglo-French Agreement of 1915, "was contrary to British undertakings to King Hussein as representing the Arabs." These undertakings, Mallet, asserted, were unconditional and irrevocable.[77] He repeated this version in another memorandum, dated 17 February 1919.[78] Subsequently, he realized that he was mistaken. Writing to Curzon on 26 May 1919, he admitted that the provisions of the Sykes-Picot Agreement were "entirely compatible with His Majesty's Government's engagements to King Hussein."[79] There is no evidence that Toynbee apprised Mallet of his joint memorandum with Ormsby-Gore, dated 25 February. So, when Mallet found out how badly he had been briefed, Toynbee's position became untenable. Late in May, Toynbee left the Foreign Office.

Balfour saw Mallet's memorandum of 4 February, but not his dispatch to Curzon of 26 May. Nor, like Mallet, was he aware of Toynbee's joint memorandum with Ormsby-Gore, and, when preparing his own memorandum of 11 August 1919,[80] he relied on Toynbee's memoranda of October and 21 November 1918, which, by that time, were outdated. Balfour was greatly perturbed by the ill-effects of the controversy on the Anglo-French relations with regard to the Syrian question. Nor did he feel at ease toward the Arabs, primarily due to, what he thought, were conflicting war-time agreements. He wrote:

> In 1915 we promised the Arabs independence; and that the promise was unqualified, except in respect of certain territorial reservations . . .
>
> In 1915 it was the Sherif of Mecca to whom the task of delimitation [of boundaries] was to have been confided, nor were any restrictions placed upon his discretion in this matter, except certain reservations intended to protect French interests in Western Syria and Cilicia.
>
> In 1916 all this seems to have been forgotten. The Sykes-Picot Agreement made no reference to the Sherif of Mecca, and . . . he has never been heard of since. A wholly new method was adopted by France and England . . . in the Sykes-Picot Agreement . . .

How strongly Balfour believed that this was the case is evident from his reaction to a leader in *The Times* (21 August 1919) which sharply criticized the Sykes-Picot Agreement, alleging that it was "not in harmony with engagements contracted by the British Government toward the King of the Hedjaz." On the following day, Eric Forbes Adam, with the Turkish section of the British Delegation and Toynbee's former departmental colleague, was quick to point out that McMahon's letter of 24 October 1915 specifically had provided for the interests of France, and that "the territorial form which the Sykes-Picot Agreement took, sufficiently show[s] that it was based on our negotiations with King Hussein." Forbes Adam wondered whether it would be advisable to brief the editor of *The Times* in this sense, but Balfour turned down his suggestion:

> It is rather dangerous to speak to *The Times* in this sense, unless we can reconcile our letter to Hussein of 1915 with the Sykes-Picot agreement of 1916. *I cannot.* Can anyone else? [81]

By contrast, as far as Palestine was concerned, Balfour emphasized in his above-mentioned memorandum, that "the Powers have made no statement of fact which is admittedly wrong, and no declaration of policy which, at least in the letter, they have not always intended to violate":

> The four Great Powers are committed to Zionism. And Zionism, be it right or wrong, good or bad, is rooted in age-long traditions, in present needs, in future hopes, of far profounder import than the

desires and prejudices of the 700,000 Arabs who now inhabit that ancient land.

"In my opinion that is right," Balfour wrote, convinced in the justice of the policy embodied in the declaration bearing his name. Nor did he ever have a scintilla of doubt about Palestine's exclusion from the promises to King Hussein.[82]

When Grey read Balfour's memorandum, he expressed surprise at Balfour's statement that the British engagements to Hussein were incompatible with the engagements to France about Syria:

> I think this statement [he wrote to Balfour] must be most unfair to those who [were] responsible for making the engagements and will do increasing mischief to the reputation of British policy and good faith. My recollection is that we promised the King of the Hedjaz and the Musselman world that Arabia and the Musselman Holy Places should be an independent Musselman Kingdom. There was nothing in this to prevent our agreeing to the demand of France for the Syrian sphere of influence under the Sykes-Picot arrangement. . . . It is impossible to allow this engagement to the King of the Hedjaz to be represented as incompatible with the engagement to France without a public contradiction.

Curzon forwarded to the Prime Minister a copy of Grey's letter to Balfour, and observed that the assurances to King Hussein "are not incompatible with a French mandate for Syria. But they do not quite square with the French conception of that mandate."[83] On 18 September, the Cabinet discussed the Syrian question, and on the following day, Lloyd George told Feisal unequivocally that there was absolutely no contradiction between the British engagements to his father and the Sykes-Picot Agreement. His father had been promised that Damascus, Homs, Hama, and Aleppo would be incorporated into the Arab State or Confederation of States, and that an identical provision had been made in the Inter-Allied Agreement.[84]

Grey tacitly agreed with Balfour's policy on Zionism. This was quite natural. In a speech in the House of Commons on 20 June 1904, he spoke movingly about the need to provide "a refuge and a home" for the persecuted Jewish people,[85] and on 9 November 1914, Herbert Samuel found him to be favorably disposed toward his proposal to found a Jewish State in Palestine after the War; the idea had always a "strong sentimental attraction to him."[86] In March 1916, he endorsed a draft declaration to be issued by the Allied Powers in favor of Jewish colonization and self-government in Palestine. Its wording was far stronger than the declaration of 2 November 1917 named after his successor.[87] If he did not specifically mention in his letter to Balfour that Palestine had been excluded from the arrangement with Sharif Hussein, it was because it was self-evident.

It would have been a measure of responsibility on Toynbee's part to prepare a revised edition of his memorandum on "British Commitments," but such a consideration did not weigh on his mind. The upshot of this negligence was that, while Toynbee himself did revise his views, his memorandum sustained a life of its own. During the Peace Conference, Toynbee befriended William L. (later Professor) Westermann, who served as an adviser on Turkish affairs to the American delegation.[88] They had much in common, and, as a token of friendship, Toynbee gave him a copy of his memorandum on "British Commitments." Whatever his motive, this was clearly a breach of the Official Secrets Act. Toynbee's conclusions made no impression on Westermann, and his memorandum was locked away in the Westermann Papers until 1935, when Professor Westermann lent them to George Antonius, who was preparing his book *The Arab Awakening*. To Antonius, Toynbee's memorandum was a god-send and served to confirm his deep-seated belief in British perfidy toward his fellow Arabs.[89] Other Arab writers, such as Dr. Fayez Sayegh[90] and Yahya Armajani,[91] made similar capital out of Toynbee's labor.

4

Pro-Arab or Pro-Zionist?

In the late forties, Toynbee acquired the reputation of being a passionate Arab protagonist and a fierce opponent of the State of Israel; by his own admission he became known as a "Western spokesman for the Arab cause."[1] But during World War I and its aftermath, he was less than sympathetic toward the Arabs. He was greatly disturbed to note that the Syrians, contrary to assurances made by Hussein, as well as by al-Faruqi, remained loyal to Turkey and "their conscripts fought dutifully on her side . . . their leaders are too prudent and the people too peaceable to allow them for a moment to contemplate rising in arms."[2] Early in the War, he ascertained that, in the Turkish Asiatic provinces, there was only "a veritable cockpit of nationalities so mutilated that they have never even achieved that [kind of] unity which is the essential preliminary to a national life."[3] By 1917, when the general Arab uprising had failed to materialize, he concluded that they had no "national consciousness. There are Arabs in name who have nothing Arabic about them but their language — most of the peasants in Syria are such . . ."[4] This view was not unique. The official Handbook prepared in 1918 to guide the British delegates to the Peace Conference gave the following description:

> The people west of the Jordan are not Arabs, but only Arab-speaking. The bulk of the population are fellahin; that is to say, agricultural workers owning land as a village community or working land for the Syrian effendi. In the Gaza district they are mostly of Egyptian origin; elsewhere they are of the most

mixed race. They have for centuries been ground down, overtaxed, and bullied by the Turk, and still more by the Arab-speaking Turkish minor official and the Syrian and Levantine landowner.[5]

In his *Survey of International Affairs for 1925* [6] — by then he was Director of the Institute of International Affairs (Chatham House) — he confirmed that, although there was "a solidarity of feeling between the Sunnis on both sides of the new Syro-Palestinian frontier," and that "Arabic was the vernacular language of all inhabitants of Syria . . . the common use of Arabic did not carry with it a corresponding sense of national solidarity. . . . Communal particularism remained . . . the dominant feature in the political life of the country."

Following the Wailing Wall riots in 1929, Palestine Arab nationalism became very much in evidence, and, in his *Survey of International Affairs for 1930,*[7] Toynbee analyzed the reasons for the Palestinian discontent fairly and accurately; their obdurate negativism, however, was not to his liking. He regretted particularly that all attempts made by the British Government to set up a Legislative Council with a majority of elected members "had been frustrated by a movement of non-co-operation on the Arab side." On 9 December 1930, in an address to a distinguished audience at the Royal Institute of International Affairs, he proclaimed unequivocally:

> We have made a number of quite sincere and serious attempts [to solve the Arab-Zionist conflict], but the intransigence of the Arabs, in their opposition to the establishment of a Jewish national home, has proved an insuperable stumbling-block every time.[8]

Nor did King Hussein of the Hedjaz earn Toynbee's respect. He referred to his staged coronation on 29 October 1916 in uncomplimentary terms. In his memorandum on "British Commitments," he reproduced the Foreign Office telegrams rejecting, on the Allies' behalf, Hussein's self-proclaimed title as "the King of the Arabs," and commented:

> His Majesty's Government avoided according Sherif Hussein a title incompatible with their commitments to other independent Arab rulers, but . . . the harm done by the Sherif's *coup d'Etat* . . .

has never been repaired. The other independent Arab rulers have not been inwardly reassured by our restriction of the Sherif's title to the Hedjaz; while he, on his part, has only accepted this restriction as provisional. The problem has been postponed, not solved.[9]

To Hussein's letter to Wingate of 28 August 1918,[10] Toynbee reacted with a mixture of disbelief and derision. He took exception to the King's habit of ignoring or refusing to take note of the reservations specified by the British Government and then carrying on as if the matter had been settled according to his own desires. "I submit," Toynbee noted, "that it is essential that we should not allow to pass unchallenged the King's memorandum. . . . He should be told clearly and unequivocally that his version of the agreement did not accord with the original one. Oriental diplomacy's seldom precise unless compelled to be so."

Toynbee's deduction in his October-November memoranda that the British Government was committed to an "Arab" and "independent" Palestine was caused, as shown above, by his misreading of the documents in question, rather than due to any pro-Arab proclivity. Once he managed to extricate himself from the maze of his self-contradictions and inconsistencies, he had no difficulty in falling in line, and, in a joint memorandum with Ormsby-Gore of 25 February 1919 to the Prime Minster, he asserted confidently that the Sykes-Picot Agreement did not conflict with the undertakings to King Hussein, and that

> Palestine, owing to the many international interests there, including Jewish aspirations, was specially excepted from Syria.[11]

In Toynbee's estimation, the Arab Revolt was of marginal importance and, unlike T. E. Lawrence, he never glamorized it. Militarily, Arab help in overthrowing the Turk was negligible. Yet, however disappointing their performance in this respect, Toynbee hoped that, at least politically, the British would be able to reap some advantages.[12] However, this expectation proved short-lived. "The militant peoples of Islam," he wrote in his *Survey of International Affairs for 1925*, "obtained political concessions, out of all proportion to their military achievements." Nonetheless, they had the temerity to attribute these achievements "to their own prowess and drew thence encouragement to continue in the same militant course" against the Allied Powers who had liberated them. The newly born Islamic Nationalism was not animated by the Western liberalism that characterized the Ottoman reformers during the nineteenth century. It was an anti-Western militant nationalism. The defeated Turks defied the victorious Allies; in the Yemen, the Iman of Saná reinvaded the Aden Protectorate late in 1918 and occupied Dála; in July 1920, the Syrians challenged the French in regular warfare; in the summer of 1920, the Iraqis rebelled against the British, as did the Egyptians; the Wahhábis raided Iraq and Trans-Jordan repeatedly from 1921 to 1925; the Afghans attempted to invade India in the spring of 1919, and even in India proper there was a Moslem insurrection in 1919 and another in 1921. "This militancy," Toynbee commented angrily, was not a demonstration of "the heroism of clearsighted courage," but a product of "the folly of ignorance." The successive uprisings in Egypt, Syria, Mesopotamia and elsewhere were eventually crushed, but ensuing political concessions granted to the native populations were interpreted by the latter. not as a gesture of generosity, but as a sign of weakness. Toynbee dismissed Moslem thinking as "another folly of ignorance."[13] However, the results were more serious than Toynbee had anticipated. Moslem antagonism, and that of the Arabs in particular, boded ill for the future status of the European Powers in the East.

Toynbee was particularly bitter against the Beduin:

> While the victorious, as well as the vanquished European belligerents, had emerged war-weary and impoverished from their life-and-death struggle, the Arab tribesmen had been profiting, as they had done thirteen centuries earlier . . .
>
> In 1914-18 . . . the belligerents had simply sought to cover their flanks by hiring Arab rulers to fight their battles for them the Arab way. [But] the Arabs' price had been high, and — with the barbarian's instinctive suspicion . . . they had insisted on being paid in gold, cash down, by all parties.

Their loyalties, however, were not necessarily reserved for their respective paymasters. They were "largely decided by the fact that their local Arab rivals were taking service with the opposite party." Consequently, they used their subsidies to conduct operations in inter-Arab warfare at their respective patrons' expense.[14] So deeply was he incensed that, even a dozen years later in an essay on T. E. Lawrence, he returned to the subject again, though in a humorous way:

> The Arabs [as the Albanians] were willing to be hired, so long as they were duly paid in gold in advance. They did not mind which side they hired themselves to. They had no intention of earning their pay by fighting seriously for any of the European belligerents. They wanted the gold in order to hire each other to fight each other, and this made economic sense. Spent in this way, the gold would circulate inside Arabia without leaving either country. The British Treasury made efforts to recover the gold that it had paid out to Ibn Sa'ûd through the India Office's nose and to King Husayn through the Foreign Office's nose. At the crisis of the German submarine campaign, the Treasury coaxed cargo-space out of the Ministry of Shipping for bringing Indian textiles to Arabian ports, in the hope that the Arabs might be tempted to part with some of their gold in exchange for these attractive foreign commodities. But there was nothing doing. Arabs could not be bribed with textiles to fight each other. Only gold would work; so the Arabs held on to their gold, and the rejected Indian textiles had to be shipped back to where they had come from.[15]

Ironically, during the given period, Toynbee was a convinced Zionist and was full of admiration for the Jewish colonization of Palestine. At that time, when Syrians and Armenians had been emigrating for the last quarter of a century, he wrote in his book, *Turkey: A Past and a Future*, that

> during the same period the Jews, whose birthright in Western Asia is as ancient as theirs, have been returning to their native land. . . . The most remarkable result of this movement has been the foundation of flourishing agricultural colonies. Their struggle for existence has been hard; the pioneers were students or tradesfolk of the Ghetto, unused to outdoor life and ignorant of Near Eastern conditions; Baron Edmund de Rothschild financed them from 1884 to 1899 at a loss; then they were taken over by the

"Palestine Colonisation Association" which discovered the secrets of success in self-government and scientific method . . .

As a result of this enlightened policy the number of colonies has risen to about forty, with 15,000 inhabitants in all and 110,000 acres of land, and these figures do not do full justice to the importance of the colonising movement. The 15,000 Jewish agriculturists are only 12 per cent of the Jewish population in Palestine, and 2 per cent of the total population of the country; but they are the most active, intelligent element, and the only element which is rapidly increasing. Again, the land they own is only 2 per cent of the total area of Palestine; but it is between 8 and 14 per cent of the area under cultivation, and there are vast uncultivated tracts which the Jews can and will reclaim, as their numbers grow — both by further colonisation and by natural increase, for the first generation of colonists have already proved their ability to multiply in the Promised Land.

"Under this new Jewish husbandry," Toynbee went on, "Palestine has begun to recover its ancient prosperity. The Jews have sunk artesian wells, built dams for water storage, fought down malaria by drainage and eucalyptus planting, and laid out many miles of road." The value of the irrigable land had risen ten-fold and the economic life of the country as a whole benefited. There was therefore "no fear that, as [Jewish] immigration increases, the Arab element will be crowded to the wall."[16]

Toynbee quoted the "Basel Programme" formulated at the First Zionist Congress in 1897, and proclaimed:

For the Zionists, Jewry is a nation, and [in order] to become like other nations it needs a Motherland. In the Jewish Colonies in Palestine they see not merely a successful social enterprise, but the visible symbol of a body politic. The foundation of a national university in Jerusalem is as ultimate a goal for them as the economic development of the land, and their greatest achievement has been the revival of Hebrew as the living language of the Palestinian Jews.

Another significant consequence of their national revival was the creation of the Zion Mule Corps by the Palestinian refugees in Egypt who participated in the Gallipoli campaign. "What is the outlook for Palestine after the War?," Toynbee asked. If the

Ottoman régime remained and Germany's long shadow persisted, the prospect would be "grave. But, if Turk and German go, there are Zionists who would like to see Palestine a British Protectorate, with the prospect of growing into a British Dominion."

Toynbee took issue with Dr. Davis-Trietsch, a German Zionist writer, who propounded a view that a Jewish settlement in Palestine would be "an asset to German influence. . . . In a certain sense the Jews are a Near Eastern element in Germany and a German element in Turkey." To this argument Toynbee had a ready reply: "Other Powers than Germany may take these possibilities to heart."[17] Toynbee's book was published in New York in mid-1917 and was meant not only to capture the sympathy of American Jews to the British cause, but to justify the dismemberment of the Ottoman Empire in the eyes of American public opinion at large. His thesis was fully in line with the directive given by the Prime Minister. On 1 February 1917, Lloyd George instructed Captain John Buchan, the newly appointed Director of the Propaganda Bureau:

> When you take in hand the question of Allied and Neutral propaganda, I am anxious you should pay special attention to the futility and iniquity of the Turk. . . . How the Turk, by his rule, made all the arts of industry and husbandry impossible, and how once rich lands have become a wilderness . . . Emphasize his incapacity for good Government, his misrule, and above all, his massacres of all the industrious populations; his brutality . . . in Armenia and Syria.
>
> I am anxious gradually to concentrate the minds of the Allied and Neutral Nations on the Turkish problem, and the importance of solving it once and for all in the interests of civilisation.

Buchan was advised to drive this *leitmotif* home and see to it that articles in the British press were spread over a considerable period of time. Until world public opinion grew accustomed to the idea of the dismemberment of the Ottoman Empire, the Turk had to be discredited and the rights of the small nationalities asserted. The impediment to social and economic progress, the ill-treatment of Jews, Armenians, Syrians, and the Balkan races, and the failure to reform the Turkish state

— these were among the principal points to be emphasized. The motto, Buchan briefed his Department, was that "the Turk must go. If Turkey . . . disappears, the German *drang nach Osten* fails and with it the major purpose with which Germany entered the War."[18]

Toynbee was fully aware of what was at stake. In an essay on Lord Bryce, his mentor on propaganda warfare, he recalled that, only by promulgating an act of sufficient "magnitude that would outweigh the Russian barbarities [against its Jewish subjects] decisively," would the British Government win over world Jewry.

> Zionism was the key. The Western powers must make themselves agents for the fulfilment of the Zionist aspirations. Here was something that might swing Jewish sympathies over to the Allies' side — at any rate in the United States, and perhaps also in Central Europe . . .
>
> When H.M.G. noticed this trump card in their hand, they were eager to play it. . . . The promulgation of the Balfour Declaration followed . . . This was indeed a trump card . . . in the internal-war game of international power politics.[19]

Sections from his book, *Turkey: A Past and a Future*, appeared in the form of an article under an identical title in the *Round Table*,[20] the organ of a group of liberal-minded British imperialists. Philip Kerr (later the Marquis of Lothian), a member of Lloyd George's Cabinet Secretariat, was its editor, and Lord Milner and Leopold Amery were members of the Board. The entire June issue was devoted to postwar problems, one of which was the future of Turkey-in-Asia. That Toynbee was asked by such exalted persons to contribute an article shows that neither his erudition, nor his sincerity with regard to Zionism were called into question. Before submitting, it he sent the proofs to Chaim Weizmann, the newly elected President of the Zionist Federation of Great Britain. Alfred Zimmern, a member of the Information Department, wrote on Toynbee's behalf to Weizmann: "Toynbee is anxious to meet you — will you be at the B'nai Brith on Sunday?"[21]

As early as 1914, before Britain's policy toward Turkey-in-Asia had been crystallized, Toynbee revealed his thoughts:

We want to break up Turkey but we assure them that peace can only be secured by giving free play to every manifestation of the spirit of nationality.[22]

Zionism fitted well into this pattern and provided a convenient vehicle to implement this policy. Weizmann's views converged with Toynbee's. From the very beginning of hostilities Weizmann had been convinced that England would win the war and that only under her wing would Zionism prosper.[23] The potential for common ground between the two existed *a priori*. There is no evidence to show whether Toynbee met Weizmann on that particular Sunday, which happened to be the 20 May 1917. If they did meet, he would have heard Weizmann's celebrated speech in which he declared that the creation of a Jewish Commonwealth was the Zionists "final ideal"; the way to this goal lay through a series of intermediate stages, one of which was that Palestine would be

> protected by such a mighty and just Power as Great Britain. Under the wing of this Power Jews will be able to develop and set up the administrative machinery which, while not interfering with the legitimate interests of the non-Jewish population, would enable [them] to carry out [their] scheme.

John Buchan subscribed to Weizmann's definition:

> I imagine that the British Government [he wrote to Lord Onslow], has no objection to a Jewish Palestine as such — at any rate to the establishment in Palestine of a very large Jewish Colony. But . . . it is not desirable to announce publicly that it should be either a sovereign Jewish State, or a British protectorate. . . . Least of all do we wish it to be a second Monte Carlo or an international banking centre.[24]

It could be safely assumed that Toynbee's views were not much different from his immediate departmental director; Toynbee's statement in his book/article, quoted already — "there are Zionists who would like to see Palestine a British Protectorate with the prospect of growing into a British Dominion" — is indicative of much. No less telling is his enthusiastic response to President Wilson's statement to Weizmann on 14 January 1919 during the Peace Conference in Paris. Wilson declared that his Government and the American people agreed that, in Palestine "shall be laid the foundation of a Jewish Commonwealth" and welcomed the idea that Britain should take over responsibility for Palestine.[25]

Toynbee's introduction to Zionism had taken place before the War at Oxford, where he befriended Leonard Stein.[26] But it was not until 1915, at the Information Department of the Foreign Office, that he was able to acquaint himself with the subject more fully. Like E. A. Gowers, its Director, Charles Masterman, the latter's assistant, as well as Leopold Amery, Toynbee was impressed with Vladimir Jabotinsky's struggle to create Jewish battalions to fight for the liberation of Palestine.[27] A few years later, he acknowledged that "the work of the Palestinian Zionist refugees in the Gallipoli campaign and later [of the Royal Fusiliers in the Valley of Jordan] . . . has been considerable in comparison with their means."[28]

In December 1917, when the Balfour Declaration first came under attack on grounds that it was inconsistent with the principle of democracy, he composed, jointly with Lewis Namier, his colleague in the Political Intelligence Department, a memorandum that served the British Government well in the years to come.

> The objection raised against the Jews being given exclusive political rights in Palestine on a basis that it would be undemocratic with regard to the local Christian and Mohammedan population is certainly the most important point which the anti-Zionists have hitherto raised, but the difficulty is imaginary. Palestine might be held in trust by Great Britain or America until there was a sufficient population in the county fit to govern it on European lines. Then no undemocratic restrictions of the kind indicated in the memorandum would be required any longer.[29]

A year later, in his 21 November 1918 memorandum already quoted, he made a further point. Explaining why, in this case, the principle of self-determination was not applicable, he stated that, as in Armenia, there would in Palestine be a mixed population, the Jewish colonists being one element of that population "which for special reasons, will be entitled to a position more than mathematically proportionate to its numbers at the start." For this and other reasons, "the desires of the inhabitants, or of the several sections of them, will have, to some extent, to take the second place." The boundaries of Palestine, which he outlined in his sketch map of 8 October 1918 and perfected on 2 December 1918, surpassed the most extreme expectations of the Zionists themselves. And it was only the objection raised by Emir Feisal that induced him, along with T. E. Lawrence, to confine the eastern border of Palestine to the River Jordan.[30] Otherwise he applauded Feisal's friendly relations with the Zionists.[31]

Throughout the Peace Conference, Toynbee was in close touch with the Zionist leaders. Weizmann, in particular, earned his admiration. Toynbee described him as a "great statesman and scientist — the most distinguished member of the Ashkenazi community in his generation." Weizmann recounted two anecdotes that made Toynbee understand, more than any philosophical essay, why an East European Jew had become a convert to Zionism. The first anecdote showed the inability of the assimilated Jew to be true to himself; the second one demonstrated Jewish homelessness.[32] But it was from the newly published *History of Zionism* by Nahum Sokolow that Toynbee learned about its origin and development. Thanking Sokolow for a copy of his book, Toynbee wrote:

> I shall look forward to the second volume which you tell me is to follow.
>
> I hope there will be a third — unless "Zionism" ends with the accomplishment of its aim and you give a new name to the work of national reconstruction in a liberated Palestine.
>
> The next stage should be the most interesting, as I hope it will be the most prosperous of all — though I cannot help thinking that, on looking back, Jewry will be most proud of the first stage of Zionism in which, in the face of so many obstacles, it reached the point it has come to now.[33]

The language employed in this letter went far beyond diplomatic niceties; the phrase "national reconstruction" gave it an added meaning. At times, Toynbee drafted letters to Weizmann on Balfour's behalf[34] and, on 10 May 1919, was accorded the unusual privilege of attending a meeting of the Zionist Advisory Committee, chaired by Herbert Samuel. Present also were David Hogarth, Col. Gribbon, and Ormsby-Gore.[35]

Toynbee's departure from the Foreign Office did not extinguish his interest in Palestine. In 1922, he fell under the spell of the Palestine Arab Delegation, then in London, and made their arguments his own. "The upshot is," he concluded, that

> Palestine was not excepted from the area in which the British government promised in 1915 to recognize and uphold Arab independence, and that the Balfour Declaration of 1917 was therefore incompatible with a previous commitment. To saddle [Britain] with [such] irreconcilable commitments is almost the worst crime of which the professional diplomatist is capable, for it compromises that country's reputation for straight-dealing.

Toynbee was also deeply troubled by what he believed was the inherent incompatibility between the obligation, enshrined in the Balfour Declaration, to make Palestine into a Jewish National Home and the clause of safeguarding the rights of the non-Jewish communities.[36]

These conclusions were strange. He seemed to have forgotten about the memorandum that he wrote with Lewis Namier on 19 December 1917, which had provided an answer to this very problem, as well as the statements he made in another joint memorandum with Ormsby-Gore on 25 February 1919.[37] He failed also to notice that the claim to Palestine at that time was not made by King Hussein, whom he described as the "spokesman of the secret anti-Turkish Arab Nationalist committee sitting in Damascus," but by a Palestinian leader, who had no status in the matter whatsoever. But the most glaring logical lapse in his thinking was his astonishing admission that the Arab leaders themselves had *a priori* excluded the Syrian littoral and Palestine. When negotiations with the Sharif Hussein (following his letter of July 1915) reached "a deadlock," owing to French traditional standing in the region, Toynbee explained,

> a prominent Arab Nationalist [al-Faruqi] advised the British government that if the inland Syrian towns of Damascus, Homs, Hama and Aleppo were expressly included in the guaranteed area of Arab independence, the Arabs would probably leave the destiny of the Syrian coast in suspense until after the war.[38]

There is, of course, no document to support the assertion that the destiny of the coastal areas, especially of Palestine, was left "in suspense until after the war."

Toynbee's errors notwithstanding, his sympathies at that time lay clearly with the Zionists. Their acceptance of the British 1922 White Paper policy "shows," he wrote in the same essay in the *New Republic*, "very praiseworthy strength of mind and consideration," and observed that, "after all the Jews have everything to gain by a régime under which they will be able to rise from being a small minority to becoming equal or even stronger than the Arabs." That the Arabs opposed Jewish immigration to Palestine, let alone their becoming a majority in the country, did not seem to impress him. Presumably this was because, in this particular case, the arguments he had advanced with Lewis Namier on 19 December 1917 remained valid. He applied the same yardstick when advocating the creation of the Armenian National Home east of Anatolia, although the Armenians did not constitute a majority in that region. Toynbee's suggestion was in line with the deliberations of the Supreme Council of the Peace Conference at San Remo. On 22 April 1920, when the frontiers of Greater Armenia were discussed, an analogy was made with Palestine. It was pointed out that the Zionists' case was not based on numerical superiority of Jews inhabiting Palestine, and that this principle could serve as a guide for Greater Armenia as well.[39]

In the same volume of Temperley's *History* (1924) in which Toynbee's article, "The Non-Arab Territories," was published, David Hogarth's "Great Britain and the Arabs" appeared, in which it was clearly stated that the Allied Governments undertook to support and recognize an Arab State only "in the interior of Syria . . . whenever established by the Arabs themselves," and under the explicit condition that they refrained from assisting the enemy and cooperated with the Allies.[40] In his introduction to Philip Graves's book, *The Land of Three Faiths*, which appeared in 1923, Hogarth endorsed Graves's view that McMahon, in his letter of 24 October 1915, had explicitly excluded Palestine from his promises to Hussein.[41]

Toynbee respected Hogarth and in all likelihood read Graves's book. As a result, he reversed his position and said nothing further about "conflicting commitments" for a number of years. Quite the contrary, in his *Survey of International Affairs for 1925*, he made it abundantly clear that

In the British Government's view, Transjordan did (while Palestine did not) fall within the area in which Great Britain had
promised King Husayn to recognize and support the independence
of the Arabs.

This was correct. In September 1922, the British Government
did use this very argument when attempting to prevail on the
Council of the League of Nations to exempt the territory of
Trans-Jordan from the application of the provisions of the Man-
date of Palestine. But Toynbee went further, stating that the
British Government

> had . . . honoured this pledge [already] by assenting to the
> inclusion of Transjordan in that Arab National State which was
> set up immediately after General Allenby's decisive victory of
> the 1st October, 1918, with Damascus as its capital and the Amir
> Feisal b. Husayn as its constitutional head.

Toynbee left no room for doubt as to which party remained in
debt to the other: "The militant peoples of Islam obtained political concession out of proportion to their military achievements," and extracted from their patrons exorbitant sums in
gold. The exclusivity and intolerance of militant nationalism in
the East dismayed him. "The general tendency in the Islamic
World at this time was for the minorities to disappear," either
by forced assimilation or by elimination. In this environment,
the attempt made by the British Government to introduce a new
minority into the area and to facilitate the establishment of the
Jewish National Home in Palestine was little short of "auda-
cious":

> This remarkable experiment appealed to the imagination and
> excited the sympathy of almost every observer who was acquain-
> ted with the long and tragic history of the Jewish people, with
> the devastating effects of the General War of 1914-18 upon the
> life of the Jews in Eastern Europe, and with the disinterested
> heroism which was displayed in Palestine — before, during, and
> after the War — by the Zionist pioneers.[42]

When the National Home had passed its experimental
stage, Toynbee did not exclude the possibility of Jews becoming

a majority in the country, Arab opposition notwithstanding.[43]

In volume II of his *Study of History*, he paid tribute to Weizmann's statesmanship and analyzed in depth the Zionist, as opposed to the assimilationist, school of thought: "The ultimate aim of the Zionists is to liberate the Jewish people from the peculiar psychological complex induced by the penalization to which they have been subject for centuries in the Gentile World." In this ultimate objective, the Zionists were in agreement with the assimilationists; they differed only in the method of curing the malady. Toynbee agreed that the assimilationists' prescription provided no solution for the Jewish problem in Eastern Europe, where there was no material prospect for a *bona fide* emancipation, while in the West, the Gentile-Jewish relationship could not be solved simply by a "social contract" under which the Gentile "emancipates" the Jew and the Jew "assimilates" himself to the Gentile. "To be a Jew," he asserted, "is to be a human being whose social environment is Jewry . . . he cannot cut off his Jewishness and cast it from him without self-mutilation":

> A Jew who, by process of emancipation and assimilation, attempts, in a social contract with his Gentile neighbours, to turn himself into a Dutchman or a Frenchman or an Englishman or an American "of Jewish religion" is simply mutilating his Jewish personality without having any prospect at all of acquiring the full personality of a Dutchman or whatever the Gentile nationality of his choice may be.

The Jews can never escape their peculiarity as a people by "masquerading" as Englishmen or Frenchmen. Hence,

> If they are to succeed in becoming "like all the nations," they must seek assimilation on a national and not on an individual basis. Instead of trying to assimilate individual Jews to individual Englishmen or Frenchmen, they must try to assimilate Jewry itself to England and France. Jewry must become a nation in effective possession of a national home, and this on the ground from which the historic roots of Judaism have sprung. When a new generation of Jews has grown up in Palestine in a Jewish national environment, then, and not till then, the Jewish problem will be solved by the reappearance in the World of a type of Jew which has been almost non-existent for the past two thousand years.

Zionist social philosophy in Toynbee's assessment was fully vindicated by results:

> In the Jewish agricultural settlements that have been founded in Palestine within the last fifty years, the children of the ghetto have been transformed out of all recognition into a pioneering peasantry which displays many of the characteristics of the Gentile European colonial type in the New World. The Zionists have made no miscalculation in their forecast of the effect which the establishment of a Jewish national home in Palestine would have upon Jewry itself. [However,] the tragic misfortune into which they have fallen, is their inability to arrive at an understanding with the existing Arab population of the country.[44]

In his address in the Royal Institute of International Affairs on 9 December 1930, already mentioned, he made some barbed remarks on the "intransigence of the Arabs, in their opposition to the establishment of a Jewish national home [which] proved an insuperable stumbling-block" to any settlement and warned that the Palestine Question could not be solved by violence. However, he prophesied that, sooner or later, the Arabs "would find themselves obliged to come to terms with Jewry," just as the Jews would have to come to terms with the Arabs:

> The Jews cannot develop Palestine economically if the country is cut off from its Arab hinterland, any more than the Arabs can develop Palestine economically if the country is deprived of the influx of Jewish capital . . . The Palestine problem can never be settled finally by force. It can only be settled by an understanding — a direct understanding — between the two parties which have a direct concern with the country.

Toynbee firmly believed that force of circumstances would drive both the Jews and the Arabs to settle their dispute by agreement. "This may happen before the termination of the Mandate or it may happen afterwards, but it will certainly happen in the end." In this matter, Toynbee carried the audience with him, but when he ventured to delve into the root causes of the Arab-Zionist conflict he provoked a commotion. He claimed that the chief culprit was the British Government: "During the War, Britain was living from hand to mouth, so she sold a pup; she sold it twice over; and it wasn't her pup to sell." And on re-flection, he commented that the territory of Palestine west of Jordan was promised "*three* times over": first to the Arabs, then to the French and the Russian Allies, and thereafter to the Jews.[45]

This was an extraordinary statement. It contradicted all that Toynbee himself had written so authoritatively in his *Survey of International Affairs for 1925*. Lieut. Commander J. M. Kenworthy, M.P., who challenged Toynbee, said that he had "never listened to so many inaccuracies of fact, judgment and sentiment in an equal time."[46] This criticism, however, fell on deaf ears. In an essay on T. E. Lawrence, apparently written shortly after Lawrence's death in 1935, Toynbee unleashed an-other assortment of inaccuracies and misconceptions. He wrote:

> I fancy that Lawrence's conscience reproached him for having promised the Arabs, in the United Kingdom Government's name, an independence that, in the event, had been withheld from them;

And went on:

> The British authorities had not told King Husayn — and, without being told, he could not have guessed — that, in a subsequent agreement with France, they were going to interpret "independence" for the Arabs to mean a substitution of British and French for Turkish political control over them.
>
> If Lawrence had been cognizant of this Anglo-French deception of the Arabs (it amounted to that), then he had been an accom-plice in the fraud; if he had not been cognizant of it, he had been the Arabs' fellow-victim. Either possibility remains open, in default of decisive evidence one way or the other; and I have no evidence on this point.

In all events, the Allied Powers had perpetrated "a fraud at the Arabs' expense . . . [who] had come out empty-handed."[47]

Only an absolute ignoramus or politically biased person could have published such nonsense. Toynbee was neither. He was familiar with the documents in question and in his memo-randum on "British Commitments" had reached entirely differ-ent conclusions about the Sykes-Picot Agreement. One need only consult his *Survey of International Affairs for 1925*, as well as another section in the same essay, quoted already, to see what truth there was in his assertion that the Arabs emerged "empty-handed" from the War. Only a psychologist could explain the curious twists of his mind. However, if one were to hazard a guess, it would be not too far-fetched to say that Toynbee must have in general suffered from an acute sense of guilt, which, in this particular case, he projected onto Lawrence. In this matter, too, he was wrong, for Lawrence did not display any feelings of guilt and self-recrimination. Quite the contrary. In his letter to *The Times* (11 September 1919), Lawrence stated categorically: "I can see no inconsistencies or incompatibilities in these four documents, and I know nobody who does."[48]

The letter made an impression at that time, and it is inconceivable that Toynbee failed to read it. He must have also been aware of the results of the Cairo Conference in March 1921, at which Lawrence acted as an adviser to Winston Churchill, then Colonial Secretary:

> He [Churchill] set honesty before expediency in order to fulfil our promises in the letter and in the spirit. He executed the whole McMahon undertaking for Palestine, for Trans-Jordania and for Arabia. In Mesopotamia he went far beyond its provisions, giving to the Arabs more, and reserving for us much less, than Sir Henry McMahon had thought fit.

Lawrence put also on record his conviction that

> England is out of the Arab affair with clean hands. Some Arab advocates (the most vociferous joined our ranks after the Armistice) have rejected my judgment on this point. Like a tedious Pensioner I showed them my wounds (over sixty I have, each scar evidence of a pain incurred in Arab service) as proof I had worked sincerely on their side. They found me out-of-date; and I was happy to withdraw from a political milieu which had never been congenial.[49]

In his essay on Lawrence, Toynbee made another statement which is even more relevant to our subject:

> It is true that the British authorities had made a territorial reservation in their correspondence with King Husayn before his

insurrection against his Turkish suzerains. The British undertaking to King Husayn to recognize and uphold the independence of the Arabs within certain territorial limits had expressly excluded the territory to the west of "the vilayets of Aleppo, Hama, Homs, and Damascus" (in whatever way this ambiguous formula is to be interpreted). This strip of territory, however, was small in extent compared to the Arab territory, east of that line, that had also been under Ottoman sovereignty or suzerainty. In respect of this far larger Arab territory, the British undertaking had been unconditional.[50]

The phrase in parentheses notwithstanding, the tenor of the whole paragraph conveys the distinct impression that Toynbee yet again had reconsidered his position and had concluded that the Syrian littoral and Palestine had been "expressly excluded." There was, of course, no "Vilayet of Damascus" — the territory in question was known as Vilayet of Syria — but this is not the only inaccuracy made by Toynbee in his chequered career. The statement that the British undertaking with regard to the vast Arab territory lying east of Palestine and the Lebanon "had been unconditional" is another example of his chronic difficulty in reading documents. However, it is worth noting that Toynbee refrained from using the controversial words "districts of . . ." and did not repeat his standard accusation of the "pup" being sold "twice."

However, if he really came to believe that Palestine had not been promised to the Arabs first, such a volte face was short-lived. During 1937, Toynbee established a good rapport with George Antonius[51] and, like a great many British intellectuals and public men, fell under his spell. Given his confused conceptions on British Middle Eastern commitments, Toynbee proved an easy target for Antonius's blandishments. Henceforth he began to veer toward the Arab camp and away from the Zionist. The Round Table Conference in London in 1939 attracted his attention, and he took keen interest in its proceedings. It was then that he learned for the first time that the word *wilāya* meant "environs," or "banlieux." It altered his outlook radically. *Wilāya* became the keyword in his campaign to prove the validity of the Arab claim.

In 1940, Toynbee told the Rev. Dr. James Parkes, who was working at that time at the Foreign Research and Press Service at Chatham House, about his October-November 1918 memoranda in which it was clearly indicated that Palestine and Syria "were within the area of Arab independence mentioned in the McMahon-Hussain correspondence" and that the Foreign Office accepted his view. Only later, he added, "as a result of Jewish pressure, H.M. Government changed their attitude and sought for arguments to show that the correspondence had failed to cover Palestine."[52]

To Parkes, who was preparing, among other things, a book on anti-Semitism, the phrase "Jewish pressure" brought unsavoury associations. He approached Malcolm MacDonald, the Colonial Secretary, and asked him to ascertain the veracity of Toynbee's statement. The Foreign Office was thereupon asked to investigate the matter, but could find no *prima facie* evidence of Jewish pressure. It existed only in Toynbee's imagination. Lacy Baggallay of the Foreign Office wrote to H. F. Downie:

> I am afraid that it would be difficult to establish that the change in the outlook of His Majesty's Government . . . was due to Jewish pressure. . . . Although Professor Toynbee is categorical [in his 1918 memoranda] about Palestine being promised as "Arab" and "independent," he qualifies it later by references to the necessity for a Mandate and to a special position for the Jews, showing that the seeds of inconsistency were there from the start.

Baggallay advised Downie to look at Childs's memorandum of 24 October 1930, where, on page 54, he referred to Toynbee's memorandum and managed "to pull the Professor's views to pieces." However, Childs's arguments, Baggallay added, were rejected by the Anglo-Arab Committee, which considered the McMahon-Hussein Correspondence during the Round Table Conference early in 1939. The Arab riposte was "based on the meaning of the words 'district' and 'vilayet', etc."[53] The person who led the Arab counter-attack was Antonius, although he was not as successful in demolishing the British case as Baggallay claimed him to be.[54]

From the early fifties, Toynbee became a determined opponent of the State of Israel, and his references to Zionism, even to Judaism, were unfriendly. However, this stage of his career lies outside the scope of the present study.

One of Toynbee's most moving essays was that on Sir Lewis Namier, an old friend and once a fellow student at Balliol College, Oxford. Toynbee felt deep affection for him. "Lewis was invincibly lovable, from first to last . . . he needed to be invincibly lovable if a friendship with him was to last, for . . . if you crossed Lewis on some issue which, for him, was of importance, he was capable of declaring total war on you, however old and close a friend of his you might be." Namier's quarrel with Toynbee was over the history of Palestine under the British mandate, which Toynbee was preparing for his (1938?) *Survey of International Affairs*. Namier objected to Toynbee's presentation "because," Toynbee explained, "by this time he had become an ardent Zionist, while I . . . was becoming more and more doubtful whether the mandatory power was going to succeed in reconciling its commitments to the Palestinian Arabs with its commitments in Palestine to the Jews. I feared that the Arabs were going to get an unfair deal. . ."[55]

When Namier angrily broke off relations, Toynbee expressed an inability to understand how he managed to reconcile his love of England with his emotional involvement with Zionism. Toynbee was also at a loss to appreciate the reason Namier reacted as he did, since he thought there was so much in common between them.

> I myself believe that what Lewis's way of working and my way have in common is something more than our common rejection of the usual way. . . We have both been trying to demythologize history. We have been trying, each along his own line, to find some way of expressing historical events in terms, not myths, out of the realities: *wie es eigentlich gewesen ist*, in von Ranke's famous words.[56]

However, if Namier parted company with Toynbee, it was not necessarily because he was becoming "an ardent Zionist," while Toynbee was cooling off, but because Toynbee was doing just the opposite of what he had claimed. Far from demythologizing history, he was consciously, or unconsciously, creating new myths — notably the myth of the "twice Promised Land."

Namier was not Toynbee's only critic. A. J. P. Taylor

thought that his method was "remote from historical scholarship," and that his voluminous *Study of History* was "not designed to serve an historical purpose." Hugh Trevor-Roper ridiculed Toynbee's claim to empirical investigation; his evidence was fitted into his own a priori theories and assumptions; while Hans J. Morgenthau stated bluntly: "Toynbee is not a historian."[57]

Replying to his critics, Toynbee said:

> I do not mind being called a minor historian, so long as it is understood that I am not renouncing the right to study history and to write some, too, when I choose. I have this right, like anyone else. It is one of our human freedoms.[58]

However, the right to freedom carries with it some responsibilities. Toynbee ignored this imperative, and that the ultimate test of an historian is how genuine is his search for the truth.

5

Sykes, Picot, and Hussein

In his essay on T. E. Lawrence, which has already been quoted, Toynbee referred to the Anglo-French Agreement as a "fraud" and a "deception of the Arabs." The document, he proclaimed, was deliberately concealed from King Hussein and flouted Britain's pledge for Arab independence and substituted British and French "political control" over the Arabs for the Turkish one.[1]

Toynbee did not produce any evidence to support his contention. In 1918-1919, when preparing his memoranda at the Foreign Office, such ideas never seemed to have crossed his mind. They developed at a later period. It does not require undue imagination to trace their paternity to George Antonius, whom Toynbee met at Chatham House in the mid-thirties, when the latter was working on his book *The Arab Awakening*.

Antonius painted the Sykes-Picot Agreement in the darkest colors[2] and claimed that, in May 1917, when Sykes went to Jeddah to see Hussein, Sykes had an opportunity to put the whole position candidly, but did not do so. It is "certain," he wrote, "that the two delegates [Sykes and Picot] left Jeddah without disclosing to King Hussein the terms of the Sykes-Picot Agreement. Subsequent events show that they did not even mention its existence except by general allusions to Anglo-French understanding and solidarity." Antonius went on to say that, in the years that followed the war, "Husain used to assert in the most emphatic terms that no mention of an Allied pact relating to Arab territories had been made at those or any other interviews, and that the first inkling he had had of it was when its existence was revealed to him by the Turks." In November 1917, when the Bolsheviks seized power in Russia, they published, among other secret documents, the text of the Agreement of 1916 and the Turks lost no time in forwarding it to Hussein. Djemal Pasha, the Ottoman Commander, pointed to it as proof that the Arabs had been duped by the Allies. "It was now proved beyond all doubt," Antonius tells us, "that the Allies harboured secret designs which were the very negation of Arab independence."[3]

This view gained wide acceptance in literature and became commonplace in history textbooks. It will be our task in the next two chapters to scrutinize all available material on this subject and to ascertain whether there was any validity in Antonius's assertions.

It should be stated straight away that it was no less a personality than Sir Mark Sykes himself who, in March 1916, recommended that the terms of the Agreement be revealed to the Arab leaders. Jointly with Picot, he was just completing the negotiations with Sazonov, their Russian counterpart, when the Foreign Office telegram of 11 March 1916 proposing to issue an Allied declaration in favor of promoting a Jewish settlement in Palestine reached Petrograd.[4] Sykes, completely unaware of the policy taking shape in London, was taken by surprise and thought that a meeting *à quatre* among the British, French, Arabs and Zionists was imperative in order to thrash out any differences of opinion. He suggested that Arab representatives, such as Aziz Bey Ali al-Misri and al-Faruqi, should be invited to London for formal discussions. When they reached London on 7 April 1916, he noted, "I believe, by May 8, the ground would be clear of the Arab-French question, and Zionist claims agreed upon... Picot [too is] anxious to deal with the problem."[5] A dialogue, however imperfect, was always preferable to Sykes than complete lack of contact. It testified to his essential honesty. It also proved prescient.

Yet, however sound Sykes's proposal was, it foundered against other calculations. At the Foreign Office, Weakley, an expert in Middle Eastern affairs, agreed in principle that the Arab leaders should be made aware of British policy and what assistance London was prepared to give to ensure the success of the Arab movement, but he believed that, until the Turks had been driven out of their Asiatic provinces, disclosure of the Inter-Allied Agreement, let alone a public declaration, was premature. Grey took note of Weakley's advice.[6] On the same day (17 March 1916), Grey had also received a message from the Russian Government requesting that the Agreement be kept secret.[7] Sensitive of his Allies position, Grey respected this wish.

The Agreement, in any case, was provisional in nature and contingent upon the Arabs' performance. Hussein undertook to mount a general rising against the Turks in the Hedjaz and in Syria, but, in spite of British promises, arms, and money, he remained elusive. The Agreement bestowed enormous benefits upon him; this was the first time in modern history that any Power committed itself to "recognize and uphold" Arab independence; but with no sign of the much vaunted rebellion in the offing, Grey did not feel obliged to accommodate him. This was particularly the case after Hussein's admission, late in March 1916, that "owing to the dispersal of chiefs," the Syrians could neither engineer a revolution, nor seize the Hedjaz railway east of the river Jordan,[8] This news was particularly disappointing, since, on 20 October 1915, McMahon advised London that Feisal (then on his way to Syria) assured him through a messenger that "the one object of the Arabs [was] to conclude an agreement with England," and that "the Syrian Arabs were under a signed compact to follow him."[9] The grandiose plan that had prompted the Cairo officials to enter into negotiations with the Sharif was now in a shambles. By implication, the failure of the Syrians to live up to their promise rendered inoperable the Allied commitment to recognize and uphold Arab independence. In these circumstances, to brief Hussein on the terms of the Agreement was hardly justifiable.

By the spring of 1917, the situation had changed. The Sharifian revolt (to distinguish it from the expected Arab revolt) was ten months old, Baghdad was in British hands, and General Murray was knocking at the gates of Gaza. Invasion of Palestine, and perhaps also of Syria, seemed imminent and the application of the Anglo-French Agreement to the territories destined to be liberated acquired greater relevance. With this in mind, both the British and the French Governments decided to dispatch their most competent diplomats, Sir Mark Sykes and Georges Picot, on a joint mission to the East. They were to act as Chief Political Officers and to advise the military on the spot. The instructions that Sykes received from the Foreign Office with regard to his status and functions in the occupied territories read in part: "The terms of the Franco-British Agreement are to be regarded as governing the policy of H.M. Government towards both the French Commissioner and the native elements in the theatre of operations of the [British] Egyptian force beyond the Egyptian-Syrian frontier."[10]

In Cairo, the animosity toward the Sykes-Picot Agreement was still strong,[11] and when Wingate suggested that the mission of Sykes and Picot to the East would provide an opportunity to consider the future of Syria *de novo*, not only did the Foreign Office reject it out of hand, but Sykes himself warned Wingate that the "mission is a joint one . . . Cordial cooperation on the strict lines of the Agreement is the basis on which I and my French colleague intend to work."[12]

In one matter Sykes deviated from the terms of the Agreement. Since October 1916, he had been convinced that a British protectorate of Palestine was an indispensable strategic requirement and that it behooved Britain to amend the agreement which he had co-authored. He believed that a British presence in Palestine and Mesopotamia and a French establishment in Syria were the basis on which to build the Anglo-French position in the Middle East. It made sense and gave more security than a mutilated Palestine and international administration in the "Brown" area. It was, however, not until the accession of Lloyd George to the Premiership in December 1916 that this concept became a cornerstone of British policy. This led to a compact with Zionism.[13]

On 3 April 1917, on the eve of the departure of Sir Mark Sykes for the East, a meeting took place at which Lord Curzon, the Lord President, and Sir Maurice Hankey, the Secretary to the War Cabinet, among others, were present. Lloyd George told Sykes, if any reminder was at all necessary, that Palestine lay outside the Arabs' concern. He warned him not to commit the British Government to "any agreement with [Arab] tribes which would be prejudicial to British interests" and underlined "the importance of not prejudicing the Zionist movement and

↺ the possibility of its development under British auspices." Sykes concurred, and commented that "the Arabs themselves probably realized that there was no prospect of their being allowed any control over Palestine." In conclusion, Lloyd George emphasized once again the importance of "securing the addition of Palestine to the British area"; no political pledges ought to be made to the Arabs, "particularly none in regard to Palestine."[14]

The day before Sykes saw Lloyd George, Picot had received meticulous instructions from Alexandre Ribot, the new French Premier and Foreign Minister. Picot's task as High Commissioner, and the task of the French military detachment, was to share the mantle of liberator with the British, and administer the occupied territories in conformity with the May 1916 Agreement. They were to demonstrate the solidarity of the Entente. With regard to Palestine, the text read:

> On your arrival in Palestine you will find numerous Jewish colonies. Right from the onset, it is necessary to display towards the Jewish settlers great benevolence and entrust them with a measure of administration of their own communities and with a share in the government of the country . . .

Picot was also instructed to show a friendly attitude toward the Christian and Moslem Arab population and to spur them on to rebel against the Turks.[15] Thus, whilst Lloyd George aimed at undermining the condominium in Palestine, Ribot's objective was to put it into effect. "You will have to organize the occupied territories so as to ensure France an equal footing to that of England," he told Picot.

Sykes and Picot were at cross-purposes here, but Palestine was an exception. In all other spheres they acted in commendable harmony. For Sykes, the indivisibility of the Entente was almost a tenet, and throughout his career he endeavored to make his French counterpart more acceptable to the Arabs.

With regard to the Arabs, Picot was guided by the memorandum of Jean Gout of the *sous-direction d'Asie* at the Quai d'Orsay. Gout maintained that concealment of the 1916 Agreement from the Syrians and the King of the Hedjaz was detrimental to French interests. Noting the preponderant British military presence in the region, the Arabs would probably veer toward them and doubt the ability of the French to protect them. Moreover, he believed that Hussein and his cohorts were lulling themselves with false hopes of resurrecting the empire of the caliphs. Hence, when they awoke to the reality, they would, Gout predicted, "blame us for the failure of their chimerical ambitions and instead of a peaceful cooperation with them, we shall be forced to act against them, perhaps even by military means. . . . Therefore," he concluded, "the moment has come that, jointly with the British, we should reveal to the Syrian leaders and to the King of the Hedjaz, what our aims are, what assistance we intend to offer, and what guarantees we are disposed to give them."[16]

The instructions that Sykes received from the Foreign Office were not as specific on this particular issue, but there was hardly any need to convince him that the Agreement should no longer be kept secret from the Syrians and the King of the Hedjaz.

Late in April, when Sykes and Picot arrived in Cairo, the British Army had suffered a serious setback on the Gaza front — the second in succession — and their joint mission to Palestine had to be shelved. They went to Jeddah instead.

Their arrival was timely, because Hussein, in the meantime, had adopted an extremist stance. The first indication of the extent of his ambitions was made when he assumed the title of "King of the Arab Nation" during his staged coronation in October 1916. Since this title also had territorial implications, the Allied Powers firmly refused to recognize him as such, addressing him merely as the "King of the Hedjaz."[17] Nonetheless, Hussein persisted in posing as the spokesman of the Arab people and "the future ruler of all Arab races." As Toynbee summed up in May 1917, "the Sherif's ambitions (both spiritual and temporal) appear to be vague but unlimited, and the British Government has been careful not to commit itself to anything beyond his sovereignty and independence of the Hedjaz itself."[18]

On 12 February 1917, Fuad al-Khatib, Hussein's Under-Secretary of State for Foreign Affairs, declared at a meeting with Hogarth in Cairo that the future Arab Kingdom ought to include Syria and Damascus. When Hogarth reminded him of French interests, especially with regard to the Syrian coast,

Fuad replied that "the Syrian interior without the coast would be of practically no value to the Arab Independent State." Nor would the King of Damascus be in a position to give up Lebanon, which was the "heart of Syria." Beirut was a commercial and cultural center, and a place where Arab ideals originated. "If the French must have something, let them take the coast northward from Junieh. Then the Arab State would have as ports Beyrout, Saida, Haifa and Jaffa."

With regard to the future of Palestine, Hogarth recorded, Fuad said that "he was in touch with a prominent Zionist and other Palestinian Jews and had full assurance of support from them. ... Arabs and Jews understood one another now," and asserted confidently that "there would be no friction."[19]

There is no hard evidence from Zionist or any other sources to corroborate Fuad's statement. That he should have referred to Jewish and Zionist support in order to buttress Arab aspirations is a matter of interest. Hogarth got the impression that Fuad was ignorant of the Allied arrangement with regard to Palestine and of the 1916 Agreement in general.[20] Clayton was also certain that Hussein himself was unaware of the terms of the 1916 Agreement and wondered "whether it would not be necessary to inform him of the general lines of that Agreement."[21]

In May 1916, British officers in Cairo unequivocally objected to Sykes's suggestion to disclose the Agreement to the Arab leaders.[22] As soon as the document reached Cairo, it came under heavy fire. Hogarth dismissed it as a "purely opportunistic measure which would offer no long-term solution." It put the British at a grave disadvantage and did not help their Arabian policy. McMahon, too, disliked the Asia Minor Agreement. Although he admitted that nothing in it conflicted with any assurances given to the Sharif, he considered it inadvisable to divulge it to the Arabs: "The moment has not yet arrived when we can safely do so without some risk of possible misinterpretation by Arabs. It might be prejudicial to our present good relations." An identical view was expressed by Captain (later Brigadier-General) Wyndham Deedes, then Intelligence Officer at Cairo Headquarters, who feared that premature disclosure might prejudice the hoped-for Arab rebellion, though he also saw no inconsistency between the Agreement and British engagements with the Sharif.

Clayton contributed two additional arguments to the armory of the objectors. First, disclosure would give an excuse to the Turkish and German propagandists to claim that the sole objective of the Allies was the division of the Ottoman Empire into war booty, in which case the Arab population would only be exchanging a Turkish and *Mohammedan* master for a *European* and *Christian* one. Second, conditions were changing so swiftly that "there can be no certainty that an agreement made today will suit the conditions of six months hence." This latter point goes far to explain Cairo's concern: disclosure, let alone its acceptance by Sharif Hussein, would have legitimized the Agreement, while secrecy held out the prospect that time would render it obsolete.[23]

However, it took the Cairo officials about ten months to realize that it was their own reasoning, not the Agreement, that was becoming obsolete. The Foreign Office was firmly committed to the Agreement and the joint mission of Sykes and Picot was designed to give it effect. (As explained already, at least as Lloyd George and his like-minded ministers and assistants were concerned, Palestine was an exception.) On the other hand, Hussein's ambitions seemed to be spiraling into a collision with the interests of the Allies. In the given circumstances, continued secrecy was bound to engender ill-will and suspicion. Both political and moral considerations called for frankness and plain talk. In mid-March, Hogarth prepared a draft of the Anglo-French-Russian Agreement to be communicated verbally to the Sultan of Egypt by the High Commissioner. In this document, Hogarth introduced the word "line" drawn from Tiberias westward, corresponding to the one along latitude 33°N. The word has caused intense hair-splitting among historians and provided fertile ground for misinterpretations; but, as already explained, Hogarth's sole purpose in using it was to delineate the British sphere of interests in southern Palestine, as well as the "Brown" zone (international) from the French sphere.[24]

It seems odd that the Sultan of Egypt, who was not concerned at all in the matter, should have been apprised of it, and not Hussein himself. The answer can perhaps be gauged from Clayton's same note; namely, that it was inappropriate to preempt the Anglo-French Mission, headed by Sykes and Picot, which was due to arrive in Cairo. It was therefore left to the Sultan's ingenuity to leak the information to Jeddah. There is no indication that the move initiated at the Residency was reported to the Foreign Office.

Clayton did not leave the matter to chance; and since, in the meantime, Hussein expressed a desire to discuss the question of Syria with C.E. Wilson, the British Representative in Jeddah, Clayton composed a comprehensive memorandum (3 April 1917), a copy of which he sent to Wilson. Reproducing the relevant section of McMahon's letter of 24 October 1915, he elucidated:

> A very important modification was made in that, while recognizing the districts of Damascus, Hama, Homs and Aleppo as Arab territory, it was expressly stated that the assurances which Great Britain was prepared to give in regard to Arab independence could only hold good in regard to those portions of the Arab territories in which Great Britain was free to act without detriment to the interests of her Ally, France. The Sherif has never been officially told of the terms of the Sykes-Picot Agreement, but it appears extremely probable that he is now to some extent aware of those terms and of the fact that those particular districts have been admitted by H.M.G. to be within the sphere of French influence. Until we are authorized to communicate to the Sherif in general terms the provisions of the Sykes-Picot Agreement it is not easy to explain to him that the districts regarding which he is evidently anxious, are outside our sphere and that it is to the French that he will have to look. He probably knows this to be the case and is therefore anxious to push the point, thinking that perhaps the matter has not yet been definitely settled and that he may secure some modification of the arrangement already come to.

Clayton presumed that the Sultan had in the meantime passed on the information which the High Commissioner had given him orally about the 1916 Agreement and added:

> Another point of importance is that no mention is made of the form which Arab independence should take, or of the nature of autonomous government which should be set up in the various districts concerned. More especially, there is no pledge whatever that all those Arab territories should come under the domination of the Sherif, and all that has hitherto been promised him in

this respect is that Great Britain would recognize him as King of the Arabs in the Hejaz.

The Sharif was the only prominent Arab with whom the Arab question could be dealt with at the time, and negotiations were therefore conducted through him; however, he "no doubt will take it to imply," Wilson was forewarned, that the British regard him as "the future ruler of all the Arab races." But, Clayton went on,

> Great Britain has never pledged herself to anything of the sort and has always treated the Sherif rather as the "Champion" (or "Spokesman") of the Arab races than as their rightful and future ruler.
>
> The only communication made by H.M.G. throughout the course of the negotiations, which could conceivably be interpreted as indicating that H.M.G. considered the Sherif as anything more than the rightful ruler of the Hejaz, is that contained in F.O. Tel. No. 303 of 31st October, 1914, conveying to Emir Abdulla a message from Lord Kitchener, in which the following words occur:
>
> "If the Arab Nation assists England in this war that has been forced upon us by Turkey, England will guarantee that no internal intervention takes place in Arabia and will give Arabs every assistance against external foreign aggression. It may be that an Arab of true race will assume the Khalifate at Mecca or Medina and so good may come by the help of God out of all the evil that is now occurring."

In order to dispel any illusions that might have lingered in Hussein's mind and to forestall any claims which he might put in the course of future negotiations, Clayton reminded Wilson of the cardinal principle of British policy in this matter:

> It is not for us to force upon the Arab races any ruler, and it is for the Sherif to make good his own position and secure for himself the choice of all the Arab peoples if he wishes to become their ruler. From the mere fact that we have recognized the independence of the Arabs it follows that we also recognize the freedom of the various Arab peoples to select their own form of independent government.[25]

Clayton's briefing proved timely, because, a few days later, when Hussein met Wilson, he accused the British of going back on their promise and of being "not perfectly open with him." He declared that he was in possession of a letter from McMahon "giving him the whole of Syria and Baghdad," and that failure to abide by this agreement would ruin his cause and force him to withdraw from the Arab movement.[26]

Clayton had anticipated some difficulties from Hussein, but the bitterness in his tone and the threatening posture came as a total surprise. In 1915-1916, during the negotiations with McMahon, it had seemed that Hussein was prepared to meet the British half way. When the first letter of 14 July 1915 proved a nonstarter, Abdullah, who wrote it, sent an oral message to Storrs emphasizing strongly the point that the restrictions "contained in his written reply [sic] should not be taken too seriously."[27] Hussein also gave the impression of being a reasonable and moderate negotiator. In his letter to Sayyid Ali al-Mirghani, the Cadi of Sudan, dated 28 December 1915, he revealed that he had raised the question of the northern frontiers merely as a "preliminary measure" and that his extensive demands originated with "the native inhabitants of those parts (concerned)."[28] Hussein's letter was written in response to al-Mirghani's letter of 17 November 1915. The latter counseled Hussein that, since the Arabian Government had not yet come into being, "discussion of the frontier question was premature."[29] Al-Mirghani also transmitted Wingate's request to remind Hussein of the nature of the reservations that McMahon had made in his letter of 24 October 1915 with regard to Syria, Palestine, and Mesopotamia.[30]

Hussein deliberately sent McMahon a copy of his letter to al-Mirghani. This made McMahon confident that the Sharif had broached the question of boundaries only as "a basis of negotiations" and that once the boundaries of the Arab Kingdom were demarcated, he would be prepared to accept "considerable modifications."[31]

However, the British misread Hussein's mind. Autocratic by nature, self-centered and impervious to advice, he was anything but moderate. He was merely biding his time. It was the Arab secret societies that exercised the most potent and lasting influence upon him. The second factor to shape his thinking was his correspondence with McMahon — not necessarily what was written there, but what he read into it.

Before the War, his ambition centered exclusively in the Hedjaz, but the visit of Fauzi Bey al-Bakri to Jeddah late in January 1915 ushered in a new era in his career. Fauzi al-Bakri was a member of a well-known family in Damascus and had been drafted by his brother Nassib into the secret society. Their father, Ata Pasha, was an old friend of Hussein. The leaders of the society charged Fauzi al Bakri with the mission of explaining to the Sharif the ideals of *al-Fatat* and to try to convince him that "the society was in a position to affect a serious revolt in Syria." Hussein was invited to take the lead. This was the kind of mission that "he had been seeking."[32] It fired his imagination.

An even stronger message was brought by Feisal following his meeting with the young Arab leaders in Damascus on 23 May 1915.[33] We know that the secret societies were only a tiny minority among the Arab population in Syria and Mesopotamia and that all their talk about a revolt against the Ottoman realm was mere fantasy, but Hussein took them seriously — perhaps too seriously. The contents, if not the language, of the so-called "Damascus Protocol" found expression in the 14 July letter which purported to represent the wishes of "the Arab nation" and demanded that England acknowledge "the independence of the Arab countries," as well as approve "the proclamation of an Arab Khalifate of Islam." How strongly he believed that he was the choice of his people for the highest office in Islam transpires from his letter to al-Mirghani of 28 December 1915, already mentioned:

> I had not claimed before [the War] to be the qualified chief of the Emirs [the Caliph] but . . . I was chosen in every quarter and even forced to take up the question of their future prospects.

This conviction was fortified by a letter he had received from al-Faruqi, dated 7 December 1915. Having identified himself as second in command to Yasin al-Hashimi and a member of the delegation that met Feisal in Damascus on 23 May 1915, al-Faruqi described how he had convinced his British interlocutors of the pervasive influence of the Young Arab societies in Syria and Mesopotamia, and that the societies aspired to form an Arab state under the leadership of the Sharif of Mecca. When the High Commissioner pointed to the reservations he had made in his letter of 24 October 1915, al-Faruqi responded, so he told Hussein, that to the best of his knowledge, and on the basis of discussions he had had with Yasin and other members of the societies, "it was impossible in any way to give up a single span of territory in Syria"; he was unaware of any land "to the west of the line Damascus-Aleppo that was not Arab"; hence, the Arab independent state should embrace Syria and Iraq and be recognized by Britain and her allies. Al-Faruqi also dwelt on the discussions he had conducted with Sir Mark Sykes, the result of which, he thought, was that the British "accepted our argument and realized that we are more useful to them than they are to us and that their interest [in the deal] is greater than ours."[34]

Needless to say, this bombastic and exaggerated testimony was far removed from reality. It will be recalled that only as a result of concessions made by al-Faruqi during his meetings with the British officers was a breakthrough possible. Reluctance to give up "a single span of territory" would have led nowhere. But al-Faruqi's concern was to improve his own standing with the Sharif, rather than stick to the facts. He also remained conspicuously silent on the Turco-German offer to the societies, which had made such an impact on the British. Was it because he feared that this particular point would cast doubt upon his credibility? Unlike the British, Hussein would have known that such a story was untrue.

Al-Faruqi was eminently successful. Hussein trusted his word and, on 1 January 1916, wrote to McMahon:

> Your honour will have realized that after the arrival of Mohammad [Faruki] Sharif . . . all our procedure up to the present was of no personal inclination or the like . . . but that everything was the result of the decisions and desires of our peoples. . . . We are but transmitters and executants.

And with regard to Syria, Hussein almost echoed al-Faruqi's language:

> It is impossible to allow any derogation [sic] that gives France, or any other Power, a span of land in those regions.

Hussein requested al-Faruqi to continue negotiations with the British authorities on his behalf[35] and, in June 1916, appointed him as his representative in Cairo.[36]

Al-Faruqi proved true to his colors. Accompanied by Jamil al-Rafi'i, his Syrian friend, who was in the employ of the British, he arrived in Jeddah on 10 June 1916. Paying fulsome praise to "our true friends the English," he reported to Clayton that the Sharif would have no difficulty in raising a force of between 160,000 to 250,000 fighters.[37] In fact, only 3,000 tribesmen loyal to Hussein joined the revolt against Turkey on 6 June 1916, while the townsmen in the Hedjaz remained quiescent.[38] Soon afterwards, al-Faruqi also reported on a revolt of the Druze in Syria under the leadership of Nuri a-Sha'lan, the powerful chief of the Ruwalla tribes.[39] The alleged "revolt" was a figment of al-Faruqi's imagination. Throughout the War, the Druze remained loyal to their Turkish overlords, even in 1917-1918, when Lawrence gave them considerable sums of money.[40]

Al-Faruqi soon quarreled with the British officers. Captain Kinahan Cornwallis of Military Intelligence and Lt. Col. C. E. Wilson, newly appointed agent in Jeddah, complained that both al-Faruqi and al-Rafai, his colleague, behaved toward them in a disrespectful and unbecoming manner. Cornwallis also discovered that al-Faruqi had fabricated a letter allegedly sent by Sharif Muhsin to Reginald Wingate requesting Wilson's recall to the Sudan. Muhsin denied any knowledge of the affair and accused al-Rafi'i and al-Faruqi of being "no better than the Turks."[41] Muhsin did not conceal his disgust with the two in front of Ruhi, then on a private intelligence mission on Storrs's behalf. Ruhi also learned from reliable sources that al-Faruqi and Jamil "were exerting their zeal to let the people here hate the English . . . I think," Ruhi observed, "that he [al-Faruqi] is a rascal [and] entirely Anglophobe."[42]

Greatly disturbed, the Residency requested that al-Faruqi and al-Rafai return to Cairo immediately. But here al-Faruqi's diplomatic misadventures did not come to an end. By then appointed as the Sharif's official representative, he tried to please his master by reporting on events that had never taken place. Perhaps the most sensational was contained in a cable, dated 10 July 1916, in which he reported that he had suggested to the High Commissioner that the British Government bestow upon the Sharif the title of "King of the Arabs," and that the High Commissioner had accepted the idea.[43]

Hussein coveted this title and, through Abdullah's instrumentality, Hussein was proclaimed "King of the Arab Lands" (*malik al-bilab al-bilah al-arabiyya*) on 29 October 1916. As mentioned earlier, the Allies rejected this title and addressed him merely as the King of the Hedjaz. Bewildered by the supposed inconsistency, Hussein complained to Wilson of the British change of heart, since formerly they had addressed him as caliph, a title which was superior to king. Wilson thereupon contacted Abdullah and the latter admitted that the British had never addressed his father officially as either king or caliph; only once had they used the phrase, as he put it, "We hope that [the] caliph be in your noble fold." As McMahon guessed correctly, Abdullah was referring to Lord Kitchener's letter of 31 October 1914, which contained the following sentence: "It may be that an Arab of true race will assume the Khalifate at Mecca and Medina." However, this pious expression of goodwill could hardly have provided the Sharif with any justifiable basis for his grossly inflated claim. Upon investigation, it was finally discovered that the culprit responsible for the misunderstanding was no other than al-Faruqi.[44] McMahon reported to Grey:

> [al-Faruqi] was in the habit — with the view doubtless of enhancing his importance — of occasionally reporting to the Sherif the purport of imaginary interviews with me and others that never took place. These came to our notice through the interception in transmission of cypher telegrams between him and the Sherif. Thus we found that on July 10th Faroki in a telegram to the Sherif said, *inter alia* "I have discussed with the high commissioner regarding the title of King of the Arabs and I saw him willing to admit this idea with the greatest facility." No such discussion ever took place. Incidentally, Faroki was in Cairo and I in Alexandria . . . [45]

Al-Faruqi's stock depreciated drastically, and, in view of the undesirability and danger of some further flights of imagination of this kind, McMahon welcomed Hussein's suggestion that he communicate directly through Wilson.[46] In December 1916, when Storrs went to Jeddah to remove any misunderstanding, "owing to irresponsible statements by Faroki," Hussein told him unequivocally that he was "far from satisfied with the person of Faroki as his Cairo representative," and wished to appoint another whom the British were at liberty to choose in his place.[47]

However, it was al-Faruqi's association with Rashid Ridā, as well as his own misdemeanors, that caused his final downfall. Mohammad Rashid Ridā was a theologian and publicist, subsequently a politician of note, who made his mark on Pan-Arab and Pan-Islamic thought. He was one of the founding fathers of the Decentralization Party and persistently stressed Arab loyalty to the Ottoman State. He accused the European imperialists of fomenting Arab separatism.[48] He impressed Sykes when the latter met him in July 1915, as an "uncompromising, fanatical Moslem." For Ridā, Turkey symbolized Mohammedan independence, but should the Ottoman army be defeated, he thought it would be necessary to set up instead "an absolutely independent" Arab-Moslem state stretching from the northern borders of Syria and Mesopotamia down to Arabia. He refused to entertain the idea of control by European powers or the appointment of European advisers exercising authority: "The Arabs could easily manage their own affairs."[49]

Intrigued by al-Faruqi's negotiations with the High Commissioner, Ridā pressed the Residency to show him the letter to Hussein of 24 October 1915. When a résumé of it was shown to him, he complained about its ambiguity, especially with regard to Syria, and remarked that most of its clauses stood "in flat contradiction to the proposals which the Arabs had put forward."[50]

In October 1916, Ridā went on a pilgrimage to Mecca. No sooner had he arrived there than an acrimonious quarrel erupted between him and King Hussein. The reasons were both ideological and personal: Hussein had rejected Ridā's request to be appointed Shaykh al-Islam in Mecca. On his return to Cairo, Ridā launched a blistering attack on Hussein, accusing him of becoming subservient to a non-Muslim power and characterizing his revolt against Turkey as "the worst disaster that has befallen Islam in this age." England was "the enemy of Islam"; "The British Government," he wrote, "has taken upon itself to destroy the religion of Islam . . . after destroying its temporal rule."51

These attacks, coming in quick succession, precipitated an irreparable rift between the two leaders. Consequently, Hussein banned *al-Manār*, Ridā's journal in the Hedjaz, and requested al-Faruqi to avoid having contact with him — a request that did not seem to have been complied with.52

Toward the end of August, Hussein received more bad news. In the opinion of British officials in Cairo, sentiment among Moslems toward himself and the Arab Movement in general had worsened perceptibly. And with regard to al-Faruqi, Wilson observed:

> From all I heard in Egypt, I regret to inform Your Highness that I do not think Your Highness's present representative in Egypt is at all suitable for the honourable position he holds, and I regret to say that I do not think he is doing Your Highness's cause any good, but on the contrary, is doing harm and part of the present feelings of Moslems in Egypt may be attributed to him.
>
> It is well known in Cairo that he is entirely under the influence of Rashid Rida and several well-known Syrian Arabs on this account do not like to have much to do with him. He is also, I am informed on good authority, too fond of the society of women of a certain class, which does not bring credit on Your Highness's Agency in Cairo, or make him respected as I consider Your Highness's Representative should be.53

Al-Faruqi was unceremoniously dismissed and his inglorious career terminated. The French representative in Jeddah attributed his dismissal to his unbecoming lifestyle, drunkenness, and the company of an Italian mistress, whereas de St. Quentin, the Military Attaché in Cairo, thought that he was "an intriguer and not popular among respected Moslem circles."54

Al-Faruqi's dismissal followed al-Misri's stormy departure.55 It is worth recalling that Yasin al-Hashimi, al-Faruqi's mentor and with whom the idea of friendship with Britain originated, continued to serve faithfully in the Ottoman army as a high-ranking officer, as did General Ali Ridā al-Rikabi, and other leading Young Arabs who survived Djemal Pasha's punitive measures.

Misled and betrayed by the leaders of the secret societies, and with the general uprising in the Fertile Crescent failing to

materialize, Hussein's status, bestowed upon him so grandiloquently by the same leaders, lapsed — the implication being
that his claim to territories outside his realm in the Hedjaz was
severely undermined, if not nullified.

Hussein was also greatly embarrassed by the universal con-
demnation of his fellow Moslems, who accused him of siding
with the infidel against a Moslem power. Logically such a setback should have sobered him and caused him to revise his
objectives; that is, to concentrate on building a viable Hedjaz
state instead of aspiring to the leadership of a nonexistent Pan-
Arab entity. However, Hussein was anything but a pragmatist.
What he did was just the opposite: to vindicate his revolt in the
eyes of his co-religionists, he reverted to his original territorial
claims and accused the British of defaulting on their "agreement" with him.

Hussein showed his hand first in April 1917, during a
meeting with Wilson, when he complained that the British were
going back on their promises. He declared that he was in possession of a letter from McMahon "giving him the whole of Syria
and Mesopotamia."[56] This extraordinary claim caused considerable perplexity in Cairo. Hussein produced no document to
substantiate his claim, and Clayton was at a loss to fathom
Hussein's unexpected change of heart. He attributed the misunderstanding to a possible mistranslation into Arabic of the
letter of 24 October. Clayton revealed his predicament to
Wilson:

> I cannot make out what the Sherif means by his interpretations
> of McMahon's letter. I have not yet succeeded in unearthing from
> the Residency files a copy of the original Arabic which was sent,
> but it is there somewhere and must be produced. I cannot imagine
> that any ambiguity can have produced the meaning which the
> Sherif has read into it and I can only think that, being very
> nervous, he is trying to do a bit of a bluff. His refusal to send
> extracts of the letters he quotes rather gives colour to this.[57]

Storrs, at that time on a mission in Basra, was contacted by
cable, but could recall no errors in Ruhi's translation and advised the Residency to examine his file which contained all the
correspondence.[58] However, a further search for a copy of this

particular document proved fruitless, and it was only in October 1919 that A. Keown-Boyd, the Oriental Secretary (Storrs's successor), found it caught in the back of a drawer in Storrs's desk. Examination of it both in Cairo and Jeddah by Colonel Vickery showed that the Arabic version of the letter of 24 October 1915 faithfully conveyed McMahon's intention. It was also Vickery who was the first British official to discover that Hussein was basing his claims on an entirely different letter.[59] Until then, the British officials felt uneasy.

Late in April, Abdullah repeated the claim, albeit without much conviction, that his father considered that "he had been promised the whole of Syria." However, when pressed by Wilson, Abdullah admitted that this was not the case.[60]

The letter on which Hussein was in fact basing his claims was not that of 24 October 1915, but one dated 10 March 1916. In 1919, during the Peace Conference in Paris, much to the British Government's surprise, Emir Feisal, on his father's behalf, quoted McMahon's letter of 10 March 1916 as proof that the latter had granted his father all his territorial demands, as well as Arab independence.[61] In this letter, McMahon had assured Hussein that the British Government had approved his requests for the supply of gold, arms, munitions, and food, but Hussein misapplied the wording to political claims on which no agreement had been reached in 1915-1916. He also misquoted McMahon by prefixing the word "all." A careful word-for-word examination is therefore necessary to ascertain whether Hussein had any grounds for his far-reaching claims and whether there was any room for a genuine misunderstanding.

It will be recalled that Hussein's letter of 18 February 1916, in which he expressed his "utmost pleasure and satisfaction at the attainment of the required understanding," terminated the discussion on political matters, and no reference to the vexed issue of frontiers was made. Subsequently, correspondence centered exclusively on money, supply of arms, munitions, and food. McMahon felt able to confirm to Grey that "the Sherif considers that negotiations are now complete and that time for action on his part has arrived."[62]

On 4 March 1916, Hussein told McMahon that, in view of the impending uprising against the Turks, it would be necessary to equip a large number of recruits:

And since [he emphasized], the country is ready and able to contribute more than a quarter of a million men from the districts which are connected with us only, there is no objection to arrangements being made for a considerable number of arms . . . to be kept in reserve as a precautionary measure in case of necessity. There is no need to repeat what is required in such operations in the way of money, stores [and] ammunition . . . [63]

This was good news, particularly as the prospect of the rising in Syria seemed to be fading. The figure of a quarter of a million of men ready to join the Sharifian force was grossly inflated, but at long last McMahon was relieved that at least in the Hedjaz the long-awaited rebellion was about to materialize. He responded promptly. On 10 March 1916, he wrote to Hussein:

I am pleased to inform you that His Majesty's Government have approved of meeting your requests [referring to gold, food, arms, etc.] and that which you ask to be sent with all haste is being dispatched . . . [64]

Several days later the Residency cabled to Hussein:

The arms, munitions and supplies promised in our letter of 10 March have been placed with the government of Port Sudan, and are now at Your Highness's disposal . . . [65]

Hussein acknowledged the receipt of McMahon's letter dated 10 March 1916, "together with the sum demanded," and added:

We have also noted the approval and acceptance of the British Government of all our demands mentioned in our letter dated 14 Rabi Tani [i.e., 4 March 1916], and the preparation of all other materials demanded in our letter in the place named awaiting our demand.[66]

At the Foreign Office, the word "demand" raised some eyebrows and a query was cabled to Cairo: "Is phrase 'our demands' in Sherif's letter correctly translated? It seems unfortunate to allow Sherif to think that he can impose his demands on H.M.G." In Storrs's absence, Lt. Colonel Parker of the Intelligence Section of the General Staff enlightened the Residency that, in his correspondence, Hussein used the words *talibat* and *matlub* interchangeably, which could be translated by "requests" just as well as by "demands." Parker did not consider the matter to be of the "slightest importance," as the meaning of the Sharif's letter was obvious, especially when read in context. In the meantime, at the Foreign Office end, an Arabic linguist also examined the text and commented: "The original Arabic does not in any way signify imposing of demands."[67]

From the above exchange, it is quite evident that the phrase "His Majesty's Government have approved of meeting your requests" in McMahon's letter of 10 March 1916 referred exclusively to the gold, food, arms, and munitions which had been requested by Hussein on 4 March, and had no political implications whatsoever. It is also crystal clear that this was how Hussein himself understood the letter at the time. What grounds he had for misapplying it to political demands is anybody's guess; though, in view of his habitual misinterpretation of documents, the matter is not too surprising. He read into documents what he wanted to read and believed in what was convenient for him to believe. He disliked taking advice, let alone accepting criticism, and kept McMahon's letters in a closely guarded chest, refusing to show them even to his own advisers and members of his family. The limits between fact and fiction were often blurred in his mind. These circumstances provided fertile ground on which a comfortable illusion that all his original territorial demands had finally been acceded to could flourish in Hussein's mind. It became almost an article of faith to which he firmly adhered practically to the end of his life.

It was necessary to deal with this issue, since it had a direct bearing on Hussein's conversations with Sykes and Picot when they were in Jeddah. It also lay at the bottom of his fatal misunderstanding with the British Government.

6

A Fatal Misunderstanding

There is no way of knowing how accurately the Sultan of Egypt apprised Hussein about the Anglo-French Agreement. Whatever the case, Hussein was "in a very uneasy frame of mind," Clayton wrote to Wilson:

> I cannot help thinking that, knowing as he does "that some arrangement" has been made with the French, and unaware of the exact terms thereof, he is fearing the worst and thinks that we have given everything away. ...He has of course interpreted our assurances to him in a way for which there is no sort of warrant, but this is not unnatural, as he no doubt feels it necessary to push us as hard as he can.

Clayton was confident that, when Wilson met Sykes, Wilson would realize that the terms of the agreement with Picot "are a good deal better" than it was thought at the time, and "that King Hussein too will be relieved at finding the arrangement much more favourable than he had feared." Sykes planned to point out to the King those areas that would be reserved: the "Blue," under French, the "Red" under British, and the "Brown" under international control. In the Vilayet of Baghdad, where Britain had some vital interests, special measures would be undertaken to ensure British "military and political predominance . . . for a considerable time."

Another important point that Sykes intended to impress on Hussein was that, although the British had recognized "the principle of Arab independence," the British Government had in no way pledged themselves to impose upon various Arab communities any particular form of government, or any particular ruler. . . . We should welcome the gradual extension of the Sherif's authority and shall do our best to help him in every possible way, but we cannot impose him upon unwilling communities.

This was particularly the case with regard to Mesopotamia, where, according to Sykes, the Arab Movement, as represented by Hussein, had no influence, and it would have therefore been counterproductive to impose him on the native population.[1]

Before going to Jeddah, Sykes had three meetings with the Syrian representatives in Cairo. Among those whom he met were Rafik Bey el-Azm, Muktar Bey el-Sulh, and Hassan Bey Hamada.[2] Picot conducted separate discussions. The result of these meetings was that the Syrians agreed to Franco-British tutelage of an Arab State or Confederation of States in areas "A" and "B," and to military protection and the employment of French and British financial and political advisers in their respective spheres of interest. No objection was raised to "a permanent military occupation" of Baghdad by Britain, or to a similar status for France in the Syrian littoral. With regard to Palestine, the delegates agreed that this area presented "too many international problems for a new and weak state such as the Arab must be to assume responsibility for . . . but that in the event of Jews being recognized as a Millet or 'Nation' in Palestine . . . actual [non-Jewish] population must have equal recognition."[3] Considering the Syrian nationalists' propensity for extremism, this was a successful outcome. The Syrians recognized the special position of Palestine and were prepared to accept a status of equality for the native Arabic-speaking population there, should the Jews be accorded special privileges for immigration and colonization. Sykes's line of argument is spelled out in a note written more than a year later:

> Palestine and Syria must be separate. It is inconceivable that an infant Syrian State should be able to cope with Palestinian problems. Palestine is of international interest to the followers of three great international religions and must be treated as such. ... In talking both to the King of the Hedjaz, to Emir Feisal, and to

Syrian intellectuals I have always found the following argument effective: "You have in view the ultimate emancipation and freedom of Syria from all tutelage and protection . . . but can you expect that the world will let you manage your own affairs without interference, if the Government of Syria is responsible for Jerusalem, Bethlehem . . . and the Jewish colonies? If you have Palestine as a part of Syria, the various elements interested in Palestine will undoubtedly control your affairs."

Picot's arrival in Egypt caused Hussein considerable anxiety and he wished to see Sir Mark Sykes. "I consider very necessary," Wingate wired the Foreign Office, "that Sherif of Mecca be now informed of general lines of our agreement with the French regarding Syria." The Foreign Office approved promptly.[5] On the following day, Wingate wired again: "I will instruct Sir Mark Sykes . . . to reassure King Hussein in regard to French aims in interior of Syria." Picot agreed to leave the matter in Sykes's hands. Moreover, Sykes was also to reaffirm the Allies' determination to support Arab aspirations, but to make it clear that the British would retain such military and political predominance in Baghdad and adjacent districts as their strategic and commercial interests would require. Hussein was also to be told that extension of his dominion beyond Hedjaz was dependent on his acceptance by the native peoples concerned.[6]

Sykes did not require any instructions from Wingate. He was superior in status and in any case intended to convey to Hussein the same message that he had delivered to the Syrian notables a few days earlier.

Sykes left Egypt for Jeddah on 1 May and on his way called on Feisal at Wejh. Feisal's misgivings were set at rest by Sykes's explanation of the nature of the Anglo-French Agreement and its relation to the Arab Confederation. "After much argument," Sykes cabled, "he accepted [in] principle and seemed satisfied." The interview with Hussein on 5 May went off equally well. Hussein was anxious lest French annexation of Syria would expose him to the charge of having led the Syrian Moslems into rebellion against the Turks only "to hand them over to a Christian Power," but Sykes reassured him. "In accordance with my instructions I explained fully the [Inter-Allied] agreement regarding the Arab Confederation or State. The King seemed relieved." Sykes also impressed on him the importance of the Franco-Arab settlement and at last got him to admit, but only after a very lengthy argument, that it was essential to Arab development in Syria.

This was a noteworthy feat which only a skillful diplomat like Sykes could have accomplished; however, Sykes credited Feisal with paving the way in a personal letter to his father. Sykes asked Wingate to tell Picot that he was satisfied with his interviews with Feisal and Hussein, "as they both now stand at the same point as was reached at our last joint meeting with the three Syrian delegates in Cairo" and that the King had expressed "an earnest desire" to meet Picot as well.[7]

Writing to Storrs, Clayton confirmed: "He [Hussein] has also been told of the general tenor of our arrangements with the French which I think has relieved his mind, as he was obviously under the impression that their intentions were for annexation on a very considerable scale."[8]

There is no indication in Sykes's cables if the question of Palestine was also discussed, but the cryptic references that he had reached "the same point" with Feisal and Hussein as he had with the Syrian delegates in Cairo, and his note of 2 August 1918 already quoted, suggest that he did. At any rate, unlike Syria, Palestine did not seem to cause Hussein much concern.

Before the second round of meetings with Hussein, Sykes and Picot conferred on their own (17 May) in order to synchronize policy. They agreed that, if the future prosperity and peaceable development of the Arabic-speaking areas was to be ensured, any inter-Power rivalry had to be eliminated. Moreover, if the Arab politicians, "versed in the arts of promoting dissension," realized that the Powers concerned were united, "they will not be tempted to endeavour to play one power against the other." Therefore, despite wide socioeconomic differences between the "Blue" zone, to be controlled by France, and the "Red" zone, to be controlled by Britain, they agreed that an identical system of administration should be adopted. The same principle should be applied to the respective spheres of interests, "A" (French) and "B" (British), which had been marked for Arab independence. In these areas both French and British advisers "should have executive authority ... and should have fixed terms of office" for about twenty-five years, to ensure the smooth running of Arab governments, and their inhabitants should be encouraged to look to the King of the Hedjaz and his successors as the titular suzerain of the Arab State or Confederation of States.9

Having reached unanimity, Sykes and Picot proceeded to Jeddah. The meeting with Hussein took place on May 19, with Feisal and Fuad al-Khatib acting as interpreters. The King admitted the Arabs' inability to achieve anything without Allied help and appealed for their close cooperation in the realization of Arab aspirations. Picot responded affirmatively and observed that France intended to assist militarily on the Syrian littoral in the same way as Britain was fighting to liberate Mesopotamia. The King did not seem to have liked this idea and repeated the argument that "he would not be a party to proceedings purporting to hand over Moslems to direct rule of a non-Moslem State." As the matter concerned Franco-Arab relations exclusively, Sykes withdrew.[10]

Hussein thereupon told Picot that he considered himself responsible for the Syrian people. Before his rebellion against Turkey, he claimed, he had received numerous letters from "leaders from all classes," some of whom also came to see him personally. All of them had proclaimed their allegiance to him and some had expressed the wish that he became their Khalifa. They had repeated their allegiance to him in 1915 when Feisal met them in Damascus. Now Moslems under Turkish influence were accusing him of selling Syria to the French. If Syria became French, his prestige would suffer irreparably. The same, he asserted, applied to the Lebanon. "If you take [it] . . . you will torture me but will gain nothing. Let the people themselves decide on their destiny."[11]

Hussein's declaration to Picot was as presumptuous as it was untrue. Those who had sworn allegiance to him were not "the leaders of all classes," as he had claimed, but members of the secret societies which constituted only a tiny minority. Nor did Hussein reveal that they had since deserted him and that, by and large, the Syrians sided with the Turks.

In all likelihood, Picot took Hussein's statement with a pinch of salt but prudently avoided a debate. When Sykes reentered the room, he proposed that France enjoy the same status on the Syrian littoral as the British did in the Baghdad Vilayet. This, it will be recalled, was in line with what Picot had agreed two days earlier with Sykes; that is, to adopt an identical policy in the "Blue" and "Red" areas to be controlled by the two Powers. Picot repeated the offer twice, but the King vehemently rejected it. Thereupon Sykes brought up the subject of departmental advisers and pointed to the importance of their having executive authority; otherwise, he stated, "Arab rule will be helpless and corrupt," whereas areas under European administration it would prosper. The King disliked the idea, but subsequently admitted, albeit reluctantly, that this might be the case. The interview closed "most inconclusively, Monsieur Picot being unfavourably impressed by the King."[12]

Picot's version of this interview is slightly different. He declared that, subject to conditions of the war, his Government was determined to give Syria "the same efficacious help as the British were providing in Iraq and Baghdad" and "through the occupation of the coast . . . to facilitate the eventual liberation of the Arab races, which is the goal of our efforts." In an oblique rebuke to the King, he pointedly remarked that, on the Syrian coast, the local population would welcome the French presence. The discussion lasted for over three hours in a confused and disjointed manner (*assez nettement fâcheuse*).[13]

On the following day (20 May), the meeting went off much better. In addition to Feisal and Fuad, Colonel Wilson was present. This time the King was forthcoming and amiable. Reaffirming his confidence in Britain, he stated that he would be content if the French pursued the same policy toward Arab aspirations in the Syria littoral as the British did in Baghdad. Picot received this statement well and relations became cordial. Before the meeting broke up, Feisal gave Sykes a separate message from his father that restated the King's position that he was ready to co-operate "to the fullest extent" with both France about Syria and England about Mesopotamia, but asking for help vis-à-vis Idrissi and Ibn Saud. "We beg that Great Britain will endeavour to induce them to recognize the King's position as the leader of the Arab movement."[14]

A manifesto signed by Feisal, as Commander of the Arab Forces, and King Hussein was thereafter issued to the Arabs in Syria promising to deliver them from Turkish tyranny. It acknowledged British support of the Arab revolt and thanked the French Government for joining England in recognizing Arab independence. "Our duty," the manifesto stated, "compels us to offer the necessary guarantees for the rights of these two Great Powers," and "when the war is over, their men and money will help us to reform our country which has been ruined by those [Turkish] tyrants."[15]

In spite of earlier arguments, Picot had reason to feel satisfied. Relations with the Arab leaders improved dramatically, and, contrary to what might have been expected, Hussein did not seem to be overly concerned with the terms of the Anglo-French Agreement when these were disclosed to him.[16] Moreover, Hussein's declaration of 20 May was seen by Picot as an implicit recognition of Anglo-French parity with regard to the future disposition of Turkey-in-Asia in the aftermath of the War. Picot was particularly delighted at so successfully linking France's status in the Syrian littoral with that of Britain in Baghdad Vilayet. That Hussein agreed, albeit reluctantly, to the appointment of advisers with executive authority in areas "A" and "B" was another tangible achievement.[17]

The latter concession by Hussein was extracted by Sykes.[18] It showed that, whenever the Allied Powers were united, the Arabs fell into line. Both Sykes and Picot gained the impression that Hussein endorsed the Agreement named after them.

Picot's report was received by the Quai d'Orsay with considerable relief. Note was taken of Picot's statement that King Hussein had been told of the Anglo-French Agreement, and that it "did not disturb him as much as had been feared." No less satisfactory was the endorsement of an operational mechanism assuring France's parity with England. Concern was expressed with regard to the newly-introduced term "Moslem Syria,"[19] but this was overshadowed by Picot's overall achievement.

The only person who was unhappy was Wilson. He was not present during the early meetings with Hussein and, by his own admission, was ill-informed about the proceedings. During his stay in Jeddah, Wilson, a fervent partisan of Hussein, had developed an exaggerated notion of Hussein's importance for British interests. On 24 May, he wrote to Clayton,

> Although Sykes and Picot were very pleased at this happy result and the Sherif had made the proposition himself I did not

feel happy in my own mind and it struck me as possible that the Sherif, one of the most courteous of men, absolutely loyal to us and with complete faith in Great Britain, was verbally agreeing to a thing which he never would agree if he knew our interpretation of what the Iraq situation is to be.[20]

Late in April, he had been assured by Clayton that, Sykes, when in Jeddah, would explain exactly how matters stood with regard to the agreement with the French, as represented here by Picot; but, to his dismay, he found himself treated by Sykes in a rather off-hand and cavalier way. He also strongly suspected that Sykes had not revealed to Hussein the nature of British policy in Baghdad Vilayet (the "Red" zone), *viz.*, that British "military and political predominance must be ensured . . . for a considerable time."[21] No other explanation was possible, Wilson thought, for Hussein's concurrence with Picot's formula of linking France's status in the Syrian littoral to that of Britain in Baghdad. He went on:

> As you know I have all along been a strong advocate of being as open as possible with the Sherif. My considered opinion is that we have not been as open and frank as we should have been at this last meeting.
>
> Special representatives of Great Britain and France came expressly to fix things up with the Sherif and when the latter agreed to France having the same status in Syria as we are to have in Iraq surely the main points of our agreement re Iraq should have been stated to prevent all chance of a misunderstanding which might have far reaching consequences.
>
> What made me feel that the Sherif and Picot had different ideas as to what the position of France in Syria was to be was:
> 1. That the Sherif agreed to France in Syria being in the same position as we in Iraq.
> 2. That Picot was so obviously delighted at getting the Sherif to verbally agree to this.

Wilson thought that, by persuading Hussein to accept the formula, Sykes had "undoubtedly taken a very heavy responsibility on his shoulders," and observed:

> I feel very strongly that the Sherif should be told exactly what our interpretation is of our future position in Iraq which position

has every right to be much more prominent than that of the French in Syria.

From George Lloyd I gather that Baghdad will almost certainly be practically British; if this is so then I consider that we have not played a straightforward game with a courteous old man who is, as Sykes agrees, one of Great Britain's most sincere and loyal admirers, for it means that the Sherif [agreed] verbally to Syria being practically French which I feel sure he never meant to do.

I must say that I think Sykes did wonderfully well in succeeding in getting the Sherif and Picot, outwardly anyhow, on friendly terms; he has had a most difficult task but I cannot help regretting exceedingly that the opportunity of the meeting was not seized upon to clear up all possible misunderstandings.

Shortly before Sykes left for Aden, he asked Wilson if he thought that the meeting with Hussein was satisfactory. Wilson responded, rather meekly, that since all agreed that it was, he too thought that "it was satisfactory."[22] And yet, on the same day he wrote the opposite to Clayton.

Lt. Colonel Newcombe, on the staff of the British Military Mission to the Hedjaz, shared Wilson's misgivings: "The Sherif agreed to the Syrian coast being governed by the French on the same terms as Baghdad by the British, having no idea what the latter are . . . and gave his consent owing to his faith in Sir Mark Sykes." Newcombe confirmed that Hussein had been apprised of the Sykes-Picot Agreement, but regretted that no copy of this document had been left with him.[23]

On the latter point, Newcombe proved right, but, on the whole, both he and Wilson were under a misapprehension. Captain George Lloyd, who served on Military Intelligence under Clayton (in the late thirties, Colonial Secretary), was superior to them both in judgment and information. He accompanied Sykes and Picot throughout their trip and, unlike Newcombe and Wilson, had a good rapport with them. He learned from Sykes that, during his earlier visit to Jeddah, it had been made clear to the Sharif that, although the British were anxious to see the establishment of "a form of Arab Government in Baghdad," he should be in no doubt about the permanency of their military occupation:

The fact that Baghdad had been used as the base of offensive[s] against us, no less than the assurance of our economic interests, demanded that the British military occupation should be recognized as a permanence.

In this interview, however, Sir Mark Sykes went further and explained to the Grand Sherif that we considered that this Arab Government, if and when set up, must be furnished by us with advisers and that those advisers must be given executive authority. To this the Sherif made considerable demur, but he eventually reluctantly gave his consent.[24]

On his return journey Sykes made a brief stop-over in Cairo. Reassured, Clayton hastened to lay Wilson's fears at rest:

I understood verbally from Sir Mark Sykes that he made it clear to the Sherif that a further large measure of control and also British military occupation would be necessary in Iraq for some considerable time to come, and this is most undoubtedly true.[25]

So, the question which inescapably comes to mind is: if Hussein knew the British position with regard to the Baghdad Vilayet, what made him consent to Picot's formula on the following day? In order to appreciate what in fact did happen and fathom Hussein's sudden volte face, it is necessary to consult Fuad al-Khatib's report in this matter. It is a unique document which illuminates the working of his master's mind.

When negotiations with Hussein reached a deadlock during the first meeting (19 May), Sykes summoned al-Khatib and urged him to prevail upon the King to become more pliant. It took al-Khatib about three hours to elicit a response. Hussein declared that he trusted Sykes because, in political matters, the British Commissioner could stand up for the Arabs better than himself, and, having the backing of the British Government, "is able to carry out his promises." However, with regard to France, Hussein's suspicions remained deep-seated, and al-Khatib experienced the greatest difficulty in persuading him to conclude a deal with the French Commissioner. Then, out of the blue, it was Hussein himself who seemed to have resolved the difficulty, exclaiming: "I have in my pocket a letter from Sir Henry McMahon which promises me all I wish . . . I know the British Government will fulfill her word." He was confident that Baghdad was "entirely his" and, therefore, by implication, the

Syrian littoral would also fall into the same category.

Al-Khatib was very much taken aback by this unexpected revelation, commenting:

> Neither I nor any one of the King's sons have seen this letter and no one besides the King knows what these promises are, but he always told us that everything as regards Baghdad is excellent.
>
> The danger therefore is that the King has a fixed idea of the meaning of this letter which may possibly differ from that held by the British Government and hence also from the interpretation given by the French Government.

Al-Khatib thought that it was imperative that the British clarify the meaning of McMahon's letter, as, otherwise, the King might at a later date consider, "rightly or wrongly, that he had been deceived."[26]

Hence, it was not "as a result of Sykes's intervention and in exchange for his promises" that Hussein changed his mind,[27] nor was it al-Khatib who managed to convince the sovereign (although he took credit for it). It was the King himself who, in the course of the conversation, convinced himself that, after all, by accepting Picot's suggestion, he could only gain.

During the second meeting (20 May), to everybody's surprise, al-Khatib went on, the King turned to Picot and, with a glimmer of irony, exclaimed: "I heard yesterday that you want to be the same in Syria as the British in Baghdad." A declaration was read out indicating the King's concurrence with Picot's formula. When the meeting ended, al-Khatib tried to seclude himself with Sykes, presumably to reveal his feelings of unease, but the King ordered him to say nothing more.[28]

At Wilson's urging, al-Khatib went to Cairo to alert the Residency of the undesirable consequences of the possible misunderstanding. He took with him Wilson's letter to Clayton of 24 May, already quoted. In its latter part, Wilson re-echoed al-Khatib's anxiety:

> The Sherif has gone trumps on a letter he has from Sir Henry McMahon the contents of which are unknown to Fuad or Feisal or any one of the Sherif's advisers.
>
> My fear is that the Sherif has possibly put one construction on the contents of this letter and we another. If this turns out to be

the case a very serious and awkward situation will certainly arise (particularly as we are unable to produce our copy which I understand has not yet been found). The Sherif's faith in us will have gone . . .

And after some reflection Wilson asked rhetorically: "Is the Sherif living in a fool's paradise? If so, he will have a very rude awakening . . ."[29]

Wilson thus produced two self-contradictory analyses: in the first part of his letter he wondered whether Sykes had been straightforward with Hussein, and in the second part pointed his finger at Hussein for living, as he termed it, in "a fool's paradise."[30] It did not take him long to realize that the second assumption was the correct one.

Clayton did not share Wilson's suspicion of Sykes:

> The Sherif is pinning his faith [he told Sykes] on a letter from Sir Henry McMahon which he states is in his possession, and which gives him all the assurances he wants. We have never seen this letter, but if it is the one originally sent defining the future arrangements regarding Baghdad, it seems very probable that the letter has either been badly translated or that the Sherif has an erroneous impression of the meaning of its contents.

Colonel Wilson's fears, Clayton went on, were that Hussein would accuse the British sometime in the future of a breach of faith.[31]

Wingate too had full confidence in Sykes. After Sykes's first visit to Wejh and Jeddah, Wingate gleefully told Lt.-General Robertson, the Chief of the Imperial General Staff, that, at a meeting with King Hussein, Sykes "outlined the arrangements made with the French regarding the future of Syria" and that "the interview seemed to have passed off as well as, or [even] better than, could be expected."[32]

About four weeks after Sykes's departure from Jeddah, Wilson learned from Feisal that his father had not understood the matter which Sykes and Picot had discussed with him during their visit in Jeddah. Wilson's suspicions of Sykes now completely evaporated. He thought that Sykes should send the King a *note verbale* of their meetings as "a proof that [British] policy has been communicated and discussed" with him. "It is very important," he added, "to give the Sherif no ostensibly good grounds on which he might make Common Cause with the Turks."[33]

Clayton held separate conversations with al-Khatib from which "it appears almost certain," he wrote to Sykes, "that the Sherif has not at all understood the situation, as explained to him by you and Picot, regarding the future of Syria and Iraq":

> He seems under the fixed impression [Clayton went on] that both will fall to him unconditionally and has given this out publicly. Of course, he may be bluffing but when it comes to the point he will inevitably maintain that his version of the interview is the correct one, and we have never given him anything in writing to the contrary.

Clayton, too, thought it advisable for Sykes to send Hussein an *aide memoire*.[34] This was all the more important since Hogarth had obtained "ample evidence" of an irrefutable nature that Hussein, "if he had ever really understood what the Commissioner said to him . . . was in no way minded to observe either the letter or the spirit of the agreement to which he was understood to have consented."[35]

A. P. Albina, a Christian Arab and Sykes's agent, interviewed al-Khatib separately. Albina was not at all surprised to hear about King Hussein's incomprehension. Nonetheless, that he should have misunderstood statements of such importance discussed with him at length both by Sykes and Picot seemed to be "hardly credible." Nor did Hussein try to discuss the issue with Feisal and al-Khatib, to whom the meaning of Picot's formula was perfectly clear.

Albina accompanied the Anglo-French team and reminded Sykes that, during the second visit to the Hedjaz, he had suggested that Picot submit in writing his Government's program concerning the future status of the Syrian littoral for King Hussein's consideration and thereafter iron out an agreement. To his dismay, Picot rejected this method and preferred to leave the matter in abeyance until after French military operations in Syria had concluded. However, "as it happened," Albina commented, "Turkish training and cunning got the best of King Hussein, and he is now ready to swear (with a mental reservation) by Allah and his Prophet, that French occupation of the Syrian littoral was never discussed." One reason for Hussein's intransigence was, Albina reasoned, his universal unpopularity amongst the Moslems. "If he publicly or tacitly consents to let the French occupy the littoral of Syria, he will be branded as a traitor to the Arab nation and Islam, and will lose his power and prestige."[36]

Sykes considered Albina's report to be of such importance that he found it necessary to reproduce it verbatim among Cabinet papers.[37] It apparently did not occur to him even at this juncture that both Picot and he himself had committed a major miscalculation in not leaving Hussein a memorandum on the result of their mission to Jeddah. It soon became clear that Hussein was taking full advantage of their omission. On 29 July, he told Lawrence that no written document had been given to him and declared triumphantly that he had trapped Picot into admitting that France would be satisfied with a parallel position in Syria to that which Great Britain desired in Iraq. Hedjaz and Syria, he declared, "are like the palm and fingers of one hand." He would not permit any French annexation of Beirut and the Lebanon either: "They are Arab countries [which] deserved independence and it is my duty to see that they get it."[38]

However, as events showed, it was not Picot who had been trapped. The British had no intention of abandoning Mesopotamia which Hussein hoped would be only temporarily occupied, and the French therefore saw no reason to curb their own ambitions in Syria. This was the origin of the conflict between the Sharifians and the French after the War, with its grim outcome for Feisal's Government in Damascus in July 1920.

To Wingate, such an interpretation of McMahon's letter of 24 October 1915 was completely "unjustifiable"; he found it incredible that King Hussein could nourish such illusions. "We must eventually take steps," he advised London, "to correct any erroneous opinion he may have or profess to have . . . in regard to the future administration of the Syrian littoral, Palestine and of the provinces of Baghdad and Basra."[39]

Wingate erred on two points. First, it was not the letter of 24 October 1915 which provided Hussein with grounds for his pretensions, but that dated 10 March 1916. This neither Wingate nor any of his colleagues could have imagined. Second, as we have seen from all the proceedings, it was not Palestine that concerned Hussein, but French ambitions, or supposed ambitions, in Syria, as well as the hostility of his neighbors in the Arabian Peninsula.

At the Foreign Office, Sir George Clerk predicted with resignation: "more future trouble," whereas Graham agreed with Wingate that sooner or later the British "must enlighten the King as to the true facts of the situation. . . Possibly he is really . . . aware of them and is bluffing."[40]

By contrast, Clayton, more familiar with the Arab mind, was spared the shock of disillusionment. As early as 7 May, he confided to Storrs:

> Sykes seems very pleased with the result of his work but your knowledge of these people will enable you to appreciate their attitude in such matters and prevent your putting too much faith in any satisfactory assurances which they may give as the result of an interview with a strong personality like Sykes. We must expect them to go back a good deal on their statements when Sykes's personal influence is removed.[41]

Clayton proved prescient, for this was exactly what happened. On 30 July, he told Sykes that Hussein had either failed to understand the tenor of the Jeddah conversations or that he was "determined not to understand it and put his own interpretation" on them. Clayton hoped that events would be too strong for Hussein and eventually impel him either "to fall into line, or fall out."[42]

The King, however, was not inclined to toe the line and in no degree lessened his pretensions. At a meeting with Wilson toward the end of November 1917, he again referred to McMahon's letters and was confident that the British Government would keep its word. According to him, Syria belonged to him also by virtue of the wishes of the Syrians themselves. Before being executed by the Turks, Arab notables had sworn allegiance to him, and he was bound in honor to secure the interests of the Moslem majority. Alarmed, Wilson urged Cairo to make yet another search for the Arabic translations which were said to have been locked up somewhere by Storrs.[43]

Wingate attributed Hussein's extravagant claims to his overweening ambition to unite all Arabic-speaking peoples under his personal leadership, and to his need to vindicate his revolt against the Ottoman Empire in the eyes of his Moslem brethren. His "highly suspicious frame of mind towards the French and, in a lesser degree towards ourselves," Wingate admitted, was another factor that governed his conduct. However, complete fulfillment of his aims were "incapable of realization," and it was also an "illusion" on his part to expect that the British Government would install him, even nominally, as an overlord of Syria. At all events, "inefficiency of the Hedjaz administration is a practical guarantee against the spread of Meccan patriarchalism."[44]

Wingate had to eat his words. For want of alternative rebels against Turkey, it was expedient for the British to cultivate Hussein and play the Sharifian card for all it was worth. As a result, Hussein felt free to take full advantage of British hesitations and pusillanimity to make ever-growing demands.

An imprecise phrase during the conversation with Picot gave Hussein yet another excuse to claim that the whole of Syria, not only its hinterland (area "A"), was his. When equality of status between the Syrian littoral and the Baghdad Vilayet was discussed, a term "Moslem Syria" (*la Syrie muisulmane*) crept in (for some reason the word Lebanon was not used). The Quai d'Orsay queried its meaning, since "Moslem Syria" would have a wider meaning, taking into area "A" the northern part of the littoral, which was inhabited predominantly by a Moslem population. This was obviously not the case.

Jules Cambon, the Secretary-General of the French Foreign Ministry, though pleased with the achievements in Jeddah, was not as trusting of Hussein as Picot and doubted whether the King's sudden turnabout on 20 May was genuine. He requested Picot, then in Cairo, to instruct Si Mustapha Cherchali, then in Jeddah, to get in touch with King Hussein in order to dispel any possible misconceptions with regard to the meaning of "Moslem Syria." Cherchali was to tell the King that, according to French understanding, Moslem Syria referred exclusively to area "A" — namely to the Syrian hinterland — and did not apply to the Syrian littoral.[45] Cherchali was an Algerian notable who was sent by Paris in April 1917 to take charge of the French Moslem pilgrims to Mecca. He was also to fulfill a semi-diplomatic mission and to disclose to Hussein the terms of the Anglo-French

Agreement. With regard to the Syrian coast, he was to be specific; that is, that it would be necessary for the French Government to maintain there a "special regime" under its "direct supervision" (*égide directe*).[46] Subsequently, it was decided that it would be more appropriate if Picot, during his joint mission with Sykes, delivered this message to Hussein, which he did.

Picot evinced some reservations with regard to Cambon's instructions. He feared that a renewed approach by Cherchali might unnecessarily irritate the King and jeopardize his achievement of 20 May. "What will materially determine the implementation of the Agreement," he told Cambon, "will be the military occupation of the territories in question." It would smooth the way with the Arabs and British alike, "because the Arabs are always inclined to accept a *fait accompli*, as they have repeatedly and ingenuously admitted to me during my recent trip to Jeddah" (*car les Arabes s'inclinent toujours devant le fait accompli*).[47]

Cambon was not convinced. He sensed, quite correctly, that inevitably a vague formulation invited misunderstandings or, still worse, misinterpretations. He repeated his original instruction and insisted that Cherchali inform Hussein unequivocally of the French Government's determination to emancipate the Syria coast and assist its inhabitants, irrespective of race or creed.[48]

Picot passed on Cambon's instruction to Cherchali, adding that the message should be delivered only in response to Hussein's enquiry in this matter.[49] Such an addendum nullified Cambon's wishes.

A meeting between Cherchali and Hussein took place on 11 July 1917, but the question of the Syria coast was not discussed.[50] As previously noted, it was eighteen days later that Hussein boasted to Lawrence that he had trapped Picot into admitting that France would be satisfied with a parallel position in Syria to that which Great Britain desired in Iraq, and that he had no intention of permitting any French annexation of Beirut and the Lebanon.[51] On the other hand, Picot believed that Hussein's declaration of 20 May legitimized the French position in the Syrian littoral and that the French prerogatives there were as secure as those of the British in Baghdad.

It could be argued that, had Sykes and Picot presented to

Hussein a joint résumé on the results of their meetings in Jeddah the fateful misunderstanding could have been avoided. Theoretically this would have met the case. However, given Hussein's peculiar interpretation of McMahon's letter of 10 March 1916, which conditioned all his thinking, and in view of his extraordinary ability to misread documents, one might be sceptical as to whether common sense would have prevailed. If nothing was settled by the Sykes-Picot mission, it was not because of lack of goodwill or frankness on their part, but because Hussein interpreted the word *understanding* according to his own convenience.

During his mission to Jeddah (8-14 January 1918),[52] David Hogarth got the distinct impression that Hussein abated "none of his original demands, on behalf of the Arabs, or in the fulness of time, of himself." To counter Turkish propaganda, Hogarth reassured the King that the Entente Powers were "determined that the Arab race shall be given full opportunity of once again forming a nation in the world," circumscribing it by a statement that "this can only be achieved by the Arabs themselves uniting."

Hogarth apprised the King anew of the 1916 Agreement, which safeguarded the interests of the Allied Powers, especially of France. The King did not demur, but treated the matter rather lightly. He referred jocularly to Fashoda and alluded to the "necessity of modifications owing to the course of the war and changes in the mutual relations of the Allies." He had full trust in Great Britain, but very little in France:

> I think [Hogarth recorded] he has some hope of forcing France's hand when it comes to the point, and expects us to back him. He lived too long in Constantinople not to have imbibed the policy of playing one Power against another. He listened to my protestations of our perfect accord with France, and the latter's good intentions towards the Arabs, with politeness but lack of conviction.

On this particular issue, Hogarth's mission was not a success. But the bombshell was yet to come. Five months later, Hussein feigned ignorance of the Anglo-French Agreement and pretended to have learnt of it from Djemal Pasha's speech in Beirut on 6 December 1917, which received wide publicity.[53]

Sykes was astounded, noting that the King had been given a comprehensive "outline and details" of the Agreement not only by himself and Picot, but later also by Colonel Bremond and Commander Hogarth, who had gone to Jeddah especially for this purpose.[54]

Sykes's confidence in Hussein was badly shaken. Hussein, for his part, stuck to his version practically to the end of his life; but it was Antonius who, in public lectures and writings, gave it wide currency. Antonius portrayed Hussein as an innocent victim of the wily and rapacious representatives of the Western Allies.[55] As all the evidence adduced above shows, this view was palpably untrue. Moreover, Antonius was consciously misleading his audiences, for it was not out of ignorance of the facts that he claimed what he did.

In 1920, Fuad al-Khatib swore on a solemn oath (*bi'l-talaq*) to Rashid Ridā that, during the visit of Sykes and Picot to Jeddah, King Hussein seemed to be quite content with the Anglo-French Agreement, and that it was due to al-Khatib's intercession that Hussein had finally accepted it.[56] Antonius must have heard about this remarkable revelation, for in the early twenties he had lived in Cairo as an employee of the Anglo-Egyptian administration. He must have also been reliably informed about this episode by General Sir Gilbert Clayton when serving as his assistant during Clayton's missions to King Ibn Saud in 1925 and 1927. In the early thirties, while preparing his book *The Arab Awakening*, he was accorded free access — a unique privilege — to the *Sledmere Papers* (the Sir Mark Sykes Papers), as well as to the *Sir Gilbert Clayton Papers,* from which any uninitiated historian would have drawn quite different conclusions than he did. But it was not the promotion of truth that dominated his writings. His primary objective was to shame and stigmatize the British in order to create in them a feeling of guilt and thereby ease the Arabs' task of wresting Palestine from the shackles of the British mandate. And it is in this light that his presentations must be seen.[57]

Whether the British Government had any obligation to the Arabs with regard to Palestine has been discussed already. The intriguing question is how Hussein himself and his sons viewed the issue. This will be the subject of our following chapters.

7

The Sharifians, the Palestinians, and the Zionists

We saw that it was not McMahon's letter of 24 October 1915 on which Hussein based his claims, but that dated 10 March 1916.[1] This letter did not refer to territorial questions at all, and certainly not to Palestine. The Arabic translation of the 24th of October letter was unambiguous for all purposes and Hussein could not have understood it in any way other than that intended by McMahon. As mentioned already, the Arabic translation was by far more specific than its English original and was free of any ambiguity.[2]

Moreover, soon afterwards, Wingate, on his own volition, explained to Sayyid Ali al-Mirghani, the Cadi of the Sudan, for Hussein's consumption, the nature of "the reservations . . . in Syria, Palestine and Mesopotamia" which McMahon had made in his letter and, since "the Sherif sets considerable store in Sayed [sic] Ali's opinions, I think," Wingate told Clayton, "that through him [Hussein] can fathom our ideas without having to apply directly to us for explanations."[3] It is worth recalling that it was al-Mirghani who had influenced Hussein to lead the revolt against Turkey and recommended him warmly to Wingate.[4] His advice, therefore, could not have remained unheeded.

In his reply to McMahon on 5 November 1915, Hussein expressed some reservations with regard to Mesopotamia and the Vilayets of Beirut and Aleppo, arguing that they were "Arab and should therefore be under Muslim Government," but he conspicuously refrained from placing Palestine in a similar category. Moreover, on 1 January 1916, he reminded the High Commissioner that, after the conclusion of the War, he would claim "Beirut and its wasted regions," but made no mention of the Sanjak of Jerusalem. Significantly, in his letter of 5 November, he used after the word "Beirut" the Arabic *sawāhil* (plural of *sahil*), which is the English equivalent of shore or coast, but without specifying where the coast began or ended. Thus, either by accident or design, he left out not only the Sanjak of Jerusalem, but also the southern part of the Vilayet of Beirut, which covered both the Lower and Upper Galilee.

Briefing General Maxwell on the contents of Hussein's letter, Clayton confirmed that the Sharif had agreed to the exclusion of Mersina and Alexandretta and maintained that the Vilayets of Beirut and Aleppo were "Arab, and should remain under Moslem Government"; but remained silent with regard to Palestine.[5]

During May 1917, when Sykes and Picot visited Hussein in Jeddah, Palestine hardly figured on the agenda. It was Syria that concerned Hussein, not Palestine. A debate on this issue was therefore superfluous. At a meeting of the Eastern Committee on 2 February 1918, Sykes recalled

> that he had personally explained to King Hussein at Jeddah the difficulties which would ensue should King Hussein be burdened with the responsibility of the inclusion of Palestine, west of Jordan, under his suzerainty. He thought that King Hussein fully realized the position with regard to Palestine . . . [6]

It is reasonable to suppose that Sykes was preaching to the converted. But the test case was the Balfour Declaration. Its publication caused a stir among the Syrian community in Cairo. They dispatched emissaries to King Hussein to urge him to protest to the British Government. However, they were made to understand by Fuad al-Khatib, Hussein's Under-Secretary for Foreign Affairs, then in Cairo, that the King "has fully acquiesced" with the British program regarding the creation of the Jewish National Home in Palestine.[7]

Hussein did not rest at that. We learn from Antonius that he "ordered his sons . . . to allay the apprehensions caused by the Balfour Declaration among their followers [and] dispatched an emissary to Feisal at Akaba with similar instructions."[8]

When Hakki Bey al-Azm, a prominent Damascene resident in Cairo, called on Feisal to try to persuade him to register a strong protest against the "wrongdoing [of the British] in giving Palestine to the Zionists," he got an evasive reply. Al-Azm pressed Feisal to prevail upon his father, who as the Sharif of Mecca and the "King of the Arab Nation," should react strongly in this matter, but to no avail.[9]

Arab notables in the newly occupied Jerusalem were, as William Yale reported, "very bitter over the Balfour Declaration. . . . They are convinced that the Zionist leaders wish and intend to create a distinctly Jewish community and they believe that if Zionism proves to be a success, their country will be lost to them even though their religious and political rights be protected."[10]

Presumably they too appealed to Hussein for support, but the latter seemed to be indifferent to their plea. In his characteristic nebulous and ambivalent style, he advised them to redouble their thanks to God for what he had given them, namely, "tranquillity and safety" for themselves and their property, and "for receiving [from the British] full rights and privileges." However, he added,

> . . . in case anything might happen which you consider harmful or the like, communicate it to Governor General at your end who will no doubt immediately give orders that such harm be made away with, this being an obligation under "agreement" . . . with Great Britain who is known for being honest.[11]

In the context of our study, this particular letter is important. It shows that even within the terms of the supposed "agreement," Palestine, from Hussein's point of view, was outside the bounds of his prerogatives and that for this reason he could not intervene on the Palestinians' behalf. Our impression is reinforced by his response to subsequent appeals.

During an interview with Colonel C. E. Wilson on 21 July 1918, Hussein revealed that he had received a number of letters from notables in Jerusalem complaining about "certain difficulties" they were experiencing and asking him to act as an intermediary with the military governor. However, Hussein stated emphatically that he was not in favour of such letters being written to him from Palestine. He could only deal with them [in his private capacity] as "Hussein ibn Ali," and he thought it undesirable that such appeals should be addressed to him.[12]

Hussein's lack of concern over the Balfour Declaration and Zionist aims was clearly demonstrated early in January 1918, during a series of conversations with David Hogarth, who came especially to Jeddah to reassure the King. Such reassurance was badly needed. The Turks were taking full advantage of the Bolsheviks' disclosure of the 1916 Inter-Allied Agreement to arouse hostility and distrust of the Western Powers, accusing them of annexationist designs and of dividing Arab lands. A Syrian Deputy to the Ottoman Parliament was driving this point home, emphasizing that the Syrians desired nothing better than to remain within the framework of the Ottoman fold: "a Turkish hell is preferable to a French [or British] paradise."[13]

Having learned from their mistakes, the CUP (Committee of Union and Progress; the Young Turks) leaders endeavored by judicious propaganda to persuade the Arabs that their only salvation lay with their Moslem brothers — the Turks. A campaign of this nature had a very disquieting effect on the British, who realized that the position of their protégé was not as secure as they thought, and that their hold over the Arabs was far from secure.[14]

Particularly disturbing were the overtures made by Djemal Pasha to Emir Feisal in Akaba and to Ja'far Pasha al-Askari, his Chief of Staff. Djemal urged that the Islamic Union be created to check the British advance in Palestine and make the realization of Arab aspirations possible. If the Arab leaders admitted that they had been deceived by their British patrons, Turkey would grant them complete amnesty.[15]

The revolt was not going too well, long-standing tribal feuds were reasserting themselves, and there were indications of a rising discontent among Sharifian forces — a precarious situation which created fertile soil for Turkish propaganda.[16] It had, as British officers in Cairo noted, "a disturbing political effect in the Hedjaz," particularly as it had been "exploited by Syrian and other 'foreign' Arabs within the Sharifian Forces."[17]

The Turks also used the Balfour Declaration as a tool to

discredit the British. They pointed out that, after the conquest of Jerusalem, the first step of the British would be to give Palestine, an Arab country, away to the Jews.[18] Expropriation of Arab landowners would follow, coupled with tutelage over and violation of Christian and Moslem holy sites.[19] Distressed, the Residency in Cairo suggested that London draft a formula to be communicated to King Hussein on the objectives of British policy in Mesopotamia, Palestine, and Syria.[20]

The task fell to Sir Mark Sykes. He drafted three formulae which were conveyed by David Hogarth to Hussein. Hogarth stayed in Jeddah from 8 to 14 January and had ten interviews with the King. The first formula was to reassure him that the Entente Powers were determined that "the Arab race shall be given full opportunity of once again forming a nation in the world," circumscribing it by a clause that "this can only be achieved by the Arabs themselves uniting." However, as far as Great Britain and her allies were concerned, they "will pursue a policy with this ultimate unity in view."[21]

"The King," as Hogarth noted, "assented cordially, saying it expressed the basis of all [the Anglo-Sharifian] agreement"; to which Hogarth responded that, owing to a long lapse of time, the Allied Powers thought it worthwhile to reiterate it.[21] It soon became apparent that the King regarded Arab unity "as synonymous with his own Kingship . . ."

> He treats our proclamations and exhortations about it as good intentions, but no more, and has no faith in their effect until we support the embodiment of the idea in one single personality — himself. "Arab Unity" means very little to King Hussein except as a means to his personal aggrandizement.

This swashbuckling posture stood in stark contrast to his feeling of insecurity in Central Arabia, and even "about the loyalty of his own Hejaz [*sic*] people." He despised Idrissi, spoke disdainfully about Immam Yehia, the Immam of Yemen, considering him "a virtual nonentity," and showed great irritability whenever Ibn Saud's name came up for a discussion:

> He both fears Ibn Saud as the centre of a religious movement, dangerous to the Hedjaz, and hates him as irreconcilable to his pretentions to be "King of the Arabs." This latter title is the

> King's dearest ambition. . . . He opposes our argument that he cannot be "King of the Arabs" till the Arabs in general desire him to be so . . . [23]

Formula No. 2, like the preceding, was intended to counter Turkish propaganda. It asserted the Entente Powers' determination that in Palestine "no people shall be subjected to another, nor would the Moslem Holy Places, particularly the Mosque of Omar, be subordinated to any non-Moslem authority."[24] Hogarth elucidated the nature of the International Administration in Palestine. "The King," Hogarth noted, "assented, saying that the brain which could formulate this, could devise a form of administration to safeguard all interests." He lauded Great Britain's policy with regard to the Omar Mosque, comparing it to Caliph Omar's protection of the Christian shrines in Jerusalem.[25] Thereafter, Hogarth read out Formula No. 3, which constituted the core of his message:

> That since the Jewish opinion of the world is in favour of a return of Jews to Palestine and inasmuch as this opinion must remain a constant factor, and further as His Majesty's Government view with favour the realisation of this aspiration, His Majesty's Government are determined that in as far as is compatible with the freedom of the existing population both economic and political, no obstacle should be put in the way of the realisation of this ideal.

Hussein was advised that the Arab cause would benefit politically from the support of world Jewry, and that, since Zionist leaders were determined to carry out their objectives by friendship and cooperation with the Arabs, their offer should not be thrown aside lightly.[26]

"The King agreed enthusiastically to Jewish settlement in Palestine," but, Hogarth commented,

> The King would not accept an independent Jew[ish] State in Palestine, nor was I instructed to warn him that such a State was contemplated by Great Britain. He probably knows little or nothing of the actual or possible economy of Palestine and his ready assent to Jewish settlement there is not worth very much. But I think he appreciates the financial advantage of Arab cooperation with the Jews.[27]

In this particular comment, Hogarth committed a double mistake. He was wrong in assuming that the British Government was contemplating an immediate foundation of an independent Jewish State in Palestine, although this was what was universally believed.[28] He was also in error in attributing Hussein's enthusiastic response to ignorance. It took him only several days to correct himself. In his article in the *Arab Bulletin* of 27 January, referred to above, Hogarth admitted that the impression that Hussein left upon him was that of "a very astute obstinate man, of . . . keen intelligence, much courage, and sometimes surprising diplomatic sense and comprehension of outside affairs." Moreover, with the exception of his outbursts against Ibn Saud, with regard to Formulae Nos. 2 and 3, he found the King to be quite "reasonable," declaring that he was "in sympathy with both International Control in Palestine and the encouragement of the Jews to settle there."

This statement, among other evidence reproduced below, goes a long way toward belying Antonius's contention that Hussein's consent to "a regulated Jewish colonization [was based solely] on humanitarian grounds," and that in his counter-draft, Hussein proposed that "Palestine be constituted into an independent [Arab] state with a national government representing all the inhabitants, including the Jews."[29]

Such a "counter-proposal" was never submitted or even contemplated by Hussein. It is plainly a product of Antonius's fertile imagination. The Hogarth reports also show beyond any doubt that it was not Palestine that caused Hussein any concern. His principal worries related to his relations with his neighbors in "the Peninsula and to his throne," which, Hogarth noted, was none too secure.

About three months later, Hussein caused an article to be published in *al-Qibla* (23 March 1919), his official mouthpiece. Palestine, the article attested, was "a sacred and beloved homeland . . . [of] its original sons [abna'ihil-l-asliyim]" — the Jews. "The resources of the country are still virgin soil" which could not provide a livelihood for the Palestinian native. But the Jewish immigrants would develop the country. "Experience has proved their capacity to succeed in their energies and their labours. . . . The return of these exiles [jaliya] to their homeland will prove materially and spiritually an experimental school for their [Arab] brethren . . . in the fields, factories and trades . . . One of the most amazing things," the article went on, "was that the Palestinian used to leave his country, wandering over the high seas in every direction . . ." It called upon the Arab population in Palestine to bear in mind that their sacred books and their traditions enjoined upon them the duties of hospitality and tolerance, and exhorted them to welcome the Jews as brethren and cooperate with them for the common welfare.[30]

This extraordinary statement which, according to Antonius, was penned by Hussein himself, shows that his enthusiastic response to Hogarth's message was not a result of a sudden impulse. It was based both on conviction and on familiarity with the conditions in Palestine.

On the eve of Hogarth's departure to Jeddah, Clayton confided to C. E. Wilson how anxious he was about the effect of Turkish propaganda on the Arab mind in connection with the Zionist movement. He hoped, however, that the Sharif was "well enough conversed in world politics" to appreciate the advantages of cooperation with the Jews. "There is little doubt that if an Arab State is to be a success, it must combine [with them] . . . The Jewish are an element of great strength if they are incorporated into [a combination with an Arab] State, but are bad enemies if a hostile attitude is taken up against them."[31]

Antonius glosses over the crucial phrases in Hussein's article and attributes the King's attitude to traditional Arab hospitality and tolerance. "The article," Antonius claims, "is historically valuable not only as an instance of his freedom from religious prejudice or fanaticism, but also as reflecting the general Arab attitude toward Jewry prior to the appearance of political Zionism on the scene."[32] It was true that Hussein and his sons were free from religious prejudice or fanaticism, but otherwise Antonius's interpretation does not stand up to unbiased examination.

Several days later, Hussein briefed Feisal, then in Akaba: "my policy is that naturally it is in our interest not to interfere in the rights or dealings, whatever they may be . . . material or mental [sic] ones, of other non-Arab races, who are very numerous in the countries concerned." He added:

If you ever meet the Zionists . . . you should remember that it is our interest to preserve their comfort and all their material rights, which we should defend with our lives. Do not think that this is merely a chance or passing through, for God willing the future will show it to be my firm resolve.

Sir Reginald Wingate, who read this letter, noted that Hussein's instructions to Emir Feisal regarding the treatment of Zionists and their non-Arab peoples are "satisfactory and show an accurate understanding of the present political exigencies."[33]

At the same time, Feisal received a letter from Sir Mark Sykes. Assuming, quite erroneously, that the Emir's disposition toward Zionism and Jews in general was unfriendly, Sykes, as a true patron and promoter of the nascent Arab movement, assumed the mantle of educator. Historical experience — mediæval Spain and Tsarist Russia being the most noted examples — showed that persecution of the Jews rebounded on the persecutors. If you challenge the Jews, Sykes warned, you will ruin yourself and your nation:

And remember these people do not seek to conquer you, do not seek to drive out the Arabs of Palestine; all they ask for is to be able to do what they have not done elsewhere, to return to the land of their forefathers, to cultivate it, to work with their lands, to become peasants once more. This is a noble thought. . . . Here are these people after 2000 years of wandering looking for something that wealth and power cannot bring — that is the soil of the earth which bore them . . .

Sykes assured Feisal that the Jews did not desire to come to Palestine by their millions; what they aspired to was "to feel that in Palestine a Jew may live his life and speak his tongue as he did in ancient times." He entreated Feisal to look upon the Jewish movement as "the key to Arab success . . . stand up for Arab rights, uphold the rights of the Palestinian peoples [but recognize the Jews as your] powerful ally."[34]

Sykes was preaching to the converted. Neither Mohammad, nor Christ, Feisal replied, desired to create hatred and controversy among people, but only peace and friendship. However, throughout ages, the position of Jews in Arab lands had been by far safer than in Christian countries. He admitted that there

were some "ignorant Arabs" who despised the Jews; this was
not his attitude. He was fully aware of their importance world-
wide, and nourished a genuine "admiration for their vigour,
tenacity and moral ascendancy, often in the midst of hostile
surroundings. So, please do not think that I will allow anyone
to turn me aside from [my] conception." Racially, Arabs and
Jews are "nearest to each other, so we can but welcome a good
understanding with them, based on solidarity of interests."[35]

At Sykes's request, Clayton endeavored through Lawrence
to persuade Feisal on the advisability of coming to terms with
the Zionists. "I have urged Lawrence," Clayton reported to
Sykes, "to impress on Feisal the necessity of an entente with the
Jews . . . I have explained that it is his only chance of doing
really big things and bringing the Arab movement to fruition."[36]
Lawrence replied:

> [As] for the Jews, when I see Feisal next, I'll talk to him, and the
> Arab attitude shall be sympathetic, for the duration of the war
> at least. Only please remember that he is under the old man, and
> cannot involve the Arab Kingdom by himself.[37]

Feisal was also advised that Palestine lay "outside the real
Arab policy . . . we have always laid down in our dealings with
him," Clayton wrote to Sykes, "that we regard [only] the
country east of the Jordan as his sphere so far as he is able to
make good in it."[38] Clayton's reservation was apposite, since
the revolt east of the River Jordan was not going as well as had
been expected despite the enormous subsidies in gold to various tribes. Lawrence tried to explain it away:

> They are, however, Bedu, and I cannot say how they will go . . . I
> have prophesied many times, and each time wrongly, so I am
> getting shy. If the Arabs had any common spirit, they would
> have been in Damascus last autumn.[39]

Concurrently, Sykes was reassuring the Syrians in Cairo,
who feared that the British Government planned to found a
Jewish State in Palestine which would be administered by a
Jewish government in the aftermath of the war.[40] They were
dismayed at the prospect of seeing Palestine, and eventually
Syria, in the hands of the Jews, whom they believed to be of

superior intelligence and commercial abilities.[41] Sykes attributed this mood to "a misunderstanding of Zionist aims and intentions . . . it was thought," he told the Middle East Committee, "that Zionism involved the expropriation of Arab proprietors and of the handing over to future Jewish tutelage of Christian and Moslem sites."[42]

It was in order to dispel any misconceptions that Sykes, as early as 16 November 1917, sent Clayton a letter to be read to the Syrian Committee in Cairo stating unequivocally that the British Government had recognized Zionism:

> Zionism is the greatest motive force in Jewry. Jewry is scattered throughout the world. If Zionism and Arab nationalism join forces, I am convinced that the liberation of the Arabs is certain. If on the other hand Zionism and Arab nationalism are opposed [to each other] . . . Arab nationalism will subside into its natural elements of desert, town, village, Christian and Moslem, and there will be nothing to pull it together.[43]

Clayton lost no time in reassuring the Syrians that the foundation of a Jewish state in Palestine was not contemplated and that it would be greatly to their advantage if they cooperated with the Jews "to throw off the Ottoman yoke." The Syrians accepted Clayton's advice.[44] On 26 December 1917, Suleiman Bey Nasif told Capt. C. A. G. MacKintosh, the Acting Director of the Arab Bureau, that the Syrian Committee had resolved that their "best and only policy was to co-operate with the Jews" on the lines that Sir Mark Sykes and General Clayton had recommended. They appreciated Jewish power and influence, and intended to advocate "Syrian-Jewish fraternity and unity as regards Palestine." Nasif gave MacKintosh the impression that he was sincere. He added that his colleagues shared his views and would abstain from "encouraging Syrian chauvinism." Nasif wrote in this sense to Clayton[45] and separately to Sir Mark Sykes.[46]

Satisfied with the Syrian response, Sykes outlined the salient features of British policy, *viz*.: (a) to guarantee the inviolability of the Holy Places; (b) to offer an honest opportunity for the Zionist colonization in Palestine; and, (c) to guarantee the existing Arab population against expropriation, expulsion, or subjection. Cooperation and consent of all the parties concerned was essential. The alternative was "Turkish tyranny or Anarchy."[47] It was left to Dr. Chaim Weizmann, the President of the Zionist Federation of Great Britain, to take advantage of Sykes's labor and build on it a structure with a sound relationship.

Weizmann arrived in Alexandria in March 20 at the head of the Zionist Commission. To his amazement, he found that the British officers were woefully ignorant of the Zionist aims:

> The authorities here [he wrote to his wife], are all convinced of one thing, namely that the Jews are getting ready to create a State of Palestine immediately and that the first thing they will do will be to requisition all the land and enslave the Arabs . . . [and] such notions are being persistently spread among the Arab masses . . .[48]

Ormsby-Gore, who accompanied the Zionist Commission as a Political Officer, was soon able to determine that this propaganda originated with certain Syrian and Palestinian individuals who, in order to inflame "sectarian and religious strife," were disseminating the idea that the Jews intended to build a temple in Jerusalem. He approached Dr. Faris Nimr, the editor of *Al-Mokattam* and an old friend of his, and acquainted him with the Zionist aspirations, which would be implemented in a British-protected Palestine. Nimr, according to Ormsby-Gore, "jumped out of his skin with delight and from that moment began to pour oil on troubled waters and did all he could to work for an accord with the Zionists."[49]

Thereafter a meeting was arranged between the Zionist Commission and the Syrian Committee. Present in addition to Dr. Nimr, were Suleiman Bey Nasif and Said Shuckair Pasha. Nimr, on the basis of what he had heard from Ormsby-Gore, was convinced that "there was nothing inimical to the Arabs in the Zionist aims and aspirations." Weizmann emphatically confirmed this. He assured the Syrians that the Commission did not desire to take over the administration or to found a Jewish State in Palestine after the War; whatever the Jews did would be to the benefit and prosperity of the country as a whole; nor did they wish to control the Holy Places, except those sacred to Jews. Nasif and Shuckair expressed their complete satisfaction with Weizmann's assurances; the latter added that "there was room for a million more people without affecting the position of the present inhabitants."[50]

Weizmann and his colleagues met separately with Kamil Abu Kasib, Abd al-Rahman Shahbandar, the editor of *El-Kawkab*, and Said Shuckair. It was a friendly, though vague, discussion about the national destinies of the two nations.[51] Major Kinahan Cornwallis, Director of the Arab Bureau (Hogarth's successor), summed up his impressions:

> There is no doubt that [Weizmann's] frank avowal of Zionist aims has produced a considerable revulsion of feeling amongst Palestinians [in Cairo] who have for the first time come into contact with European Jews of good standing. They had the conviction forced upon them that Zionism has come to stay, that it is more moderate in its aims than they had anticipated, and that by meeting it in a conciliatory spirit they are likely to reap substantial benefits in the future.

Before the arrival of the Commission, the attitude of the leading Syrians and Palestinians in Cairo with whom Cornwallis spoke was that of "uncompromising opposition." The radical change of heart that ensued boded well for the future.[52] Clayton, who, in the meantime, had been promoted to the rank of Brigadier-General and appointed Chief Political Officer in the newly occupied territories, shared this belief. "I feel convinced," he wrote to Sykes, "that many of the difficulties which we have encountered owing to the mutual distrust and suspicion between Arabs and Jews will now disappear." Weizmann's policy, he went on,

> will undoubtedly go far towards removing the fears of Arabs, both in Occupied Territory and elsewhere. Already his conversations in Cairo with Dr. Nimr and others have had satisfactory results and I feel sure that the same will be the case when he meets the leading Moslems in Jerusalem.[53]

However, this expectation proved misplaced. In Palestine, as in Egypt, the Balfour Declaration came as a "bombshell." Both Moslem and Christian populations interpreted it as "an intention of the British Government to set up a Jewish Government at the end of the War, to deprive the Arabs of their land and oust them from the country. They looked upon the Commission as the advanced guard of Jewish capitalists and expropriators" and viewed it with suspicion.[54]

Weizmann lost no time in allaying these fears. Accompanied by Ormsby-Gore, he called on Ismail Bey al-Husseini, a leading notable in Jerusalem, where he also met al-Husseini's cousin, Kamal Bey al-Husseini, who served in the dual capacity of Grand Mufti and Grand Cadi of Jerusalem. In a thorough conversation, he told his hosts that it was not part of the Zionist policy to found a Jewish state or Jewish government after the War. On the contrary, the Zionists preferred "a British Administration, under which Jews and Arab could work harmoniously for the development of the country on a basis of equality and justice." He also assured his hosts that the Zionists intended to respect the Holy Places, Moslem or Christian; nor did they wish to expropriate, let alone to drive the population out of, the country: "There was room in Palestine for Jew as well as Arab . . . there was land in many districts lying idle and unproductive for want of people to cultivate it." The two Arab notables were greatly relieved by these statements and expressed their desire to live in peace and friendship with their Jewish neighbors. The Grand Mufti later related his favorable impression of Weizmann's personality to Colonel Storrs, the newly appointed Governor of Jerusalem.[55]

Weizmann enlarged on the theme during a dinner party given in his honor by Colonel Storrs in Jerusalem on April 27. In addition to the Grand Mufti and his cousin, Musa Kazem Pasha al Husseini, the Mayor of Jerusalem, was present, as well as repre-sentatives of all ecumenical sectors and some British officers. Weizmann reiterated the points made since his arrival and emphasized the historical connection of the Jews with their ancestral home and warned his audience not to give credence to misrepresentations and allegations maliciously disseminated by the "common enemy." The Zionists desired that the supreme political authority in Palestine be vested in one of the civilized Democratic Powers, and that this Power would "hold Palestine in trust until such time as the population became capable of self-government."[56]

Weizmann's speech was translated by the Governor into Arabic and was greeted with applause. The Grand Mufti expressed confidence in the sincerity of the Zionist declaration and looked forward to close cooperation with them in the future development of the country.[57] Two weeks later, at the invitation of the Military Governor of Jaffa, Weizmann met with local Moslem and Christian leaders and made identical statements.[58] As in Jerusalem, the response was friendly, but, as Weizmann revealed to his wife, "it is difficult to trust them."[59] As early as April 16, he confessed to Ormsby-Gore that he had found among the Arabs, or certain sections of them, "a state of mind which seems . . . to make useful negotiations impossible at the present moment,"[60] and was soon able to detect that, parallel to an anti-Zionist sentiment, there was also an anti-British sentiment.[61]

This impression was confirmed by A. Albina, a Jerusalem Catholic and Sykes's local agent. Weizmann's speech at the official dinner in Jerusalem did not, in his opinion, allay the fears among the population. "Jewish predominance is a nightmare to Moslems and Christians alike," and the presence of the Zionist Commission strengthened them in their belief that the British Government intended to grant the Jews far-reaching privileges in Palestine. To an outsider, the political situation seemed fairly smooth on the surface, but a person like himself, who was mixing with the people, could only foresee trouble. "The Moslem population, in its majority, although outwardly friendly or indifferent [toward the British Military Administration], is still holding aloof and watching events with suspicion. It cannot conciliate [sic] itself to Christian domination."[62]

Here lay the crux of the matter, for, unlike the Syrians in Cairo, who were, or appeared to be, British-oriented, those in Palestine were to a man pro-Turk. Weizmann's speech merely tended to confirm their fears that both the British and the Zionists had come to stay.

Before the War, the Arab population in Palestine, as elsewhere, on the whole, lived contentedly under Ottoman administration.[63] Whatever their grievances, a sense of loyalty to Islam and to the Caliphate always prevailed. This was the case during the Hamidean period,[64] as it was during the Young Turk regime. Despite the grumblings and complaints against the policies of the latter, there was no widespread and organized attempt by the Arab inhabitants of Palestine to secede from the Ottoman Empire. Before the War, the Decentralization Party was a tiny group with a limited appeal and devoid of any influence. The landowners (*effendis*) and senior bureaucrats subscribed to Ottomanism and believed that the preservation of the Ottoman Empire was the best means of defending Islam against the encroachments of the European Powers.[65]

During the War, the Palestinian population remained loyal to the Empire. The proclamation of *jihad* (holy war) by the Sultan Muhammad Rashad against the Allies at the start of hostilities was universally applauded. Leading notables and religious functionaries in Nablus demonstrated by word and deed their unswerving allegiance to the Sultan. In Jerusalem, the Husseinis, Nashashibis, and other leading families paraded their patriotism. The fiery speeches for the Ottoman cause of al-Shaykh Abd al-Quādir al-Muzaffar attracted large crowds. Asad al-Shuqayri of Acre served as a Mufti of the Fourth Army in Sinai, Palestine, and Syria during the War.[66] Hajj Said al-Shawa of Gaza, one of the most influential landowners, became Djemal Pasha's "right-hand man." In charge of conscription in the Gaza District for the Ottoman army, he served as chief of propaganda and country-espionage, and actively assisted the war effort.[67] In Beer-Sheva District, the *effendis* encouraged Beduin to come out against the British and the Sharifians.[68]

Even Djemal Pasha's high-handedness and repressive measures against the secret societies did not fundamentally affect the loyalty to the Ottoman realm.[69] Shekib Arslan, a Druze notable from the Lebanon and editor of *El-Shark*, fully justified el-Zahrawi's execution. Both he and Sheikh Abdel Aziz Shawish, a Jerusalemite Seminar teacher and editor of *el-Alam al-Islam*, sang the praises of the Turks and of the courage of the Ottoman troops. They heaped abuse on the British and played a conspicuous role in the Pan-Islamic propaganda. After June 1916, they attacked Sharif Hussein with unusual vehemence and labeled him a traitor and a renegade.[70]

Sharifian proclamations, which were disseminated in Palestine, fell on deaf ears. The proclamations called all those who were "labouring for the sake of religion and freedom of the Arabs" to join the revolt "so that the Arab Kingdom may again become what it was in the time of your fathers."[71] On 28 May 1917, Emir Feisal issued a manifesto to the Arabs in Syria, promising to deliver them from Turkish tyranny.[72] And from Akaba in October 1917, Feisal intensified his propaganda against the Turks, calling on the Arabs in the Sinai Peninsula and Palestine to rally to his banner.[73] Their response was negligible. They preferred to serve another master. Djemal Pasha had only praise for the loyalty of the Arab regiments in his army. He could find no better proof of his conviction that "the Arab would not revolt and turn traitor."[74]

Ronald Storrs recalled that, when the British forces were crossing the Sinai and advancing into Palestine, they met "with no active military cooperation from Arabs,"[75] while the Syrian-Palestinians would rather see the Judean Hills "stained with the blood of the London Territorials" than take sides in the fight for their own freedom.[76] Philip Graves, a member of the Arab Bureau and subsequently on the Arab Section of the General Headquarters of the Expeditionary Force in Palestine, had some words of praise for the Arabs of the Hedjaz and their Beduin allies, but those in Syria and Palestine "remained passive or aided the Turks."[77] C. S. Jarvis, formerly Governor of Sinai, expressed himself in even less complimentary terms: "The Syrians as a people did nothing whatsoever towards assisting the Arab cause . . . beyond hold secret meetings and talk. The inhabitants of Palestine did rather less."[78] Despite much encouragement, when the British troops were already firmly entrenched in Jerusalem, the results of recruiting for the Sharifian forces were disappointing: no more than 150 Arabs were enlisted.[79]

This unenthusiastic response was symptomatic of the mental make-up of the Palestinians and of their attitude toward the liberating British army. In Rafa, south of Gaza, as early as 2 December 1917, a comment made by Colonel Richard Meinertzhagen, a Military Intelligence Officer on General Allenby's staff, is illuminating:

> The Arab [he noted] is dominated by his religion. However much he appreciates the benefits of British rule . . . he always remembers that we are unbelievers and as such must not be tolerated. He rejoices at the temporary relief we have given him . . . but the joy is temporary and he will soon long for the return of his old masters; he has not yet thought of Nationalism. His hatred of us is partly suspicion and partly religious. He is sensible to our justice and honesty, but even this cannot weigh against fanaticism, and so it will remain . . .[80]

By April 1918, the Allied strategic situation had changed for the worse. Russia had collapsed and the German drive in the Western Front was in full swing. Allenby was ordered to dispatch his best troops to France. This caused the Arabs in southern Palestine to rethink their attitude toward the Turk. "It is my firm conviction," Ormsby-Gore wrote from Jaffa-Tel-Aviv, "that the Zionists are the one sound firmly pro-British, constructive element in the whole show. The Arabs in Palestine are, I gather, showing their old tendency to corrupt methods and *backsheesh* . . . "[81]

Ten days later, he wrote angrily to Sir Maurice Hankey, the Secretary to the War Cabinet:

> Mark's blessed Arabs are a poor show in this country — they may be better on the other side of the Jordan. . . . We are getting reports that the Arabs in territory occupied by us are beginning to forget what they suffered under the Turks (political memories are short) and think we should do more for them. Gratitude in the East is largely limited by what you get out of people in hard cash![82]

And in his report No. 5, dated 19 May 1918, he quoted a statement made by the British Intelligence Officer in Jaffa:

> Anti-British talk is frequently reported from the neighbouring villages. The majority of the *fellaheen* are neither pro-British nor pro-Turk, but the *Mouktars* and more influential men are generally in favour of the old regime.

Given this atmosphere, Ormsby-Gore wondered whether it was worthwhile for Dr. Weizmann "to continue going to Canossa at the feet of the Arabs. The Arab Effendis of Palestine . . . will never be an asset to the British Empire. . . . Sooner or later we shall find that we cannot do as we are trying to do now, to ride both horses in Palestine: the Arab Moslem and the Jew." He pointed to the "striking lack of interest shown by the [Palestinians] in the Sherifian movement," and concluded that "any anti-Jewish feeling on the part of the Arabs is equally, if not more, anti-British."[83]

No less disconcerting to Ormsby-Gore was the attitude of the ruling elite, which was also anti-Sharifian:

> The *Effendi* class, and particularly the educated Moslem-Levantine population of Jaffa, evince a feeling somewhat akin to hostility towards the Arab movement . . . [this] class has no real political cohesion, and above all no power of organisation. . . . As long as the war continues, it will sit on the fence, and while regretting the piping time of Turkish rule . . . will not dare to do anything to embarrass a British military administration backed with British bayonets.[84]

Only the peasants, poor townsmen, as well as the Beduin, developed some sympathy toward the Sharifian movement.

Clayton shared Ormsby-Gore's convictions. "The Palestinian Arab," he wrote to Balfour, "is not greatly interested in events outside his own country," and with the exception of the Beduin in the south, the Palestinians, by-and-large, looked upon the Sharifian movement with "comparative indifference."[85] This was one of the reasons that Clayton — probably in conjunction with Ormsby-Gore — arranged a meeting between Weizmann and Feisal. Weizmann was thoroughly pro-British and the Jewish community in Palestine embraced his policy unreservedly.[86] Weizmann and Feisal were to serve as the twin pillars upon which British influence in the East was to rest. The idea was a modified version of Sykes's Grand Design of the Arab-Zionist-Armenian entente under Anglo-French aegis "to render Pan-Islamism innocuous" and form an antidote to the Turco-German combination.[87]

At the end of April 1917, before leaving Cairo for Jeddah, Sykes urged Weizmann to join him to meet Feisal and King Hussein,[88] but a whole year elapsed before Weizmann could go to the East. While in Cairo, he was privately told by Clayton that the Arabs (i.e., the Sharifians) would not oppose a Jewish presence west of the Jordan.[89] Weizmann was aware of the "pledges" which the British Government had given to the Arabs, but these, he wrote to Ormsby-Gore, concerned the Hedjaz, and therefore, in his opinion, "the political centres of gravity of the Arab problem lay in the Hedjaz and not in Palestine."[90] When Lt. Colonel Alan Dawnay saw Weizmann in Jerusalem, he found him

> very anxious to see Feisal and talk over Zionism. . . . We are arranging to send him down with Billy Gore to meet Feisal at

Akaba. . . . From what I gathered of Zionist aims, I think there should be no difficulty in establishing friendly and sympathetic relations between them.[91]

Ormsby-Gore fell ill and Lawrence, whom Clayton wished to be present during the interview with Feisal,[92] was away in the north. His place was taken by Colonel P. C. Joyce. The meeting between Weizmann and Feisal took place on 4 June at the Arab Army headquarters at Wadi Waheida north of Akaba. After a cordial exchange of greetings, Weizmann stated that he had been sent by British Government to study the conditions in Palestine, to lay plans for the future, and get into contact with the representatives of the Arab nation. A close cooperation between the Jews and Arabs in Palestine and elsewhere was essential for the progress of both nations: "a Jewish Palestine would assist in the development of an Arab Kingdom and [it] would receive Jewish support." The Zionists, Weizmann explained, did not propose to set up a Jewish Government; they wished to colonize and develop the country under British suzerainty without encroaching on the legitimate interests of the local inhabitants; there was no intention of ousting anybody; there was enough room in the country for everybody.

Feisal alluded to the historical traditions of both races, and pointed to the need for close cooperation between them. He recognized the value of the Jews to Palestine and admitted being "quite sympathetic to Jewish national aspirations." However, in the absence of authority from his father, he could not express any definite opinions on political matters. He had also to be very guarded in his public utterances, since Turkish and German agents were only too ready to make capital out of any statement that might affect Arab interests in Palestine, especially as the Palestine Arabs, as well as the Beduin, were prone to exaggerate. However, personally, "he accepted the possibility of future Jewish claims to territory in Palestine," and reemphasized "the absolute necessity of an intimate collaboration" between the Jews and the Arabs for their mutual benefit.

Weizmann concurred that the interests of both people ran parallel. He intended to proceed to the United States, where Jewish influence could be brought to bear in favor of the Arab movement and establishment of an Arab State. Feisal applauded this proposal warmly. The possibility of Weizmann meeting King Hussein was also discussed, but no firm decision was taken.

Colonel Joyce, who acted as a translator, was also very satisfied with the results of the interview. He was convinced that Feisal "really welcomed Jewish cooperation and considered it essential for [realization] of future Arab ambitions." Feisal fully realized "the future possibility of a Jewish Palestine and would probably accept it if it assisted Arab expansion further north. . . . In that point they [Weizmann and Feisal] are a strong combination."[93]

Weizmann was impressed with Feisal's personality. He wrote to his wife:

> He is the first real Arab nationalist I have met. He is a leader! He's quite intelligent and a very honest man, handsome as a picture! He is not interested in Palestine, but on the other hand wants Damascus and the whole of northern Syria. He talked with great animosity against the French, who want to get their hands on Syria. He expects a great deal from collaboration with the Jews! He is contemptuous of the Palestinian Arabs, whom he doesn't even regard as Arabs.[94]

Weizmann reiterated his tribute to Feisal at a meeting of the Zionist Commission, commenting sarcastically that "all others seemed to be fluctuating people who could cry out and complain when they thought their interests were affected and from whom we could never expect any real cooperation."[95] And on the following day, in Ormsby-Gore's presence, he declared:

> I have seen Sherif Feisal, the Arab Commander-in-Chief, and, after my interview with him, I am justified in stating that it is possible to find a *modus vivendi* for the thorny political Arab problem; for, with the Arabs, we wish to live on the best of terms.[96]

The sentiment was mutual. The interview at Wadi Waheida left an indelible mark on Feisal. Six weeks later, in a letter to Sykes, he admitted that, although bivouacked far away from the world's centers, he had "a perfect notion of the importance of the Jewish position, and admiration for their vigour and tenacity and moral ascendancy, often in the midst of hostile surroundings," adding that, on general grounds, he would welcome "any good understanding with the Jews." And Lieutenant Abdin Husheimi, an officer in the Sharifian army, could hardly conceal his delight with the Weizmann meeting "the leader of our troops, Feisal . . . I am sure," he told a friend, "the consequences of this meeting will be to the benefit of our common cause."[97]

On 12 June, Weizmann arrived in Alexandria and reported on his Akaba encounter to Wingate, Clayton, and Colonel George Stewart Symes.[98] All greeted the news with unconcealed jubilation, particularly as it contrasted with some disturbing information about Feisal's secret negotiations with Djemal Pasha on a possible defection to the Ottoman fold. In response to Djemal Pasha's overtures, made from Salt on June 5, Feisal had conceived a plan for the creation of a unified Arab Army composed of Arab units currently serving in the Ottoman forces, combined in order "to fight side-by-side against the [British] enemy, the Arab Army to be under its own Commander"; to form an independent Syria linked to Constantinople on the model of the Austro-Hungarian monarchy; and to cease requisition of grain and foodstuffs in Syria." A copy of this plan was stolen by Lawrence from Feisal's secretariat and internal evidence showed that it had been influenced or dictated by the Syrian officers in his entourage.[99] Although Weizmann was completely ignorant of this move, he had, by opening new vistas for Feisal, inadvertently tipped the balance in favor of the British.[100]

Clayton hoped that the cordial relations that had developed between the two leaders would bring positive results: it would neutralize enemy propaganda among Sharifian adherents, while a combined desire of both Arabs and Jews to emancipate themselves from Turkish domination would have "a very considerable effect at the Peace Conference." Feisal demonstrated "an intelligent appreciation of the larger issues involved," and it was evident that he regarded "mutual cooperation between Jews and Arabs as an important factor in attaining Arab ambitions in Syria." The Sharifian interests "do not lie in Palestine . . . their aims lie in the direction of Damascus and

Aleppo." Clayton thought that a conference between Weizmann and King Hussein sometime in the future should be
arranged.[101]

Zionist and Arab policies "are not necessarily incompatible," Clayton assured Gertrude Bell. The Zionists did not contemplate establishment of a Jewish state, at least in the immediate future (an aspect which was not apparent until the arrival
of the Zionist Commission), and this "has put a very different
complexion on the whole idea in the eyes of our Arab friends
. . . " He continued:

> There is little doubt that the main ambition of the Sharifian
> Arab lies (at any rate of Sherif Feisal) in Syria. His eyes are
> fixed on Damascus and Aleppo and nothing else seems to matter
> to him. . . . It is this that leads him to welcome Jewish
> cooperation as he is quite prepared to leave Palestine alone
> provided he can secure what he wants in Syria. He is wise, I
> think, in endeavoring to enlist Jewish sympathy on his side.

In any event, Palestine itself, Clayton went on, lay "outside the
real Arab policy":

> The so-called Arabs of Palestine are not to be compared with the
> real Arab of the Desert or even of other civilised districts in
> Syria. . . . He is purely local and takes little or no interest in
> matters outside his immediate surroundings. The Sharifian
> movement leaves him absolutely cold . . .

The class composed of small traders, landowners, and ex-
Ottoman employees "is against anything which spells progress
or development . . . they are shiftless and corrupt by inclination," and abhor a situation in which they would have to com-
pete with "more energetic and enterprising elements." On the
other hand, as far as the *fellah* was concerned, "Jewish expansion in Palestine, for which there is ample room . . . will greatly
improve [his] condition . . . provided it is on moderate and
liberal lines sketched out by Dr. Weizmann."

Britain too was and would be benefiting considerably from
its Zionist policy.

> A Palestine in which Jewish interest is established and which is
> under the aegis of Great Britain will be a strong outpost to Egypt,

the invasion of which would raise even more bitter feelings all over the world than did that of Belgium.[102]

This concept had been advanced first by Leopold Amery, a member of the War Secretariat, in a memorandum dated 11 April 1919.[103] Clayton must have learned of it from Ormsby-Gore. The latter, too, was satisfied that neither King Hussein nor his son were overly concerned with the Zionist movement; nor was there "any desire to include cis-Jordan Palestine in their dominions." The cordiality which marked the meeting between Weizmann and Feisal in Akaba was "quite genuine on both sides." The Zionist leader realized that the peaceful future of Palestine depended upon the success of Feisal's military and political objectives. "With the Arab movement centered at Damascus, Zionism in Palestine would be a help rather than a hindrance to it." On the other hand, he went on, both Feisal and Lawrence, his principal British advisor, realized that, in the hands of a well-wisher to the Arab movement such as Dr. Weizmann,

> an element of strength and stability will be introduced in Palestine which will help to bridge the gulf between the East and the West, and enable the Arabs to learn from the Jews how best to develop the country, not in the interest of concessionaires living in Paris, but of the population resident in the East.[104]

In an extraordinarily frank conversation with Symes, Lawrence disclosed his concern about the difficulties that Feisal would face in the future. He feared that it would be "exceedingly difficult" for Feisal to control the territories liberated from the Turks; "the *effendi* class, the educated class, the Christians, and the foreign elements will turn against him." His movement was popular only among the peasants, the Beduin tribes, and the poor Moslems of the towns. Hence, Lawrence reasoned, if British and American Jews, securely established in Palestine, offered the Arab State in Syria to Feisal, he would accept it, and "with Anglo-Jewish advisers would dispense with the *effendim* and buy out the foreigners. This," he hoped, "would give time for a development of an Arab spirit in Syria from below, and might be preferable to a Syrian-*Effendi* regime."[105]

Formerly, Lawrence had distorted views and some reservations about Zionism,[106] but, following a long discussion with Weizmann at Allenby's headquarters in Cairo on June 16,[107] he agreed with Weizmann on "main principles . . . ," Clayton told Sykes, "Both are looking far ahead, and both see the lines of Arab and Zionist policy converging in the not too distant future."[108] Lawrence was quick to grasp that Weizmann hoped for "a completely Jewish Palestine in fifty years, and a Jewish Palestine, under a British facade, for the moment."[109] Such an outcome did not alarm him unduly. He nourished little sympathy for the Palestinians, and was angry at their indifference to Feisal's call to arms.[110] Despite the differences between Arabs and Jews, he was certain that, in the long run, the Zionist experiment would bring about improvement in the standard of living of the existing Arab population in Palestine, whilst on a wider plane, "the consequences might be of the highest importance for the future of the Arab world. It might well prove a source of technical supply rendering them independent of industrial Europe, and in that case the new confederation might become a formidable element of world power."[111]

Lawrence's views were important, since they had a bearing on Feisal's political education. It was probably under the influence of Lawrence's ideas that Symes struck a philosophical note:

> Ought not Jewish genius exercised in every kind of human aptitude, to be engaged upon a task of a Semitic renaissance? Could not the masters of monetary exchange, of science, and the arts, become political brokers between the Western and a revivified Near-Eastern civilisation? Might not a Jewish leaven securely lodged in the body politic raise the latter's status and enhance its significance?

This concept, Symes tells us, was not merely a visionary one, but was "conceived as an act of constructive statesmanship, which appealed to many great and generous [British] minds. . . . There was a practical synthesis in the idea." From this perspective, Symes commented, "the Palestine question might properly be regarded as the *gage d'amour* of a great alliance; the suggestion that it might also entail the excision of a pound or more of Arab territorial flesh was dismissed as monstrous."[112]

Shortly after Weizmann left Cairo for Palestine, Wingate received a letter from Hussein from which he was able to deduce that the King envisaged the foundation, with British assistance, of the Federation of Arab States "comprising of the Arabian Peninsula, Syria, the Gezira, and Mesopotamia," but not of Palestine; the component parts of the Federation would look to Mecca as their political and spiritual center. Wingate reasoned that Weizmann's offer to assist the Arab State, both financially and politically, would be welcome to the King, since this would obviate the need to depend on a Christian Power which was offensive to Moslem susceptibilities.[113]

Weizmann, of course, did not command even a minuscule of the financial resources comparable to those of a European Power, but this was the notion which apparently lingered in the mind of the Sharifians. "Sherif Feisal," Clayton briefed Weizmann, "sees in Zionism a force which, if enlisted on his side, may furnish him with the necessary economic support, but which bears what may be described as an 'un-national' complexion." With the help of Zionism, he hoped to be able to counter penetration of foreign concessionaires of the Vitali stamp and politically to garner international support for the future Syrian State.[114]

Given such a conducive atmosphere, Weizmann was able to tell Balfour confidently that the success of the Arab movement as represented by Feisal would reduce the likelihood of an Arab-Zionist conflict in the future. "I foresee — and Feisal and his counselors fully agree on this point — a possibility for a sincere cooperation between the two Nations, which will lead to a mutual benefit and to consolidation of the British in the Near East." The British authorities and all experts with whom he had an opportunity to discuss the position, agreed that "the real Arab movement is developing in Mecca and Damascus" and that Feisal, if and when he entered Damascus, "will consolidate the Arab position. He will need support, and the Zionist movement can give him all the elements of which he stands in need . . . We shall serve as a bridge between you and him." In this context, the Arab question in Palestine would assume "only a purely local character."[115]

Adroitly, Weizmann was trying to minimize the importance of the Palestinians. At the seventeenth meeting of the Zionist

Commission on 16 June, he declared that if the Arab movement were to achieve anything after the War, "its centre of gravity must move up to Eastern Syria. It is only in the territory of which Damascus is the centre as far as Homs, Hama, and Aleppo in the north that it can found a real nation and a real people." When at Akaba, he was told that even the Beduin were "disgusted with the so-called Arabs of Palestine; with their failure . . . to come to [Feisal's] assistance either morally or militarily. There is no community of ideal between the Arab movement and [the *effendis*] . . . In fact, there is a great divergence of aim . . . which it seems still almost impossible to bridge," he concluded, on an almost prophetic note, that, if the Arab movement led by the Sharifians was to make good in Syria, it must impose itself on this sector of population.[116]

Clayton almost despaired of reconciling the Palestinians to the Sharifians, as well as to the Zionists. All efforts to dissipate the former's distrust and apprehension were of no avail: "It is not a question of national feeling, for I have detected but few signs of real patriotism amongst the population of Palestine, but the [ruling] classes . . . will spare no effort to induce in the peasantry a hostile attitude towards the Jews." They were in close touch with the lower strata of society and it was not difficult for them "to persuade an ignorant and gullible population that Zionism is only another word for robbing them of their lands and even of their means of livelihood."[117]

Clayton erroneously equated "patriotism" with the struggle of liberation from the Turks. He failed to realize, like many of his British contemporaries, that the Palestinians, as subsequently also the Syrians, did not regard the supposed liberation as a boon. They remained, at least at heart, Ottoman loyalists and saw in the British-Sharifian-Zionist combination a threat to the status quo. Resistance to what they regarded as "foreign intruders" served as a powerful impetus to the birth of Arab nationalism which was of an entirely different genre than the British had expected.

An episode related by Aref el-Aref, one of the chief founders of the Palestine Arab national movement, an historian and a diarist, substantiates this assumption. The central figure emerging from this story is Amin al-Husseini (later Hajj), a scion of the Husseini family and a younger brother of the Mufti of Jerusalem. During the War, he served in the Ottoman army as a junior officer, but following the capture of Jerusalem by Allenby, he crossed the lines and offered his services to British Intelligence. Trusted by the British, he was put in charge of recruiting for the Sharifian army in Jerusalem. When in Akaba, he had an acrimonious encounter with Lawrence, who bitterly complained to him about the Palestinian contingent in Feisal's Army: "They were unreliable, undisciplined, and they incited the Hedjazi Arabs to disobey their commanders." Feisal too resented their conduct and told al-Husseini that he would never appoint a Palestinian to any political position. Al-Husseini concluded that if Feisal, assisted by the British, emerged victorious, the Arabs in Palestine and Syria would have to submit to the rule of the Bedou-Hashemites, as he called them. He also realized that Feisal was ready to cooperate with the Jews in order to resist "the French invasion of Arabia."

On his return, Amin al-Husseini conveyed his anxieties to Musa Kazem al-Husseini, his elder cousin and the Mayor of Jerusalem. At a meeting of notables convened at Kazem's home, Amin accused Feisal and his father of becoming "the servile instruments of the British." He warned that "there was no prospect of winning Arab objectives in Syria and Palestine if the Arab cause re-mained tied and controlled by the British." who, he went on, assisted by Feisal and the Zionists, conspired to defraud the Palestinians. Unless the Palestinians succeeded in driving a wedge among their adversaries, "the British will establish their rule over the Arab World with the help of international Jewry centered in Palestine."[118]

There is no evidence from any other source, British or Zionist,[119] to corroborate this story, but it would be idle to dismiss it as fictitious. As an intimate colleague of Amin al-Husseini and a collaborator, Aref el-Aref was privy to his thoughts and witnessed his political activity at close quarters. Moreover, he kept a diary and it does not seem that he harbored an ulterior motive in relating the story. It fits well into the general pattern of the Palestinian attitude toward the British, the Sharifians, as well as the Zionists.

David Hogarth, one of the most sagacious British officers, like Lawrence, foresaw the difficulty that the Sharifians would have to encounter in the future. He pointed to the likelihood of a disastrous collision between Ibn Saud and King Hussein in the south, and the growing opposition of the Syrians in the north. Last, but not least, it was "quite impossible to maintain the revolt except on a bullion basis... If Feisal should score a conspicuous military success this autumn," he prophesied, "he may be able to keep the lead and control of the Arab Movement; but even so, he is going to find in the hour of success" some vested interests leagued against him: the Syrians, the pro-Turks, and the French.[120]

This was the crux of the matter, since on the viability of the Sharifian movement hinged not only the British position, but also the survival of the nascent Arab-Zionist entente.

8

The Declaration to the Seven
and Lawrence's "Capture" of Damascus

In his book *The Arab Awakening*, George Antonius claims that the Foreign Office statement of 16 June 1918, known as "The Declaration to the Seven," "proved to be extremely important, both for what it contained and for the effect it had." And in the following paragraph, he reiterated that this document

> is by far the most important statement of policy publicly made by Great Britain in connection with the Arab Revolt. ...Its significance lies in this: that it confirms England's previous pledges to the Arabs in plainer language than in any former public utterance, and, more valuable still, provides an authoritative enunciation of the principles on which those pledges rested.[1]

Strangely, Antonius makes no mention of the memorandum submitted by the seven anonymous Syrian notables in Cairo,[2] although he saw it among the *Papers of Sir Mark Sykes*, as well as in its original Arabic text when interviewing the Syrians in Cairo.[3]

For an historical inquiry, the Syrians' memorandum is important, since it shows what had made the British Government issue the Declaration. It also enables us to judge whether this document bore a unilateral nature, as Antonius tries to present it, or whether, like McMahon's "pledge" in his letter of 24 October 1915, it was conditional on the Arab's doing their part of the deal. In the case of the Declaration to the Seven, the reference is specific: "Territories liberated from Turkish rule by the

195

action of the Arabs themselves." It is only after examining how the Arab inhabitants in Syria and Palestine responded to the call to liberate themselves from Turkish rule that one could pass judgment on the validity of the British Declaration to the Seven.

The document was penned by Sir Mark Sykes and approved by Lord Hardinge, the Permanent Under-Secretary for Foreign Affairs. It was issued in response to a memorandum presented by seven anonymous Syrian notables in Cairo who were members of a newly formed party, the Party of Syrian Unity. These notables had succeeded in gaining the ear of Osmond Walrond, in the employ of the Arab Bureau, and who recommended them to Wingate.[4]

The memorandum began grandiloquently. The signatories claimed to act as spokesmen for the various Arab Political Societies, membership of which was composed of all classes: the enlightened ones, the nobility, the religious leaders, as well as Beduin chiefs, who together represented "four-fifths, or more, of the total inhabitants of Syria [including those] behind the enemy lines." They asked the British Government to give them "a guarantee of the ultimate independence of Arabia." By the term "Arabia," they meant the territory which, besides the Arabian Peninsula, included the Gezira, Syria, Mesopotamia, Mosul, and a large part of the province of Diarbekr. Palestine and the Lebanon were not listed, and it appears that these territories were excluded from the petitioners' desiderata. Nor did Wingate, who in his covering note summarized the memorandum, notice anything to the contrary. In view of the name of their Party — "Syrian Unity" — this exclusion is all the more important.

In return for meeting their request, the signatories offered to provide the Allies with whatever services they needed. They were speaking not only in the name of the Arabs in general, but "particularly the Syrians, whether here in Egypt, or in the countries still under the Turkish yoke, or in parts where the British Army is operating." By the term "services," they had in mind military service. On this point, their statement was crystal clear:

> We consider the formation of a national army in the Arab territories occupied by the British of prime importance, as it would

result in strengthening the Arab Frontier and weakening the Turkish. For this reason, we ask to be allowed to form Committees which would work for this end in those territories and, as soon as they form a sufficient force, to send it to the Northern Arab Troops under the leadership of the Princes, the sons of His Hashemite Majesty.

Although the revolt against Turkey broke out in the Hedjaz, the *fons et origo* of the Arab national movement was in Syria. On the strength of the agreement that had been concluded early in the War between the Arab Secret Societies and Hussein, the Seven Syrians were certain that their plan would meet with his and his sons' approval. They hoped that the British Government would accept their proposal, "for . . . our people stretch forth the hand of friendship and sincerity to Great Britain and its mighty people." As proof of their friendship, they pointed out that, soon after the outbreak of the War, "the Syrian Societies had sent their delegate to Egypt" in order to reassure themselves of the British support for the realization of Arab national aspirations.

The "delegate" in question was none other than Muhammad Sharif al-Faruqi, whose extraordinary career has already been extensively discussed in this work. The signatories thus unwittingly admitted that al-Faruqi was not a person of little consequence, as Antonius and his followers claimed, but an authorized representative of the Secret Societies who had been dispatched to Cairo on a specific mission. As we know, al-Faruqi's subsequent conduct could hardly serve as "proof" of friendship toward the British, but this was apparently the only example that the signatories could quote.

Wingate overlooked this fact. By his own admission, he was unable to verify to what extent their statements reflected accurately the attitude of their co-religionists behind enemy lines, but was correct in pointing out that the proposed action against the Turks was conditional on a British "guarantee of the ultimate independence of Arabia."

This condition was met in the Declaration to the Seven, in which it was emphasized that the British Government would recognize "the complete and sovereign independence of the Arabs inhabiting those territories [which would be] liberated from Turkish rule by the action of the Arabs themselves" (item II). This was a reaffirmation of the standing British policy grounded in McMahon's letters of 24 October and 14 December 1915; namely, that British recognition of Arab independence was conditional upon Arab military performance against the Turks. The territory in question lay east of the River Jordan and in the Syrian hinterland. Territories liberated from Turkish rule by the action of the Allied armies (item III), such as Palestine, fell into an entirely different category. That this was so may be seen from Clayton's earlier letter to Sykes, dated 4 April 1918:

> We have always laid down in our dealings with [Feisal] that we regard the country east of the Jordan as his sphere, so far as he is able to make good in it.[5]

It would have certainly been inconceivable for Sykes to issue a document which would have in any way impinged upon the validity of the Balfour Declaration, as Antonius implies.[6] Sykes's primary motive was to provide some tangible incentive for a Syrian insurrection against the Turks. Like Wingate, he had no way of knowing how reliable the signatories were and how correct their information was about the prevailing mood among their compatriots in Syria, but, as the promise he had made was conditional on the Syrians doing their part, no undue risk, he might have thought, was involved. This was the thinking that lay behind the Declaration to which Antonius ascribed so much importance.

Antonius claimed that "a wave of jubilation swept the Arab world as the contents of the Foreign Office statement became known," and that "the despondency that had settled upon the forces of the revolt gave place to a fresh outburst of enthusiasm."[7] There is no evidence that this was what actually happened. Quite the contrary, the atmosphere that prevailed was that of indifference bordering on total rejection. As C. S. Jarvis, formerly Governor of Sinai, put it bluntly, "The Syrians as a people did nothing whatsoever towards assisting the Arab cause . . . beyond hold secret meetings and talk. The inhabitants of Palestine did rather less."[8]

On July 4th, a dinner party was given in Jerusalem by the Arab Recruiting Committee of the Emir Feisal at which two hundred notables, the Mufti of Jerusalem, and a number of British officers were present. Lieutenant Adib Wahbi, Head of the Recruiting Committee, spoke about the Arab Movement and read a message from Emir Feisal. Colonel Storrs, the Military Governor of Jerusalem, paid a glowing tribute to King Hussein and proclaimed that the Arab Movement "would bring back the ancient luster of past Arab greatness." He commented thereafter on the performance of Shakespeare's *Hamlet*, given by Arab volunteers, and quoted the famous epigram "To be or not to be, that is the question." He applied this saying to the Arab Nation, and said that "the Arab Nation will become great or remain lowly in proportion to her efforts during the present opportunity."[9]

In spite of all the encouragement and the fanfare, the results were disappointing. The total number of recruits to the Sharifian forces only reached 534. In Jaffa, only 160 were recruited, and in the Hebron area, the position remained "at standstill."[10] On 11 August, Feisal appealed to Clayton to facilitate the recruitment of Arabs and to remove all the obstacles hindering its success,[11] but could obtain no solace from the General. It was only in mid-December, during Hogarth's visit to Syria, liberated by Allenby's forces, that the stark truth emerged:

> It cannot be said too strongly [Hogarth warned] that mere liberation from Turks does not appear to Syrian Arabs nearly such a boon as the European Press represents it. It has been for them, only a means to . . . independence. If they are not to have the latter in full measure, they would rather have the Turk back and will scheme to get him.[12]

The seven Syrian notables in Cairo were either out of touch with the prevailing undercurrent among their co-religionists in Syria, or were deliberately misleading the British authorities, as al-Faruqi did in 1915, in order to extract far-reaching promises. Their friendly reference to King Hussein sounds rather peculiar, since, as Amin Sai'd, an Arab historian, tells us, members of their Party "had gradually dissociated themselves from Hussein in the first two years of the revolt, owing to inflexibility and obstinacy they encountered in him, and to his disinclination to listen to the advice of those qualified to give it."[13]

This attitude reflected the one held by the Syrians in general. Dr. Faris Nimr found it necessary to warn the Arab Bureau (24 February 1918) of the great anxiety that existed in Syria about Hussein's aspirations to become the King of all Arabia and Syria with British assistance. "The Syrians," he stated emphatically, were "strongly opposed to Hussein's Kingship; they were willing to accept Feisal as a constitutional ruler, though not as a deputy to his father."[14] Dr. Nimr was the editor of the newspaper *al-Mukattam* and the *al-Muqtataf* monthly. He was staunchly pro-British and the Residency valued his opinion. Subsequently it became clear to Clayton that the seven Syrian notables, as well as their Party, were anti-Sharifian. They resented the idea of any separation of Palestine from Syria and were also "averse to any close connection with Arabia, as represented by the King of the Hedjaz and his sons." They were opposed not only to the Zionist aspirations, but "also to the Arab Movement as represented by the Sharifian leaders. Their programme envisages an autonomous Syria, including Palestine, under the protection of . . . some great Power."[15] The term "autonomous" Syria, as well as the principle of "consent of the governed" in the territories freed from Turkish rule by the Allied armies laid down in their memorandum of 7 May 1918, was meant to keep Syria free from Sharifian control.[16]

The memorandum must have come to Feisal's attention[17] and caused considerable displeasure. Lawrence aired the resentment, describing the signatories in uncomplimentary terms as "an unauthorized committee of seven Gothamites in Cairo."[18]

Hussein's reaction is not known, but it would be not too farfetched to assume that it was this memorandum that prompted him, on 28 August 1918, to submit to Wingate far-reaching territorial claims.[19] Hussein's ambitions were not new. As shown above, they were based on his misreading of McMahon's letter of 10 March 1916. He intended to present them well after termination of hostilities and this was apparently why he had left his correspondence with McMahon in abeyance. However, rival demands from the Syrians called for a pre-emptive move. The cardinal question that comes to mind in the wake of his letter of 28 August is, did Hussein's territorial demands for Arab independence include Palestine. On the basis of the evidence adduced above, as well as Feisal's statements during the Peace Conference and those made by himself,[20] the answer is in the negative. On this particular issue, Hussein remained consistent.

The person who made the correct deduction from the Declaration to the Seven was Lawrence.[21] He realized that only in areas liberated by the Arabs themselves could an independent Arab government be set up. The goal of his ambition, as Colonel Joyce testified, was "the great Arab drive north and the capture of Damascus"[22] — a Damascus that was to be free and unfettered by control of a Great Power. Early in 1918, Lawrence reached the bitter conclusion that a spontaneous rebellion in Syria was "an impossibility: the local people will take no action till the front tide of battle has rolled past them. If it is a Sherifian tide," they would enlist in Feisal's cause, but if the front line was that of Allenby's forces, "they will get on with the ploughing of the fields, feeling no gratitude, and no obligation towards us." In all events, the outcome of "the Sherifian invasion of Syria," as he put it, would affect the future of the region and would determine "the European rivalry in the East."[23]

With such high stakes, a supreme effort was needed to ensure Feisal's success. With this objective in mind, Lawrence got in touch with Syrian members of the Secret Society of Arab Nationalist, many of them officers in the Turkish Army, such as Ali Ridā al-Rikabi, President of the Syrian branch of the Secret Society, at that time serving in the Ottoman Army as General of the Engineers Corps.[24] However, the idea of a rebellion had little appeal for them. Quite the contrary, Yasin al-Hashimi, promoted, at the recommendation of Kaiser Wilhelm II to the rank of Major-General in recognition of his gallantry, commanded the Ottoman troops at Salt and Amman in the spring of 1918 and proved, according to the British, "too good a strategist for us."[25] It was he who was largely responsible for the defeat of the Australian cavalry unit ordered by General Allenby to establish a bridgehead east of the River Jordan.[26] Yasin was the head of the Secret Arab Societies, who, it will be recalled, sent al-Faruqi to Cairo in 1915 to win over the British.[27]

Feisal must have been deeply disappointed, for in May 1915, when he had met the leaders of the Secret Societies on his return from Constantinople, they had "pledged themselves that, if his father were to raise the standard of revolt, they would bring about a mutiny of all the Arab regiments in the Turkish Army."[28] It was for this purpose that Syrian and Mesopotamian prisoners-of-war were incorporated into Feisal's Regular Army.[29] However, it was not appreciated at that time that "they were rapidly developing into red-hot [anti-Allied] nationalists."[30] How hazardous the position was of British officers attached to the Sharifian forces was attested by Lieutenant-Colonel W. F. Stirling: "We realized that if Allenby's push failed, we should lose little or no chance of escaping . . . The Arabs would be sure to turn against us."[31]

The Beduin tribes east of the River Jordan could also not be relied upon. German Military Intelligence described them as "extraordinary vacillating in character," devoid of any national aims, and constantly feuding among themselves. Although open to Turkish Islamic propaganda, they were in equal measure easily lured by British gold and material benefits.[32]

Albina, the well-informed agent of Sir Mark Sykes, assessed that there were only two ways of winning them over: "Money and Force":

> It is no use showering gold on them unless we can make them feel that we actually hold the supremacy in the field . . . Arab Chiefs are cunning and evasive. German gold is just as good to them as English. They will pocket it from both parties and back the winner. We must not expect them to help us against the Turks unless the latter are defeated and then they will only attack for plunder's sake.[33]

In September 1918, when Allenby launched his decisive offensive, it was the Australian cavalry divisions, augmented by Indian troops, that bore the brunt of the battle. If any services were given by the local tribes, it was only for "a prize in gold and the prospect of loot."[34] There was no general uprising.

On the night of 30 September, when the Australian Cavalry unit was converging on Damascus, Lawrence seemed to be very despondent and depressed[35] — and for a good reason. The goal of his ambition was "the great Arab drive north and the capture of Damascus."[36] Now, to his consternation, the Australians were about to deprive him of this privilege. And this was exactly what had happened.

At dawn on October 1st, the Third Australian Light Horse Brigade, headed by Brigadier-General Wilson, entered Damascus in pursuit of the retreating enemy troops. At 7 A.M., in front of the *Serai* [the City Hall], Emir Said al-Jazairi "surrendered Damascus to Major Olden." Said al-Jazairi had been appointed by Djemal Pasha to take care of the city before the latter's retreat.[37] General Wilson attested most emphatically that "there were none of the Arab Forces in Damascus when his Brigade passed through on the early morning of the 1st October," an opinion with which Lieutenant-General, Sir Henry Chauvel fully concurred.[38]

General Chauvel was the Commander-in-Chief of the Desert Mounted Corps. On 25 September, he was ordered by General Allenby to take command of the whole of the operation for the capture of Damascus and of its subsequent administration through the local Turkish *Wāli*. On 30 September, having issued instructions to surround Damascus, he rode to join General Barrow, the Commander of the Fourth Cavalry Division, under whose command Feisal was also. On his arrival at 7:30 A.M. on October 1st, General Barrow informed him that Lt. Colonel Lawrence, who acted as liaison officer, had slipped off early that morning without saying anything to him and had ridden into Damascus with some Arab followers on the heels of the advance guard of the Fifth Cavalry Division. By that time, Wilson's Light Horse Brigade was vigorously pushing the enemy columns toward Homs, leaving no troops in the city.[39]

Apart from Arab regulars, 600 in all, nearly all the tribesmen, who joined Lawrence, were natives of the country north of Dera'a. "At their heels," the official historian tells us, "came swarms of the meaner Bedoins of the desert, lured by the splendid prospect of looting the wealth of the town. Accompanied by their women and camels and asses, they streamed across the plain lusting for an orgy of pillage."[40] There was neither honor, nor bravado, in this kind of entry, but sufficient material for Lawrence to create the myth that it was the Arabs who had captured Damascus.

Chauvel recalled how disgusted Barrow was with Lawrence's conduct in Dera'a and that he had told him so. "After all," Chauvel commented, "Barrow and his division did all the real fighting with the IVth Turkish Army from Irbid to Damascus and, had it not been for them, Lawrence would not have got to Damascus when he did."[41]

When Chauvel arrived unexpectedly in Damascus (8:30 A.M. October 2nd), he caught Lawrence by surprise. Lawrence resorted to some lame excuses for his unceremonious departure and introduced him to Shukri al-Ayyubi as the Governor of Damascus. Chauvel wished to see the Turkish *Wāli*, Emir Said al-Jazairi, who had formally surrendered the city to Major Olden, for this was the procedure that he had to follow under General Allenby's instructions. Lawrence responded that the *Wāli* had fled before Djemal Pasha's retreat and that al-Ayyubi, a descendant of Saladin, "had been elected Governor by a majority of citizens." Chauvel was subsequently to discover that on both counts Lawrence had lied to him. Al-Jazairi had been deposed and his brother, Emir Abd al-Qadir, assassinated, while al-Ayyubi had been elected only by the Hedjazi supporters, much to the dismay of the local population, "who were terrified at the prospect of Hedjaz domination."

It was Captain Hubert W. Young, a Senior Supply Officer with the Hedjaz Forces, who opened Chauvel's eyes as to the deeper motives for Lawrence's moves. Unlike al-Jazairi, al-Ayyubi was an Arab, and his appointment was meant to prejudge the administration in the Sharifian's favor. The Hedjazi endeavored to minimize the military contribution of the British army and to create the impression that "it was the Arabs who had driven out the Turk."

The Hedjazi administration proved to be an instant failure. The city was in a state of total chaos, looting became rampant, and the population felt intimidated. Young thought that a show of British force was imperative. Chauvel acted upon this advice and drove through the streets of Damascus at the head of a large contingent, composed of representatives of every unit, including artillery and armored cars. The effect was electric; law and order were restored. Lawrence strongly objected to this march, but subsequently yielded, requesting that the British Army salute the Hedjazi flag at the *Serai*. Chauvel resolutely declined.

On the following morning, the 3rd of October, Lawrence informed Chauvel that Emir Feisal would arrive in Damascus in the early afternoon and that "he wished to have a triumphal entry, galloping in like an Arab conqueror of old at the head of about 300 horsemen." Seeing that Feisal had very little to do with the "conquest" of Damascus, the idea of "triumphal entry" had very little appeal to Chauvel.[42]

In the meantime, General Allenby, briefed on the events by Chauvel, hurriedly arrived in Damascus and urgently summoned Feisal, then in Dera'a. In the presence of high-ranking British and Sharifian officers, Allenby rebuked Feisal, reminding him of the terms of the Sykes-Picot Agreement,

1. That France was to be the Protecting Power over Syria.

2. That he, Feisal, as representing his Father, King Hussein, was to have the Administration of Syria (less Palestine and the Lebanon Province) under French guidance and financial backing.

3. That the Arab sphere would include the hinterland of Syria only and that he, Feisal, would not have anything to do with the Lebanon, which would be considered to stretch from the Northern boundary of Palestine (about Tyre) to the head of the Gulf of Alexandretta.

4. That he was to have a French Liaison Officer at once, who would work for the present with Lawrence, who would be expected to give him every assistance.

Feisal, according to Chauvel,

> objected very strongly. He said that he knew nothing of France in the matter; that he was prepared to have British Assistance; that he understood from [Lawrence] . . . that the Arabs were to have the whole of Syria including the Lebanon but excluding Palestine; that a Country without a Port was no good to him; and that he declined to have a French Liaison Officer or to recognise French guidance in any way.

Thereupon, Allenby turned to Lawrence, asking him whether he had advised Feisal that "the French were to have the Protectorate over Syria" and whether he told him also that "Feisal was to have nothing to do with the Lebanon." Lawrence answered in the negative. After some discussion, Allenby told Feisal that he "must accept the situation until the whole matter was settled at the conclusion of the War. Feisal accepted this decision and left with his entourage." In contrast, Lawrence demurred, stating categorically that he would not work with the French and would rather return to England.[43]

Several days later, Allenby wrote to his wife, "I had a long talk with [Feisal] . . . He is nervous about [the] Peace Conference, but I told him he must trust the [Allied] Powers to treat him fairly."[44] And to the War Office, he reported on the policy that he had been adopting:

> I am recognizing Arab independence in Areas "A" and "B"; advice and assistance is being given by French and British respectively. French interests are recognized as being predominant in the "Blue" Area.
>
>   Feisal is being warned that if he attempts to control the "Blue" Area, the settlement of which must await the Peace Conference, he will prejudice his case. He is also being told that the Lebanon's status is a peculiar one, and was guaranteed by the Powers, so that he will be treading on delicate ground if he attempts undue interference in that area.[45]

Our narrative invalidates Kedourie's thesis, in his otherwise masterly study,[46] that "the Arab 'capture' of Damascus had been deliberately contrived" in order to enable the Sharifians to gain control of the city and thereby to prejudge the issue in their favor, and that the whole object of this device was to undermine the French position in the Syrian hinterland. "Thus the chief responsibility for what took place in Damascus on 1 and 2 October," Kedourie concluded, "falls on Allenby." The evidence reproduced above shows that the main culprit was Lawrence, not Allenby.[47]

In this particular issue, Allenby acted in conformity with the instructions he had received from the War Office. They were meant to put into effect the terms of the Sykes-Picot Agreement, which provided the recognition of the "Arab independence" within the respective French (area "A") and British (area "B") spheres of interest.[48] By recognizing and supporting the Arab Government, Allenby, on behalf of the Allied Powers, was fulfilling McMahon's pledge to the Sharif. The instruction that Allenby received from the War Office on this matter read:

> In accordance with the engagements into which His Majesty's Government have entered with the King of Hedjaz, and in pursuance of the general policy approved by them, the authority of the friendly and allied Arabs should be formally recognised in any part of the areas "A" and "B" as defined in the Anglo-French Agreement of 1916 . . . [49]

The British Government saw no inconsistency between its engagements to King Hussein and those to France, as provided in the Asia Minor Agreement. The Arab State or Confederation of States was to cover the area of the Syrian hinterland and that east of the River Jordan. Both the Lebanon and Palestine were excepted. In the context of our study, it is worth pointing out that, unlike their claims to the Lebanon, throughout the War, neither Feisal nor his father laid any claim to Palestine.

Lawrence made his way to England via Cairo, where he announced to the world news services that the Arab troops had entered Damascus first. The first unsigned article appeared in the *Palestine News* (10 October 1918), and the second appeared under the caption "The Arab March on Damascus" in *The Times* of 17 October.[50] Damascus, he stated in the latter, was entered on the night of 30 September, "the Arabs being the first troops in."

It was at that time that Hubert Young was asked "two or three times . . . who had really taken the town. Was it the British [Army] or our noble Lord Sherif Feisal? The object of these enquiries was presumably to establish a claim to complete and sovereign Arab independence in the Syrian hinterland." Young, who witnessed the events at close quarters, replied that "as Feisal had at least 400 men with him and [General Chauvel] had not more than 15,000, it must clearly have not been the Sherif who captured the town."[51]

Chauvel himself lodged a strong protest at the obvious travesty of facts:

> In order to avoid the risk of any such misrepresentation being handed down to history, I, as General Officer commanding the

troops that captured Damascus from the Turco-German forces, hereby definitely state that no Arab troops entered the city of Damascus until after Australian, British and Indian troops had moved right through it and all organised enemy forces had either been killed, captured or dispersed.[52]

Neither Young nor Chauvel made their views public at that time, so Lawrence's version traveled unchallenged far and fast, gaining currency both in official circles and in the Press. It was therefore natural for Nahum Sokolow to congratulate King Hussein, on behalf of the Zionist Organization, on the "triumphant victory . . . [in] liberation of Damascus, the most ancient and precious jewel of the crown of Arabia." As friends and admirers of Arab civilization and imbued by the spirit of Semitic solidarity, the Zionists shared the Arabs' aspirations in the revival of the East. Hussein responded warmly: "I pray God to enable me to fulfill my duty towards you which is incumbent on me to perform on account of noble and good feelings expressed in your message."[53]

Lawrence considered Arab-Zionist cooperation to be of vital importance for the advancement of the Arab cause. On 28 October, when meeting Lord Robert Cecil, the Under-Secretary of State for Foreign Affairs, he suggested that "it would be well to have both Arab and Zionist representatives present" when the future of the Middle East was discussed. He denounced the folly of the Sykes-Picot Agreement, the boundaries of which, he said, were "entirely absurd and unworkable." He also declared that "Damascus had been militarily at the mercy of Feisal ever since November [of 1917], and that he could have taken it then and made peace with Turks upon terms which would have been very favourable."[54]

He harped on this tune at the War Office and elsewhere, and, during a meeting of the Eastern Committee (29 October), reminded its members that in the June Declaration to the Seven, upon which Feisal and the Arab leaders relied, "we had promised unlimited Arab sovereignty" for areas which would be captured by Arab arms. Feisal would reconcile himself to French presence in the coastal region of Syria, including the Lebanon (the Blue area), but would oppose their penetration to the Syrian interior (area "A") and would reject their advisers there. "He was anxious to obtain the assistance of British or American Zionist Jews for this purpose. The Zionists would be acceptable to the Arabs on terms."[55]

When Lawrence met Weizmann, he was preaching to the converted:

> The establishment of an Arab Government in Damascus and in certain parts of the North of Syria [Weizmann wrote to Brandeis] may be of great benefit to us if we continue to carry out the policy as laid down in the conversation with Ameer Feyzal [sic] during my visit to his headquarters last summer [near Akaba]....
>
> An intimate co-operation [Weizmann went on] between the Arab Government and the Zionist Organization to be established on the basis that Palestine is the Jewish sphere of influence (within boundaries still to be determined) and development. The Zionists to assist in the development of the new Arab States by supplying technical and political and financial advisers. It is obvious that such an arrangement would lead to a consolidation of the Near Eastern policy on a proper and rational basis, and it would be left to the two races interested in the Near East to settle ultimately their own destiny without very much interference from the outside.

The stumbling block to such a promising prospect was the notorious Sykes-Picot Agreement and the "exaggerated claims of the French in Syria." It was therefore the duty of the Jews in the United States to solicit President Wilson's support in foiling its implementation.[56]

Weizmann had separate discussions with Ormsby-Gore, Hogarth, and a number of other British officials, and reached "complete agreement" on the policy outlined above; the only question that was left in abeyance was that of boundaries. Lawrence was of the opinion that it would be advisable for Weizmann to discuss it first with Feisal.[57] But in fact it was Lawrence himself who sketched (in all likelihood with Feisal's prior concurrence) the boundaries separating the Arab State from the Jewish National Home. The demarcation line ran along the River Jordan; the Arab State was to cover the Syrian hinterland and the area that was to later become Trans-Jordan. He regarded Trans-Jordan as an integral part of Syria, reflecting the Ottoman administrative division; that is, Vilayet of Syria, synonymously referred to in British official circles as the district of Damascus.[58]

It would be observed that, unlike Allenby, who followed the division which had been demarcated in the Sykes-Picot Agreement, Lawrence made no distinction between the French and British spheres of interest. It was perhaps not accidental that on November 18th Clayton submitted a memorandum advocating the amalgamation of Areas "A" and "B," presumably under British aegis. Such an arrangement, he reasoned, "would greatly facilitate the settlement of the Zionist question."[59]

The Lawrence-Clayton territorial model provided a blueprint for the Weizmann-Feisal Agreement, which was concluded on 3 January 1919 during the Peace Conference in Paris. However, three weighty questions hovered in the background which were to determine its viability:

1. Would France willingly forego her rights in Area "A"?

2. What was the measure of support that Feisal enjoyed among the Syrians?

3. Was there sufficient vitality in the nascent Damascus regime to ensure its development into statehood and eventual independence?

The answer to these three questions proved to be negative.

When Allenby was on the point of entering Syria, the War Office advised him of the undertaking that the British had given to the French Government that it would abide by the terms of the 1916 Agreement, and that, should Syria "fall into the sphere of interest of any European Power, that Power should be France." With regard to Area "A," the British Government reiterated the declared policy that, in that area, France "shall have priority of right of enterprise and . . . shall alone supply advisers or foreign functionaries at the request of the Arab State or Confederation of States."[60] On 30 September, a Convention was signed between the British and the French Governments obliging General Allenby to appoint a French representative as his Chief Political Adviser on Syria. Both governments undertook also to issue a declaration, which became known as the Anglo-French Declaration of 8 November 1918, to the effect that:

neither Government has any intention of annexing any part of the Arab territories, but that, in accordance with the provisions of the Anglo-French Agreement of 1916 [colloquially known as the Sykes-Picot Agreement], both are determined to recognise and uphold an independent Arab State, or Confederation of States, and . . . to lend their assistance in order to ensure the effective administration of those territories under the authority of the native rulers and peoples.[61]

France's equal status to that of Britain in that region was thereby re-endorsed, her inferior military contribution in this particular theater of war notwithstanding.

On 1 December 1918, during Clemenceau's visit to London, Lloyd George struck a deal. Against a concession that Palestine would pass into British control and Mosul be attached to Mesopotamia, Lloyd George promised his support for a French mandate of Syria, which included not only the "Blue zone" in the littoral, but also the four towns in the Syrian hinterland (Area "A").[62] On 9 January 1919, the Foreign Office told General Clayton that, in view of the uncompromising French position, annulment of the Sykes-Picot Agreement was impractical.[63] Thus, Arab independence in areas "A" and "B" could be implemented only within the framework of the 1916 Agreement, albeit in a modified form in line with the new spirit of the times.

Internal conditions in Syria militated against the Lawrence-Clayton scheme. The country had been severely devastated by war and economic activity was at a standstill.[64] Nonetheless, until 30 September, the Turks managed to preserve law and order. The decisive factor in the smooth running of the country had been "the organising genius of the Germans." But once they retreated, administration collapsed into chaos, thousands of the inhabitants were starving, others were "turbulent and in no mood for work."[65]

The task of reconstruction would have taxed the capacity of a Western Power accustomed to managing the affairs of great cities; "to the Arabs, it was impossible." The Hedjazi, from Feisal down, had been accustomed only to the control of unsanitary little desert towns and squalid villages, not of a city of 300,000 inhabitants such as Damascus. The newly appointed officials were incompetent and corrupt.[66]

Emir Said al-Jazairi, whom Djemal Pasha had appointed Governor, could have provided administration of the city and a modicum of stability. But Lawrence, suspecting him of a "French connection" and a potentially adverse influence on Feisal, dismissed him, while his brother, Emir Abd al-Qadir, known as the strong man, was assassinated.[67]

The Jazairis represented also the dominant faction of the Damascene political leadership and, inevitably, their removal from the pedestal provoked the deep-seated hostility of leading Damascene notables to the Sharifian regime.[68] Shukri al-Ayyubi, whom Lawrence appointed instead to govern the city, proved to be "useless," fanatical, and not too intelligent.[69] He was soon after replaced by Ali Ridā Pasha al-Rikabi, who stayed in this post until the end of Feisal's regime. Gertrude Bell described him as "inefficient, corrupt, [though] courteous." He was known to be a staunch upholder of "Arab independence, but except for an ardent hostility to the French, he appeared . . . to have no political principles."[70] His loyalty to Britain was dubious.[71]

David Hogarth, during his visit to Syria in December 1918, was very much disturbed by what he found. The Arab administration was a miserable imitation of the Ottoman. Though in Damascus there were some men of good intention and energy, in the provinces the officials were idle and ineffective. The gendarmeries and the soldiers of the regular Arab Army were "dregs of a Turkish army, ill-disciplined and unfit." The Hedjazi who had been introduced into the administration and imposed as an unofficial ruling class on the Syrian population, were "an evil" which urgently called for removal. With the exception of Feisal and his brother, Zeid, they "should be sent back to the Hedjaz. They have assumed a privileged and oppressive role, and their influence is obscurantist and vicious." Their presence produced an anti-Sharifian feeling, which would not bar Feisal from constitutional leadership of an Arab state in Syria, but would oblige him to rule as "a Syrian, relying on neither Sherifian, nor Bedouin support."

To breathe some life into Syria's "dry Turkish bone," Hogarth maintained, it must be administered by some external Power. "If left to itself, [Syria] will either have Turks back, or will become an inferior Turkey, where institutions do not function":

> In any case [Hogarth reasoned], the de-Turkization of the Arab Government and the education of Syrians to political independence will be so difficult and ungrateful a task that I, for one, would gladly see Great Britain absolved from it. If the majority of Syrians would accept French tutelage . . . we might thankfully leave them to our Ally!

At the root of the difficulty was their hostility to France. They regarded French predominance as "wholly incompatible with the independence they have fought — or plotted — to gain, and as a betrayal of them by us." Hogarth concluded despondently that, contrary to the view presented in the European Press, the Syrian Arabs did not consider at all their "liberation" from the Turks as a "boon"; they regarded it merely as a means to achieve their independence. If they failed to achieve it, "they would rather have the Turk back and will scheme to get him."[72]

Sykes was equally disturbed on his tour of the region early in January 1919. "Intrigue, corruption, incompetence, and vanity have marked almost every act" of the Damascus government. Ambitious paper schemes were drawn up, but nothing was done; promises were made but there was no attempt to keep them; practical business was subordinated to political theories; and money had been wasted on propaganda and bribery: "In fact, from top to bottom, where the Syrian Arabs are left to themselves, graft and rascality and ambitious designs are the only things one is able to see."

The country as a whole was riven by ethnic and religious dissent. Moreover, the large number of Mesopotamian officers and functionaries who had attached themselves to the Arab movement were becoming a source of embarrassment to the native population. The Iraqi officers were abler and more energetic than the Syrians and occupied numerous coveted posts. As a result, there was a general desire to see the Mesopotamians return to their own country, but they were not eager to do so.

What was particularly disconcerting to Sykes was the growing tendency among the educated Moslem Syrians "to cut themselves adrift as far as possible from Sherifian influence, and to shake off all idea of subjection of any kind to the King of the Hedjaz."[73]

Lawrence's attempt to impose the Sharifian regime on the unwilling Syrian population was ill-conceived. He was, as William Yale, the American Agent, described him, a "brilliant and courageous young man, who will stand out as one of the romantic heroes of the War, for his unbelievable feats with the Arabs." However, he "dislikes the Syrians and has no faith in them. He has become a true son of the desert and his heart is all with the Bedouins. . . . His love for [them] is sincere and it was because of it, that he encouraged the Arabs in their ideas of conquest and domination of Syria."[74]

Both Lawrence and Feisal underestimated the depth of feeling among the Syrians. Feisal in particular was puzzled by the reserved attitude of the notables. He expected them to rally to his side and assist him to run the country, but to his dismay "the Damascene notability distrusted him almost as much as they did his nationalist followers. Excluded from their traditional positions of authority, the notables were unwilling to cooperate directly with forces bent on eroding their power." Throughout the War, they retained their administrative posts and viewed the Sharifian rebellion "with alarm and disdain, and even treason." They regarded the Arab tribes culturally inferior and socially backward. They were hostile to King Hussein and his sons and mistrusted their political ambitions.[75]

Like the Palestinians, the Syrians did not recognize the right of the King of the Hedjaz to rule over Syria and speak on their behalf. They regarded the Hedjazi Arabs as a "foreign group" and intruders. Moreover, it was "preposterous," they claimed, that the European Powers, who had just proclaimed their adherence to the principle of self-determination, should "thrust upon [them] by force of arms the Sharifian Government."[76]

Ill-feeling toward the Sharifians was not limited to politicians. Dr. Alois Musil, a noted Austrian Orientalist who, from the turn of the century, had studied the Arab mind and lived among Arabs (he married an Arab woman and embraced Islam), revealed that the conservative Arabs would never forgive Sharif Hussein for having betrayed the Caliph, whereas Feisal was reproached for perjury. In 1915, on the Holy Stone at the Mosque of Omar in Jerusalem, he swore an oath of allegiance to Turkey, but a year later reneged on it. "Not a single member of the *Ulema*," Musil maintained, "has any good opinion of Hussein and his sons. They are publicly denounced as traitors, not only in Arabic-speaking countries, but throughout Islam."[77]

Little wonder that some time after the fall of Damascus its notables declared unequivocally that they would not submit to the King of the Hedjaz. Ja'far al-Askari, Feisal's Chief of Staff, warned them that if they disobeyed, they would be forced by the sword. The Damascenes averred that an attempt to impose the Hedjaz government on Syria would result in a civil war. Al-Askari remained adamant that "Syria would be compelled to accept the King of the Hedjaz."[78]

Ja'far al-Askari was a Baghdadi of humble origin, then thirty years of age. In 1916, he was taken prisoner by the British while fighting with the Sanusi on the Western Egyptian front and joined Feisal's staff. Intoxicated by the capture of Damascus, he, like other officers in the Sharifian army, seized power and were, in Miss Bell's words, "in a fierce pursuit of an exaggerated political ideal for the attainment of which, or on the off chance of its attainment, they were prepared to set the Syrian province in a blaze . . . "[79] Their unabated ambitions defied realism and stood in inverse ratio to their ability to govern. Predominantly alien, they made concerted efforts to keep the Damascus notables and other men of local standing away from Feisal and thereby became the virtual rulers of Syria.[80]

Unable to reach a *modus vivendi* with the native social elite, Feisal, per force, had to rely on his officers and the sprouting nationalist parties and clubs — though at a price. Unlike the conservative group, which was appreciative of the European contribution to the economic development of their country, the nationalist groups, such as *al-Ahd* and *al-Fatat*, since their establishment "were preaching hatred against the foreigners in general and against the British in particular." They were prepared to accept Hussein and his sons only as "champions of emancipation from European authority" and declared unequivocally that they would support Feisal "only so far as he fought for Syria's independence. . . . Feisal is a weak character," Musil commented. "He is influenced by his [entourage] and is unable to take up a leading role. . . . Afraid of deposition, he always relies on the more radical elements and thereby is alienating the more prudent elements."[81]

Musil's assessment tallies with that given by two of his contemporaries. William Yale characterized Feisal as a person of a "pleasing manner and of [striking] appearance, liberal minded and kindly disposed to all parties. But," he observed, "he is not a strong man and is surrounded by clever and unscrupulous politicians, who can easily influence him."[82]

Colonel Richard Meinertzhagen also had some words of praise for Feisal's amiable nature and his intelligence. But, he told the writer of the present study, "he was no leader."[83] He was definitely not cast in the mold of Ataturk as Professor Khoury put it, and "his effort to build a strong centralized Arab government in Damascus anchored in the 'national principle' was doomed to failure from the outset."[84]

Late in November, when Feisal sailed for Europe to present his case at the Peace Conference, his position at home was very insecure, but few, if any, of the leaders in European capitals were aware of his dire predicament.

9

The Weizmann-Feisal Agreement
and After

Feisal arrived in London on 10 December 1918 and on the following day, accompanied by Lawrence as interpreter, called on Balfour. Having expressed the gratitude of the Arab peoples to the British Government for the support given during World War I, he stated that the Arabs wanted only "one protecting Power, whether in Syria or in Mesopotamia, and this Power must be Great Britain." Any other would be intolerable; his followers would rather perish in the struggle than tamely submit to it. Throughout the conversation, he was "as violently anti-French as . . . indisguisedly pro-British."

Balfour responded that Feisal was in error as to the true nature of French policy and pointed to Clemenceau's recent announcement that the French Government was determined to enable Syria to work out its own salvation and progress.[1]

Balfour was the least suitable person before whom one could air anti-French sentiments. The previous week, he had stated most emphatically to the Eastern Committee that Britain could not go back on the Sykes-Picot Agreement: "I am quite certain that we ought to be most careful not to give . . . the French . . . the impression that we are trying to get out of our bargains with them made at an earlier and different stage of the war. . . . If the Americans choose to step in and cut the knot, that is their affair, but we must not put the knife into their hand."[2]

Hence, Feisal's only hope was President Wilson. Wilson, it

was thought, was the only leader who would be able to exert pressure on the Allies to scrap the secret agreements. The Foreign Office, however, was helpful in other ways, particularly in enabling Feisal to obtain a hearing at the Peace Conference. It was agreed also that Lawrence would act as his advisor, though unofficially, since he was to serve as a member of the British delegation.[3]

On 27 December, accompanied by Lawrence, Feisal called on Edwin Montagu, the Secretary of State for India, and reiterated his attack on the Sykes-Picot Agreement. Throughout the War, he maintained, he had had no idea of its existence, and that Arab right in Syria "had been bargained away in advance . . . The Arabs dislike and distrust French methods . . . and they have no desire to come under their influence." When questioned about Palestine, Feisal said that the Arabs were under deep obligation to Great Britain and that it would ill become them to cause any difficulties:

> There are conflicting interests in Palestine, but the Arabs admit the moral claims of the Zionists. They regard the Jews as kinsmen whose just claims they will be glad to see satisfied. They feel that the interests of the Arab inhabitants may safely be left in the hands of the British Government.[4]

To a rabid anti-Zionist like Montagu,[5] Feisal's statement must have come as a surprise, but with regard to the Sykes-Picot Agreement, Montagu remained silent.

In between these meetings, Feisal met Weizmann again on 11 December, with Lawrence acting as interpreter. He found in Weizmann a sympathetic partner. Feisal was indignant at the Anglo-French Agreement, which, in his opinion, was "equally fatal to Arabs and to Jews"; the position of the former was "extraordinary [sic] dangerous" and they feared that they would be pushed back into the desert. He divulged that his government in Damascus was "extremely weak, It had no money and no men. The Army was naked and had no ammunition. His great hope was in America, which he thought would be able to destroy the agreement."

Weizmann replied that, since he had become aware of the Agreement, he had been unremittingly acting against it, both in England and in the United States. A strong contingent of

American Zionists was on its way to Europe and at the Peace Conference they would use their influence in favor of both Jews and Arabs. "Our policies," Weizmann assured Feisal, "[are] absolutely identical." Feisal expressed the desire to acquaint himself with the Zionist program, which Weizmann unfolded in great detail:

1. The Zionists expected that the Peace Conference, as well as Feisal, would recognize the national and historical rights of Jews to Palestine.

2. They would ask that Great Britain be appointed a Trustee Power with due representation of the Jews in the administration of Palestine.

3. They would demand reform of the Land Laws in Palestine in order to render the land in the hands of absentee *effendis* and usurers available for colonization. This would enable extensive public works to be carried out which could absorb four to five million Jewish immigrants "without encroaching on the ownership rights of Arab peasantry." Nor was there any intention of interfering with the Moslem Holy Places.

4. In return for Feisal's acquiescence, the Jews would be prepared "to render him every assistance in brain and money, so as to help to revive his country."

5. The question of boundaries was to be left until after larger political issues were settled.

At this juncture, Feisal remarked that "it was curious there should be friction between Jews and Arabs in Palestine." Currently, the unrest was being promoted by Turkish and pro-Turkish propaganda, to which the Arabs in Palestine were still susceptible. Feisal was confident that he and his followers would be able to convince them that "the advent of the Jews into Palestine was for the good of the country, and that the legitimate interests of the Arab peasants would in no way be interfered with. . . . He did not think for a moment that there was any scarcity of land in Palestine." As to the big absentee landlords like the Sursuk family, who lived in Beirut, he would not trouble about them. Finally, he assured Weizmann "on his word of honour that he would do everything to support Jewish demands, and would declare at the Peace Conference that Zionism and the Arab Movement were fellow movements, and that complete harmony prevailed between them."[6]

After this meeting, Weizmann briefed Dr. David Eder, Acting Chairman of the Zionist Commission, that Feisal was "in complete agreement" with the Zionist proposals.[7] Feisal, on his part, made his views public. On the following day, he told the Reuters Agency unequivocally:

> The two main branches of the Semitic family, Arabs and Jews, understood one another, and I hope that as a result of interchange of ideas at the Peace Conference, which will be guided by ideals of self-determination and nationality, each nation will make definite progress towards the realisation of its aspirations. Arabs are not jealous of Zionist Jews, and intend to give them fair play and the Zionist Jews have assured the Nationalist Arabs of their intention to see that they too have fair play in their respective areas. Turkish intrigue in Palestine has raised jealousy between the Jewish colonists and the local peasants, but the mutual understanding of the aims of Arabs and Jews will at once clear away the last trace of this former bitterness.[8]

The Emir expressed himself in a similar vein at a banquet given in his honor by Lord Rothschild on 21 December 1918. He recalled his meetings with Dr. Weizmann in Akaba and in London and, in unmistakable terms, emphasized the kinship between the Arabs and the Jews, to whom he referred as "our cousins by blood." Arab friendship toward the Jews had been consistent since the Middle Ages at the time when the attitude of the Christian peoples toward them left very much to be desired: "No true Arab can be suspicious or afraid of Jewish nationalism . . . and I do say to the Jews — welcome back home . . . Dr. Weizmann's ideals are ours." In return, he expected help, since no state could be built up in the Near East without the goodwill of European Powers. He saw no better intermediaries who could best transmit European ideals, knowledge, and experience than the Jews. On behalf of the Arab State, he pledged cooperation with them to the best of his ability.[9]

Feisal's speech, which Lawrence had helped to draft, made a profound impression on the audience, which also included

British statesmen and public men. However, the big test still awaited him at the Peace Conference in Paris.

King Hussein was known to be extraordinarily jealous of his prerogatives, and it was only following Lawrence's urgings, as well as C. F. Wilson's repeated requests, that he finally agreed to delegate his authority to Feisal, in a document entitled *Pleines Pouvoires*, to represent him at the Peace Conference. He conditioned his consent, however, on compliance with the terms of his so-called "Agreement" with the British Government, as it had been spelled out in his letter of 28 August 1918 to Sir Reginald Wingate. This "Agreement," it will be recalled, was based on the King's erroneous understanding of McMahon's letter of 10 March 1916. British officials in Cairo and Jeddah were still at a loss to fathom on what grounds Hussein made his far-fetched deductions and attributed it to the supposedly mistranslated Arabic version of McMahon's letter of 24 October 1915, a copy of which was thought to be lost. Hussein's claims at the time, and throughout the Peace Conference, related primarily to Syria and Mesopotamia, not to Palestine.[10] Feisal regularly reported to his father on the proceedings at the Peace Conference, and his statements made there could be taken as reflecting the King's views, or at least to have been approved by him.

The Allied Powers rejected Hussein's self-styled title "King of the Arab countries," but, after a lengthy debate in 1916-1917, reluctantly agreed to refer to him merely as "King of the Hedjaz"; nor did they acknowledge his claims to any territory beyond his kingdom, unless agreed to by the Arab populations concerned. Hence, at the Peace Conference, Feisal could act only as the Representative of the Arab Kingdom of the Hedjaz. If he was granted a hearing on behalf of other Arab provinces as well, it was apparently on grounds of being recognized as the leader of the Arab national movement and as an ally who had participated in the War.

The Conference was a meeting of the victors who were to decide on the fate of the vanquished Powers. It is therefore understandable that Feisal, like Lawrence, should have extolled his contribution to the victory in excessive terms. "All [Arab] provinces," he declared at Lord Rothschild's banquet, "have

sent their best men to our forces for this revolt. My officers were
Syrians, Palestinians, Mesopotamians. They did not join me
and the allies to get rid of one master for another . . ." And in a
memorandum submitted to the Peace Conference on 1 January
1919, he stated: "As an old member of the Syrian Committee
[of the Secret Societies], I commanded the Syrian revolt, and
had under me Syrians, Mesopotamians and Arabians."[11] He
endeavored thus to give the impression that he enjoyed the
support of all his fellow-Arabs in the Fertile Crescent, not only
from the Hedjazi and other Beduin tribes. He drove this point
home on countless occasions, thereby laying the foundation of
the myth that there was a general Arab revolt, not merely a
Sharifian uprising.

The cherished Arab goal, he wrote in his memorandum of 1
January 1919, is "unity," economic and social differences between various Arab provinces notwithstanding. Syria, he insisted, was "sufficiently advanced politically to manage her own
affairs." However, as valuable as foreign technical assistance
would be, it should not be at the expense of "the freedom we
have just won for ourselves by force of arms."

On 6 February, accompanied by Lawrence, he demanded
from the Council of Five recognition of Arab independence and
sovereignty from the line Alexandretta-Diarbekr in the north to
the Indian Ocean in the south under the guarantee of the League
of Nations. He justified his claim on the grounds of the Arab
participation in the War and on the principles enunciated by
President Wilson.[12]

Palestine was excepted. On this point, Feisal was unmistakably clear. In his memorandum of 1 January 1919, referred to
already, he declared:

> In Palestine the enormous majority of the people are Arabs. The
> Jews are very close to the Arabs in blood, and there is no conflict
> of character between the two races. In principles we are abso-
> lutely at one. Nevertheless, the Arabs cannot assume the respon-
> sibility of holding level the scales in the clash of races and
> religions that have, in this one province, so often involved the
> world in difficulties. They would wish for the effective super-
> position of a great trustee, so long as a representative local
> administration commended itself by actively promoting the
> material prosperity of the country.

This was an unequivocal admission that Palestine was not to be part of the Arab State and that, since the Jews constituted at that time a minority, protection of a trustee was required to ensure their security and unhindered development. He recognized the unique character of Palestine and that, for this reason, the principle of self-determination was inapplicable. "Palestine, for its universal character," he declared before the Council of Five, "[should be] left on one side for the mutual consideration of all parties interested." With one exception, David Miller remarked, "he asked for the independence of the Arabic areas enumerated in his memorandum. . . . The Arabs asked for freedom only and would take nothing less . . . "

It stands to reason that Feisal could not have excepted Palestine without his father's prior consent. Its exclusion is all the more remarkable, since, on 11 December 1918, the Central Syrian Committee in Paris adopted a resolution in favor of a United Syria, which included Palestine.[13] Feisal also ignored the Congress of the Palestinian Nationalists on 1 February 1919, which adopted a similar resolution and pressed for the definition of Palestine as "Southern Syria."[14] Nor, as late as March, was his position affected when the Syrian Party in Damascus decided to approach the United States and ask them for support and protection for a United Syria.[15]

On 3 January 1919, when Feisal signed his famous Agreement with Weizmann, his mind was fixed that the Jewish National Home in Palestine and the Arab State were to be two separate entities. The Agreement was a formal confirmation of what had been already agreed upon between these two leaders on 11 December 1918, with one exception. According to Toynbee, "Feisal altered the 'Jewish State' of Weizmann's draft to 'Palestinian State' throughout."[16]

The preamble of the Agreement reaffirmed "the good understanding" existing between the signatories and stated that the surest way to realization of their respective national aspirations was through "the closest possible collaboration in the development of the Arab State and Palestine." To this end, Arab and Jewish accredited agents shall be exchanged (Article I), and boundaries delimited by a Commission to be agreed upon by the parties concerned (Article II). It is laid down (Article III) that the Constitution of Palestine shall "afford the

fullest guarantees for carrying into effect the British Government's Declaration of the 2nd November 1917"; and (Article
IV) that "all necessary measures shall be taken to encourage
and stimulate immigration of Jews into Palestine on a large
scale," and to enable their close settlement on land through
intensive cultivation of the soil. Provision was to be made
(Articles IV, V) for the protection of Arab peasants and tenant
farmers in Palestine and for Moslem custody of the Moslem
Holy Places. The Zionist Organization undertook, on its part
(Article VII) to "use its best efforts to assist the Arab State in
providing the means for developing the national resources and
economic possibilities thereof." Finally, the parties agreed
(Article VIII) "to act in complete accord and harmony on all
matters . . . before the Peace Congress."[17]

Weizmann deposited a copy of this document with the
British delegation to the Peace Conference[18] and with David H.
Miller, the legal adviser to the American delegation. The latter
published it in his *Diary* in 1928.[19] The British, as Toynbee's
minute indicates, were fully aware of it. Clayton welcomed it
warmly. The Zionists, he advised the headquarters in Cairo,
have come to a "definite agreement with Feisal with whom they
are in close cooperation. These two factors will form a strong
combination and intend to bring all their influence to bear on
American opinion."[20]

The Agreement was seen as the embodiment of the mutual
recognition between Arab and Zionist national aspirations in
their respective territories. However, the proviso, which Feisal
appended in Arabic, tended to detract from its importance.
Lawrence, who was present, translated it cursorily:

> If the Arabs are established as I have asked in my manifesto of
> Jan. 4 addressed to the British Secretary of State for Foreign
> Affairs, I will carry out what is written in this agreement.

Antonius translated the reservation with great precision:

> Provided the Arabs obtain their independence demanded in my
> Memorandum dated the 4th of January, 1919, to the Foreign
> Office of the Government of Great Britain, I shall concur in the
> above articles. But if the slightest modification or departure
> were to be made, I shall not then be bound by a single word of the

present Agreement which shall be deemed void and of no account
of validity, and I shall not be answerable in any way whatsoever.[21]

There was obviously a slip of the pen. Feisal had in mind his
memorandum dated 1 January 1919, which he had submitted to
the Peace Conference, not to the Foreign Office, as he erroneously noted. All the same, the reservation did not augur well
for the Agreement, for there was hardly any prospect that the
Peace Conference would accede to his demand for a complete
"independence and sovereignty." As early as January 1919, it
was made clear to him that "Great Britain had no intention of
falling out with France on Syrian questions," and he was
advised to accept French control in Syria,[22] a solution which
was not to his liking. He pinned his hope, therefore, on the
United States, the foremost upholder of the principle of self-
determination, and adamantly against the 1916 Inter-Allied
Agreement. Here was a common denominator between him and
the Zionists. This was why Weizmann's offer, made in Akaba
and later in London, to represent the Arab case in America
made such a strong appeal to him.

Weizmann did his best to assist Feisal. At his urging, Rabbi
Stephen Wise prevailed upon President Wilson to grant an
audience to the Emir.[23] Wise was the Chairman of the American Provisional Committee for General Zionist Affairs and a
close friend of the President. In 1919, he was a member of the
Zionist delegation to the Peace Conference.

Wilson received Feisal on 6 February 1919, but throughout
the meeting he was reserved and noncommittal. It was a formal
conference rather than an exchange of views. Lawrence, who
acted as interpreter, later told Stephen Bonsal, a member of the
American delegation, that Feisal was greatly disappointed:
"We merely established a ceremonial contact and that to the
Arabs is a great sorrow."[24] A week later, Feisal met Yale, who,
in the meantime, had been attached to the American delegation
as an expert. He told Yale that America seemed to him "the
most disinterested Power" and that he really preferred her to
accept the mandate for Syria, but "he did not say so openly, as
he had received no encouragement from America."[25] Nor did he
receive any encouragement from Yale. Yale was not convinced

that Syria was ripe for independence; nor did he believe that an Arab Confederation was a feasible idea.[26]

The American delegation was guided by a document entitled "Outline of Tentative Report," dated 21 January 1919. The Report found it was "hard to gauge" the strength of the Arab movement, and maintained that the mandatory principle should be applied to Syria, but no recommendation was made as to the Power to be selected to carry out this principle.[27]

The mandatory principle was the corollary of the idea of trusteeship which was deeply ingrained in President Wilson's mind. He envisioned the League of Nations as a "residuary trustee" for the German and Turkish Empires,[28] which should exercise responsibility "until the day when the true wishes of the inhabitants could be ascertained."[29] Wilson's concept was analogous to General Smuts's formula that was adopted by Britain and the Dominions. Smuts proposed that the German colonies and the territories severed from the Turkish Empire should be entrusted to the tutelage of "advanced nations" as a "sacred trust of civilization." With regard to the latter, which had reached a stage of development, their independence could be "provisionally recognized, subject to the rendering of administrative advice and assistance" by a mandatory power until they were ready to stand alone.[30] Smuts's formula was adopted by the Supreme Council and was enshrined in the celebrated Article 22 of the Covenant of the League of Nations, to which President Wilson subscribed.

The idea of trusteeship and the principle of the mandate signaled a demise of colonialism,[31] but the Arabs have never really understood it and suspected that the old colonial system had been clothed in a new guise. To Feisal, the principle was totally incomprehensible. He was stunned at the meeting of the Council of Ten on 6 February, when President Wilson, responding to his demand to recognize the Arabs as "independent and sovereign peoples," asked whether he "would prefer for his people a single mandatory or several." He found no solace either when he met the President later on the same day.[32]

Feisal's diplomatic venture misfired. Nonetheless, his interest in Zionism did not wane. Early in 1977, Philip Noel Baker, M.P., a leader of the Labour Party, revealed to an interviewer his extraordinary experience of being converted to Zionism by

Lawrence and Feisal. During the Peace Conference, Baker was head of the League of Nations section of the Foreign Office working under Lord Robert Cecil. He remembered Feisal speaking with conviction: "Of course we want the Zionist to come into Palestine." They will bring capital and know-how,

> . . . all the greatest scientists are Jewish — and the territory of Palestine now so arid and . . . a desert will be transformed; it will become a garden and will blossom like a rose. We shall borrow their experts, we shall work together and we shall do the same in all [Arab] countries which have turned into deserts. We shall make them flourish again as they used to be in the past.

And after a pause, in a pensive mood, Feisal added, "After all, why should not we? We are both Semitic, we are cousins . . . we ought to be able to work with them and we will."[33]

This was why the Zionists were so shocked when Feisal made an unfriendly statement to Le Matin (1 March 1919), which quoted him as saying that, "if the Jews desire to establish a State and claim sovereign rights in the country, I foresee and fear very serious dangers and conflicts between them and other races."[34] Lawrence, too, was nonplused by this statement, and rushed to Weizmann to reassure him that Feisal was preparing a démenti.[35] Weizmann and Professor Felix Frankfurter of the Harvard Law School, and a leading member of the American Zionist delegation, sought for a clarification of the Emir's position. Feisal's secretary elucidated that what Feisal had in fact said was that, "If the Zionists wished to found a Jewish State at the present moment, they would meet with difficulties from the local population."[36]

The emphasis in the Secretary's reassurance was on the words "at the present moment." All the same, Feisal's statement was out of tune with his declared general line of policy. Was it a slip of the tongue, or a sign of things to come? We can only conjecture.

The Quai d'Orsay was as disturbed by Feisal's Pan-Arabism as it was offended by the Zionists' bias toward the British. In an Arab-Zionist combination under British patronage, they sensed danger to their position in the East. No wonder the French Press was less than sympathetic. It would be reasonable to suppose that Le Matin asked Feisal some provocative questions in order to elicit the kind of reply that would sour his relations with his newly won friends. He might have also heard about protests coming from Damascus against his recent public declarations.[37] Whatever the case, he was more than accommodating when invited to state his position in writing. On 1 March 1919, he wrote to Frankfurter:

> We feel that the Arabs and Jews are cousins in race. ...We Arabs, especially the educated among us, look with the deepest sympathy on the Zionist movement. Our deputation here in Paris is fully acquainted with the proposals submitted yesterday by the Zionist Organisation to the Peace Conference, and we regard them as moderate and proper. We will do our best, in so far as we are concerned, to help them through: we will wish the Jews a most hearty welcome home.
>
> With the chiefs of your movement, especially with Dr. Weizmann, we have had, and continue to have the closest relations. He has been a great helper of our cause, and I hope the Arabs may soon be in a position to make the Jews some return for their kindness.
>
> We are working together for a reformed and revived Near East, and our two movements complete one another. The Jewish movement is national, and not imperialist: our movement is national and not imperialist, and there is room in Syria for us both. Indeed I think that neither can be a real success without the other.
>
> People less informed and less responsible than our leaders and yours, ignoring the need for co-operation of the Arabs and Zionists, have been trying to exploit the local difficulties that must necessarily arise in Palestine in the early stages of our movements. Some of them have, I am afraid, misrepresented your aims to the Arab peasantry, and our aims to the Jewish peasantry, with the result that interested parties have been able to make capital out of what they call our differences.

He was convinced that these differences were not on matters of principle, and that by mutual goodwill, they would disappear in due course.[38]

Feisal, it seems, had not only consulted the Zionist Proposals which had been submitted to the Peace Conference, but also attended the meeting of the Supreme Council on 27 February 1919, during which both Sokolow and Weizmann presented their case.[39]

Frankfurter expressed satisfaction that Feisal considered the Zionist proposals "'moderate and proper'. . . we have in you a staunch supporter for their realization." He assured Feisal that Arabs and Jews, animated by similar purposes, would be working together as friends. They are "neighbors in territory [who] cannot but live side by side as friends."[40] On the same day, Frankfurter wrote to Brandeis:

> The locus of trouble from the Arabs is Palestine and not Paris. . . . I think we can regard Prince Feisul as a genuine friend. At all events, at the least, we must deal with him on the basis that we are his genuine friends and the friends of his people. I do not think the Arab question is out of the way; I do not even say that it is easy of solution; I do insist, however, that it can be solved by cooperative effort. Feisul's letter states the matter as I see it and should be our governing outlook.[41]

Frankfurter took care to give Feisal's letter the utmost publicity. It was reprinted in the *New York Times* (5 March 1919), *The Times* in London (6 March), the *Jewish Chronicle* (7 March), and in scores of other leading papers. Arthur Ruppin hailed it in the *Jüdische Rundschau* as "a document of historic importance" and pointed out that it was "the first Arab voice which had expressed sympathy with national Jewish aims."[42] Samuel Tolkowsky, a member of the Zionist delegation, brought a French translation of Feisal's letter to the editor of *Le Matin*, but the latter refrained from publishing it,[43] which confirms our assumption that the editor nourished ulterior motives when interviewing Feisal.

Among personalities to whom Frankfurter sent copies were: Professor William L. Westermann, Dr. Sidney Mezes, head of the Western Asia Division of the American delegation, William Yale, Director of the Intelligence Section, and Ormsby-Gore for the British delegation.[44] Weizmann sent a separate copy to Balfour.[45] Significant was also Frankfurter's instruction to Robert Szold, the Acting Chairman of the Zionist Commission in Palestine, to give Feisal's letter every possible publicity,[46] presumably in order that the Arab population too would become cognizant of it. The Arab press was soon to pick up the issue, albeit in a negative way. Thus, in its issue of 26 March, the *Suriya-el-Jadida*, a daily in Damascus, greeted the news with disbelief and questioned the authenticity of Feisal's letter.[47]

Regardless, Feisal continued to act in the spirit of his accord with the Zionists. On 15 April, he received a delegation of the Palestinian Jewish community, headed by David Yellin, Aaron Eisenberg, Meyer Dizengoff, the mayor of Tel-Aviv, and other prominent public figures. He greeted them affably and, addressing them as "brothers," proclaimed himself a staunch supporter of the Zionist idea. As an Arab, his first duty, he declared, was to his fellow Arabs, but "since they [the delegates] were Semites, not Frenchmen or English," he would speak to them freely. He confided being criticized by some Arabs for leaving Palestine alone, but "this I did after careful calculations. My primary interest lay in the Hedjaz and in Syria. Why should I get involved in a complicated problem like Palestine, to which the Jews lay claim as well?" He hoped, on his return to Syria, to be able to convince the Palestinians (with whom he was thought to have some influence) to cooperate with the Zionists and invited his visitors to see him in Damascus in the near future.[48] Feisal's statement sounded like an echo of Sykes's advice given to the Syrians in Cairo in April 1917, as well as to King Hussein and himself while in Akaba.[49]

Also present during Feisal's meeting with the delegation of the Palestine Jews was Auni Bey Abdul Hadi, Feisal's Secretary-General and a member of the Hedjazi delegation at the Peace Conference. A scion of the well-known Nablus family and a graduate of the Sorbonne University, he became a leading national activist of the Palestinian Arabs during the Mandate period. Five days after this meeting — that is, on 20 April — there was yet another meeting at Feisal's residence between Abdul Hadi and the same Jewish delegation in order to discuss the mutual relationship between Arabs and Jews in Palestine. After an exchange of views, it was decided unanimously to found a joint Arab-Jewish Committee, the objectives of which would be:

1. Creation of a "rapprochement and an entente between the two communities in Palestine" with a view to further the political and economic development of the country.

2. To prevent any manifestations of hostilities of one part of the population against the other.

3. To define the privileges and duties for all the ethnic groups in Palestine with regard to the future administration of the country and all other aspects of communal life.

4. To establish a Central Committee composed of twelve members: six Arabs and six Jews. The former would be appointed by Abdul Hadi and his colleagues, whereas the latter would be appointed by those Jewish representatives listed at the end of the document. The committee would be established in Jerusalem.

5. The Central Committee would appoint regional committees in various centers of the country with the above-mentioned objectives.[50]

This accord was to serve as the first step toward the implementation of the Weizmann-Feisal Agreement of 3 January 1919, but, whereas the Agreement had been drafted from a regional perspective, the accord was meant to regularize the inter-communal relations in Palestine proper and to assuage the fears of Arab Palestinians of Jewish domination and deprivation of their rights. It was to form a basis for future negotiations after Feisal's return to Damascus.

Abdul Hadi also attended the meeting during which Feisal signed his letter to Frankfurter. Present at that time were also Nuri Said (later Prime Minister of Iraq), Rustum Haidar, General Haddad Pasha (a Syrian who served during the War in the British Administration in Egypt and Jerusalem and who was later appointed to be Feisal's political representative in Europe), as well as Fuad el-Khatib, the Under-Secretary of State of the Hedjazi Government. All of them were members of the Hedjazi delegation. At no time did they disagree with Feisal's moves.[51]

In 1922, Ittamar Ben-Avi, the son of Eliezer Ben-Yehuda, the celebrated Hebrew linguist and author, met Feisal, now the King of Iraq, in Paris. Three Arab personalities made this meeting possible: Najjar Pasha, Feisal's aide-de-camp, Riad Bey el-Sulh of Beirut, and Auni Abdul Hadi. Ben-Avi wished to revive the moribund Arab-Zionist *rapprochement*, whereas Feisal was angling for financial largesse from the Rothschild family. The conversation throughout was cordial and informal. When Ben-Avi steered it to the correspondence with Frankfurter, the King unhesitantly confirmed the content of his letter to Frankfurter (3 March 1919), and added: "I shall repeat and reemphasize it in the coming years." But in a veiled reproach, he pointed out that, so far, the Jews had failed to make their promised financial and territorial assistance good. He suggested that a joint venture be set up for "mutual assistance . . . so that every Arab . . . will be your faithful friend." When James de Rothschild joined the party, toasts were exchanged to "the Semitic Covenant" between the respective "Arab and Jewish Kingdoms." However, the financial aid that Feisal expected for Iraq surpassed even the Rothschilds' ability to meet.[52]

It was not before the Summer of 1923, when the Third Palestine delegation was visiting London, that Musa Kazim Pasha al-Husseini, its head, questioned the authenticity of Feisal's letter. The Zionists were embarrassed, because the original was mis-laid and could not be located.[53] The Shaw Commission, which had been appointed to investigate the causes of the 1929 riots, raised the matter again during their inquiries. Subhi Bey al-Khadra, a lawyer and a member of the Arab Executive, denied any knowledge of Feisal's letter and could not believe that a document of this nature would ever have been written by Feisal. He also made a bizarre remark that the accredited representa-tives on the Hedjazi delegation were Rustum Haidar and Abdul Hadi, not Feisal. Abdul Hadi confirmed al-Khadra's revelation, remarking that all that the Zionists had produced was a second typewritten copy, which, he alleged, was "a forgery." Feisal, then King of Iraq, was contacted and Rustum Haidar, Chief Political Secretary, cabled the following:

> His Majesty does not remember having written anything of this kind with his knowledge.[54]

The Zionists were outraged. Meyer Weisgal, the Secretary-General of the Zionist Organization in the United States, urged Frankfurter to put the record straight for presentation to the Shaw Commission.[55] With his characteristic precision and

clarity,[56] Frankfurter described the background to the correspondence with the Emir. The interview, he recalled, took place
on March 3rd at Feisal's residence in the presence of members
of the Hedjazi delegation, while Lawrence acted as interpreter.
Frankfurter set forth the Zionists' attitude, particularly those in
America, toward the realization of Arab aspirations and about
their mutual relationship. Feisal was in full accord with Frankfurter's views and "voiced his support of the Zionist program
as it had been submitted to the [Supreme] Council very
recently."

It was deemed desirable to make a record of what passed,
Frankfurter continued, and it was agreed that Lawrence was to
frame in English the substance of Feisal's views *pari passu* with
Frankfurter's affirmation of the Zionists' position. This procedure was carried out to the full satisfaction of both parties.
Feisal's letter was cabled on the same day to Justice Brandeis,
as well as the Zionist Bureau in London, and had been kept
since among their respective records. It was published widely in
the press and attracted lively comment:

> It is utterly grotesque [Frankfurter went on] now to raise the
> slightest question in regard to the authenticity of Prince Feisal's
> letter. It was a document prepared under the most responsible
> conditions. It received important publicity at the time. It has
> ever since been treated without question as one of the basic docu-
> ments affecting Palestinian affairs and Arab-Jew relations.[57]

Frankfurter published this statement in the *Atlantic Monthly*
(30 October 1930) in order to rebut the points made by Professor William E. Hocking in the same journal in its July 1930
issue.[58] In his article, Hocking, a distinguished American philo-
sopher, formerly a pro-Zionist and later a fervent Arabophile,
had repeated almost verbatim al-Khadra's and Abdul Hadi's
version propounded before the Shaw Commission.

In 1930, Professor Nathan Feinberg, of the Hague Academy
of International Law, happened to meet King Feisal in Geneva.
"The King," Professor Feinberg recorded, "did not deny the
authenticity of his letter to Frankfurter, but claimed that he
could not remember having written it."[59] It would perhaps be
unfair to accuse Feisal of dishonesty for his diplomatic
forgetfulness, since, strictly speaking, it was Lawrence who

drafted the letter in English; Feisal only signed it. In contrast, William Yale, then Professor of Near Eastern History at Yale University, remembered it well when approached by Frankfurter in the same year. "I first became familiar with this correspondence," he responded, "in Paris in 1919," and confirmed Feisal's letter to be authentic.[60]

In December 1964, when the Jewish Agency in London moved to its new residence, Mr. Joseph Fraenkel, an historian, by chance found the original of Feisal's letter. A photostatic copy of it appeared thereafter in the Press[61] and in a number of publications. An intriguing episode thus came to a close.

Unlike Feisal's correspondence with Frankfurter, the Agreement with Weizmann was kept secret, evidently at Feisal's request. In September 1930, when it came to his knowledge that the Zionists had deposited a photostatic copy of it at the Colonial Office, he became most anxious lest it was made public. Through Jacob Landau, the Director of the Jewish Telegraphic Agency in London, he conveyed to Dr. Weizmann that he still considered the Agreement with him as a "Treaty of Amity," but pointed to the detrimental effect its publication would have on Arab opinion.[62]

It was only on 10 June 1936, after Feisal's death (8 September 1933), that Weizmann published this document in full in *The Times*.[63] On 26 January 1937, he submitted it to the Palestine Royal Commission (the Peel Commission). Its publication fell like a bombshell in the Palestinian camp. Bewildered, Hajj Amin al-Husseini, the Mufti of Jerusalem, requested that Emir Abdullah issue a formal denial. Abdullah declined. Upon examination of the photostatic copy of the Agreement, he easily identified his brother's signature, as well as his handwriting, in the reservation, which was replete with characteristic calligraphic errors that Feisal had retained since childhood. An appeal by the Arab Executive Committee to Abdullah to issue a statement to the effect that the Agreement was not binding fell on deaf ears. Thereupon, a delegation, headed by Izzat Darwaza and Abdul Hadi, called on the Emir in Amman to voice its displeasure. On his part, Abdullah counseled them to exercise prudence. The Jews in Palestine were an economic and political factor which he, as a realist and statesman, could not ignore. The Palestinian Arabs could blame only themselves for selling land to the Jews.[64] It is noteworthy that the famous McMahon "pledge" was not raised during the encounter with Abdullah, although the issue was being hotly debated at that time with the British.

Abdul Hadi tried to make another point during his testimony given to the Anglo-American Committee of Inquiry, 1947. He suggested that the Emir Feisal "did not know what he was signing, because the agreement [with Weizmann] was not in Arabic." Bartley Crum, a member of the Committee, asked him point blank, "Are you suggesting that Colonel Lawrence deliberately muddled Feisal?" Abdul Hadi nodded in agreement. "Certainly. I know it. . . . Lawrence was careful not to allow any Arab to be present during the meeting. . . . he had tricked Feisal deliberately and with foreknowledge. And . . . presumably Weizmann, too, was in the plot."

Crum noted in his memoirs, which appeared in the same year:

> It was incredible that Feisal should be ignorant of what was in the statement, because he had initialed an Arab translation, and added a postscript in his own hand saying that he could not be held to his promise if certain conditions were not carried out.[65]

Abdul Hadi's testimony was in line with that of Said Rustum Haidar, his colleague in the Hedjazi delegation. Reacting to a statement made by Malcolm MacDonald, the British Colonial Secretary, about the Weizmann-Feisal Agreement, Haidar wrote,

> I can recall no knowledge of it and it would be of interest if the Arabic text were published . . . it is generally known that the late King Feisal knew not a word of English at that time, and I fear lest there should have been an intrigue in the matter which may have been secretly contrived for obvious motives.

The letters which King Feisal might have written to certain Zionists, Haidar went on, were inspired by "a sense of courtesy" with a view of creating a conducive atmosphere for advancement of the Arab cause. But, he emphasized,

> A gesture of this kind is one thing — to concede Palestine as a

National Home for the Jews is another. I can definitely say that
the late King Feisal did not do anything of the kind, nor could he
ever possibly have thought of doing it.[66]

Arab protagonists did their best to minimize the importance
of this episode and to absolve Feisal of having made such
statements. Antonius attributed Feisal's docility to being subjected to "pressure," to his ignorance of English, and to his
unfamiliarity with the methods of European diplomacy. He
gives Feisal credit, however, for his "positive belief in the possibility of Arab-Jewish co-operation . . . so long as that did not
conflict with Arab independence," which, in Antonius's view,
included Palestine.[67]

Antonius was silent about the Feisal-Frankfurther correspondence; nor did he mention Feisal's positive exclusion of
Palestine from his desiderata, both in his 1 January 1919 memorandum and in his statement to the Supreme Council on 6
February. This was not a casual oversight, since all the relevant
documents were at his disposal.[68]

Suleiman Mousa was not the first, and not the last, among
Arab historians to claim that the two documents in question
were "forgeries." "Feisal," Mousa wrote, "could not possibly
have put his signature on anything that would have harmed the
Arab cause,"[69] while Tibawi is not short of disparaging remarks on the first document, and, with regard to the second,
implies that it was Lawrence who actually signed it for Feisal.
Even when a photostat of Feisal's original letter to Frankfurter
was published (e.g., in the *Jerusalem Post* of 16 December 1964),
he continued to question its authenticity. "Faisal's usual signature was in larger, bolder and clearer hand . . . This revelation,"
he went on, "goes a long way to confirm 'Auni 'Abdul-Hadi
that the letter was a forgery."[70]

Feisal's signature, which appears on numerous documents
in other matters, is a testimony to the contrary. So is its unmistakable identification by Emir Abdullah early in 1937.[71] Any
uninitiated scholar would confirm that the version propounded
by Antonius, Mousa, Tibawi, and others is a flagrant distortion
of the events. The portrayal of Feisal as an innocent victim of
pressure exerted on him, and of deception, is nonsensical. And
had Feisal really been unaware of what he was signing, as

Antonius and his followers claimed, he would not have appended his reservation to the Agreement with Weizmann. Such an imputation, albeit inadvertently, against Feisal's character is an offense to his intelligence and good sense, for, his limitations notwithstanding, Feisal, more than any of his Arab contemporaries, was well-versed in international politics. Equally unjust is the comment on Lawrence, whose devotion to the Arab cause was unquestionable. There was no other person than Lawrence to whom Feisal owed his career during the War and thereafter in the Council of Nations.

There remains the question of Feisal's status. Henry Cattan, a Palestinian jurist, contended that the Emir Feisal only took part in the Paris Peace Conference of 1919 "to secure political support for the claims of Hedjaz," and that "he possessed no representative capacity that entitled him to speak on behalf of the Arabs of Palestine or of the Arabs generally."[72] A Palestinian historian, Bayan N. al-Hout, also concluded that Feisal had no legal right to negotiate on behalf of the Palestinians.[73] This is a variant of what Abdul Hadi declared before the Shaw Commission in 1929. Clearly, it is an afterthought rather than historical reasoning. Although officially Feisal stood at the head of the Hedjazi delegation, he did not make demands of the Supreme Council specifically for the Hedjaz, which had already been recognized, but, with the exception of Palestine, he asked for the "independence of all the Arabic speaking peoples in Asia."[74] In his memorandum, dated 1 March 1919, in the section dealing with the Arab national movement, Feisal expressly emphasized that King Hussein, his father, "became [its] leader in war after combined appeals from the Syrian and Mesopotamian branches," and that his father had a "privileged place among the Arabs, as their successful leader . . . as Sherif of Mecca."[75]

As curious as it may be, Antonius endorses this view. He defined the status of King Hussein, in whose name Feisal appeared and acted at the Peace Conference, as "the authorised spokesman of the [Arab] national movement."[76] It should be borne in mind that only the Conference was entitled to define the legality of any delegation and, as we saw, none of its members disputed Feisal's status.

Feisal's standing at the Peace Conference was sounder than

it was at home, where his position was woefully weak. Following his return to Syria, his relations with the Zionists underwent a gradual transformation. Consequently, the Agreement with Weizmann was not implemented. This was not necessarily because of diminution of interest — Feisal always had a sneaking affection for Weizmann — but because he was not master in his own house and lacked the necessary qualities of leadership to impose his will on his followers. It should be pointed out, however, that, in spite of fierce opposition at home, he never disavowed the Agreement, either publicly, or in private. In an interview with the *Daily Mail* of 30 March 1921, he declared: "As for the Zionist question, I arrived at an understanding satisfactory to us both, with Dr. Weizmann, and I am ready to carry it out."[77] In Feisal's eyes, the Sharifian-Zionist accord of 3 January 1919 remained valid, although, ironically, by 1921, its value was only academic, since Feisal was no longer the ruler of Syria.

The Agreement proved to be abortive. Nonetheless, historically it is an important document. In it, as well as in his letter to Frankfurter, Feisal recognized the Balfour Declaration and the legitimacy of the Zionist aspirations. Consonant with his father's standing policy, he excluded Palestine — consciously and deliberately — without disregarding the interests of the Palestinian Arabs, which were to be safeguarded. He believed that, in the long run, the Palestinian Arabs would benefit from Jewish colonization. His calculations, however, were made from a wider perspective. In Arab-Jewish cooperation, an idea to which he referred again and again, he saw the key to the revival of the Near East and a means to build Arab independence without the interference of the European Powers.

10

The King-Crane Commission and the Unmaking of the Weizmann-Feisal Agreement

At the time that Feisal was consolidating his entente with the Zionists, Sykes was touring in the East. There the picture was totally different. Since Feisal's departure for Europe, Palestinian opposition to Zionism had increased. Clayton attributed it to Pan-Arab sentiment.[1] The old generation, the ruling elite of the *effendis*, was primarily concerned with maintenance of their privileged positions rather than with national aspirations.[2] Materialistic and pragmatic, they were prepared to accept "the control of a European Power and even to conclude an entente with the Jews on a federative basis," provided their own interests were safeguarded. In contrast, the young generation, which was imbued with an extreme brand of nationalism, aspired to the complete independence of all Arabic-speaking provinces. They were as fiercely anti-Zionist as they were anti-British. They were also anti-Sharifian. However, following the conquest of Damascus, they made a sharp reversal and discovered in the "independent" Arab government a vehicle to combat Zionism. In Damascus, unlike Palestine, they could freely engage in politics and were unhindered in their propaganda activity. The slogan that came to dominate the Young Palestinians' activity was "United Syria," an artificial creation, the purpose of which was to wrest Palestine from Zionist "domination" and parry European encroachment.[3]

The Young Arabs of Palestine were organized into clubs, of

which the most prominent were *al-Muntada al-Arabi* (the Literary Club) and *al-Nadi al-Arabi* (the Arab Club). The former was led by the al-Nashashibis, and the latter by the al-Husseini family. The number of members was small, not exceeding 500 in each club, but their influence by far surpassed their numerical inferiority. They were vocal, resolute, and dedicated. Constant perennial feuding separated the two clubs, but ideologically there was little difference between them. The moving spirit of the *al-Nadi al-Arabi* was Hajj Amin al-Husseini, who served as its president, whereas among the *al-Muntada al-Arabi* ranks, the most prominent member was Izzat Darwaza, its secretary, who later became Secretary of the General Syrian Congress.[4]

The head of the *al-Muntada al-Arabi* branch in Damascus was Shaykh Abd al-Qādir al-Muzaffar. In 1915, he served as the Immam (Chaplain) of an Ottoman Battalion on the Sinai front. An inspiring orator, his task was to propagate the gospel of the *jihad* against the Allied forces. He continued his anti-British campaign even after World War I ended, describing them as "the meanest nation in the world which never keeps its word." He was fanatically hostile toward the Jews, not only those who lived in Palestine, but even those in Damascus.[5] At the War Office, he was regarded as "a dangerous . . . man" who had been responsible for organizing anti-Jewish demonstrations and riots.[6]

The test of strength within the Palestine community took place at the First Palestine Congress (27 January-10 February 1919) in Jerusalem. In general, the Palestinians felt little affinity with Syria.[7] The older generation in particular was concerned with parochial matters,[8] but the Young Arabs won the day, and it was under their pressure that the slogan of "United Syria" finally triumphed at the Congress. It was resolved to rename "Palestine" "Southern Syria." Other resolutions called for Syrian independence and for measures to counter the Zionist enterprise.[9] Protests to this effect were sent to the Peace Conference.[10]

On his arrival in Jerusalem in mid-November 1918, Sir Mark Sykes found the atmosphere tense. The Zionists complained that the Arabs were becoming aggressive and were taking advantage of the partiality which the Military Authorities displayed toward them, while the Arabs accused the Zionists of being provocative and pointed their finger at London for "acting in such a way that the Palestinian Arabs will sooner or later become subject to Jewish rule."

The Moslems, Sykes reported, feared Jewish brain-power and enterprise. Infected by Arab nationalist effervescence, they "are imbued with a tincture of race hatred," whereas the Christians disliked the Jews on religious and racial grounds and were disappointed not to gain the dominant position they had expected when a Christian Power took over the country. Moreover, Turkish agents and other intriguers, who proliferated in the country, were "doing their best to make the situation as bad as possible." He thought that it should be made clear to the Palestinian Arabs that, while the British Government was determined to watch over their interests, the Balfour Declaration was "a settled part of the policy of His Majesty's Government" and was confirmed by the Entente as a whole.[11]

Sykes soon discovered that the anti-Zionist agitation originated in Damascus; the most prominent activists were Hajj Amin al-Husseini and Abd al-Qādir al-Muzaffar, both leaders of the *al-Nadi al-Arabi* club. The former was based in Aleppo, a stronghold of the pro-Turks, and the latter resided in Damascus, which became the center of Palestinian activity:

> Syrian agitators went down to Palestine and Palestinian agitators came up to Syria, and a campaign was [unleashed] which threatened to become serious.[12]

Sykes was known to be sympathetic to both Arab nationalism and Zionism, and was a firm believer in Armenian independence. "I want to see a permanent Anglo-French Entente," he wrote in August 1917, "allied to the Jews, Arabs and Armenians which will render Pan-Islamism innocuous."[13] He expected that the Arab national movement in particular would constitute an effective antidote to Pan-Islam. Now this "grand design" was in ruins. Arab nationalism was assuming a Pan-Arab and a Pan-Islamic character. Islam was becoming the core of the Arab movement. Calls for "complete independence from any form of Foreign control" were eliciting violent and passionate applause at public meetings:

> There can be no doubt [Sykes warned] that if [the spirit of
> religious fanaticism] gets firm hold of the people, the position of
> the Christians and Jews will become intolerable.

He felt bound to stress this point because he had noticed that
some British officers failed to appreciate that the anti-Jewish
and anti-French sentiments, to which they sometimes listened
with complacency, were "really only forerunners of anti-British
feelings and indeed anti-Foreign and anti-non-Moslem feeling":

> My experience is that if only the British will stand up to the
> Syrian Arabs and make it plain that certain things will not be
> tolerated, the agitation will collapse, providing always that
> the Zionists do not ask for more than justice or reason can
> demand.[14]

One of Sykes's assignments during his stay in the East was
to coordinate Anglo-French policy and to assist in promoting
good relations between the French and the Arabs.[15] This was in
line with the instructions that the Foreign Office had given to
Clayton on 12 October 1918:

> The guiding principles which should govern your policy should
> be (1) to promote good relations between Arabs and French; (2) to
> encourage to your utmost Arab confidence in the sincerity of En-
> tente's purpose in [their] policy of liberation.[16]

The British officers, however, were slow to comply with these
instructions. Nor did they take much heed of Sykes's warning.
The *fait accompli* established by Lawrence in Damascus on 1
October 1918[17] marred Anglo-French relations in the years to
come. Sykes reasoned: "Had the French conquered the country,
or been in a position to occupy it by force at an early date, the
natural stimulus of self-interest would have produced a large
number of Francophile Muslims." But the contrary had happened and the installation of Feisal in Damascus "without the
knowledge of the French Government, which is now an open
secret, put Franco-Syrian Moslem relations on an even more
difficult basis."[18]

The French were fully cognizant of what was afoot, and, as
Young revealed several years later, they suspected that "by

introducing a foreign ruler [i.e., Feisal] into their sphere [the British] were trying to undermine French legitimate influence."[19] Captain Young, as mentioned already, was privy to the events leading to the capture of Damascus.

British officers in the East did little to assuage French grievances and the Parisian Press was bitterly critical. On 31 January 1919, Stephen Pichon, the French Minister for Foreign Affairs, complained to Balfour about the unfriendly attitude that certain British officers adopted toward their French counterparts. It was alien to the spirit of the Entente Cordiale. Pichon listed a number of incidents, the cumulative effect of which was to create a *fait accompli* which harmed French standing and showed the native population that France was merely "a minor Power." Particularly offensive was the conduct of the Sharifians toward the French and their dissemination of rumors that England was bent on creating an Arab-Sharifian Empire.[20]

Sykes returned to Europe a frustrated and dispirited man. The way the Middle East was now shaping was not to his liking. His mission had failed. He painted a gloomy picture of the situation in Palestine to Aaron Aaronsohn, an old friend of his, when they met at the Peace Conference in Paris. British Military officers in charge of administration were biased toward the Arabs and hostile toward the Jews, while the Husseinis and their supporters were intriguing and becoming more insolent.[21]

On 16 February 1919, Sir Mark Sykes died. (During his stay in the East, he had contracted a fatal infection.) With him died his brain-child: an Arab-Zionist-Armenian entente under British and French aegis in their respective spheres of influence. In the absence of a conducive atmosphere in the Middle East, the Weizmann-Feisal Agreement was doomed.

When the anti-Zionist protests reached the Peace Conference, Balfour relayed them to Lawrence. Thereupon, Feisal cabled to Emir Zeid, his brother, who was deputizing for him in Damascus during his absence:

> I see anti-Zionist articles in your Damascus papers. Please explain privately to Ali Riza [sic] that the Zionist Committee is helping us very much here in Paris and that I am most anxious to

retain their goodwill. Do your best to control the press on this point.[22]

Feisal left Paris on 23 April in order to meet the International Committee of Inquiry which was scheduled to arrive in Syria. It was Feisal who had asked President Wilson, when they met in Paris,[23] to send a commission to ascertain the wishes of the Syrian people as to their choice of a mandatory Power. He aired this idea a month after the capture of Damascus, although at that time only with regard to the disputed area which covered the Kazas of Hazbeya, Rasheya, and Ba'albek. Otherwise, he accepted without reservation General Allenby's administrative division of the Occupied Enemy Territory Area (the O.E.T.A.), according to which Palestine was separate.[24] It was, however, Dr. Howard Bliss, an American born in Syria and the President of the Syrian Protestant College (from 1920, the American University of Beirut), who won the President over to the idea. Bliss "laid the essential foundations for the sending of a Commission of Inquiry to the East."[25] Its purpose was "to give an opportunity to the people of Syria, including the Lebanon, to express their political wishes and . . . desire as to what Power, if any, should be their Mandatory Protecting Power." He based his plea on the Wilsonian principles, as well as on the Anglo-French Declaration of November 1918. Palestine, on which President Wilson had strong opinions, was to be excluded from the scope of the inquiry.[26]

On March 20, when the disagreement between Lloyd George and Clemenceau over Syria came into the open, President Wilson intervened, observing that the wishes of the people concerned should be the determining factor in the choice of the mandatory, and espoused the proposal made by Feisal and Bliss. Clemenceau acquiesced in principle, though on condition that the inquiry not be confined to Syria. Lloyd George agreed reluctantly.[27] Thereupon, Wilson drafted the terms of reference for the proposed investigatory body.[28]

No sooner had the decision of the Council of Four been taken, than a meeting of experts convened by Wickham Steed, the editor of *The Times*, warned of the adverse effect that sending an international commission to Syria would have: "It would unsettle the country [and] make it appear that the Conference had been unable to reach any decision. It would also open the door to intrigues and manifestations of all kind." Present during the meeting were Gertrude Bell, T. E. Lawrence, and Sir Valentin Chirol of the Foreign Office, while the French were represented by Robert de Caix, Henri Brénier, and others.

Lawrence, the leading light during the discussion, suggested that it would be far more profitable if all the parties concerned reached an agreement on "general principles" and only there-after dispatch a competent commission to Syria to examine the details on the spot. He made it clear that "the movement for Arab unity possesses no serious political value for the present or, indeed, for the future." French representatives concurred with Lawrence, and it was finally agreed by all present that the French Government should approach Feisal and reach a settle-ment on the following lines:

1. France would receive a Mandate for Syria.
2. The Syrians would elect their own Prince; the obvious candidate was Emir Feisal.
3. French status in Syria would be analogous to that of British Agent *vis-à-vis* the Sultan of Egypt.[29]

Lawrence's change of heart with regard to French predomi-nance in Syria is puzzling, but he must have been aware that under no circumstances would the British Government accept a mandate over Syria and that it would be counter-productive to pit Feisal against the Quai d'Orsay.

Yale, who was intimately acquainted with the proceedings of this conference, thought that there was sufficient information on hand and it was superfluous to dispatch a special commis-sion of inquiry; it would cause an unnecessary delay in the settlement of a complicated problem. Professor Westermann, the Chief of the Western Asia Division of the American delegation, thought the same.[30] Gertrude Bell took the unpre-cedented step of approaching Stephen Bonsal directly and told him, for Colonel House's consumption, that it would be useless to carry out an enquiry, "for the Oriental does not speak freely to people whom he does not know. And the net result is that there is no real opinion."[31] Bonsal commented humorously, "Gertrude had studied the problem quite closely and, not

entirely without reason, she was inclined to think that our legis-
lators in Washington often forgot their responsibility for our
wards in the Philippines."[32]

Curzon, then in London, thought that if the dispatch of the
Commission could not be prevented, Britain should ensure that
Palestine and Mesopotamia were excluded from its scope of
enquiry.[33]

Balfour, the statesman-philosopher, questioned the wisdom
of the principle of self-determination being applied to the East:
"The language of the Covenant [Article 22 of the League of
Nations] may suit the longitude of Washington, Paris, or
Prague. But in the longitude of Damascus it will probably get us
into trouble." There were only three eligible mandatory Powers
for Syria: England, America, and France. England had refused,
America would refuse, "so that whatever the inhabitants may
wish, it is France they will certainly have. They may freely
choose, but it is Hobson's choice after all." And with regard to
Palestine, the Peace Conference did not suggest that the native
inhabitants be consulted at all, since

> The four Great Powers are committed to Zionism. And Zionism,
> be it right or wrong, good or bad, is rooted in age-long traditions,
> in present needs, in future hopes, of far profounder import than
> the desires and prejudices of the 700,000 Arabs who now inhabit
> that ancient land.[34]

The justification for ignoring the principle of self-determination,
Balfour wrote to Lloyd George,

> . . . is that we regard Palestine as being absolutely exceptional;
> that we consider the question of the Jews outside Palestine as one
> of world importance, and that we conceive the Jews to have an
> historic claim to a home in their ancient land, provided that
> home can be given them without either dispossessing or oppres-
> sing the present inhabitant.[35]

Three decades later, Quincy Wright, an authority on the
mandates under the League of Nations, expressed an analogous
view at a scholarly conference:

> Palestine is perhaps the outstanding area of the world in which
> self-determination is inapplicable because of the greater weight

of external, as compared to internal, political forces in shaping its destiny.[36]

Application of the principle of self-determination to the peoples in the East came under fire as early as 5 December 1918 at a meeting of the Eastern Committee of the War Cabinet. Lord Robert Cecil, the Under-Secretary of State, cautioned that one should not be over-pedantic when the future of Syria was discussed: "In territories of this kind we should not attempt to leave it to the populations" alone to decide their destiny. Lawrence was even more incisive:

> Self-determination . . . is a foolish idea in many ways. We might allow the people who have fought with us to determine themselves. People like the Mesopotamian Arabs, who have fought against us, deserve nothing from us in the way of self-determination.[37]

The same criterion applied to the Syrian and to the Palestinian Arabs.

President Wilson acquired a reputation for being inflexibly doctrinaire. However, on this particular issue, he was not as obdurate. Robert Lansing, the American Secretary of State, noted that, on a number of occasions during the Peace Conference, Wilson considered it expedient to abandon the principle of self-determination, realizing that, if applied indiscriminately, it would create difficulties in the solution of problems in many parts of the world, such as in North Africa, Syria, and Palestine. Lansing, for his part, subjected it to severe criticism. However important the idea was, he thought it should not become the determining factor in the decision-making process. There were additional elements that should be taken into account: strategic, economic, as well as ethnic. Palestine was a case in point. Lansing asked Wilson pointedly: "How can [the principle] be harmonized with Zionism, to which the President is practically committed?"[38] Wilson, however, saw no difficulty. Like General Smuts, Balfour, Robert Cecil, and others, he regarded Zionism to be consistent with the principle of self-determination. This was also the view taken in 1917 by the Russian Provisional Government, particularly Prince Lwow, the Prime Minister and a strong upholder of this principle.[39]

When Wilson appointed Dr. Henry C. King, President of Oberlin College, and Charles R. Crane, a Chicago millionaire, as members of the Inter-Allied Commission,[40] he could not envisage that their report would sharply diverge from his own approach. In all likelihood, he must have been unaware of their bias toward the Arabs, and that Crane, in particular, nourished a prejudice against Jews. On 24 November 1933, Crane gave a luncheon party in Cairo for a number of leading Moslem notables and clerics in order to present his *Weltanschauung*. He expressed his belief that "the age of European domination over the Moslem world has gone . . . leaving the field clear for Islam to take charge of its own destiny." He accused the Jews of conducting a world campaign against other religions. Their endeavor to return to Palestine and to establish themselves there with the aid of British force was a palpable manifestation of this campaign:

> They were not the old Hebrews . . . but an altogether different sort of Jew, who were impregnated with communistic and atheistic ideas, and whose arrival in the Holy Land of Palestine was primarily another move in the anti-God campaign which they had started in Russia and elsewhere, and by which they hoped to achieve the annihilation of established religion and indeed of all belief in God.

Crane went on to say that the Jews constituted a menace, both to Christianity and to Islam, and it was incumbent upon them to unite in order to counter this danger. Hajj Amin al-Husseini, the Grand Mufti in Jerusalem, shared his ideas. Influential circles in the Vatican also responded favorably to his overtures. The Papal Secretary, when he saw him in Rome, emphasized the importance of working out a practical plan.[41]

These ideas of Crane, expressed in 1933, had already been simmering in his mind earlier. They were noticeable from his method of investigation during the summer of 1919, and detectable from his statement that Emir Feisal was "a real lover of Christians [and that he] could do more than any other [leader] to reconcile the Christians and Islam . . . [He] even talks seriously of an American college for women at Mecca."[42] Not one word did Crane emit about Feisal's sympathy toward the Jews, although the Jewish delegation in Palestine, which appeared before the American Commission, emphasized this point a number of times.

In May 1933, Crane wrote to Hamilton Fish, Jr., a member of the House of Representatives, Washington, D.C., that, soon after his investigation on the Commission, he visited King Hussein of the Hedjaz, who showed him two documents: one in which Hussein asked the British High Commissioner in 1915 specifically whether the British promise for Arab independence also included Syria and Palestine; and the second one, signed by the High Commissioner, answering in the affirmative:

> These papers [he added] are still in existence. Not only were these promises not kept, but as a Mandatory power in Palestine, Britain has practically abdicated—turning over the whole power . . . to the Jews, and Palestine is practically under a Jewish Mandate.[43]

He repeated the story in a letter to Sir George Young in England, observing that Allenby's appeal to the Arabs to join him during his campaign was based on these "promises." Nevertheless, the final result was that the Jew was substituted for the Turk: "the present actual situation is that the Jews are absolutely in control of every bit of the machinery. . . . It is really not any longer a British Mandate, but a Jewish Mandate."[44]

Crane could not possibly have visited the Hedjaz in 1919. Soon after completing his investigation, he went with Dr. King to Constantinople and thereafter to the United States. His version of a British commitment to Hussein with regard to Palestine is pure fabrication. The King-Crane report makes no mention of the McMahon-Hussein Correspondence; in all likelihood, at that time Crane must have been totally ignorant of it.

Wilson justified his selection of commissioners on the grounds, as White, the Secretary to the Commission, confided, that "these two men were particularly qualified to go to Syria because they knew nothing about it"[45]—a statement which inevitably invites the question whether ignorance is a prerequisite for competence and impartiality.

Wilson was, as a matter of course, indebted to Crane for furnishing sizable sums for his presidential campaign in 1916, but the most plausible explanation for his laxity in choosing him and King was the plain fact that, *a priori*, he did not expect Palestine to be included in the investigation. It was Syria—more precisely, the Syrian hinterland—that constituted the bone of contention, not Palestine. It was perhaps not accidental that Palestine was not specifically mentioned in the terms of reference of the Commission as proposed by Wilson and confirmed on 25 March 1919 by the Council of Four. The Commission was requested "to make enquiries in certain portions of the Turkish Empire which are to be permanently separated from Turkey and put under the guidance of governments acting as Mandatories for the League of Nations."[46] The key word in this phrase is "enquiries," as distinct from recommendations. It was also understood at that time by all concerned that Palestine was specifically excluded from the Commission's terms of reference.[47] Frankfurter's correspondence in this matter is illuminating. On March 28, 1919, he cabled to Brandeis:

> Great deal of opposition to such commission, and differences may still be adjusted here without Commission. In any event, I have direct assurances of President, through the Colonel, as well as Colonel's [personal assurances], that Palestine wholly outside Commission's jurisdiction. Our Commissioners will be so instructed.[48]

And to Robert Szold, the Acting Chairman of the Zionist Commission in Palestine, Frankfurter wrote that the Zionist Delegation received assurances that "Palestine will be set aside as the foundation for the Jewish homeland and that Great Britain will be named mandatory."[49] Agitation in Damascus for a United Syria was becoming more vocal, and Frankfurter, concerned lest it adversely affect the Commissioners, turned to House again. The latter advised him to speak to Crane directly. When they met (30 April), Frankfurter found Crane forthcoming:

> He wishes me to say to you [Frankfurter briefed House] that he and Dr. King are endeavoring to have the field of inquiry of the Syrian Commission . . . restricted so as to begin from Syria northward. Specifically, he thinks it is important to have territory about which there is no contention, like the Hedgaz [*sic*] and

Palestine, excluded from the scope of the Commission's inquiry.[50]

President Wilson was about to return to the United States, and Frankfurter sought repeated reassurances. On 16 May 1919, Wilson replied,

> I never dreamed that it was necessary to give you any renewed assurance of my adhesion [sic] to the Balfour Declaration, and so far I have found no one who is seriously opposing the purpose which it embodies . . . I see no ground for discouragement and every reason to hope that satisfactory guarantees can be secured.[51]

In fact, Wilson went beyond support of the Balfour Declaration. On 14 January, 1919, when he met Weizmann, he declared that his Government and the American people agreed that in Palestine "shall be laid the foundation of a Jewish Commonwealth." He offered Weizmann his "entire support . . . full and unhampered."[52]

King and Crane were fully aware of Wilson's position. On 2 March 1919, Wilson received a deputation of the American Jewish Congress consisting of Stephen Wise, Judge Julian Mack, and Louis Marshall and expressed his confidence that the Allied nations, with the fullest concurrence of the American Government, were agreed that in Palestine "shall be laid the foundations of a Jewish Commonwealth." The statement also appeared in the Egyptian press, and some of the State Department officials, as well as the Commissioners, expressed concern about its effect on the Palestinian Arabs. An enquiry showed that Wilson's statement was authentic and, after a consultation with the Commissioners, it was decided not to ask the President to issue a *démenti*.[53]

In all likelihood, King and Crane were also briefed about the report of the Intelligence Section of the American Delegation to the Peace Conference, which recommended that "there be established a separate state in Palestine," and that "it will be the policy of the League of Nations to recognize Palestine as a Jewish state, as soon as it is a Jewish state in fact." In the discussion that followed, it was declared:

> It is right that Palestine should become a Jewish state, if the Jews, being given the full opportunity, make it such. It was the

cradle and home of their vital race, which has made large spiritual contributions to mankind, and is the only land in which they can hope to find a home of their own; they being in this last respect unique among significant peoples.

At present, however, the Jews form barely a sixth of the total of 700,000 in Palestine, and whether they are to form a majority, or even a plurality, of the population in the future state remains uncertain. Palestine, in short, is far from being a Jewish country now. England, as mandatory, can be relied on to give the Jews the privileged position they should have without sacrificing the rights of non-Jews.

The holy places and religious rights of all creeds in Palestine were to be placed under the protection of the League of Nations, and its mandatory. The Intelligence Section also recommended that "there be established a Syrian state" and that the mandatory principle should be applied to it, but no recommendation was made "as to the Power to be selected to carry out this principle."[54] It was in this particular province that the International Commission was expected to conduct its enquiries.

The Commission's departure for the East was hanging fire because of the disagreement among the Allies. The French were willing to join the investigation provided Syria was garrisoned by French rather than British troops, and their financial subsidy of the Arab Government in Damascus was substituted for the British. This, Allenby resisted strenuously. Clemenceau remained, however, adamant. "As long as Syria remained entirely under British military occupation," he said, "it was useless to send French Commissioners." Lloyd George was equally emphatic: ". . . he would not send Commissioners if the French did not."[55] In these circumstances, Westermann thought it wiser not to send the American members. A rump commission would do a great deal of harm, without achieving anything constructive or adding to the information already available in Paris. But Wilson made up his mind and instructed the American Section to go on their own. They left Paris for Constantinople at the end of May and were accompanied by three experts from the Intelligence Section: Professor Albert Lybyer, an eminent Orientalist, the Reverend George Montgomery, a Protestant missionary who resided in the East, and William Yale.[56]

Events proved Westermann right. The appearance of an American, as distinct from Inter-Allied, Commission, gave the native inhabitants the erroneous impression that, if requested, America would not refuse to accept a protectorate over Syria, which was, obviously, not the case. The entire venture turned into an exercise in futility. Miss Bell, in her 15 November 1919 memorandum,[57] condemned the rump Commission as "a criminal deception."

Feisal arrived in Beirut on 30 April. During his absence, the economic position in Syria had deteriorated and the country was crippled by a growing political malaise. Disorder prevailed. Europeans complained that they could get no justice, and there were serious riots in the north between Moslems and Armenians.[58] Three formidable tasks confronted the Emir: to consolidate his position; to prepare his testimony for the Commission; and, to put into effect his agreement on Arab-Zionist cooperation.

On 9 May, Feisal addressed a large gathering of Syrian notables and briefed them about the claims that he had presented to the Peace Conference. "I asked that el-Hedjaz, Syria, and el-Irak should each have an independent Government by itself, but all united within the great union of Arab countries." Significantly, he did not mention Palestine, nor did he include it within the area of Arab independence. All the delegates present expressed individually their confidence in his leadership.[59]

Buoyed by such unanimous support, Feisal hoped to be able to bring about an Arab-Jewish reconciliation and make Zionism acceptable to his fellow Arabs. On 11 May, Clayton cabled the Foreign Office:

> Feisal has already begun [?work] of reconciling Arabs to Zionist policy. He informed an Arab delegation in Damascus that he would not consider Arab and Zionist aims to be incompatible and delegation seemed favourably impressed. Members of Zionist Commission are being invited to visit Feisal who may also ask few leading Palestine Arabs to attend with a view to rapprochement. Urgent necessity for moderate and conciliatory attitude should be impressed on Zionists both here and in Europe in order that Feisal's efforts may not be nullified.[60]

Feisal, on his own accord, cabled the Zionist Commission in Jerusalem:

> Many thanks for your congratulations on my return . . . shall consider it a great pleasure to see a deputation of your committee in Damascus at an early date.

Clayton, who relayed this message, asked the Commission to let him know how soon the deputation would proceed to Damascus.[61] Delighted, Weizmann and Frankfurter responded instantly,

> We learn, with deep gratitude, of your continued efforts towards friendliest relations between Arabs and Jews. We wish you to be assured that, on our part, we shall further the happiest co-operation.[62]

However, this was not to be. The Weizmann-Frankfurter joint cable had hardly reached its destination when Lt. Colonel Kinahan Cornwallis, Deputy Chief Political Officer in Damascus, reported:

> Feisal is beginning to realise the difficulties which he will have in reconciling Palestinians and Zionists, and no longer treats the question as a minor one. He has abandoned his idea of having a conference here [Damascus] but he intends to ask various notables to visit him separately and endeavour to convert them. He will also try to induce the Zionist Commission to moderate its demands, and will probably propose a conference to the [King-Crane] Peace Commission.[63]

Feisal was taken aback by the vehement reaction of the Palestinians. Some of their leaders were "advocating the defence of Arab independence in Palestine by the sword," while al-Muzaffar's opinions had not mellowed with time. On 15 May, during a meeting in Feisal's honor, speeches were made demanding Palestine's "independence and [its] inclusion in the Syrian State."[64]

The political power did not rest with the assembly of notables, but with the extra-governmental organizations which, in the absence of an authoritative central administration, were becoming more assertive. Among the most influential organizations during the short-lived Arab regime in Damascus were *al-*

Ahd, al-Fatat, and *al-Nadi al-Arabi.* They dominated local political life in Syria and no major policy decisions could be taken without prior consultation with them.[65]

In 1915, the leaders of *al-Ahd* and *al-Fatat* swore allegiance to Feisal, as well as to his father, only to desert them soon after. Those who were spared execution or banishment by Djemal Pasha faithfully served their Turkish master throughout the War. Now, demobilized from the Ottoman Army, they flocked to Feisal's camp to reap the benefits of his victory. They enjoyed the subsidy provided by the British Treasury (amounting to £150,000 monthly), conscripted men, distributed jobs, and became the effective governors of Syria.

Perhaps the best example was the career of Yasin al-Hashimi, the founder and moving spirit of *al-Ahd.* It was on his own initiative that, late in 1915, al-Faruqi defected to the British to profess the Young Arabs' friendship for Britain,[66] while he himself rejoined the Ottoman Army. There, as a high-ranking officer, he excelled in his military exploits against the British on the Palestinian front.[67] When the Turks retreated from Damascus, al-Hashimi, like other Iraqi prisoners of war, changed his allegiance and joined Feisal. In the meantime, the Hedjazis and other tribesmen melted away and Feisal appointed al-Hashimi as Chief-of-Staff. The new Arab army in Syria was largely al-Hashimi's creation. He exerted a tremendous influence on Emir Zeid and on Feisal himself. He impressed Miss Bell as "the most forcible personality" she had ever met.[68]

Yasin al-Hashimi soon became one of the most extreme exponents of Arab independence, and, on the eve of the arrival of the Commission of Inquiry, he circulated a letter to the tribal chiefs in Mesopotamia asking them to demand "complete independence as one nation, with the assistance [as opposed to a Protectorate] of a single Power."[69] The Political Officer in Baghdad sounded an ominous note:

> The Arab movement is becoming steadily more anti-foreign and more anti-British. It shows, however, no sign of being constructive, nor does it promise to develop on peaceful lines. Arabia never has and never can be united.[70]

Another group that came into prominence in Damascus was that of the Palestinians. They idolized al-Hashimi. They

regarded him as "a true Arab nationalist" and a model to follow.[71] However, unlike the Iraqis, who were primarily officers
in control of the army, the Palestinians were predominantly
political activists. Formerly anti-Sharifian, they joined Feisal
with the explicit purpose of using his regime to combat Zionism
and wrest Palestine from a British tutelage. Among Feisal's
followers in Damascus, they were "the strongest advocates of
an Arab State without foreign control of any kind."[72] Ali Ridā
al-Rikabi was noted for his partiality toward them and gave
them posts in the Damascus Government.[73] Consequently,
members of the Executive Committee of the Arab Club (al-Nadi
al-Arabi) reached key positions in the administration, including
that of chief of Police in Damascus and the Commander of the
Gendarmerie.[74] The Palestinian activists were therefore in a
position to exert constant pressure on Feisal.[75]

There was yet another factor that nipped in the bud Feisal's
attempt to effect an Arab-Zionist rapprochement. On 15 May,
Clayton told Dr. Eder that,

> . . . the Commander-in-Chief does not consider it desirable that
> any conference should take place at present between Emir Faisal,
> the Zionist Commission and Palestinian Notables. Any such con-
> ference would trench [sic] upon the sphere of the Peace Commis-
> sion which is shortly arriving.
>
> At the same time the Emir Faisal is using every effort
> privately to influence any Palestinians who may visit him to
> moderate their antagonism to the Zionist policy. Emir Faisal
> trusts that the Zionist Commission will assist him by exercising
> influence in the direction of avoiding any extravagant demands
> or undue pushing of Zionist claims.[76]

Strangely enough, the cable was sent only a few days after
Clayton had relayed Feisal's explicit invitation to the Zionist
Commission to see him in Damascus.[77] Moreover, on 11 May,
Clayton made it clear to Eder that "there is no objection to your
visiting Emir Feisal as requested, but you should make arrangements to do so as soon as possible, as he may be absent from
Damascus shortly. Please wire me a date convenient to you
. . ."[78] Embarrassed, Eder cabled to Feisal: "Authorities have
asked us to postpone official visit. Regret we are unable to
leave tomorrow as we wired you yesterday we were doing."[79]

Clayton had to be corrected by Eder that it had not been pro-posed to hold a tripartite conference between Emir Feisal, the Zionist commission, and Palestinian notables;[80] at this stage, only a bilateral meeting with the Emir was intended: "the visit . . . had the Emir's approbation." All the same, the Military authorities would not budge. Major Waley, on Clayton's behalf, replied:

> . . . It is still considered by the Commander-in-Chief undesirable at the present juncture that any definite meeting should take · place between Emir Feisal and Representatives from your Com-mission. At the same time steps are being taken to inform Emir Feisal of the necessity of your working on the most friendly terms with each other and in closest sympathy, and we feel sure that we can rely on your considering the necessity of such cooperation in your future policy.[81]

The Zionists did not give in, and on 23 June informed Feisal that in their statement to the American Commission (which had arrived in Palestine on 10 June), they pointed to their "contin-ued cooperation" with the Emir and to their desire "to work harmoniously with the Arab population for the good of Pales-tine . . . You will recall," they added sarcastically, "a visit to you of our Commission was postponed on advice of the Chief Political Officer." Feisal responded tersely, "We will expect your arrival and will be happy to meet you."[82] However, the matter rested neither with Feisal, nor with the Zionists. "It is odd," Eder wrote to Weizmann on July 2, 1919, "that we should still be debarred from meeting Feisal. Allenby is less favourable to us than before the Armistice."[83] Eder had detec-ted this adverse trend two months earlier:

> As regards the [Military] Administration, there is decidedly more antagonistic feeling towards the realization of the Bal-fourian policy. . . . There are . . . influences at work who do not wish to see this Arab-Jewish entente.[84]

The question that inescapably comes to mind is what caused Allenby to become so antagonistic to the Zionists and what made him object so strenuously to their meeting with Feisal? In 1918 he gave his blessing to the Weizmann-Feisal meeting at Akaba and impressed Weizmann as being sympathetic to the Zionist idea.

Neither Allenby, nor his Political Officer, briefed the Foreign Office about the drastic change of policy; the move, in fact, was made without London's knowledge, let alone approval. No records have survived in the War Office files[85] that could enlighten us about this issue. The present author has been fortunate, however, in finding a number of documents that provide a clue to the thinking of the Military authorities.

In his letter to Weizmann of July 2, Eder wrote, "The Administration is now very keen on Palestine and Syria being under Gr. Britain." While Storrs diligently inquired what the Zionist attitude would be to such a scheme, Clayton approached the Zionist Commission directly, intimating that there would be no settlement and no peace in the region unless Syria and Palestine were "under one control, preferably British." General Money, the Chief Administrator of O.E.T.A. South, made a similar statement. "It is quite clear," the Zionist intelligence report concluded, "that Great Britain wants the union of Palestine, Syria, and Mesopotamia (Cairo-Baghdad axis) under one Moslem flag and under her protection." At this juncture, the Military authorities decided to "go slow" on Zionism, which, in Robert Szold's opinion, was tantamount to a "complete defeat" for the Zionist cause.[86]

During his investigation as a member of the American Commission, William Yale ascertained that the British intended not only to keep Palestine, but would have liked to control Syria as well:

> They do not wish the French even in Mount Lebanon. However, realizing that without an open break with France they cannot single-handed force France to give up her claims, they would be pleased if the United States stepped in and took Syria. They have allowed and encouraged the Young Arabs to carry on a United Syria propaganda . . .[87]

Propaganda of this nature constituted a flagrant contravention of the principle of status quo, of which the Military Administration claimed to be a faithful guardian.

Throughout the War, Allenby adhered strictly to the instructions of his superiors in London. We saw that it was Lawrence who had single-handedly engineered Feisal's "capture" of

Damascus, not Allenby. Even after hostilities ended, he showed no intention of dislodging the French from Syria. Quite the contrary. He agreed with Hogarth's recommendation made in his memorandum of 18 December 1918 that Britain should keep clear of Syria. "He is a great authority on Eastern matters and a man of cautious and sound judgment," Allenby wrote General Sir Henry Wilson, the Chief of Staff,

> I am entirely at one with him, in the view he expresses, and I think the paper is worthy of your careful perusal. I am doing everything in my power to help the French, especially in the areas where their interests are held to be paramount.[88]

On 4 February, he assured the Director of Military Intelligence that he had worked with strict adherence to the Allied cause and wholeheartedly supported the legitimate aspirations of the French. "I have worked untiringly to promote a better understanding and with some success. . . . This is well known to the French Military Administrator and to my political adviser, Monsieur Picot."[89] And a month later, in Picot's presence, he severely reprimanded Ali Ridā al-Rikabi, Chief Administrator O.E.T.A East, for the obstructive and even hostile attitude of his administration toward the French. "Nothing can be more harmful to Arab interests," Allenby rebuked al-Rikabi, "than to promote the idea that the French and English are not working in complete accord":

> The French and English have fought side by side in this country [i.e., Syria] for the principles of justice and freedom and it is out of the question to think that the action of self-interested intriguers can disturb an alliance which has been cemented for over 4 years of war and suffering. The Arab administration appears to forget at times that they are merely a provisional administration. . . . No independent Arab Government can exist unless set up by the Peace Conference, which has not yet given its decision regarding those territories which have been liberated [by the Allied forces] from Turkish domination.[90]

Such blunt words could have come only from a determined and impartial commander, loyal to his Government's policy, such as Allenby unquestionably was. Yet, only several weeks later, a total transformation in his approach took place. No document has come to light to show how it occurred, but what is certain is that he embraced the doctrine current among the Military establishment in the East that, for strategic reasons, it was essential for Britain to control both Palestine and Syria to ensure territorial contiguity from Cairo to Baghdad.

One can detect the change from his comments during the meeting of the Council of Four on March 30, to which he had been invited. But it was not until mid-May, following Feisal's return from Paris, that his policy had finally crystallized. On 12 May, he had a long conversation with Feisal about the forthcoming enquiry of the Commission. Asked whether Britain, if offered, would accept a mandate for Syria, Allenby answered rather disingenuously that he "did not know."[91] A few days later, Feisal revealed to Clayton that, on Lawrence's advice, he had agreed verbally with Clemenceau to persuade his people to accept a French mandate for Syria "on the understanding that France recognized Syrian independence." Although Feisal said that he "had never any intention of carrying out this arrangement,"[92] Allenby, knowing how weak and unstable Feisal was, might have suspected that Feisal would be in no position to resist the French offer.

If this was the case, it explains the Military's gravitation toward the Arab nationalists, the Palestinians in particular, who were the most zealous exponents of United Syria. It explains also why the attitude toward Zionism hardened. In January, the Weizmann-Feisal Agreement was welcome, but from spring 1919, it no longer suited British interests as the Military saw it. A British mandate in Palestine inevitably strengthened the French claim to Syria, while support of a Jewish National Home alienated the Young Arabs, whose goodwill British officers were trying to cultivate. In these circumstances, it becomes understandable why Allenby objected to Feisal's wish to meet the Zionist delegation.[93]

It took Allenby several months to realize that he had been mistaken. Arab extremists were not only anti-French and anti-Zionist, but also anti-British.[94] Nor did the grand design of *Pax Britannica* behind an Arab facade prove a realistic policy. The idea had been conceived in Cairo and Khartoum early in the War, but Sir Edward Grey, faithful to the alliance with the

French, foiled it.[95] There was equally no chance in 1919 of it being approved by the British Government. "I am totally opposed to trying to diddle the French out of Syria," Lord Milner, the Colonial Secretary, wrote to Lloyd George (8 March 1919), and added: "If we are to play the honest broker between the French and Feisal, the French must fulfil their promises to us over Palestine and Mosul."[96]

Milner was preaching to the convinced. Lloyd George had no interest in Syria[97] and, like Milner, was committed to Zionism. On 30 March, at the Council of Four in Allenby's presence, Lloyd George made his position crystal clear.[98] On 17 May 1919, *The Times* re-echoed the Prime Minister's view:

> There should be no reason for the minds of our Allies to be perturbed about our policy in the Levant. Great Britain has always recognized France's right to Syria as a sphere of influence. . . . Now some Power has got to have the Mandate for Syria. Great Britain does not want it. Mr. Lloyd George has told the world so. The only other Power interested is France . . .

And yet, Allenby totally ignored the Prime Minister's solemn declaration at the Council of Four. He resisted strenuously the replacement of British troops by the French in Syria on the grounds that this would be "a serious blow to British prestige,"[99] and that he would consider himself "irresponsible" [*sic*] for what would occur if the International Commission would not come and if the French force was increased "even by one soldier."[100]

Allenby's motive transpires from yet another telegram to the War Office:

> You know my views regarding the political danger and economic disadvantages of separating Palestine and Syria, which is contrary to the wishes and interests of the great majority of the population.[101]

Whatever the rights or wrongs of Allenby's arguments, the War Office would not listen to them. "In view of P.M.'s determination not to accept Syria," it would be next to "impossible" to implement Allenby's proposal, reads a Minute by Colonel Richard Meinertzhagen, a member of the Military Delegation to the Paris Peace Conference. However, when Allenby allowed

Feisal to believe that Britain might after all undertake a mandate for Syria, provided the American Commission showed that this was consonant with the wishes of the people concerned, Balfour felt duty bound to remind the recalcitrant General that "H.M.G. have not departed from the view expressed orally by Prime Minister . . . in your presence, to M. Clemenceau, in the presence of President Wilson, Signor Orlando and myself that in no circumstances would Great Britain become mandatory for Syria," and that, on 29 May, General Clayton had been explicitly advised to this effect.[102]

However, it was to no avail. Balfour was bitter. "The British officers in Syria," he complained, "have not always played up to the British Ministers in Paris" and had inflicted an incurable injury to Anglo-French relations. The Prime Minister had formally announced that "under no circumstances would England either demand the mandate for Syria or take it; he valued too highly the friendship of France." "Yet," he went on,

> at the very moment when the declaration was made, and ever since, officers of the British army were occupied in carrying on an active propaganda in favour of England. Rumours were spread . . . regarding France's unpopularity with the Arabs, and though the rumours were false, everything was done to make them true. There could be but one object in these maneuvers, namely, to make the British mandate, which had so solemnly, and doubtless so sincerely, [been] repudiated in Paris, a practical necessity in the East.[103]

Allenby's purpose was to use the Commission of Inquiry as an instrument to legitimize the claim for a United Syria and foist it upon the Peace Conference. Balfour, however, was too astute to let the General have his way. He rebuked him sternly:

> You appear to think that the Commission will decide the future of the various ex-Turkish territories. That is not correct. They will have no power to decide, but after examining all the facts of the case will tender their advice to the Council of the Principal Allied Powers, who will have to take the final decision.[104]

Feisal, too, believed, or wanted to believe, that the recommendations of the forthcoming Commission would be decisive for the future of Syria. In his speech on 9 May at the Damascus

Town Hall,[105] and thereafter, he encouraged this belief. As a result, unbridled propaganda was unleashed throughout Syria and Palestine. Demonstrations, inflammatory speeches, and distribution of pamphlets became the order of the day. "The agitation," Friedenwald reported, "is primarily Pan-Arabic and anti-European . . . [it] is largely forced and is not a natural expression of genuine popular will . . . secret societies . . . are very active; the behaviour of some of them is considered by local people as provocative and insolent." In addition, "there are plenty of foreign interests here engaged in stirring up" mutual hostility. Some French and British officers behaved as if the 1904 Entente Cordiale did not exist, but the *fons et origo* of all the agitation and intrigue was Damascus.[105]

On May 24, 1919, the Moslem-Christian Association convened in Jerusalem and resolved that:

1. Syria, extending from the Taurus Mountains in the North to Raffah in the South, should be "absolutely independent."
2. Palestine (renamed "Southern Syria") constituted an indivisible part of Syria.
3. Zionist immigration should be stopped and the Jewish National Home policy abandoned. Only the native Jews domiciled since the prewar period were to be entitled to equality of rights.

"These demands," the Zionist Intelligence Bureau remarked, "were inspired by Damascus, and many facts prove that they were looked upon by the British Military Authorities here with no disfavour." Early in June, al-Muzaffar, who had formerly been expelled to Damascus as persona non grata, was allowed to return to Jerusalem and was received by Colonel Storrs and General Money. Soon after, al-Muzaffar launched a vigorous propaganda campaign.[106]

After a considerable delay, the Commissioners landed in Beirut, from whence, surprisingly, they went down to Jaffa (10 June), rather than to Damascus. This was contrary to the schedule charted by Colonel House and in violation of Crane's unequivocal assurance to Frankfurter to exclude Palestine from the scope of investigation.[107] As late as 28 May, Frankfurter, who was usually well informed, called to Friedenwald in Jaffa: "American members of Interallied Syrian Commission . . . leaving for East over Constantinople. Doubtful if and when they will reach Palestine. French and English [members] will not join."[108]

What made King and Crane deflect from their original itinerary is a mystery. What appears to be certain, however, is the ease with which they uncritically embraced the arguments of the British military officers. Only two days after their arrival, they dispatched an alarming telegram from Jaffa expressing doubts that "any British or American official here believes that it is possible to carry out the Zionist program except through the support of a large army."[109] During the inquiry, the Zionist representatives gained the impression that the Commission appeared to be interested primarily in the way that the Jewish National Home would affect the well-being of the local Arab inhabitants. They opined that Palestine was inextricably "tied up with the problem of Syria. . . . The Commission," Szold reported, "found undoubtedly a very strongly organized demand for a United Syria, [but] the stereotyped character of the requests coming from all over Palestine must have shown the Commission the artificial character of the demands which were made." Nonetheless, opinion was by no means unanimous. Certain notables were averse to the idea of a United Syria; others, who were in a minority, welcomed Jewish immigration; while the *fellahin* from certain Arab villages protested against the self-appointed representatives of the *effendi* class. Szold hoped that the Commission would realize that the organized opposition to Zionism was worked up largely by the *effendis*, who "do not represent the great mass of the *Fellahin*."[110] Unlike the big landowners, the farmers realized that they would benefit from the Jewish enterprise in Palestine and steered clear of the nationalists' propaganda.[111]

Dr. Montgomery, who accompanied the Commission as an expert, was of the same opinion,[112] while Lybyer, another expert, testified:

> A great active system of propaganda has been carried on for the program [for a United and independent Syria] . . . This program has been shaping under our eyes, and to certain extent has been

influenced by a desire to meet the supposed inclinations of the Commission. . . . Agents [from Damascus] have been working very hard for it. Differences of opinion have been skilfully accommodated, certain formulas have been distributed in manuscript and print and taught orally. The Press has been influenced in various ways . . .[113]

More penetrating were Yale's comments. His long sojourn in the region—before the War as a representative of the Standard Oil Company, and from 1917 as a special agent in Cairo of the State Department—his acquaintance with the local personalities, as well as his command of Arabic, made him uniquely qualified to gauge local opinion. He thought that Syria and Palestine were anything but united. Both countries formed a kaleidoscope of ethnic and religious communities riven by mutual rivalry, fear, and jealousy: "Even up until November 1918 there was but little thought of union [of Palestine] with Syria or of independence." The idea had ever since been actively encouraged by British officers, who had tried to create a situation that "it would be impossible for the French to occupy the country." The Damascus Government, with tacit British approval, carried out an aggressive campaign against France, while the Palestinian nationalists were not slow to take full advantage. They launched a most able propaganda campaign throughout Palestine and Syria. They appealed to the Beduin by making use of Feisal's prestige as a Beduin leader; among the ignorant *fellahin* and Moslems in general, they made use of *hodjas* (a teacher; a respected member of the community) and appealed to their deep-rooted religious sentiments; whereas, to the liberal Moslems, and to the Christians they preached Syrian Unity and Syrian Nationalism. However, the purpose of the Young Arabs, Yale went on, was not to build a liberal, multinational, and multireligious entity. Their ultimate aim was to create "a Moslem Arab State and eventually a Moslem Arab Empire. . . . They succeeded in duping many Syrian Christians," and of taking advantage of Feisal's weakness as "an instrument . . . to secure their aims."

Yale characterized Feisal as a "liberal and open-minded leader who wished all the sects and denominations in the country to cooperate for the best interests of the State."

However,

> ... he has not enough power and influence in the country to make his ideas prevail ... he is loved but not feared; he is courted but not obeyed. Should the Emir fail to satisfy the Young Arab Party they would dispense with him.[114]

The Syrian social and economic elite, primarily the big landowners, resented the rise of the Young Arabs to power. Under the Ottomans, they had enjoyed a privileged position, but now they were "constantly rebuked, insulted, ignored or pushed aside ... Damascus notables were conspicuously absent from government, often passed over for Palestinians and Iraqis."[115] The notables disliked, as Miss Bell aptly wrote, "the upstart band of Baghdadis and Palestinians who are in authority over them ... the aliens ... [who] are in fierce pursuit of an exaggerated political ideal for the attainment of which ... they are prepared to set the Syrian province ablaze."[116]

The conservative landowners were interested primarily in the maintenance of peace and stability of their own country. Palestine and Mesopotamia concerned them but little. When Feisal called for elections for the Syrian Congress, which convened on 2 July 1919, the powerful group of land-owning notables won a resounding victory. It was a heated contest. Yet, in spite of "bribery and intimidation" employed by the Arab Independence party,[117] the conservatives won the day. Then the unexpected happened. The land-owning representatives of Aleppo, Hama, and Homs, who for years had been at odds with their Damascene counterparts, decided, for entirely regional considerations, to join the nationalist bandwagon to ensure that their personal interests and those of their constituents were represented. They tipped the balance of power in favor of al-Fatat and the Istiqlal Party, who henceforth dominated the Congress. "The Damascus old guard's appeal to moderation and stability was drowned out by louder demands of nationalist delegates calling for absolute and uncompromising independence."[118]

Feisal faced one of his most severe tests of leadership. Unlike the nationalist hotheads, he realized that an Arab state would not be able to hold its own without external support, and that, without the effective assistance of a Mandatory Power, Syria would slide into chaos.[119] In his speech to the Congress, he pressed for a British Mandate for the whole of Syria. This was his overriding motive for convening the Congress. However, he miscalculated badly. The Arab Independence Party fomented a storm of indignation, and demonstrations were held in the streets. "Feisal was branded as a traitor and the British were cursed." Michel Bey Lotfullah, President of the "Union Syrièn" of Cairo and in the employ of the O.E.T.A. South, who reported on the proceedings to the British Military authorities, saw in it the hand of Egyptian and Mesopotamian agents who had been secretly supported by Yasin al-Hashimi.[120] Conspicuous among those who were clamoring for independence were also Palestinian activists.[121]

The extreme nationalist tenor of the Congress embarrassed Feisal.[122] To parry the rising tide of extremism, it would have made more sense for him to side with Syrian notables and construct a united camp of the four cities. The moment for such a move was opportune. Concerned with the growing assertiveness of the "strangers to the territory of the four towns . . . the notables of Damascus and its wise men sent a delegation [to Feisal] to advise him to follow a policy which would be in the general interest, but," Kurd Ali, a local chronicler lamented, "he paid no attention to their words."[123] Instead, Feisal chose the line of least possible resistance. In a speech at a banquet, he now demanded "complete independence and no mandate." This volte face was warmly applauded, and his popularity among the nationalists resurged; but by the same token, he became captive to them. Henceforth, it was Yasin al-Hashimi, Nassib al-Bakri, and their crew who became the masters of the situation. They controlled all appointments in the administration, the press, and the army, and kept leaders of other parties at bay. Associated with them were Emir Zeid and Ali Ridā Pasha.[124] In addition to al-Hashimi, the influential Steering Committee consisted of Palestinian activists such as Rafiq al-Tamimi and Muhammad Izzat Darwaza.[125]

The resolutions adopted by the Congress on 2 July 1919, to be presented to the Commission of Inquiry, were dictated by the extremists. The Congress presented a list of demands to be submitted to the Peace Conference:

1. Recognition of "immediate and complete political independence for Syria without protection or tutelage" by a foreign Power. Syria was to include Palestine, as well as the Lebanon, and to cover the area from Mount Taurus in the north to Raffah and Akaba in the south.
2. Mesopotamia should also be completely independent.
3. The Congress would reject Article 22 of the League of Nations on the grounds that Syrians were themselves sufficiently advanced and did not require a mandatory.
4. As a last resort, the Syrians would be content to accept technical and economic assistance from the United States; failing that, from Britain, as the second choice, but the French claims in any form were to be rejected.
5. With regard to the Jewish National Home, the resolution read:

    > We oppose the pretensions of Zionists to create a Jewish commonwealth in the southern part of Syria, known as Palestine, and oppose Zionist migration to any part of our country; for we do not acknowledge their title but consider them a grave peril to our people from the national, economical, and political points of view. Our Jewish compatriots shall enjoy our common rights and assume the common responsibilities.[126]

Rejection of Article 22 was an act of defiance against the League of Nations and an affront to President Wilson; it clashed with the Commission's terms of reference. More serious was the confrontational stance on the question of Palestine. In this matter, the conflict between the Congress and the Peace Conference was absolute. But the most bizarre aspect of the resolutions taken by the Congress was its peroration. The Congress declared that the Syrians, and for that matter also the Palestinians, "would have not risen against the Turks" and would have not "shed so much blood in the cause of . . . liberty and independence" had they not been confident that, after the War, the Allied Powers would recognize the political rights which they had enjoyed hitherto under the Turks and "secure the realisation of [Arab] aspirations."[127] Any uninitiated reader would be stunned by this perversion of the truth. If blood had been shed by the Syrians on the battleground, it was not against Turkey, but in its defense.

On the following day, the 3rd of July, Feisal appeared before the Commission. He said that, in order to satisfy Arab aspirations, it would be desirable if all Arab countries, including Syria, Palestine, and Mesopotamia, be placed under the influence of the same Power. Separation between Syria and Palestine was unacceptable. With regard to Zionism, "some months ago he was prepared to accept it in its limited sense" — that is, only "a certain amount of immigration and extension of existing Jewish colony. However," he went on, "the wider Zionist aspirations . . . frightened the people" and they were "determined not to have any form of it." On the whole, Colonel French noted, Feisal did not say much to the Commission, nor did he express himself very strongly in this matter.[128]

Hard-pressed by the nationalists on the one hand, and discouraged by Allenby on the other, Feisal's attitude toward Zionism had undergone a radical transformation. However, strange as it may seem, at heart he still nourished a sneaking sympathy toward Weizmann and was convinced of the merits of cooperation with the Zionists. Toward the end of July, he made a point of calling on Yosef Abbadi, a leader of the Jewish community in Damascus, and expressed his satisfaction with his "brother Jews." He acknowledged that the Jews, especially the Zionists, had supported him in Europe, and that Dr. Weizmann was very much interested in assisting the Arabs. He hoped that the misunderstanding between the Jews and some of the Arabs, "whose only purpose in their writings is to fish in troubled waters, will soon disappear." He promised to do everything in his power to bring people closer to each other. He was confident that Jewish immigration to Palestine would prove beneficial to the country and make it prosper: "The Jews possess intelligence, money, and experience." On 9 August, Abbadi called on Feisal in the presence of Emir Ali, his elder brother. The conversation revolved on the same theme and was throughout cordial.[129]

Feisal was speaking in two languages: one to the Jews, and the other to his fellow Arabs. His dilemma was vividly described by Colonel French, the Acting Chief Political Officer in Cairo:

The situation is exceedingly difficult for the Emir Feisal whom I believe to have made honest attempts to hold the balance between the moderate and extreme sections of the Arabs and who desires to fulfill his promises both to His Majesty's Government and to the Zionists; and this very honesty has to a certain extent undermined his influence which for the moment is probably decreasing rather than increasing.[130]

More realistic was Major Camp, Assistant Political Officer, who analyzed Feisal's position from the Palestinians' perspective:

In my opinion [he reported], Dr. Weizmann's agreement with Emir Feisal is not worth the paper it is written on or the energy wasted in the conversation to make it. On the other hand, if it becomes sufficiently known among the Arabs, it will be somewhat in the nature of a noose about Feisal's neck, for he will be regarded by the Arab population as a traitor. No greater mistake could be made than to regard Feisal as a representative of Palestinian Arabs (Moslem and Christian natives of Palestine who speak Arabic); he is in favour with them so long as he embodies Arab nationalism and represents their views, but would no longer have any power over them if they thought he had made any sort of agreement with Zionists and meant to abide by it. But it seems that he is capable of making contradictory agreements with the French, the Zionists and ourselves, of receiving money from all three, and then endeavouring to act as he pleases. This is an additional reason why his agreement with Weizmann is of little or no value . . . [131]

Weizmann was bitterly disappointed with Feisal's statement to the Commission. It was "not fair," he told Eder, and stood in "flagrant contradiction" to his accord and pronouncements made in London and Paris.[132]

The Weizmann-Feisal Agreement was dead, but Feisal, too, was on the losing side. The extreme nationalists, as Colonel French reported, were "perfectly prepared to try complete independence and [were] quite indifferent as to the results of their experiments on the country, provided that they [could] become a Power in politics."[133] As we shall see in the second volume of our study, Feisal's alliance with the Palestinian and Mesopotamian nationalists eventually resulted in his own downfall.

We must now return to the King-Crane Commission.

The Commission stayed in Palestine and Syria six weeks, received petitions, and interviewed individual delegations. From Damascus, they went to Constantinople, where they completed their report, which, on 28 August, was submitted to the American delegation to the Peace Conference, as well as to President Wilson. Though the hands that signed it "were the hands of King-Crane, the voice was the voice of Crane,"[134] the most forceful member of the Commission. He did not, and could not have gone, to Jeddah to see King Hussein, as he claimed in his letters to Hamilton, as well as to Sir George Young.[135] Nor was any member of the Commission aware at that time of the McMahon-Hussein Correspondence. Feisal made no mention of it during his testimony.

Their stay was marked by an orgy of political agitation fueled by the belief that the results of the inquiry would determine the future of the region. In Palestine, al-Muzaffar, who came down from Damascus, was exhorting the population to demand "absolute independence," implying that Sharifian troops stationed at Amman were poised to take over the country and replace the British troops.[136] In Damascus, thousands of pamphlets under the heading "Freedom or Slavery" were distributed which contained detailed instructions about the evidence to be submitted to the Commission.[137] It was alleged that the Damascus Government used censorship to suppress any friendly references to France and had picketed the offices of the Commission for the purpose of intimidating the delegations of the Christian communities.[138] The powerful chieftain of the Aneizeh Beduin, following a quarrel with Feisal, came out in favor of France. Yale quoted the case as "indicative of the facility with which large groups of Moslem Arabs can be won over by one faction or the other when it suits the personal interests of those groups or their leaders."[139] The Commissioners themselves, in a special supplement to their report entitled "For the Use of Americans Only," gave instances of pressure that had been employed by the British, French, and Arabs to influence the witnesses, and admitted:

> We were not blind to the fact that there was considerable propaganda; that often much pressure was put upon individuals and

groups; that sometimes delegations were prevented from reaching the Commission; and that the representative authority of many petitions was questionable.[140]

In the circumstances, it would have been extremely difficult even for the most competent investigator to gauge the true will of the population, but neither King nor Crane were in any way qualified for such a complicated task. An attempt to apply yardsticks customary in democratic countries to an area where democracy was unknown, where a *sheikh*, landlord, or government official had the determining voice, was folly.

One would have thought that rejection of Article 22 of the League of Nations by the General Syrian Congress would have made the work of the Commission redundant. But this logic was lost on the Commissioners. Instead, they embraced the demands of the Congress and modified them in such a way as to make them palatable to the Peace Conference. Thus, the Syrian Congress clearly and unequivocally expressed the desire for "full and absolute independence for Syria," but King and Crane recommended placing it under a single Mandatory Power, specifying that, "from the point of view of the desires of the 'people concerned', the Mandate should clearly go to America"; with England as second choice. This was a flagrant misrepresentation, since the "people concerned" abhorred the notion of a Mandate and specifically asked merely for "assistance."

Nor was the Damascus Congress a "representative [body speaking] in the name of the Syrian people," as the Commissioners described it in their report. The participants were elected by the old electorate system for the Ottoman Parliament of 1909, and only sixty-six of the eighty-eight representatives were able to meet in Damascus; most of those absent were from the French-dominated "Blue" zone area. There was no one representative of the Jewish settlement in Palestine. The Commissioners took hardly any notice of the haphazard and undemocratic procedure in the Congress's decision-making processes.

The method of investigation employed by the Commissioners was of dubious merit. The questions that they put to the interviewees were phrased in such a manner as to elicit the desired answers. Abraham Elmaliyach, who watched its work from close quarters, produced a number of examples.[141] More-

over, the Council of Four instructed the Commissioners to acquaint themselves with the conditions of the regions concerned,
"a knowledge of which might serve to guide the judgment of the
Conference,"[142] but King and Crane took license in making their
recommendations, which were often based on faulty or inadequate information.

All these defects, however, pale into insignificance when
compared to the breach of faith committed with regard to
Palestine. Crane, in particular, reneged on his pledge made both
to Frankfurter and Colonel House to confine the inquiry to the
area from Damascus northwards. The Commissioners erred
also in applying the principle of self-determination to Palestine.

In their report, they declared that, "the Zionists looked forward to a practically complete dispossession of the present
non-Jewish inhabitants of Palestine, by various forms of pur-
chase," although the material which the Zionist delegation had
submitted to them showed quite the contrary. They continued:

> no British officer . . . believed that the Zionist programme could
> be carried out except by force of arms [and] that a force of not less
> than 50,000 soldiers would be required even to initiate the pro-
> gramme. That of itself is evidence of a strong sense of injustice of
> the Zionist programme . . .

They dismissed out of hand the claim that the Jews had
historical rights to Palestine on the grounds that neither the
Christians nor the Moslems could accept the Jews as "the
proper guardians of the Holy Places or the custodians of the
Holy Land as a whole." To the Jews, the sacred places,
particularly "those having to do with Jesus are . . . abhorrent to
them." Ergo, the proposal to create "a Jewish State, however
gradually that might take place," was inadmissible. They
recommended that

> only a greatly reduced Zionist programme be attempted by the
> Peace Conference, and even that, only very gradually initiated.
> This would have to mean that Jewish immigration should be
> definitely limited, and that the project for making Palestine
> distinctly a Jewish Commonwealth should be given up. . . . There
> would be no reason [they added] why Palestine could not be
> included in a united Syrian State, just as other portions of the
> country . . .

These ideas echoed the attitude prevalent among Arab nationalists, as well as in the British Military circles. The King-Crane proposal, if implemented, would have condemned the Jewish community in Palestine to a status of a permanent minority in Greater Syria, which was an antithesis of Zionism. It ran counter to the recommendations made by the American delegation to the Peace Conference and was a blatant disregard of President Wilson, who had advisedly and publicly used the term "Jewish Commonwealth."[143]

This was not the kind of material the American Delegation had expected, and soon after, it was buried in the State Department's vaults. On 24 September, the British Delegation asked their American counterparts for a copy of the report, but the latter adamantly refused;[144] evidently it was thought that no useful purpose would be served if the report was disseminated, even privately.

The King-Crane Report was published first in 1922,[145] but remained practically unnoticed. In 1932, in his book *The Spirit of World Politics*, Professor William E. Hocking, an Arab sympathizer, referred to it scathingly as "mischievous" and obliquely blamed President Wilson for sending "the bootless Commission" in the first place.[146] In the judgment of the Committee on Foreign Affairs of the House of Representatives, which discussed the whole issue in 1944, the King-Crane Report was a piece of propaganda.[147]

Antonius thought otherwise:

> The King-Crane Report [he wrote] is a document of outstanding importance. It is the only source to which the historian can turn for a disinterested and wholly objective analysis of the state of feeling in Arab political circles in the period immediately following the War. The investigation carried out by the American commissioners was the only attempt made on behalf of the Peace Conference to establish the facts relating to Arab aspirations by actual ascertainment on the spot: in that alone, their findings merit special attention. But it added greatly to the value of the inquiry that it was undertaken by a body with no national ambitions to promote, who approached their task with open minds, and that it was conducted by two men of recognised independence of judgement, in whom the qualities of insight and sanity were remarkably combined. Of that, the Report bears ample evidence

throughout: perhaps its most outstanding characteristics are the shrewdness of its findings and the unmistakable honesty of its recommendations.[148]

As all the evidence adduced above shows, the work of the Commission merited none of the words of praise which Antonius so lavishly heaped upon it. For an historian, it would be rather risky to rely upon it.

Antonius ignored the reports of the advisers, Montgomery and Yale, although he got hold of them.[149] Montgomery's association with the Jews during his long sojourn in the East is not known, but it seems that he was imbued with deep admiration for their "remarkable history . . . qualities . . . and the preservation of their nationality. . . . May we not say that they regard Palestine not only as a refuge from persecution but as a place for trying out an experiment in nationalism?"

Montgomery thought that Syria's political union with Palestine was not essential to its economic development and that British officers, who were endeavoring to steamroll it, were implacably antagonistic to the Jews. The question of Palestine should be judged from a wider perspective. "What has been already accomplished by the Zionists in Palestine speaks very hopefully for their future." The entire country, and the *fellahin* in particular, would benefit from Jewish enterprise, the apprehensions of the large private land-holders notwithstanding. There was also little ground for fear with regard to the preservation of the Christian and Moslem Holy Places, especially if the country was to be placed under the trusteeship of the League of Nations. From the geopolitical point of view, a wedge between a militant Egypt and Syria would check the development of an unfriendly Moslem bloc.

Montgomery recommended that Palestine be autonomously administered with Great Britain as the Mandatory; that immigration of the Jews be encouraged for the benefit of the country; and that appropriate arrangements be made for safeguarding the Christian and Moslem Holy Places. Lebanon, too, should be autonomously administered, with France as the Mandatory, while Syria should be run by Emir Feisal under a joint Franco-British Mandate. America, in his opinion, should not get involved at all.

By far superior in analysis was Yale. As already mentioned, he was an old hand in Middle Eastern affairs, and his command of Arabic stood him in good stead. Without mentioning King and Crane by name, his disagreement with their thinking is evident practically from every page of his report. United Syria, in his view, was not a viable proposition. Although Syria, Palestine, and Mount Lebanon were economically and commercially interdependent, politically they did not form a unit. Palestine, for its unique character, "must be considered apart," while the Lebanon, which was overwhelmingly Christian, so profoundly different in its civilization and ideals from the interior, politically did not form a part of Syria. Syria was a motley of religions and sects, "each jealous of one another, each more fanatical than the other and intolerant of all others . . . [a] mixture of races [which] adds nothing to its unity," while socially the gap between the Beduin, the sedentary town-folk, and *fellahin* was wide. The allegiance of the great majority of the people was local and religious. National spirit, which could have served as a cohesive force, "does not exist [in Syria] . . . the Syrians have no national history, no national traditions, no national sentiment."

The same characteristics applied to the population of Palestine, the vast majority of which were illiterate, and in such centers as Hebron, Nablus, and Jenin, "profoundly fanatical, anti-Jewish, anti-Christian, and anti-European." However, the *fellahin* in the villages were for the most part docile and easily managed. In Yale's judgment, the expressions of national feeling which the Commissioners had heard from Beer-Sheva in the south to Damascus and Ba'albek in the north, should not mislead one into assuming that this sentiment was genuine. It had been cleverly orchestrated by the Young Arabs; but,

> the masses of *fellaheen* and bedouins, who do not even understand the word Nationalism, support [it] because they believe that it means Moslem supremacy and independence, and because they are ordered to. Among the *effendi* class in general in the cities [it] has received support because it will, they believe, maintain their position . . . as over-lords, [while] the Moslem clergy and fanatics were pleased to see in it Moslem supremacy and independence . . .

There existed among some younger men a vague but acute sense of nationalism, but the majority of the people were fanatically Islamic:

> I am firmly convinced [Yale continued], and this conviction has come from what I have seen and heard during the past month, that the present movement in Syria and Palestine is not really a national movement [but that] of pan-Arabism and Pan-Islamism [and] that it is a very dangerous movement. . . . it is almost certain that the present Arab movement or Syrian national movement will turn into fanatical Islamism.

In the section "Recommendations," Yale expressed the opinion that Palestine should be separated from Syria and constituted as a National Home for the Jewish People under the Mandate of Great Britain, acting as the custodian in the name of the League of Nations. This was a replica of the recommendation made by the American Delegation to the Peace Conference in January 1919. The novelty was in argumentation, based on his recent enquiry.

He recognized that such a disposition would be contrary to the wishes of the majority of non-Jewish populations in Palestine. However, injustice that would be done to "individuals" should be weighed against injustice to the Jewish people, who, unlike the Palestinian population, were recognized as a nation. Furthermore, "the wishes and desires of 14,000,000 Jews who have a national history, national traditions, and a strong national feeling must be taken into consideration." On this point, Yale followed closely the line taken by President Wilson, Balfour, Jan Smuts, and other statesmen with whom the prin-ciple of self-determination had originated. The United States and the Allied Governments, he emphasized, had made definite and formal promises to the Jewish people. To retract such promises now would be "unjust and unwise. These promises must be fulfilled and the Jews must be given their chance to found in Palestine a Jewish Commonwealth." Looking toward the future, Yale envisaged that,

> Jewish energy, Jewish genius and Jewish finance will bring many advantages to Palestine and perhaps to all of the East. Modern Western methods and civilization will be brought to Palestine

[and] with the immigration of the Jews . . . a new element will be
introduced into the Orient . . . a Jewish Commonwealth in Palestine will develop into [a European and American] outpost in the
Orient.

Yale was not oblivious to the difficulties that lay ahead,
but, in the same breath, dismissed the talk of "wholesale
massacre of Jews," as well as that maintenance of a very large
armed force would be required if the Zionist program was to be
carried out, as "exaggeration due in part to the fact that those
who make such statements are opposed to Zionism and are in
general anti-Semites." When the Palestinians learned that the
Western Powers were determined to implement the Jewish
National Home policy, and when the Mandatory Power
suppressed with a strong hand any disturbances and demonstrations against the Jews, "the danger of a wide-spread uprising will be dissipated. The Arabs," he concluded, "may never
become reconciled to Jewish immigration, but they will become
reconciled to the fact that they must accept it as inevitable."
    With regard to Syria and Mount Lebanon, Yale's recommen-
dations were similar to those made by Montgomery.

The King-Crane Report was suppressed, perhaps in consequence of the Montgomery and Yale papers, but the unsettling
effects of the Commission's stay in the Middle East reverbe-
rated in the region for a long time. The ill-consequences vindicated fully the Middle East experts who, to a man, had warned
against sending the Commission to the East.[150] Before his departure, Crane himself, as the Commissioners' Secretary noted
on 16 April, doubted whether, "considering the existing attitude of the occupying Powers in Syria, Palestine, and Mesopotamia, and the state of feeling of the population there, the
appearance of an American Commission of inquiry might not
arouse hopes which it would not be possible to fulfill."[151] And
yet, neither Crane nor King did anything to lower the level of
expectations among the native population. The result was
devastating: the trust in the West had gone and the tense situation became even more exacerbated. Miss Bell commented bitterly: "The American Commission did nothing, and could do
nothing, but encourage vain hopes. The result has been a disas-

trous prolongation of unrest and intrigues on the part both of the Arabs and of the French, and increased bitterness on either side." She did not absolve the British either from responsibility:

> Rightly or wrongly, I came to a sharply defined conclusion that the chapter of Arab history which comprises the last twelve months is not one in which we figure with credit. The initial mistake for which we were responsible . . . was the setting up of an Arab Government in Damascus . . .

This Government presented only an "outward appearance of a national Government." Formally, it was independent, but in practice, this was hardly the case. It had been "artificially financed by [British] subsidy" and its administration "has left much to be desired." Had Syria been left to itself, she speculated, it "would have remained stationary for decades" and national organizations would have remained in a state of "decay." But the aftermath of the armistice had produced "a remarkable crop. It is open to doubt whether it springs from seed grain or from dragon's teeth; if from the latter," she commented sarcastically, "very inadequate provision has been made for the harvest."[152]

The kind of teeth Miss Bell described so graphically had been cultivated assiduously by the Turks. The atmosphere of resentment against the Allies created a favorable atmosphere for the dissemination of Turkish Pan-Islamic doctrines, against which the British had "no effective antidote."[153]

The man who was the standard-bearer for liberation of Mesopotamia from British tutelage was none other than Yasin al-Hashimi. He was in touch with the leaders of the Committee of Union and Progress, and his sympathies were pro-Turkish.[154] During the summer of 1919, a drastic increase of anti-Sharifian propaganda took place in Mesopotamia which bore "an anti-British and anti-foreign nature." It assumed an even more ominous character following the formation of a Turkish-Arabic Pan-Islamic League, about which the Director of the Military Intelligence reported on 16 August 1919. This League was created in consequence of negotiations between Emir Feisal and Kutchuk Djemal Pasha, who acted on behalf of Mustapha Kemal Pasha.[155] The purpose of the League was to liberate the Arabic-speaking provinces from Christian domination, with Feisal being appointed as the overlord.[156] In September (shortly before his departure for Europe), when Miss Bell met Feisal "in one of his less responsible moments," as she put it, the Emir had declared that "if the nations of Europe attempted to separate Palestine from Syria, he would proclaim a jihad."[157]

During the spring of 1918, when it was discovered that Feisal (then in Akaba) was conducting secret negotiations with Djemal Pasha, the Commander of the Fourth Ottoman Army (not to be confused with his namesake, Kutchuk Djemal Pasha, the Minor), Sir Ronald Graham, the Assistant Under-Secretary for Foreign Affairs, noted:

> Feisal's natural instinct is pro-Turk . . . and we must not be surprised at his tendency to hedge, more especially now that General Allenby has withdrawn from the East of the Jordan. . . . We should discourage Feisal from making any arrangements for "after the War" . . . with the Turks.[158]

It was in order to detach Feisal from the Turkish embrace, among other reasons, that General Clayton arranged the Weizmann-Feisal meeting at Akaba,[159] but by now Zionism had lost its earlier attraction for Feisal; other considerations were simmering in his mind. He believed, as Colonel French reported, the British Government's decision to accept the Mandate for Palestine was tantamount to the "division of Arab countries and a return to the 'Unjust Agreement of 1916.'"[160] Volunteers were being enrolled and sworn to "defend the country against partition." At this juncture, Feisal expressed his wish "to repudiate his agreement with Weizmann for fear it may be construed as acquiescence in partition of Syria."[161] At the Foreign Office, A. D. Paterson commented sarcastically,

> Feisal is far too much the political opportunist to let it [his Agreement with Weizmann] stand in his way after it has ceased to be of use to him.

W. S. Edmonds, Paterson's colleague, tried to explain that it was perhaps in order to increase his influence with his supporters that Feisal proposed "to disavow his arrangements with the Zionists," but S. Kidston, an old hand at the Foreign Office, was downright condemnatory. He characterized Feisal's decision as a "rush move" that was likely to cause "great complications" for the British Government.[162]

On 9 September, Colonel Meinertzhagen, Clayton's successor, accompanied by M. LaForçade, who succeeded Picot as the French Political Officer, called on Feisal in Damascus. LaForçade, in an effort to improve relations with the Emir, was exceedingly conciliatory. In contrast, Meinertzhagen was firm and told his host unequivocally that British policy was based on: (a) refusal to accept a mandate for Syria; (b) establishment of Zionism in Palestine; (c) the Anglo-French Declaration of November 1918 (which did not apply to Palestine); and, (d) that any attempt to breach the peace "would bring Feisal into direct conflict with Allies" to the detriment of his cause. Feisal responded that unity of Syria was a "vital issue" for the Arabs, and defined Syria's boundaries as extending from Gaza in the south to the Taurus Mountains in the north. Thereafter, he laconically made a surprising statement that "he accepted Zionism."[163]

How Feisal reconciled his claim for a United Syria with acceptance of Zionism became clear during a private and informal conversation with Meinertzhagen on the following day. Feisal reaffirmed his policy of a United Syria to the "absolute exclusion of France and everything French. He and his people would fight on these points." However, with regard to Zionism, Meinertzhagen gathered that,

> Feisal's ultimate aim is an Arab Federation embracing Mesopotamia and a Jewish Palestine — all under a British mandate. He is inclined to ignore British refusal of Syrian Mandate and intends to force the hand of His Majesty's Government in this respect.

Meinertzhagen thought that recent Arab military preparations "need not be taken too seriously," but, like Yale, he was more concerned with the Arab movement drifting into "religious fanaticism and massacres."[164]

Feisal's policy seemed to be full of contradictions, but if, on the basis of all the data gathered, we were to fathom what was Feisal's (as well as his followers) ultimate aim, we should be able to construct the following:

1. To free Mesopotamia from British tutelage. (In this respect he counted on Turkey's assistance accompanied by a general uprising against the British—the *jihad*—which, in fact, materialized several months later.)

2. To dislodge the French from Syria resorting to guerrilla warfare, as well as forcing Britain's hand to exert pressure on France.

3. To persuade the Zionists to do away with the British Mandate in Palestine and instead accept Arab patronage of "the Jewish Palestine" within the framework of United Syria.

If such a devious scheme was indeed lingering in his mind, he must have been woefully underestimating the political realities of the day and courting his own demise. At any rate, "a Jewish Palestine in a United Syria" without a British Mandate, as he presented it to the Zionist leaders in London in October 1919,[165] was obviously a nonstarter.

Notes

Preamble

* The Preamble is composed of two parts — "The McMahon-Hussein Correspondence and the Question of Palestine," and the dialogue, entitled "The McMahon-Hussein Correspondence: Comments and a Reply," that ensued between myself and Arnold Toynbee following the article's appearance — both of which were published in the Journal of Contemporary History in vol. 5, no. 2, 1970, and vol. 5, no. 4, 1970, respectively. I am grateful to Professor Walter Laqueur, the Editor-in-Chief of the *Journal of Contemporary History*, for permission to reprint this material as the Preamble of this volume.

Minor corrections or omissions have been rectified, and the format of the original document and Notes has been changed to conform to that of the other chapters of this book.

1. *Hansard, Lords*, 1 March 1923, col. 232, statement by the Colonial Secretary.
2. F.O. 371/14495, Pol. Eastern General (1930), Minute by W. J. Childs, dated 16 July 1930; Minute by G. W. Rendel, dated 21 July 1930. Transcripts and quotations of Crown copyright material appear by permission of the Controller of H.M. Stationery Office (hereafter HMSO). For brevity's sake, the prefix P.R.O. (Public Record Office) before the relevant Foreign Office files (F.O.) and Cabinet papers (CAB) is omitted.
3. The McMahon-Hussein correspondence was first published in George Antonius, *The Arab Awakening* (London, 1938), and in Cmd. 5957 (1939). Now freely available at the Public Record Office in F.O. 371/2486/34982, Turkey (War), Pol. 1915, and F.O. 371/2767/938, Turkey (War), 1916.

4.   CAB 37/155/33, Grey to Rodd, 21 September 1916.

5.   F.O. 371/2486/34982, Grey to McMahon, 14 April 1915, Confidential; McMahon to F.O., 30 June 1915; F.O. 371/2774/42233, p. 140075 (draft announcement); *The Times*, 28 July 1916.

6.   This term, used in Grey's Note to Cambon of 16 May 1916 *(Documents on British Foreign Policy, 1919-1939* [hereafter *D.B.F.P.*] First Series, vol. IV, p. 247, para. 10, E. L. Woodward and R. Butler, eds. [London, HMSO, 1952]), was later, at Cambon's suggestion *(ibid.,* p. 249) modified to "uphold" *(soutenir).* However, this verbal change did not imply any diminution in the status of Britain and France.

7.   CAB 42/6/10, Evidence of Lt.-Col. Sir Mark Sykes on the Arab Question before the War Committee, 16 December 1915, G. 46, Secret.

8.   See Hussein's letters to McMahon, 14 July, 5 November 1915.

9.   McMahon to Hussein, 14 December 1915. In Antonius, the date of this letter is erroneously given as 13 December.

10.   D. G. Hogarth, "Wahabism and British Interests," *Journal of the British Institute of International Affairs,* 1925, p, 72.

11.   F.O. 371/2486/34982, McMahon to Grey, 26 October 1915, Secret; same to F.O., 5 November 1915; same to Grey, 14 May 1915, Confidential.

12.   Clayton Papers, Clayton to Jacob (Aden), 11 March 1916, private letter; same to Beach, 17 April 1916, private letter. I am very grateful to Mr. S. W. Clayton and to Lady Clayton for permitting me to study these papers.

13.   Ronald Storrs, *Orientations* (London, 1939), pp. 160-161.

14.   F.O. 371/2786/34982. "Verbal message of Muhammad Ibn Arif, on Sherif Hussein's behalf," to Storrs, Alexandria, 18 August 1915, and R[onald] S[torrs] Note dated 19 August, Secret; encl. in McMahon to F.O., 26 August 1915, Secret. In this dispatch, Hussein's letter of 14 July is enclosed.

15.   McMahon to Hussein, 30 August 1915.

16.   "Exactly how much territory should be included in this State it is not possible to define at this stage" (Grey to McMahon, 14 April 1915, as above, note 5).

17.   On whom see Antonius, *The Arab Awakening,* pp. 168-169; Elie Kedourie, *England and the Middle East* (London, 1987[1956]), pp. 36-40, and an illuminating article by the same author, "Cairo and Khartoum on the Arab Question 1915-18," *The*

Historical Journal, No. 2, 1964.

18. F.O. 371/2486/34982, "Memorandum on the Young Arab Party," dated 11 October 1915, and "Statement of Muhammad Sharif el-Faruqi," 12 October, encl. in McMahon to Grey, 12 October 1915, Confidential.

19 Antonius, *The Arab Awakening*, pp. 153, 157-158.

20. *Auswärtiges Amt Akten* [hereafter A.A.A.], *Türkei*, no. 177: *Der Libanon* (Syrien), Bd. 12, Prüffer to Djemal Pasha. Memorandum dated 5 December 1915 (in French), encl. in Prüffer to Metternich (Ambassador in Constantinople), 10 December 1915; Bd. 13, Loytved-Hardegg (Damascus) to A.A., 6 May I916.

21. Djemal Pasha, *Memories of a Turkish Statesman, 1915-1919* (London, 1922), pp. 213, 167.

22. F.O. 371/2486/34982, "Memorandum on the Young Arab Party," by Lt.-Col. G. F. Clayton, Confidential, encl. in McMahon to Grey, 12 October 1915.

23. Storrs, *Orientations*, pp. 155.

24. About which Balfour complained at a meeting of the War Committee on 20 November 1915; see CAB 42/5/17.

25. F.O. 371/2486/34982, Maxwell to Kitchener, 12 October 1915, encl. in War Office (W.O.) to F.O., 15 October 1915; see also same to same, 16 October, encl. in W.O. to F.O., 18 October.

26. *Ibid.*, Kitchener to Maxwell, 13 October 1915, encl. in W.O. to F.O., 15 October; McMahon to F.O., 18 October 1915; same to Grey, 18 October 1915, Personal; same to F.O., 20 October 1915; same to same, 20 October, tel. no. 627.

27. *Ibid.*, Grey to McMahon, 20 October 1915; McMahon to Grey, 26 October 1915, Secret (enclosed also Hussein's letter dated 24 October); same to F.O., 26 October 1915.

28. "As you rightly say, it is very much to the High Commissioner's credit that he boldly took the responsibility on himself of replying to the Sherif without further reference, and I greatly hope that the latter will not stick out about the frontiers" (Wingate to Clayton, 1 November 1915, Private, Wingate Papers, Box 135/5). I am grateful to Mr. Richard Hill, formerly of Durham University, and Mr. I. J. C. Foster, Keeper of Oriental Books, for permitting me to consult these Papers.

29. F.O. 371/2486/34982, India Office (I.O.) to F.O., 4 November

1915; same to same, 22 October 1915.

30.   F.O. 371/2486/34982, "Negotiations with the Grand Sherif," Memorandum by Secretary of State for India, dated 8 November 1915, initialed A[usten] C[hamberlain].

31.   F.O. 800/58, Private Papers of Sir E. Grey, Crewe to Bertie (Paris), 17 December 1915; Private; copy in CAB 42/6/11.

32.   F.O. 371/2486/34982, undated minute on p. 181834 of 30 November 1915.

33.   *Ibid.*, McMahon to F.O., 30 November 1915.

34.   "In your desire to hasten the movement we see . . . grounds for apprehension . . . First . . . is the fear of the blame of the Moslems of the opposite party . . . that we have revolted against Islam and ruined its forces" (Hussein's letter to McMahon, 5 November 1915); McMahon's letter to Hussein, 14 December 1915 (in Antonius, mistakenly given as 13 December). Antonius's transcription (or translation) of this section (p. 424) is faulty and distorts McMahon's intention. This transpires also from McMahon's dispatch of 24 January 1916 to Grey that "everything will depend . . . on the extent and success of Arab co-operation during the war," as well as on the nature of the conditions under which both the British and the Arabs might find themselves at the conclusion of the war. Hussein to McMahon, 1 January 1916. Again, Antonius's translation —"noted its contents" (p. 424) — is at variance with the British one.

35.   Antonius glosses over this aspect of the correspondence (p. 173) and highlights only "Great Britain's pledge." He admits, however, that the obligations with regard to military performance "had been debated orally with the Sharif's messenger" (p. 176).

36.   On 18 October 1919, Lloyd George told M. Clemenceau that one of the conditions on which the whole agreement was based was that "the Arabs should fulfil their part." Lloyd George went on to impress upon the French Prime Minister that the Arabs did fulfill this condition (*D.B.F.P.*, First Series, vol. IV, p. 483). However, as this statement was motivated by Lloyd George's desire to undermine the French claim to the interior of Syria, it should not be accepted as an impartial assessment, particularly when compared to his own testimony, on which see below.

37.   F.O. 371/2773/42233, Walton to Secretary of Government of

India, 29 May 1916, encl. in I.O. to F.O., 27 June 1916; "The Sherif of Mecca and the Arab Movement," Memorandum prepared by the General Staff, dated 1 July 1916; Copy in CAB 42/16/1 and in Clayton Papers.

38.   F.O. 371/2768, Hussein to McMahon, 18 February 1916 (received early in March). Printed p. 69301 (heretofore unpublished).

39.   *Ibid.*, Note to the Sherif dated 10 March 1916; enclosed also in McMahon to Grey, 13 March 1916; F.O. 371/2768/938, I.O. to F.O., 24 March 1916; Sykes to D.M.I., encl. in Buchanan to F.O., 13 March 1916. On Aziz Ali Bey al-Masri, founder of the *al-'Ahd* society, subsequently Chief of the Hedjaz Staff, see Antonius, *The Arab Awakening*, 118-73, 159-161, 212; *D.B.F.P.*, vol. X, Part II, pp. 832-838; Storrs, *Orientations*, pp. 183-202.

40.   F.O. 371/2768/938, Report of General Lake (Basra), 30 March 1916, encl. in I.O. to F.O., 31 March; F.O. (on Grey's instruction) to McMahon, 5 April 1916; McMahon to F.O., 18 April 1916, where Hussein's letter of 29 March is quoted. A translation of this letter is enclosed in McMahon to Grey, 16 April 1916, Secret.

41.   F.O. 371/2768/938, Clayton to Sykes, encl. in McMahon to F.O., 20 April 1916; Arab Bureau Note on "The Arab Question" (undated), encl. in McMahon to Grey, 19 April 1916, Secret. The Bureau was established on 17 February 1916. On its administration and staff, see F.O. 371/2771/18845.

42.   F.O. 371/2768/938, McMahon to F.O., 30 April 1916.

43.   Indicative of the attitude held at that time in Cairo and Khartoum is the Wingate-Clayton correspondence. On 15 November 1915, Wingate wrote to Clayton: "If the embryonic Arab state comes to nothing, all our promises vanish and we are absolved from them. . . . if the Arab State becomes a reality, we have quite sufficient safeguards to control it" (cited in Kedourie, "Cairo and Khartoum on the Arab Question," p. 285). And on 22 May 1916, Clayton wrote to Wingate: "Luckily we have been very careful indeed to commit ourselves to nothing whatsoever" (*ibid.*, p. 288). The impression of William Yale, the American Intelligence Officer in Cairo, and later attached to the American delegation at Versailles, was that the British were "exceedingly careful not to promise the Sharif too much" (The William Yale Papers,

rep. no. 2, dated 5 November 1917, p. 10). The original Yale documents are in General Records of the Department of State, Record Group 59, File 763, 72/13450, National Archives, Washington, DC. They are also deposited at the Yale University Library, New Haven, CT, USA, and a microfilm of the Yale Papers is at St. Antony's College, Oxford.

44.   F.O. 371/2768/938, Minute dated 3 May 1916, p. 80305. An observation to similar effect was minuted by Grey and O'Beirne; see F.O. 371/2767/938, p. 51288.

45.   See note 37.

46.   F.O. 371/2773/42233, McMahon to F.O., 11 June, 3 July, 9 July, 13 September, 27 October 1916; Viceroy of India to I.O., 6 July 1916, encl. in I.O. to F.O. 7 July, 8 July 1916; also CAB 42/15/15, W.O. meeting, 30 June 1916. F.O. 371/2775/42233, Wingate to C.I.G.S., 24 October 1916, encl. in W.O. to Hardinge, 27 October. A report produced for the War Council (CAB 42/23/3) revealed that the Arabs were incapable of defending Rabeqh.

47.   F.O. 371/2773/42233, "The Sherif of Mecca and the Arab Movement." Memorandum prepared by the General Staff dated 1 July 1916; see also CAB 42/15/5.

48.   CAB 37/161/9, meeting of the War Council, 9 December 1916; also CAB 42/24/8 and CAB 42/24/13, W.O. meetings on 16 and 20 November 1916; CAB 42/20/8, Gen. Robertson's memorandum dated 20 September 1916.

49.   F.O. 371/2775/42233, W.O. to Grey, 5 October 1916; F.O. 371/2776/42233, W.O. to F.O., 9 November 1916, Secret; F.O. 371/2781/201201, Appreciation by Sykes of the Arabian Report, 27 September 1916, Secret.

50.   F.O. 371/2775/42233, "Situation in Syria," Memorandum by Sykes, 14 October 1916.

51.   Clayton Papers, Private letter dated 15 December 1917.

52.   T. E. Lawrence's military contribution has been greatly exaggerated in some writings. Commenting on *The Seven Pillars of Wisdom*, General Sir H. G. Chauvel, formerly Commander of the Australian Division in the Egyptian Expeditionary Force, wrote: "Lt. Colonel Joyce has been kept in the background. He was in charge of the Hedjaz Mission, while Lawrence was only the liaison officer between Feisal and General Allenby. Joyce was the organizer of the only fighting force of any real value in the whole of the Arab Army, and I always thought that he

had more to do with the success of the Hedjaz operation than any other British officer." Chauvel to the Director of the Australian War Memorial in Canberra, 1 January 1936, Allenby Papers, copy at St. Antony's College, Oxford. I should like to thank Miss Elizabeth Monroe, Senior Fellow of the College, for allowing me to consult and quote from these papers; see also Hubert Young, *The Independent Arab* (London, 1933), pp. 145, 198. For the total expenditure on subsidy of the Arab Revolt, see below note 64. For the numbers and use of the Northern Arab Army see Kedourie, *England and the Middle East*, pp. 117-118.

53. Philip Graves, *Palestine, the Land of Three Faiths* (London, 1923), pp. 40, 112-113. Before 1914, Graves was *The Times* correspondent in Constantinople and later Staff Officer in Eastern theaters of war; from 1916, he was a member of the Arab Bureau in Cairo and was subsequently in the Arab section at the General Headquarters of the Expeditionary Force in Palestine.

54. C. S. Jarvis, *Three Deserts* (London, 1936), p. 302.

55. Lloyd George, *The Truth about the Peace Treaties* (London, 1938), vol. II, pp. 1026-1027, 1119, 1140. See also statement by Winston Churchill, Hansard, 23 May 1939, col. 2174.

56. F.O. 371/3391/4019, Clayton to F.O., 15 June, 15 September 1918; Hansard, 19 June 1936, col. 1379, statement by James de Rothschild.

57. *Palestine Royal Commission Report,* July 1937, Cmd. 5479, 22.

58. Antonius, *The Arab Awakening*, pp. 433-434; Kedourie, *England and the Middle East*, pp. 113-115, 119-122; Kedourie, "The Capture of Damascus, October 1918," *Middle Eastern Studies*, October 1964, p. 76.

59. *Palestine Royal Commission*, Minutes of Evidence . . . Colonial, no. 134 (London, 1937), p. 292.

60. F.O. 371/2781/193557, *Arabian Report,* 29 November 1916, citing Wingate's telegram of 22 November.

61. Djemal Pasha, *Memories of a Turkish Statesman*, pp. 167, 213.

62. F.O. 371/3384/747, Wingate to Balfour, 21 September 1918.

63. C. K. Webster, "British Policy in the Near East," in *The Near East*, P. W. Ireland, ed. (Chicago, 1942), p. 156. Professor Webster served in Military Intelligence under General Macdonogh.

64. Storrs, *Orientations*, pp. 160-161. Storrs estimated that the to-

tal cost of the Arab Revolt to Britain amounted to £11,000.000 in gold (*ibid.*, 160, note 1). This tallies with official records (F.O. 371/3048/22841).

65. Though it did not "shatter" the solidarity of Islam or endanger materially the Khalifat, as Clayton claimed in his Note, dated 28 September 1916, in the Clayton Papers.

66. *The Letters of T. E. Lawrence*, David Garnett, ed. (London, 1938), p. 576.

67. See e.g., Antonius, *The Arab Awakening*, p. 176-182.

68, *Statement of British Policy in Palestine*, 3 June 1922, Cmd. 1700, p. 20.

69. The statements are reproduced in the Jewish Agency for Palestine, *Documents Relating to the McMahon Letters* (London, 1939), pp. 14-19; *Documents Relating to the Palestine Problem* (London, 1945), pp. 22-27.

70. The Committee's report is published in Cmd. 5974 (1939); see pp. 10, 24, 46.

71. Letter to McMahon dated 9 September 1915.

72. F.O. 371/2486/34982, "Memorandum on the Young Arab Party," by Lt-Col. G. F. Clayton, 11 October 1915, Secret, encl. in McMahon to Grey, 12 October, Confidential.

73   *Ibid.*, McMahon to Grey, 16 October 1915, encl. in W.O. to F.O., 18 October; same to same, 18 October 1915, telegram no. 623.

74. *Ibid.*, Sykes to D.M.O., encl. in McMahon to F.O., 20 November 1915; also in F.O. 371/2767/938, encl. in Nicolson's "Memorandum on Arab Question," dated 2 February 1916. Al-Faruqi's statement to Sykes was appended to Nicolson's memorandum as an indication that the Arab leaders' claim was confined to the Syrian hinterland.

75. Lloyd George, *The Truth* . . ., vol. II, p. 1032.

76. F.O. 371/2486/34982, McMahon to Grey, 18 October 1915, Personal. The translation of the Sharif's note to McMahon differs from that of Antonius; McMahon to F.O., 18 October 1915.

77. As early as 1907, the Consul estimated the number of Jews "in the whole of Palestine. . . at 100,000 out of total population of 400,000-450,000"; F.O. 371/356 no. 40321 (no. 62), Blech to Sir N. O'Conor, 16 November 1907, reproduced in *British Consulate in Jerusalem, 1838-1914*, A. M. Hyamson, ed. (London, 1941), vol. II, p. 570. German sources, both Consular and

Zionist, confirm this figure. A. Ruppin's figure of 85,000 in his *The Jews in the Modern World* (London, 1934), pp. 55, 389, is slightly underestimated.

78. *Palestine, the Land of Three Faiths*, 53-54.

79. F.O. 371/7797 (1922), E. 2821/2821/65, McMahon to Shuckburgh, 12 March 1922, encl. in Shuckburgh to Forbes-Adam, 13 March.

80. F.O. 371/2486/34982, McMahon to Grey, 26 October 1915, Secret.

81, CAB 27/1, 30 June 1915, C.I.D., Secret, 220 B.

82. F.O. 371/2486/34982, F.O. (Grey) to McMahon, 20 October 1915.

83. Edgar Suarès was a prominent businessman and head of the Jewish community in Alexandria. For his proposal, see F.O. 371/2671/35433, McMahon to Grey, 11 February 1916, and encl. report dated 27 January 1916. On receipt of Suarès's scheme, the Foreign Office considered a suitable formula for an Allied declaration in order to win the sympathy of Jews, particularly in Russia. Its central phrase reads: "held out to them the prospect that when in course of time the Jewish colonists in Palestine grow strong enough to cope with the Arab population they may be allowed to take the management of the internal affairs of Palestine . . . into their own hands" (F.O. 371/2817/42608, Minute dated 14 March 1916). The author of the Minute was Hugh O'Beirne, a senior official at the Foreign Office. Before the World War I, he was Counsellor at the British Embassy in St. Petersburg and in 1915 chargé d'affaires at Sofia.

84. F.O. 371/2486/34982; the copy is enclosed in McMahon to F.O., 26 August 1915, Secret.

85. F.O. 371/2817/42608, Minute dated 23 March 1916.

86. F.O. 371/2671/35433, Minute dated 28 February 1916.

87. Letter to *The Times*, 12 July 1922.

88. P.R.O., 30/57.

89. CAB 42/6/9; CAB 42/2/5, meeting of the War Council, 10 March 1915; CAB 42/1/10, Memorandum by Lord Kitchener, 16 March 1915, Secret, G. 12.

90. CAB 24/9, G.T. 372; copy in Sir Mark Sykes Papers, MSS Library, Hull University, Hull (formerly Sledmere Papers), confidential reel, microfilm copy at St. Antony's College.

91. The first memorandum, CAB 27/36, E.C. 2201, is not signed or

dated, but is presumably November 1918; for the second, see CAB 24/72/I, G.T. 6506, "Memorandum respecting the Settlement of Turkey and the Arabian Peninsula," Secret. On the Hogarth message see below.

92.   Letters to the author, 27 October, 3 November 1969.

93.   Professor Toynbee's arguments are identical with those advanced by the Arab Delegation to London in 1922.

94.   F.O. 371/14495 (1930), "Memorandum on the Exclusion of Palestine from the Area assigned for Arab Independence by McMahon-Hussein Correspondence of 1915-16," Confidential.

95   F.O. 371/6237 (1921), "Summary of Historical Documents from . . . 1914 to the outbreak of Revolt of the Sherif of Mecca in June 1916," Secret, no. 10812. Printed in January 1921; original typescript dated 29 November 1916. Now in the Arab Bureau file 28 E(4) under the title *Hedjaz Rising Narrative*. In vol. I, pp. 110-112, there is a summary setting out what was and what was not agreed with Hussein; reproduced in a General Staff memorandum of 1 July 1916, CAB 42/16/1, and in Childs's "Memorandum on the Exclusion of Palestine . . .," pp. 51-52. Childs noted, quite correctly, that by substituting the word "line," which was not used by McMahon, for "districts," the author of the *Hedjaz Rising Narrative* committed a serious error. One reason why it was printed and resubmitted in 1921 was to draw attention to the mistranslated passage in McMahon's letter of 24 October 1915, which corrupted its meaning.

96.   See above, p. 104; see Hogarth's Introduction to Graves, *The Land of Three Faiths*.

97.   Childs, however, errs in putting Sykes in the same category as the author of the *Hedjaz Rising Narrative*, who influenced Toynbee. On the contrary, Sykes's telegram of 20 November 1915 indicates clearly that he well understood al-Faruqi's outline of the boundaries of the Arab state. So does his cable on the following day. It implied Sykes's recognition of the traditional French standing in the Syrian littoral and Palestine, qualified only by the British claim to Haifa and its environs, to be obtained from the French in the form of a concession. Moreover, the task of the British, Sykes added, would be "to get Arabs to concede as much as possible to the French," in return for the latter's concession to Arab desiderata

in the Syrian hinterland.

Again, Childs pushes his argument too far by suggesting that the Arab Bureau had some ulterior motive in misinterpreting McMahon's letter of 24 October 1915. This, it seems, was a genuine mistake, as can be seen from a comparison with statements made elsewhere in the memorandum, which convey the distinct impression that Palestine was meant to be excluded. Thus, in the paragraph listing the regions where the British "have *not* agreed to recognize Arab independence in Syria," the author significantly added: "or in any other portion . . . in which we are not free to act without detriment to our ally, France," which, in the given context, could be applicable only to Palestine. Further on, when discussing the Sykes-Picot Agreement, the author stated: "Palestine, west of Jordan, to be internationalized. Acre and Haifa to be British . . . Independent Arab State to consist of the remaining area [i.e., Cis-Jordanian Palestine and the Syrian hinterland], but to be divided into two spheres of influence . . . French and British." This inconsistency apparently accounts for McMahon's failure to notice the Arab Bureau's error when forwarding the memorandum, under the title "The Arab Question" (undated), which was its prototype (enclosed in McMahon to Grey, 19 April 1916, F.O. 371/2768/938).

98.   CAB 27/24. Philip Knightley and Colin Simpson in their recent book, *The Secret Lives of Lawrence of Arabia* (London, 1969), took Curzon's statement as well as that of the Arab Bureau as "conclusive" evidence that "Britain *did* knowingly, first promise Palestine to the Arabs as part of an independent Arab area," and thereafter published the Balfour Declaration (p. 106). This is, of course, quite erroneous. Dr. Fayez Sayegh made a similar mistake when consulting a copy of Toynbee's memorandum "The British Commitments to King Hussein," found among the Westermann Papers, now at the Hoover Institution at Stanford University. Dr. Sayegh's findings were published in an article in the Lebanese magazine *Hiwar* (summarized in a leading article in *The Times*, 17 April 1964). Significantly, Toynbee's conclusion made no impression on the late Professor Westermann, who served as an adviser on Turkish affairs to the American delegation to the Paris Peace Conference. Nor did they make any impact on William Yale (see

below).

99. *Hansard*, 19 July 1920, col. 147.

100. F.O. 371/5066, E. 14959/9/44, "Memorandum on Palestine
     Negotiations with the Hedjaz," by H[ubert] W. Y[oung], dated
     29 November 1920. Its circulation was authorized by Curzon,
     the Foreign Secretary. See *Hansard*, 11 July 1922, cols. 1032-
     1034, statement by Winston Churchill, Colonial Secretary, and
     Cmd. 1700, 3 June 1922, p. 20; Lloyd George, *The Truth* . . ., vol.
     II, pp. 1142-1149.

101. Letter to *The Times*, 23 July 1937; see Philip Graves, *The Land
     of the Three Faiths*, p. 54. In October 1916, Hussein proclaimed
     himself "King of the Arab countries," but the Allied Govern-
     ments recognized him as "King of the Hedjaz" only.

102. Wingate Papers, Box 135/5, Wingate to Clayton, 1 November
     1915, Private.

103. But duly rejected by McMahon in his reply, dated 30 January
     1916. The messenger who brought the Sharif's letter to Sir
     Henry brought also a letter from the Sharif to his friend,
     Sayyid Sir Ali al-Morghani. One passage is of particular in-
     terest. It reads: "We have no reason for discussing the question
     of the frontier other than a preliminary measure," which con-
     firms our earlier evidence that the correspondence served only
     as a *basis* for negotiations on the boundaries. Their precise
     definition was left in abeyance. Hussein did not raise the ques-
     tion of boundaries until 1918.

104. CAB 24/10/447, 6.7.447, Secret, Ormsby-Gore's memorandum on
     Zionism, dated 14 April 1917.

105. Yale Papers, Reports 3 and 5, dated 12, 26 November 1917;
     Lloyd George, *The Truth* . . ., vol. II, p. 1142; Antonius, *The
     Arab Awakening*, p. 269.

106. For the full text, see Cmd. 5964 (1939); Cmd. 5974 (1939), 48*ff*;
     also Leonard Stein, *The Balfour Declaration* (London, 1961),
     pp. 632-633.

107. Quoted in Jewish Agency for Palestine (JAP), *Documents
     Relating to the McMahon Letters* (London, 1939), and
     Documents Relating to the Palestine Problem (London, 1945),
     pp. 161-167; briefly mentioned by Antonius, p. 269, who had
     reason to believe that the article was written by King Hussein.

108. Letter to *The Times*, 21 February 1939, reproduced in JAP,
     Documents Relating to the McMahon Letters, pp. 18-19.

109. Clayton Papers, Clayton to Sykes, 4 February, 4 April 1918; Clayton to Miss Bell, 17 June 1918; private letters.

110. Allenby Papers, "Meeting of Sir Edmund Allenby and the Emir Feisal . . . in Damascus on October 3, 1918" a copy of a record written by General Sir H. G. Chauvel. An identical copy is found in Chauvel's *Comments on the Seven Pillars of Wisdom*, pp. 11-14, dated 31 October 1935; see Hubert Young, *The Independent Arab*, pp. 255-257.

111. D. H. Miller, *My Dairy at the Conference of Paris* (New York, 1924), vol. IV, pp. 226; Lloyd George, *The Truth* . . ., vol. II, p. 1042.

112. For the text, see Jewish Agency for Palestine, *Memorandum Submitted to the Palestine Royal Commission* (London, 1936), pp. 296-298; Antonius, *The Arab Awakening*, pp. 437-439; and for a discussion, Stein, *The Balfour Declaration* , pp. 641-643. The original text of the Agreement has not survived. Carbon copies in Central Zionist Archives, Jerusalem, and F.O. 608/98, Peace Congress, 1919, Pol. no. 159, File 375/2/2; "Feisal altered the 'Jewish State' of Weizmann's draft to 'Palestinian State,' throughout." Minute by Toynbee, dated 18 January 1919 (*ibid.*, no. 227, File 375/2/1).

113. Yale Papers, Report dated 27 October 1919. The passage relating to Palestine reads: "to set up a separate political unit under the Mandate of Great Britain, under whose guidance the Zionists will . . . be allowed to carry out their projects to make of it a National Home for the Jewish people." Rustum Haidar, a member of the Arab delegation, told Yale that, with certain modifications with regard to Syria, Feisal would be "ready to accept his solution." McMahon said that Yale's proposals were in accordance with the agreements he had made with King Hussein and urged Yale to see Lord Allenby. Yale's scheme is reproduced in full in David Garnett, ed., *The Letters of T. E. Lawrence,* 286, but the version on Palestine is given in an abridged form.

114. H. W. V. Temperley, *History of the Peace Conference* (London, 1920-1924), vol. VI, p. 175.

115. F.O. 371/6237, E 986/4/91, "Report on Conversation . . . 20 January 1921." Present were R. C. Lindsay, Major H. W. Young, Col. Cornwallis, Emir Feisal, Brig. Gen. Haddad Pasha, Rustum Haidar; see also F.O. 371/6238, E 2133/4/91, F.O. to

Herbert Samuel (Jerusalem) 22 February 1921, referring to the Lindsay-Feisal conversation; Winston Churchill's statement, *Hansard*, 11 July 1922, cols. 1032-1034.

116.   Article XI of the Asia Minor Agreement (May 1916) stated that "the negotiations with the Arabs as to the boundaries of the Arab State or Confederation of States shall continue"; Major Young wrote in his memorandum that "no actual agreement was ever arrived at . . . although . . . certain definite undertakings were given . . . by Sir H. McMahon in his letter of 25 [*sic*] October, 1915." Mr. Harmsworth, Under-Secretary of State for Foreign Affairs, in a speech in the House of Commons on 24 October 1921, stated categorically that "no formal Treaty was concluded between His Majesty's Government and the King of the Hedjaz in 1915. . . . These undertakings were embodied in a long and inconclusive correspondence; and on certain points no specific agreement was reached."

117.   See Hogarth, "Wahabism and British Interests," p. 73.

118.   Toynbee, "Memorandum on British commitments to King Hussein," on which see note 91.

Comments and Reply

Toynbee's Comments (pp. lii-lx)

1.   Cab. 27/36, E.C. 2201, cited by Mr. Friedman in his note 91, p. xliv.

2.   Cab. 24/72/I, G.T. 6506, also cited by Mr. Friedman in his note 91, p. xliv.

3.   Friedman, p. xxiv.

4.   Clayton in F.O. 371/2486/34982, cited by Mr. Friedman on his p. xxxvii-xxxviii.

5.   F.O. 371/6237 (1921), cited by Mr. Friedman in his note 95, p. xlv.

6.   See Friedman, p. xxxviii, and note 74.

7.   F.O. 371/2768/938, cited in Mr. Friedman's note 97, p. xliv.

8.   F.O. 371/5066, E. 14959/9/44, cited by Mr. Friedman, p. xlvi.

9.   F.O. 371/7797 (1922), E. 2821/2821/65, quoted by Mr. Friedman p. xl.

10.   F.O. 371/14495 (1930), cited by Mr. Friedman, p. xlv.

Friedman's Reply (pp. lxi-lxviii)

1. CAB. 24/72/1.
2. F.O. 882/5. Arab Bureau Papers, 121-326. "Summary of Historical Documents from the outbreak of War between Great Britain and Turkey, 1914, to the outbreak of the Revolt of the Sherif of Mecca in June, 1916." Cairo, Arab Bureau, 29 November 1916.
3. F.O. 882/2, Arab Bureau Papers, "The Arab Question," Note by Cdr. Hogarth.
4. "What we were asked to promote, was simply independence to the Arabs from their present over-Lord, the Turk." See also Hogarth's article cited in the Preamble, p. xxii (also note 10, above), and other evidence, *ibid.*, pp. xx-xxiii.
5. F.O. 371/2768/938, McMahon to Grey, 19 April 1916, dis. no. 83 Secret; see my article p. xliv, note 97, where "Cis-Jordanian Palestine" in square brackets should be corrected to "east of the river Jordan."
6. F.O. 882/14, Anglo-Franco-Russian Agreement. Hogarth (Cairo) to Hall (London), 3 May 1916.
7. F.O. 371/3054/865526, Note on Anglo-Franco-Russian Agreement, by D. G. Hogarth dated 10 July 1917.
8. D. G. Hogarth, "Wahabism and British Interests," *Journal of British Institute of International Affairs*, 1925, p. 73.
9. F.O. 371/6237, Eastern (1921) E. 155/4/91. P. Knightley and C. Simpson in *The Secret Lives of Lawrence of Arabia* (London, 1969), p. 106, overlooked the minute sheet that accompanied the "Summary" and were trapped into the same error.
10. Prof. Toynbee consistently substitutes for it "wilayahs," a term not used by McMahon. This method was employed earlier by the Arab Delegation for the obvious reason that, in vernacular Arabic, it stands for "environs" — a narrower meaning than district or the Turkish "vilayet."
11. F.O. 882/14, Palestine Political, Memorandum by W. O(rmsby) G(ore), dated 12 January 1917, p. 267.
12. George Antonius, *The Arab Awakening* (London, 1938), p. 179, pp. 262-263; Cmd. 5974, p. 27; Leonard Stein, *Promises and Afterthoughts* (London, 1939), pp. 9-10; Childs, "Memorandum on the Exclusion of Palestine . . .," pp. 60-61.

Introduction

1. Margaret Cole, ed., *Beatrice Webb's Diaries, 1924-1956* (London, 1936), p. 256.
2. Geoffery Furlonge, *Palestine is My Country: The Story of Musa Alami* (London, 1969), pp. 57-58, 222-227.
3. J. R. Colville, *Man of Valour: The Life of Field-Marshal The Viscount Gort* (London, 1972), p. 259.
4. The Committee's report is published in Cmd. 5974 (1939); see pp. 10, 24, 46.
5. Hugh Foot, *A Start in Freedom* (London, 1964), pp. 35-36.
6. Elizabeth Monroe, *Britain's Moment in the Middle East, 1914-1956* (London, 1963), p. 43.
7. Isaiah Friedman, *The Question of Palestine 1914-1918: British-Jewish-Arab Relations* (London, New York, 1973). A second expanded edition was published by Transaction Publishers (New Brunswick, NJ) in 1992.

Chapter 1   A Follow-up to the Dialogue with Arnold J. Toynbee

1. Arnold J. Toynbee, *Study of History*, vol. XII, *Reconsiderations* (Oxford, 1961), p. 245. Hugh Trevor-Roper accused Toynbee of a "terrible perversion of history. ... [His] theories are not deduced from facts, nor tested by them: The facts are selected, sometimes adjusted, to illustrate the theories, which themselves rest effortlessly on air. ... He compares himself with the Prophet Ezekiel; and certainly, at times, he is just as unintelligible" (*The Sunday Times*, 17 October 1954), reprinted in M. F. Ashley Montagu, ed., *Toynbee and History: Critical Essays and Reviews* (Boston, MA, 1956), pp. 122-124.
2. Arnold J. Toynbee, *Reconsiderations*, p. 47.
3. Isaiah Friedman, *The Question of Palestine, 1914-1918. British-Jewish Arab Relations* (London & New York, 1973), p. 89; an expanded second edition was published by Transaction Publishers of Rutgers University, New Brunswick, NJ, in 1992. See also "Comments" by Arnold Toynbee, which has been reprinted here in the Preamble (pp. lii-lx).

4.   Below, Chapter 3, pp. 61-88.
5.   Ulrich Jasper Seetzen, *Reisen durch Syrien, Palästina, Phoni-cien, die Transjordan Länder . . . herausg.* vom Prof. Dr. Fr. Kruse (Berlin, 1854), 2 Bande.
6.   M. C. Volney, *Travels through Syria and Egypt in the Years 1783, 1784 and 1785*, transl. from French (Dublin, 1788).
7.   Karl Baedeker, *Palestine and Syria, Handbook for Travellers*, transl. from German (London, 1876).
8.   F.O. 371/3059/162432, *The Turkish Provinces in Asia* by Gertrude Bell, 23 June 1917, Section on Syria, p. 3. Similarly, in a French document, "Geography of Syria," where its author gives a detailed description of Damascus and of its neighborhood — the word *wilāya* does not appear at all. A translated digest of the document is found in W.O. 106/194, fos. 105-108.
9.   Gertrude Bell, *Syria* (London, 1907), p. 140. In 1919 and 1928, there appeared second and third impressions.
10. F.O. 882/26, *Arab Bureau Bulletin*, no. 42, 15 February 1917, "Syria, The Raw Material," by T. E. Lawrence, p. 112 (written in 1915, but not circulated).
11. H. A. R. Gibb and H. Bowen, *Islamic Society and the West* (Oxford, 1950), 2 vols.
12. Abdul-Karim Rafeq, *The Province of Damascus, 1723-1783* (Beirut, 1966).
13. Karl K. Barbir, *Ottoman Rule in Damascus, 1708-1758* (Princeton, NJ, 1980).
14. Moshe Maoz, *Ottoman Reform in Syria and Palestine, 1840-1861* (Oxford, 1968).
15. Cmd. 2700 (1922) vol. 23, *Correspondence with the Palestine Arab Delegation*, p. 26.
16. Cmd. 5974 *Report of a Committee set up to consider certain Correspondence between Sir Henry McMahon and the Sharif of Mecca in 1915 and 1916*, 16 March 1939, (HMSO, 1939), paras. 10, 11, p. 14. For the reason why Antonius used this argument in 1939, see Isaiah Friedman, *Palestine: A Twice-Promised Land?* vol. 2 — *The Creation of the Historical Myth, 1920-1939*, Transaction Press, forthcoming.
17. Cmd. 5974 *Report of a Committee*, pp. 32, 34. On McDonnell, see Friedman, *Palestine: A Twice-Promised Land?* vol. 2, forthcoming.

18.   M. Th. Houtsman, H. A. R. Gibb, and others, eds., *Encyclopedia of Islam*, vol. IV (Leiden, 1934).

19.   H. A. R. Gibb and J. H. Kramers, eds. (Leiden, 1953), p. 633.

20.   Bernard Lewis, *A Handbook of Diplomatic and Political Arabic* (London, 1947).

21.   Philip Khoury, *Urban Notables and Arab Nationalism. The Politics of Damascus 1860-1920* (Cambridge, UK, 1983), see glossary, pp. 244-245.

22.   Welga Rebhan, *Geschichte und Funktion einiger politischer Termini im Arabischen des 19, Jahrhunderts 1798-1882* (Wiesbaden, 1986), Seiten 42-43.

23.   Hans Wehr, *A Dictionary of Modern Written Arabic*, Milton Cowan, ed. (Ithaca, NY, 1961).

24.   I am grateful to Dr. Dafna Tsimhoni, Lecturer in Modern Middle Eastern History, Ben-Gurion University of the Negev, Beer-Sheva, Israel, now at the Technion, Haifa, for examining Arab dictionaries on my behalf.

25.   Professor D. Kushner to the author, 22 January 1990. Also statement by Dr. B. Abu-Manneh, Senior Lecturer in Middle Eastern History at the University of Haifa.

26.   Listed in the bibliography of A. L. Tibawi, *Anglo-Arab Relations and the Question of Palestine, 1914-1921* (London, 1978), p. 513.

27.   F.O. 371//2140/5867, tel. no. 264.

28.   CAB 42/2/8, "Note on the Defence of Mesopotamia," 16 March 1915.

29.   CAB 42/2/14. On this meeting, see Friedman, *The Question of Palestine*, pp. 27-18.

30.   CAB 27/1, 30 June 1915, Minutes of meetings. On this Committee, see Friedman, *The Question of Palestine*, pp. 19-21.

31.   All the above documents are found in F.O. 371/2486 /34982.

32.   F.O. 371/3384/747.

33.   F.O. 141/587/545, Memorandum (in ms. undated), received by Storrs on 6 March 1916.

34.   F.O. 371/2140/5867, cited in Mallet to Grey, 14 October 1914, tel. no. 976.

35.   F.O. 882/12, fo. 157, Wingate to Clayton, 15 November 1915.

36.   I am grateful to a colleague, who requested anonymity, for assisting me to read the documents in Arabic, on which see

Appendices.
37. Letter to the author, 21 September 1989.
38. This is the official translation as it appears in Cmd. 5957 (1929), p. 9. In the original Arabic, the word *wilāyat* in dual number was used and translated in Cairo in 1915 to "Vilayets of Mersina and Adana." In his book, *The Arab Awakening* (New York, 1965, 5th impression), George Antonius translated this as "districts of . . . ," (p. 420) and "provinces of Aleppo and Beirut" (p. 421).
39. Barbir, *Ottoman Rule in Damascus*, p. 16.
40. Gibb and Bowen, *Islamic Society*, I, pp. 142-144.
41. Barbir, *Ottoman Rule in Damascus*, p. 16.
42. Vital Cuinet, *Syrie, Liban et Palestine. Geographie Administrative* (Paris, 1896), p. 303; Salnami, *Turkish Official Year Book for 1920.*
43. Cuinet, *Syrie, Liban et Palestine*, pp. 384-385; Gibb and Bowen, *Islamic Society*, I, p. 8; Rafeq, *The Province of Damascus*, p. 58.
44. See map facing p. 1 in Cuinet, *Syrie, Liban et Palestine*; F.O. 141/587/545, fo. 59, "The Historical Connection between Egypt and Syria," Memorandum by M. Pyrie Gordon, Intelligence Department; an official French document defined Syria's boundaries as from the Gulf of Alexandretta in the north to the Isthmus of Suez in the south. "Geography of Syria," 1919, digest, translated into English in W.O. 105/194, fos. 105-108.
45. Volney, *Travels through Syria and Egypt*, pp. 178-179; Baedeker, *Palestine and Syria*, pp. 55-56, 465, 468; Fr. Barnabas Meistermann, *New Guide to the Holy Land*, trans. from French (London, 1923), p. 574.
46. This is the Arabic title of Sufuh Khar's book *The City of Damascus. Studies in the Geography of Cities* (Damascus, 1969), listed in the bibliography of Khoury's *Urban Notables* . . . , p. 135.
47. *Proceedings of the Second International Congress on the History of Greater Syria*, 2 vols. [in Arabic] (Damascus, 1980), listed in Khoury's bibliography, *ibid.*
48. Below, pp. 40-42.
49. Friedman, *The Question of Palestine*, p. 87.
50. F.O. 371/2486/34982, p.375, no.18, 15 November 1915.
51. F.O. 882/13, fo. 442, Sykes (Cairo) to Cox (Mesopotamia), 22 November 1915.

52. F.O. 882/26, *Arab Bureau Bulletin,* no. 42, 15 February 1917, "Syria" by T. E. Lawrence, 8 January 1917 (but written early in 1915), p. 112.

53. F.O. 371/2768/938, McMahon to Grey, 25 April 1916, dis. no. 86.

54. F.O. 882/14. p. 179, "Notes on the country beyond the Jordan," November 1917, issued by G.S. Intelligence, G.H.Q., E.E.F. The memorandum was widely distributed.

55. F.O. 882/14, p. 267, Palestine. Political Memorandum by W. O[rmsby] G[ore], 12 January 1917.

56. F.O. 371/3385/747, p. 192, Memorandum dated 11 November 1918.

57. *Ibid.,* Sykes (Damascus), 27 November 1918, tel. no. 14, Secret.

58. F.O. 372/3383/747, p. 583, "Sketch Map relating to . . ." by AJT, dated 8 October 1918. For the boundaries as marked by Toynbee, see P.R.O., Map room, MFQ 379(1). The F.O. Handbook no. 60, *Syria and Palestine* (HMSO 1920) uses Vilayet of Damascus as equivalent to the "Turkish official [term of vilayet of] Syria," p. 1.

59. *A.A.A., Türkei* 177, Syrien, Bd. 46, Loytved-Hardegg to Bethmann-Hollweg, Damascus, October 1918, dis. no. J., no. 896.

60. F.O. 371/2486/34982, Memorandum on "The Arab Question," dated 21 December 1915, on which see Friedman, *The Question of Palestine,* pp. 105-106.

61. Meistermann, *New Guide to the Holy Land,* p. 12.

62. There is some mistake. The Vilayet of Syria (district of Damascus) included the sanjak of Ma'an. Hence, the boundary separating it from the Vilayet of Hedjaz ran, not from Ma'an, but eastward from Akaba. As elsewhere in the Ottoman Empire, internal boundaries were subject to constant changes. In 1886, the sanjak of Ma'an was transferred from the Vilayet of Syria to the Vilayet of Hedjaz. In 1891, the *status quo ante* was restored. In 1915, Djemal Pasha pushed it southward to the line of Wejh-El-Ala in the Hedjaz; but near the end of 1916, it was moved again to the latitude of Akaba, which remained the southern border of the Vilayet of Damascus to the end of the war. The F.O. Handbook, *Syria and Palestine,* delineates the southern boundary of the Vilayet of Damascus from a point starting "south of Akaba and running north-eastwards toward Ma'an and the depression of El-Jafa, separ-

ating the Vilayet of Damascus from the Vilayet of the Hedjaz" (p. 2).

63. Friedman, *The Question of Palestine*, p. 94; Cmd. 1700, vol. 23 (1922), p. 26; Cmd. 5974 (1939), pp. 14-15; Antonius, *The Arab Awakening*, pp. 78-179; Toynbee, "Comments," pp. xxiv-xxv.

64. Friedman, *The Question of Palestine*, pp. 82-83, and below, pp. 36-38.

65. F.O. 371/14495, E 6491/427/65, "Memorandum . . ." by W. J. Childs, 24 October 1930, p. 49.

66. F.O. 78/760 Rose (Beirut) to Sir Stratford Canning (Constantinople), 28 August 1948, dis. no. 18.

67. See note 10, above.

68. Cited in *The Letters of T. E. Lawrence*, David Garnett, ed. (London, 1938), pp. 283-284.

69. Barbir, *Ottoman Rule in Damascus*, pp. 16, 102-103, where a table appears; also, Rafeq, *The Province of Damascus*, p. 4.

70. Thus, during the eighteenth century, the sanjak of Nablus was attached for a short time to Sidon (in the Lebanon), although the two were not even contiguous. See Amnon Cohen, *Palestine during the 18th Century* (Jerusalem, 1973), p. 164.

71. Reproduced in Friedman, *The Question of Palestine*, pp. 84-85.

72. F.O. 371/5053, E 6685/2/44. Note by Samuel, 16 June 1920. Smith had in mind, as a matter of course, the ancient period.

73. F.O. 608/98, fo. 375/2/1, no. 588, "Palestine," Minute by Ormsby-Gore, dated 23 January 1919.

74. See below, pp. 83-84, 94-95.

75. Map V. Delimitation of boundaries of this scheme, as well as that of "Spheres of Interests" or "Partition of Turkey," did not correspond to the Ottoman administrative division. On this Report, see Friedman, *The Question of Palestine*, pp. 18-21.

76. See "Preamble," above.

77. F.O. 371/7797, E 2821, pp. 182-185, Shuckburgh to Forbes Adam, 13 March 1922; Forbes Adam to Shuckburgh, 20 March 1922.

78. Philip Graves, *The Land of Three Faiths* (London, 1923), pp. 53-54. See also Friedman, *Palestine: A Twice-Promised Land?* vol. 2, forthcoming.

79. *France and the Levant*, Handbooks prepared by the Historical Section of the Foreign Office, no. 95 (London, HMSO, 1920).

80. On which, see Isaiah Friedman, *Germany, Turkey and*

Zionism, 1897-1918 (Oxford, 1977), pp. 32-34.

81. On which, see W. N. Medlicott, *The Congress of Berlin and After* (London, 1938), pp. 112-113; Foreign Office Handbook no. 254, *The Congress of Berlin 1878* (HMSO, 1920).

82. Arnold J. Toynbee, *Nationality and the War* (London, 1915), p. 446.

83. Arnold J. Toynbee, *Turkey: A Past and Future* (New York, 1917), p. 63. Curiously, Toynbee did not take this and other data into account in November 1918 when assessing British commitments to King Hussein.

84. G. P. Gooch and H. W. V. Temperley, eds., *British Documents on the Origins of the War, 1898-1914*, vol. X, pt. 11, no. 201 (15 February 1914); *Ibid.*, (10 April 1914), p. 367; *Die Grosse Politik der Europäischen Kabinette 1871-1814* (Berlin, 1922-1927), vol. XXXVII (2).

85. F.O. 371/2767/938, "Arab Question," Note by Arthur Nicolson, 2 February 1916.

86. Cited in Leonard Stein, *The Balfour Declaration* (London, 1961), p. 53.

87. Friedman, *The Question of Palestine*, pp. 100-102.

88. CAB 27/1, "Remarks by the Secretary of State for India ...," 6 April 1915, App. VIII, p. 99 to the de Bunsen Report.

89. Friedman, *The Question of Palestine*, pp. 20-21.

90. *Ibid.*, pp. 57-61. Similarly, in 1917, before issuing the Balfour Declaration, the British Government had to consult President Wilson, as well as her other Allies.

91. Friedman, *The Question of Palestine*, p. 102.

92. F.O. 371/2480/2506, Grey to Bertie, 14 November 1915, tel. no. 875, Urgent.

93. Friedman, *The Question of Palestine*, p. 100.

94. F.O. 800/48, Grey Papers, Grey to McMahon, 8 March 1915.

95. P.R.O. 30/57/47, Kitchener Papers, Storrs to Fitz[gerald], 8 March 1915.

96. F.O. 608/93, no. 5353, where copies of minutes of negotiations with the French are reproduced.

97. George M. Trevelyan, *Grey of Fallodon* (London, 1937), memorandum dated 18 February 1916, pp. 317-318.

98. Friedman, *The Question of Palestine*, p. 15.

99. CAB 37/155/33, Grey to Rodd, 21 September 1916.

100. F.O. 371/2486/34982, McMahon to F.O., 22 August 1915, tel. no.

450, Secret; Hirtzel (I.O.) to Grey, 24 August 1915, Pressing.

101. F.O. 141/587/545, fos. 79-80, Wingate (Khartoum) to McMahon (Cairo), 15 May 1915; a copy in the Sudan Archive, University of Durham, SAD 134/30.

102. Antonius, *The Arab Awakening*, pp. 157-158. On p. 70 in my book, *The Question of Palestine*, I erroneously gave the date as 26 March, 1915. On that date, Feisal met the leaders of the societies on his way to Constantinople.

103. Elie Kedourie, *In the Anglo-Arab Labyrinth. The McMahon-Husayn Correspondence and Its Interpretations 1914-1939* (Cambridge, UK, 1976), pp. 130-131. Kedourie erroneously states that the meeting took place in the autumn of 1915, but the fault seems to be Amin Said's, the author of *The Secrets of the Great Arab Revolt* [in Arabic], whom Kedourie quotes.

104. Turco-Sharifian relations lie outside the scope of this study.

105. Al-Faruqi (Cairo) to Sharif Hussein (Jeddah), 27 Muharram 1334 (7 December 1915), reproduced in Muhammed Tahir al-Umari, *Mugaddarat Al-Iraq As-Siyasiyya* [the Political Destinies of Iraq] (Baghdad, 1925), vol. 1, pp. 218-224. I am grateful to Mr. (now Dr.) Jeffrey Rudd for translating this letter for me. Translated excerpts appear in Tibawi, *Anglo-Arab Relations*, App. 2, pp. 498-499. When interviewed by Clayton on 11 October 1915, al-Faruqi said that the meeting with Yasin took place in Aleppo, not in Constantinople.

106. Al-Faruqi to Sharif Hussein, as in note 105, above.

107. T. E. Lawrence, *Seven Pillars of Wisdom* (London, 1938), p. 59.

108. F.O. 882/16, fo. 192, Maxwell to Kitchener, 4 November 1915. According to Lutfallah, his brother and a number of other "Young Arabs" tried to join the British in Iraq (*ibid.*, fos. 185-186, G.H.Q, London, citing Athens, to G.O.C., Egypt, 17 October 1915), but there, it seems, they vanished.

109. F.O. 371/2486/34982, "Memorandum of the Young Arab Party" by G. F. Clayton, 11 October 1915; a copy in F.O. 882/13; above, pp. 69-70.

110. Sudan Archives, W 135/4/10, Clayton to Wingate, 9 October 1915. On Ridā, see, Friedman, *The Question of Palestine*, pp. 98-99, 223-224. See also below, Chap. 5, pp. 138-139, and Friedman, *Palestine: A Twice-Promised Land?* vol. 2, forthcoming.

111. F.O. 371/2486/34982, Maxwell to Kitchener, 16 October 1915; a copy in F.O. 882/13.

112. Friedman, *The Question of Palestine*, p. 101.
113. See note 109.
114. F.O. 371/2486/34982, McMahon to F.O., 18 October 1915, unnumbered, Personal.
115. F.O. 882/14, fos. 185-196, Maxwell to H.M.'s Minister (Athens), 1 November 1915. For his cable to Kitchener. See Friedman, *The Question of Palestine*, pp. 71-72.
116. *Ibid.*, fos. 284-291, "Personal Views on the Arab Situation" by Aubrey Herbert, M.P., dated 30 October 1915. A copy of this memorandum was sent to Kitchener. For the other part of this memorandum, see below, p. 38.
117. F.O. 371/2490/128226, F.O. to W.O., 15 September 1915. The instruction was given in response to the report by General Hamilton, the G.O.C., of the M.E.F. to the W.O., dated 25 August 1915, on the interrogation of al-Faruqi soon after his defection at Gallipoli (*ibid.*).
118. F.O. 371/2140/46261, p. 198, Viceroy to I.O., 8 December 1914.
119. *Ibid.*, p. 340, Mallet (Constantinople) to Grey, 14 October 1914, citing the above report.
120. See note 10.
121. See Friedman, *The Question of Palestine*, pp. 70-71.
122. See Note 105, Tibawi omitted this passage in his Appendix.
123. F.O. 371/2486/34982, Statement of Muhammed Sharif el al-Faruqi, 12 October 1915, encl. in McMahon to Grey, 12 October 1915, Confidential. Also F.O. 882/15, fos. 28-38.
124. F.O. 882/24, fo. 113; Note by the Arab Bureau on the A.H.D. Committee . . . , April 1919.
125. C. Ernest Dawn, *From Ottomanism to Arabism* (Chicago, IL, 1973), pp. 152-155. In Appendices 1-IX, pp. 174-179, Prof. Dawn provides lists of the members of Arab nationalists, and of their social background.
126. Khoury, *Urban Notables* ...,pp. 74, 78. Also Ann M. Lesch, *Arab Politics in Palestine, 1917-1929* (Ithaca, NY, 1979), p. 25.
127. F.O. 371/3059/162432, "Turkish Provinces in Asia." Memorandum by Gertrude Bell, 23 June 1917, p. 3.
128. *A.A.A., Weltkrieg*, Nr. 11G, K196694, Mutius to Bethmann-Hollweg, 31 July 1916; same to same, 12 October 1916, dis. no. J., no. 2076. See also Friedman, *The Question of Palestine*, pp. 70-71. On Mutius, see Friedman, *Germany, Turkey and Zionism*, pp. 184-187.

129. A. L. Tibawi, *A Modern History of Syria* (London, 1969), pp. 200-205. The Porte ignored the societies' demands at this Congress because it felt that they represented only "a negligible element in Arab society," Lesch, *Arab Politics*, p. 25.

130. Majid Khadduri, "Aziz Ali Misri and the Arab Nationalist Movement," *St. Antony's Papers*, Middle-Eastern Affairs (1965), no. 17, pp. 140-150. Professor Khadduri challenges the accepted view advanced by Antonius and other Arab writers— who praise Aziz Ali as "the revolutionary leader *par excellence*" who championed the Arab cause against Turkish domination—and shows that, on the contrary, his idea was Turco-Arab unity. His quarrel with Enver Bey, was stirred up, not by national differences, but by personal jealousy. Al-Misri was accused of embezzlement and sentenced (on 15 April 1914) to fifteen years hard labor. Pressure on the Ottoman Government by the British Embassy brought about his release, and, when he arrived in Egypt on 22 April 1914, he was welcomed as an Arab national hero (*ibid.*, pp. 140-145).

131. *A.A.A.*, Weltkrieg, Nr. 11G K197010-11, Report by the Hamburg Colonial Institute on the Arab Question, December 1916.

132. Antonius, *The Arab Awakening*, pp. 152-153. Antonius received this information personally from Feisal, then King of Iraq (see *ibid.*, note 1).

133. Dawn, *From Ottomanism to Arabism*, p. 155.

134. F.O. 882/23, fos. 123-124, Intelligence Report, "Personalities . . . ," probably composed by Miss Bell, March 1920.

135. Friedman, *Palestine: A Twice-Promised Land?* vol. 2, forthcoming.

136. Below, Chap. 5, pp. 136-138.

137. F.O. 882/4, fo. 267, Note from R[uhi] to R. S[torrs], Jeddah, 2 August 1916, Storrs sent the report to Clayton for his perusal (marginalia, dated 8.8.16). On Ruhi, see below, pp. 39-42, 136.

138. Khadduri, "Aziz Ali Misri and the Arab Nationalist Movement," pp. 151-156. Al-Misri told Prof. Khadduri that before the revolt in 1916 he had been unaware of Hussein's objectives and that the British tried to win him over by offering the throne of Iraq (or Yemen) if he consented to lead an expeditionary force against the Turks. However, he declined the offer, since, according to his testimony, he was "neither interested in the throne, nor was [he] of the opinion that Britain

could win the war" (*ibid.*, pp. 152, 155, note 40). In addition to the interview (1958), Khadduri refers also to a statement made in *al-Ahram* (21 July 1959, p. 3) to this effect. Although Khadduri did not consult the Foreign Office files, he had no hesitation in dismissing al-Misri's claim as absolutely "fantastic."

139. F.O. 882/13, Sykes to D.M.O., 20 and 21 November 1915.

140. F.O. 882/4, fos. 82-83, Hardinge (Delhi) to Maxwell (Cairo), 28 November 1915. Private. Earlier he told the India Office, "I regard scheme [of an Arab rebellion] as unlikely to materialise, both owing to quality of leaders and because tribes and Sheiks concerned are too backward to pay attention to 'Young Arab' propaganda." Among the leaders mentioned were Sayyid Talib (on whom see below, note 142) and Nuri al-Said. Hardinge dismissed the former as "utterly untrustworthy" and the latter as a "highly Europeanised delicate Arab, aloof, about 25, apparently a visionary socialist" (F.O. 371/2130/5867, p. 198, Viceroy to I.O., 8 December 1914). Nuri al-Said subsequently joined the Sharifian army and in the thirties became a leading statesman in Iraq.

141. Friedman, *The Question of Palestine*, p. 76.

142. F.O. 882/15, fo. 74, Lawrence (Basra) to Intrusive [an Intelligence Branch agent] (Cairo), 9 April 1916. Sayyid Talib was a leading Arab personality in the Lower Iraq. In 1908, he joined the CUP (the Committee of Union and Progress) and was elected to the Ottoman Parliament. Shortly after, he fell out with the Young Turks and formed the Moderate Liberal Party (*Hur el-Mu'tadil*), the forerunner of the "Young Arabs." In 1912, he came to Egypt to court the British. He saw Lord Kitchener and, on his return journey, Lord Hardinge at Simla. British Intelligence described him as "a vicious man and a heavy drinker ... a bad man." In March 1917, Clayton objected to his coming to Cairo on the grounds of his "doubtful morals ... and tendency to intrigue" (F.O. 882/14, fos. 119-121) Clayton to Symes, 5 March 1917 and a note on Talib, same date.

143. Friedman, *The Question of Palestine*, pp. 76-77.

144. F.O. 882/19, fo. 84-85, translation of a verbal message, (undated and unsigned), encl. in Wilson (Port Sudan) to Clayton, 19 March 1916.

145. Clayton to Wingate, 22 April 1916, tel. no. 299 quoted in F.O.

371/6237 (1921) "Summary of Historical Documents from . . . 1914 to the outbreak of Revolt of the Sherif of Mecca in June 1916," Secret, no. 10812. Printed in January 1921, pp. 53-54; original typescript, dated 29 November 1916, in the Arab Bureau, F.O. 882/5, file 28 E/4, under the title "Hedjaz Rising Narrative."

146. The Sudan Archive, Durham, 145/3/33, "Note on a telegram no. 219 from the Foreign Office to the High Commissioner, dated March 6, 1917," initialed by Clayton.

147. F.O. 882/2, fo. 203, Memorandum by David Hogarth, 16 April 1916.

148. F.O. 800/381, fos. 134-135, Nicolson to Hardinge, 16 February 1916.

149. F.O. 882/3, fos. 51-3, Memorandum by Miss Bell, 23 June 1917.

150. F.O. 371/2486/34982, McMahon to Grey, 18 October 1915, Personal, unnumbered.

151. *Ibid.*, same to F.O. 18 October 1915, tel. no. 623. McMahon was referring to Hussein's letter of 9 September 1915.

152. *Ibid.*, McMahon to F.O., 7 November 1915, tel. no. 677, where the High Commissioner related his conversation with al-Faruqi, on 18 October 1915.

153. See note 150, above.

154. See note 123, above. It is possible that the secret societies learned the contents of Grey's cable to McMahon of 14 April 1915 from Hussein. Grey stated that the British Government "will make it an essential condition in the terms of peace that the Arabian Peninsula and its Holy Places should remain in the hands of an independent Moslem State." Exactly how much territory should be included in this state, he added, "it is not possible to define at this stage" (F.O. 371/2486/34982, Grey to McMahon, 14 April 1915, tel. no. 173).

155. See note 152, above.

156. Friedman, *Germany, Turkey and Zionism*, p. 192; Friedman, *The Question of Palestine*, p. 84, An authoritative French document quoted a figure of 120,000 Jews (W.O. 106/194, fos. 105-106, "Geography of Syria").

157. Above, note 48; also P.R.O. 30 57/45, Kitchener Papers, Storrs to Fitzgerald, 28 December 1914.

158. F.O. 371/2486/34982, F.O. to McMahon, 20 October 1915, tel. no. 796, drafted by Grey.

159. *Ibid.*, Wingate to Grey ("My dear Sir Edward"), Private, 15 May 1915.
160. Above, pp. 17-18, and below, pp. 39, 42.
161. F.O. 882/13, fos. 378-381, "Note on British Policy in the Near East," by Wingate, 25 August 1915; a copy in F.O. 371/2486/34982.
162. F.O. 882/2, fos. 132-133, Wingate to Clayton, telegram dated 23 October 1915.
163. See note 158.
164. F.O. 371/2486/34982, McMahon to Grey, 26 October 1915, dis. no. 131, Secret.
165. *Ibid.*, McMahon to F.O., 7 November 1915, tel. no. 677.
166. *Ibid.*, McMahon to F.O., 26 October 1915, tel. no. 644, Secret; copy in F.O. 141/461/1198.
167. F.O. 882/2, fos. 134-137, Clayton to Tyrrell, 30 October 1915.
168. F.O. 882/16, fos. 188-189, Maxwell to H.M.'s Minister, Athens, 1 November 1915.
169. Friedman, *The Question of Palestine*, pp. 72-73.
170. F.O. 371/2486/34982, Memorandum by G. W. Aubrey Herbert, M.P., 30 October 1915. A copy was sent to Kitchener. The memorandum was inspired by Clayton; see Margaret Fitzherbert, *The Man Who Was Greenmantle* (London, 1983), p. 169. When Herbert saw Grey, he found him very changed and "infinitely weary" (p. 170).
171. F.O. 371/2486/34982, Grey to Bertie, 10 November 1915, tel. no. 878.
172. Friedman, *The Question of Palestine*, p. 103.
173. Cmd. 5479, p. 20, para. 9.
174. Ronald Storrs, *Orientations* (London, 1939), pp. 15, 149, 159.
175. F.O. 882/6, fos. 367-370, Wilson to Clayton, 28 May 1917; below, pp. 136-137.
176. A copy of the Arabic translation of McMahon's letter of 24 October 1915 in Ruhi's handwriting, with Storrs's covering note (25 October 1915), was kept among the High Commissioner's files (F.O. 141/461).

   In 1937, when the Peel Commission was preparing its report, the question of publication of the Correspondence was revived, and on 2 June 1937, the Cabinet decided that the documents should be assembled and made ready for publication. Thereafter, the Embassy in Cairo supplied "certified ... copies" of the Arabic translations of the McMahon-Hussein Correspondence. The letter of 25 January 1916 was missing from the set and the Arabic texts of the Kitchener and Abdullah Correspondence could not be found (F.O. 371/2087, E 3034, 3194 and 3529/22/31, Lampson to Eden, 16, 19 June 1937). Arabic texts of McMahon's letters of 24 (erroneously indicated 26) of October, 14 December 1915, and 10 March 1916 are reproduced in Appendices 1, 2, 3; see also 4.

A. L. Tibawi examined the Arabic text of McMahon's letter of 24 October 1915 when it was still in its original file, F.O. 141/461 (Tibawi, *Anglo-Arab Relations* (London, 1978), p. 85, note 15), but the document has since disappeared. Only Storrs's covering note remained. For a critique of Tibawi's analysis, see Friedman, *Palestine: A Twice-Promised Land?* vol. 2, forthcoming.

177. See above, pp. 10-11.
178. F.O. 371/5067/9, E 16103/9/44, Minute by Young, 25 December 1920; see also Friedman, *Palestine: A Twice-Promised Land?* vol. 2, forthcoming.
179. L. Grafftey-Smith, *Bright Levant* (London, 1970), p. 156.
180. Sudan Archive, Durham, 135/5, Wingate to Clayton, 1 November 1915, Private.
181. Friedman, *The Question of Palestine*, p. 91, and vol. 2, forthcoming.
182. Grafftey-Smith, *Bright Levant*, p. 155.
183. F.O. 686/42, fo. 86, Vickery to Arbur, 3 October 1919. The whole episode, as well as Vickery's encounter with Abdullah, is related in Friedman, *Palestine: A Twice-Promised Land?* vol. 2, forthcoming.
184. *Ibid.*, fo. 57, Vickery to Arbur, 20 November 1919.
185. Grafftey-Smith, *Bright Levant*, p. 155; also F.O. 141/726 /76, where it states that the Arabic letters were eventually found by Keown-Boyd "among some rubbish" left by Storrs (Note dated 21 February 1931).
186. *Sudan Gazette*, no. 120.
187. Grafftey-Smith, *Bright Levant*, p. 50.
188. F.O. 686/42, fos. 67-68. "Literal translation of original Arabic letter sent by Sir H. McMahon to King Hussein." See Appendix 4. The name of the translator is not given. In the typescript, the word "gave" is an error for "have," or rather, "has."

189.   Grafftey-Smith, *Bright Levant*, p. 155.
190.   See below, Chap. 5, pp. 141-143.

Chapter 2   The "Pledge" to Hussein and the Sykes-Picot Agreement

1.   Arnold J. Toynbee, *Acquaintances* (London, 1938), pp. 196-197.
2.   David Garnett, ed., *Letters of T. E. Lawrence* (London, 1938), pp. 280-282.
3.   The William Yale Papers, 1917-1919; in microfilm, St. Antony's College, Oxford, Report dated 27 October 1919. In 1917-1918, Captain Yale served as an American Intelligence Agent in Cairo. Also reproduced in Garnett, *Letters of T. E. Lawrence* , p. 286, but the version on Palestine is given in an abridged form.
4.   Garnett, *Letters of T. E. Lawrence*, pp. 285-287, Lawrence's draft letter to Lloyd George, dated 9 October 1919, was found among his papers after his death, but there is no evidence that it was sent.
5.   See Chap. 3 below, pp. 95-96.
6.   See *Toynbee and History, Critical Essays and Reviews*, M. F. Ashley Montagu, ed.; *Toynbee, Reappraisals*, C. T. McIntire and Marvin Perry, eds. (Toronto, 1989).
7.   George Antonius, *The Arab Awakening* (London, 1938), pp. 248-249.
8.   *Ibid.*, pp. 169, 178.
9.   On one occasion, McMahon complained: "Sherif's requirements . . . are often expressed in vague terms and sometimes unintelligible . . . impossible to follow" (F.O. 371/2774/4223, McMahon to F.O., 15 July 1916, tel. no. 587.
10.   Lloyd George Papers, House of Lords, E 2/13/12, Grey to Lloyd George, 2 November 1916.

    To Wingate, Grey cabled: "Lord Kitchener's death has made the consideration of an appointment necessary. . . . In my opinion there is no-one so well fitted as yourself . . . to fill the post" (Ronald Wingate, *Wingate of the Sudan* [London, 1955], p. 201). Lady Wemyss, the Admiral's wife, wrote: "McMahon was ruthlessly chucked out from here . . . [The Foreign Office] had been furious at his being given the appointment at all . . ." (Lady Wemyss, *The Life and Letters of Lord Wester Wemyss* (London, 1935), p. 340). McMahon was Kitchener's protégé, and after Kitchener died with the sinking of *H.M.S. Hampshire* on its way to Russia (5 June 1916), McMahon had nobody to support him.

11. F.O. 371/2767/939, encl. in McMahon to Grey, 7 February 1916, dis. no. 26; copies in F.O. 141/461 and F.O. 882/5.

12. F.O. 371/2767/938, "The Arab Question," a note from Nicolson to Grey, 2 February 1916.

13. *Ibid.*, F.O. to Buchanan, 9 February 1916, tel. no. 377.

14. F.O. 800/381, Nicolson Papers, Nicolson to McMahon, 8 March 1916, Private.

15. F.O. 371/2768/938, Sykes to Clayton, 14 April 1916, tel. no. 287. For reasons why Cairo officials objected to sending al-Faruqi and al-Misri, see Friedman, *The Question of Palestine*, pp. 116-118.

16. F.O. 882/16.

17. F.O. 371/2768/938, McMahon to F.O., 4 May 1916, tel. no. 329.

18. Friedman, *The Question of Palestine*, pp. 108-109.

19. F.O. 882/14, fo. 35, "Anglo-Franco-Russian Agreement," Hogarth to Hall, 3 May 1916.

20. F.O. 371/2486/24982, fos. 379-384, Sykes to D.M.O., nos. 19, 20, cited in McMahon to F.O. 20, 21 November 1915, tel. nos. 707, 709. See also Friedman, *The Question of Palestine*, pp. 84-85.

21. Friedman, *The Question of Palestine*, p. 105.

22. *Ibid.*, pp. 103, 108.

23. For the provisions of the Agreement see *D.B.F.P.*, First Series, vol. IV, pp. 241-251. At Cambon's suggestion, the word "protect" was altered to the less obtrusive "uphold" (*soutenir*). Cambon to Grey, 25 August, and Grey to Cambon, 30 August 1916, *ibid.*, pp. 248-249; see also Lloyd George, *The Truth . . .*, vol. II, pp. 1023-1024.

24. Lloyd George, *The Truth . . .*, vol. II, p. 756.

25. F.O. 371/2410/46261, R. E. M. Russel, Intelligence Department, Cairo, 17 August 1914, "Precis of Conversation with . . ."

26. F.O. 371/2767/938, Hussein to al-Mirghani, 28 December 1915, encl. in McMahon to Grey, 7 February 1916, dis. no. 26; a copy in

F.O. 141/46/1198 and in F.O. 882/5.

27.   F.O. 371/2486/34982, Sykes for D.M.O., no. 18, encl. in McMahon to F.O., 15 November 1915, tel. no. 706.

28.   F.O. 371/2486/34982, Sykes to D.M.O., no. 19, encl. in McMahon to F.O., 20 November 1915, tel. no. 707, appended to Nicolson's note, "Arab Question," of 2 February 1916.

29.   Friedman, *The Question of Palestine*, p. 223.

30.   F.O. 371/2676/936. Ganem was interviewed by Albina, an Arab Christian agent of Sir Mark Sykes. Note, dated 7 March 1916. Copies sent to D.I.D. and D.M.I.; perused by E. G.[rey].

31.   F.O. 371/2767/938, "Arab Question," Note dated 4 February 1916; also CAB 37/142/10.

32.   *Ibid.*, An Outline of the Agreement, dated 2 February 1916.

33.   F.O. 800/106, Grey to Curzon, 22 February 1916.

34.   F.O. 371/2768/938, Grey to Bertie, 11 May 1916, tel. no. 350. Rodd, the Ambassador in Rome, was briefed on 21 September 1916 (CAB 37/155/33).

35.   *D.B.F.P.*, First Series, vol. IV, p. 245, Grey to Cambon, 16 May 1916. On May 23, Grey repeated the same text to Count Benckendorff, omitting mention of the four cities, which were of no concern to Russia.

36.   F.O. 371/2767/938, F.O. 371/2667/938, p. 23579, Nicolson to Grey, 4 February 1916.

37.   Friedman, *The Question of Palestine*, p. 73.

38.   F.O. 371/2486/34982, F.O. to McMahon, 11 November 1915, tel. no. 874, quoting Chamberlain's letter verbatim. Nicolson minuted: "Chamberlain's memorandum represents in my opinion a true state of the case."

39.   *Ibid.*, fo. 338, Viceroy to I.O., 11 November 1915.

40.   F.O. 371/2767/938, McMahon to F.O., 1 March 1916, tel. no. 152[?].

41.   F.O. 371/2768/938, McMahon to F.O., 18 April 1916, tel. no. 272, where Hussein's letter of 29 March is quoted. A translated copy of this letter is enclosed in McMahon to Grey, 16 April 1916, dis. no. 79, Secret.

42.   F.O. 371/2768/938, p. 80305, Minutes dated 3 May 1916. In my book, *The Question of Palestine* (pp. 117-118), I expressed an opinion that the decision to maintain secrecy was "a major blunder of policy." However, I have since revised my judgment.

43.   See below, Chap. 5, pp. 130-131, and Chap. 6, pp. 145, 147-162.

Chapter 3   Toynbee *versus* Toynbee

1.   F.O. 371/3384/747, p. 183770; copies in F.O. 371/3411/161891; F.O. 882/13; and CAB 27/36, E.C. 2201.
2.   F.O. 371/4368/4352, P.I.D.; a copy in CAB 24/72/I, G.T. 6506.
3.   F.O. 371/3384/747, p. 171983; F.O. 371/3411/161891 p. 175294, Wingate to Balfour, 21 September 1918, dis. no. 219, Secret. Enclosed: Hussein's letter of 28 August; Clayton's Note of 8 September; Cornwallis, Note of 10 September and "Notes on King Hussein's Statement of the Agreement . . ." Attached is also a note by General B. T. Buckley, the Director of Military Intelligence, Cairo. Buckley wrote: "This document is King Hussein's version of the agreement and makes no mention of the various important points raised in the letters sent to him by the High Commissioner of Egypt on this subject." Wilson's letter to Symes of 15 September 1918 is quoted in his own letter to Cheetham (copy for T.E.L.) dated 31 January 1919, F.O. 608/97, fos. 473-6.
4.   F.O. 371/3384/747, fos. 83-85, Minutes by Sir Eyre Crowe and Robert Cecil, dated 16 October 1918.
5.   F.O. 366/787, p. 91660.
6.   William H. McNeill, *Arnold J. Toynbee, A Life* (Oxford, 1989), p. 69.
7.   F.O. 371/3411/161891, p. 175294, Minutes by Toynbee, dated 23 and 28 October 1918. Attached are: Wingate's dispatch to Balfour, 21 September, and letters of Hussein, Cornwallis, and Clayton, on which see note 3, above.
8.   F.O. 882/5, fos. 121-216.
9.   F.O. 371/3384/747, *Papers Relating to King Hussein's Version of His Agreements with His Majesty's Government*, 5 November, 1918, 21 September 1918, and other documents, on which see note 3, above.
10.   F.O. 371/4368/443, pp. 125-130, Minutes by A. J. T[oynbee], 9 October 1918, and Crowe. On the *Manchester Guardian's* policy, as well as that of *Palestine*, see Friedman, *The Question of Palestine*, pp. 128-129.
11.   F.O. 371/4353, P.C. 3l, Minute by Toynbee, dated 18 November 1918. Toynbee feared that Feisal might use the "Declaration to the Seven" of 11 June 1918 to further his cause.
12.   F.O. 371/3385/747, "Memorandum on Changes in the General

International Situation . . . the Main British Commitment Regarding the Middle East," Confidential, Printed; undated; presumably mid-November 1918.

13.   *Ibid.*, 19 December 1918. The memorandum was prepared at the request of Sir Louis Mallet.

14.   "Comments," see pp. lii-lx," above. The request was rela-ted to the 19 December 1918 memorandum, not, as Toynbee erroneously claimed in his "Comments," with regard to *British Commitments to King Hussein.*

15.   McNeill, *Arnold J. Toynbee, A Life*, pp. 75, 77.

16.   Jukka Nevakivi, *Britain, France and the Arab Middle East, 1914-1920* (London, l969), pp. 91-93.

17.   Toynbee, *Acquaintances* (London, 1938), pp. 211-212. Toynbee recalled this episode to illustrate his point that the British Government "went back on its agreement" with Hussein and that "Lloyd George had left out the rights and wishes of the Arabs themselves" (*ibid.*). By that time (*Acquaintances* was published in 1967), Toynbee had altered his views radically and lost no opportunity to criticize the British Government, and Lloyd George in particular.

18.   McNeill, *Arnold J. Toynbee, A Life*, p. 80.

19.   *Ibid.*

20.   *Ibid.*, p. 81.

21.   Toynbee, *Acquaintances*, p. 181.

22.   F.O. 371/4363, Cecil's Minute on Toynbee's "Memorandum . . . on Preparation of Draft Treaty with Turkey," noted.

23.   F.O. 371/3384/747, fo. 424, Memorandum by R. C., 28 October 1918.

24.   Entitled "Reconstruction of Arabia," reproduced in David Garnett, ed., *The Letters of T. E. Lawrence* (London, 1928), pp. 267-269.

25.   CAB 27/37, fo. 75, "Policy in Arabia," Memorandum by Sir A. Hirtzel, 20 November 1918.

26.   Below, pp. 95-96.

27.   Toynbee, *Acquaintances*, pp. 211-212.

28.   Above, pp. 65-67.

29.   F.O. 371/3057/108112, "Situation in the Ottoman Empire, Arabia, etc.," Memorandum by Toynbee, 29 May 1917.

30.   David Hogarth, "Great Britain and the Arabs," H. W. V. Temperley, ed., *History of the Peace Conference*, vol. VI (Lon-

don, 1924), pp. 126-129.

31.   A. J. Toynbee, *The Murderous Tyranny of the Turks* (London, New York, 1917), p. 21. The MS for this book was prepared late in 1916.

32.   *Turkey: A Past and a Future,* (New York, 1917), see pp. 26-29.

33.   Above, Chap. 1, p. 30.

34.   F.O. 608/96, p. 2753, Minutes, dated 24 & 25 February 1919.

35.   F.O. 371/3386/747, pp. 103-110. Neither Toynbee's memorandum, nor that of Hirtzel, were dated; presumably mid-December.

36.   F.O. 371/3383/747, fo. 583; the map is kept in the Map Room, MFQ, 379(1). For its section on Palestine, see Map 4.

37.   F.O. 371/4368/4352, pp. 330-341. Unlike the "Memorandum on British Commitments," this had only a limited circulation.

38.   Below, Chap. 4, p. 110.

39.   See note 37, Note by E[ric] D[rummond] on Balfour's behalf, dated 2 December 1918.

40.   *Ibid.,* p. 353, L. Storr to Oliphant, 26 November 1918.

41.   *Ibid.,* p. 352, Toynbee to Nicolson, 26 November 1918.

42.   Above, pp. 62-63.

43.   See "Preamble," above.

44.   See note 37, p. 352; Minute 27 November 1918.

45.   F.O. 371/3044/1173, Memorandum by H. Nicolson, 13 July 1917, and Minute by Graham.

46.   Friedman, *The Question of Palestine,* p. 251. Nicolson also misled Leonard Stein into thinking that, when the formula for the Balfour Declaration was first considered at the Foreign Office end, the key-words seemed to have been "asylum" or "refuge" (*ibid.*).

47.   New edition, 1944, pp. 140-141. However, when the State of Israel was proclaimed, he unequivocally aired his satisfaction "at this realization of the hopes of Zionism" (*ibid.,* Friedman, *The Question of Palestine,* p. 251; see also p. 327).

48.   Toynbee, *Acquaintances,* p. 198. On Forbes-Adam's views, see Friedman, *The Question of Palestine,* pp. 320-321.

49.   See note 37, pp. 354-355, "Note on . . . Territorial Negotiations between H.M.G. and King Hussein: (undated).

50.   Antonius, *The Arab Awakening,* p. 177.

51.   F.O. 371/3384/747, p. 18168, Clayton (Cairo) to F.O., 31 October 1918, tel. no. 154. Minutes by Ormsby-Gore (2 November

1918) and Toynbee (7 November 1918).

52.   F.O. 371/14495 (1930) "Memorandum on the Exclusion of Palestine from the Area assigned for Arab Independence by Mc-Mahon-Hussein Correspondence of 1915-1916," Confidential, dated 24 October 1930.

53.   *Ibid.*, p. 54.

54.   For my disagreement with Tibawi and Kedourie, see Friedman, *Palestine: A Twice-Promised Land?*, vol. 2, forthcoming.

55.   See "Preamble," above, where the relevant section of Hogarth's note is reproduced.

56.   F.O. 371/2486/34982, tel. no. 736, p. 448.

57.   David G. Hogarth, *The Nearer East* (London, 1902), p. 264.

58.   F.O. 882/24, Anglo-Franco-Russian Agreement, Hogarth (Cairo) to Hall (London), 3 May 1916. On Hall, see Friedman, *The Question of Palestine*, pp. 110-111.

59.   F.O. 371/2768/938, McMahon to Grey, 19 April 1916, dis. no. 83, and enclosed the memorandum of the Arab Bureau (Hogarth), dated 16 April 1916.

60.   *Ibid.*, Minutes by Clerk, Nicolson, and Grey, 3 May 1916. Also above, p. 59.

61.   The Sudan Archive, Durham, 145/3/23. The note appears under the Residency's letterhead and is titled "Communicated verbally to Sultan by H. C. Very secret." It is undated and not signed but the handwriting is unmistakable. It is Hogarth's. The archivist was probably right in inserting the date "([?] March 1917)."

62.   F.O. 371/3385/747, pp. 168-69.

63.   *Ibid.*, Clayton to F.O., 18 November 1918, tel. no. 190, Minutes by Ormsby-Gore (22 November 1918) and Toynbee (26 November 1918).

64.   On which see above, Chap. 1, pp. 10-11.

65.   Friedman, *The Question of Palestine*, pp. 91-92.

66.   P.R.O. Map Room, MPI 720. The map is undated, but all indications are that it was prepared toward the end of November 1918. See Map 3.

67.   See above, pp. 83-84, and Map 4.

68.   F.O. 371/3398/27647, pp. 583-84. During the Ottoman period, the Arabah [now Aravah] region in the eastern Negev was part of the Hedjaz Vilayet.

69.   Friedman, *The Question of Palestine*, p. 301.

70. F.O. 608/98, fo. 375/2/1. no. 588, Memorandum by Ormsby-Gore, 23 January 1919.

71. Toynbee, *Acquaintances*, p. 181.

72. David Hunter Miller, *My Diary at the Conference of Paris* (New York, 1924), vol. IV, p. 226; Lloyd George, *The Truth . . .*, vol. II, pp. 1142-1149.

73. F.O. 608/93, fo. 360/1/1, p. 3051, Memorandum, dated 25 February 1919, Confidential; for information of the Press, but not for publication. In a minute dated 3 March 1919, Toynbee noted that the memorandum had been prepared at short notice and that there was no time to show it to anybody except Mr. Philip Kerr, who had asked for it.

74. F.O. 608/97, fo. 375/1/3. p. 2921, Minute by Toynbee dated 2 March 1919; Cheetham to Curzon, 9 February and enclosed letter from Hussein of 29 January 1919. On the "Agreement," see above, p. 62.

75. F.O. 371/3385/747, p. 192, "Memorandum on . . . Settlement of Western Asia" by David Hogarth, 11 November 1918.

76. CAB 27/24; also Friedman, *The Question of Palestine*, pp. 89-90.

77. F.O. 608/105, fo. 384/1/1, "Our Promises to the Arabs," Memorandum by Mallet, Paris, 4 February 1919.

78. P.R.O. 30, 30/10, Milner Papers; a copy is in Bodleian Library, Oxford.

79. F.O. 371/4180/2117, p. 7998, Mallet to Curzon, Paris, 26 May 1919, dis. no. 809.

80. *D.B.F.P.*, First Series, vol. IV, pp. 340-349, no. 242, Memorandum by Balfour (Paris) with respect to Syria, Palestine and Mesopotamia.

81. F.O. 608/93, fo. 360/1/11, p. 5840, Minutes, 22 August 1919.

82. This is implicit, among others, in the phrase "we promised the Arabs independence . . . except in respect of certain territorial reservations," such as the Syrian littoral and Palestine. On Balfour's attitude, see Friedman, *The Question of Palestine*, pp. 325-326.

83. Lloyd George Papers, F 12/1/43, Grey to Balfour, 9 September 1919; Curzon's Minute, 17 September 1919.

84. *D.B.F.P.*, First Series, vol. IV, doc. no. 286; see also Friedman, *Palestine: A Twice-Promised Land?*, vol. 2, forthcoming.

85. H. C., 20 June 1904; O.R., col. 571.

86. Friedman, *The Question of Palestine*, p. 9.
87. *Ibid.*, pp. 53-58.
88. Toynbee, *Acquaintances*, pp. 198-200.
89. See Friedman, *Palestine: A Twice-Promised Land?*, vol. 2, forthcoming.
90. Sayegh's findings were published in an article in the Lebanese *Hiwar* magazine, which was summarized in *The Times* of 17 April 1964, p. 15.
91. Yahya Armajani, "The Awakening of the Arabic Speaking People," *Middle East Past and Present* (New Jersey, 1970), pp. 293-294.

Chapter 4   Pro-Arab or Pro-Zionist?

1. Toynbee to Talmon, 3 July 1967, "An Exchange between Arnold Toynbee and J. L. Talmon," *Encounter*, October 1967, reprinted in Walter Laqueur, ed., *The Israel-Arab Reader. A Documentary of History of the Middle East Conflict* (London, 1969), p. 260.
2. Above, Chap. 3, p. 79.
3. Arnold J. Toynbee, *Turkey: A Past and Future* (New York, 1917), p. 6.
4. Arnold J. Toynbee, *Nationality and the War* (London, 1915), p. 379.
5. Foreign Office Peace Handbook, no. 60, *Syria and Palestine*, (HMSO, 1920), pp. 56-57. It was probably prepared by Ormsby-Gore, who, during his service on the Arab Bureau in Cairo, was gathering information on Syria and Palestine. The MS was circulated early in 1919.
6. Arnold J. Toynbee, *Survey of International Affairs for 1925* (Oxford, 1927), vol. 1, p. 351. He referred to the Foreign Office Handbook, quoted already, as well as to the Admiralty Handbook, *Syria (including Palestine)*, (HMSO, 1920), pp. 175-235, and to a number of other authoritative publications.
7. Arnold J. Toynbee, *Survey of International Affairs for 1930* (Oxford, 1931), pp. 223-224, 254-255.
8. *International Affairs, Journal of the Royal Institute of International Affairs*, vol. XX (January 1931), p. 56.

9.	On this memorandum, see above, Chap. 3, pp. 66-67. The Allied Powers recognized Hussein only as "the *titular head* of the Arab peoples in their revolt against Turkish misrule," and as "the lawful and *de facto* ruler of the Hedjaz" (F.O. to Wingate, 6 November 1916, cited in Toynbee's memorandum, pp. 13-14).

10.	On which see above, Chap. 3, pp. 62-63.

11.	Above, Chap. 3, pp. 96.

12.	See note 9, above.

13.	*Survey of International Affairs for 1925* (Oxford, 1927), pp. 6-12, 103.

14.	*Ibid.*, p. 273. See also Arnold J. Toynbee, *The Islamic World since the Peace Conference* (London, 1927).

15.	Arnold J. Toynbee, *Acquaintances* (Oxford, 1967[1938]), p. 190.

16.	Toynbee, *Turkey: A Past and a Future*, pp. 64-66.

17.	*Ibid.*, pp. 66-71. Davis-Trietsch aired his views in an article "Die Juden der Türkei" (Leipzig, 1915), Pamphlet no. 8 of the *Deutsches Vorderasienscomitee's* series: *Länder und Völker der Türkei*. On Trietsch, see I. Friedman, *Germany, Turkey and Zionism*, p. 254.

18.	F.O. 395/139/15729, Lloyd George to Buchan, 1 February 1917; Buchan to Montgomery, 25 March 1917; Friedman, *The Question of Palestine*, pp. 170-171.

19.	Toynbee, *Acquaintances*, pp. 152-153.

20.	June 1917, no. 27, pp. 532-536. The article appeared anonymously. Professor Toynbee was good enough to tell me that he wrote it (Letter, dated 3 November 1969, to the author).

21.	Alfred Zimmern (on Toynbee's behalf) to Weizmann, 16 May 1917. Reginald (later Sir Reginald) Coupland, the Acting Editor of the *Round Table*, asked Jabotinsky to convey his thanks to Weizmann for reading the proofs (22 May 1917). The letters are deposited at the Weizmann Archives, Rehovot, Israel.

22.	Toynbee, *Nationality and the War*, p. 411.

23.	Friedman, *The Question of Palestine*, p. 11; Leonard Stein, *The Balfour Declaration* (London, 1961), Chap. 6 and *passim*.

24.	Friedman, *The Question of Palestine*, pp. 250-251.

25.	*Ibid.*, pp. 301, 313.

26.	Toynbee, Stein, and Julian Huxley were the only students to receive Senior Scholarships to the University of Oxford in 1906. I am grateful to Mrs. Leonard Stein for this information. In the

1920s, Toynbee invited Stein to contribute a sub-section to his *Survey of International Affairs for 1925* on the development of the Jewish National Home in Palestine and referred to him as "a distinguished member of the Zionist Organization" (p. 23, note 3 of p. 22).

27.   Friedman, *The Question of Palestine*, pp. 43-47, 171.

28.   F.O. 371/4368/443, p. 302, Memorandum on "Changes in the General International Situation . . . ," undated, presumably mid-November 1918. During a ceremony to present decorations to some members of the Jewish Battalions, General Chaytor, the Commander-in-Chief of the Australian Cavalry Division, said:

> . . . I was particularly struck with your good work on the Mellalah front, and by your gallant capture of the Ummesh Fort and defeat of the Turkish rearguard when I gave you the order to go, for I was then enabled to push my mounted men over the Jordan at that cross, and so you contributed mightily to the capture of Es Salt and of the guns and other material which fell to our share; the capture of Amman; the cutting of the Hedjaz railway, and the destruction of the 4th Turkish Army, which helped considerably toward the great victory at Damascus.

Cited in Lt. Col. Henry J. Patterson, *With the Judeans in the Palestine Campaign* (London, 1922), pp. 186-187; see also, F.O. Handbook, *Syria and Palestine*, pp. 62-63.

29.   F.O. 371/3054/84173, Minute by A. J. T[oynbee] and L. B. N[amier], dated 19 December 1917, on a despatch from Sir H. Rumbold to the F.O.; Friedman, *The Question of Palestine*, p. 326.

30.   Above, Chap. 3, pp. 83-84.

31.   F.O. 371/3386/747, p. 206913, Memorandum by Toynbee, undated.

32.   Arnold J. Toynbee, *Study of History* (Oxford, 1934), pp. 242-243.

33.   Toynbee to Sokolow, Paris, 7 March 1919. The late Dr. Celina Sokolow kindly showed me this letter. It is now deposited at the Central Zionist Archives, Jerusalem, file A18 706.

34.   F.O. 608/99, p. 6950: ". . . I have no doubt that we are on the road toward a satisfactory settlement," Balfour to Weizmann, 21 April 1919.

35. F.O. 608/100, p. 11752, encl. in Weizmann to Forbes Adam, 4 June 1919.

36. Arnold J. Toynbee, "The Trouble in Palestine," *The New Republic* (New York, 6 September, 1922), vol. XXXII, no. 405, pp. 38-40. Earlier he stated that British commitments to Hussein and to other parties were incompatible only "in spirit"; Arnold J. Toynbee, *The Western Question in Greece and Turkey* (London, 1922), pp. 48-49.

37. For a discussion, see Friedman, *The Question of Palestine*, pp. 324-332.

38. Arnold J. Toynbee, "The Non-Arab Territories," in H. W. V. Temperley, ed., *History of the Peace Conference*, vol. VI (London, 1924), p. 56.

39. *D.B.F.P.*, First Series, vol. VIII, p. 110.

40. Above, Chap. 3, pp. 78-79.

41. On Graves's book, *The Land of the Three Faiths*, with Hogarth's introduction, see "Preamble," above, Note 53, and Friedman, *Palestine: A Twice-Promised Land?*, vol. 2 — *The Creation of the Historical Myth, 1920-1939*, forthcoming.

42. *Survey of International Affairs for 1925*, pp. 12, 21-23, 272, 361.

43. *Survey of International Affairs for 1930* (Oxford, 1931), pp. 229, 254.

44. Arnold J. Toynbee, *Study of History* (Oxford, 1934) vol. II, pp. 252-254.

45. See note 8 above, pp. 43-45, 56, 59, 67.

46. *Ibid.*, p. 59.

47. Toynbee, *Acquaintances*, pp. 196-197.

48. D. Garnett, *Letters of T. E. Lawrence*, pp. 281-282. The four documents were: McMahon's letter of 24 October 1915; the Sykes-Picot Agreements; Statement to the Seven Syrians in Cairo, 11 June, 1917, and the Anglo-French Declaration of 8 November, 1918.

49. *Ibid.*, pp. 345-346.

50. Toynbee, *Acquaintances*, p. 196.

51. On Antonius's relations with Toynbee, see Friedman, *Palestine: A Twice-Promised Land?*, vol. 2, forthcoming.

52. F.O. 371/24569, E 1897/1897/31, record of a telephone conversation between L. H. Baggallay (F.O.) and H. F. Downie (C.O.), 18 April 1940.

53. *Ibid.*, pp. 95-96, Baggallay to Downie, 10 May 1940.

54.   For a discussion, see Friedman, *Palestine: A Twice-Promised Land?*, vol. 2, forthcoming. Dr. Parkes read the exchange between Toynbee and myself in the *Journal of Contemporary History* (vol. 5, no. 4, 1970) and told me thereafter how delighted he was that it was not Toynbee who had the better of the argument (letter dated 5 November 1970).

55.   Toynbee, *Acquaintances*, pp. 68-73.

56.   *Ibid.*, pp. 76-77.

57.   M. F. Ashley Montagu, ed., *Toynbee and History: Critical Essays and Reviews* (Boston, MA, 1956), pp. 116, 123, 192.

58.   *Ibid.*, p. 385.

Chapter 5   Sykes, Picot, and Hussein

1.   Above, Chap. 2, p. 47.

2.   Above, Chap. 2, pp. 49-50.

3.   Antonius, *The Arab Awakening*, pp. 252-54.

4.   Friedman, *The Question of Palestine*, pp. 52-61, where the whole episode is discussed.

5.   F.O. 371/2767/938, Sykes to F.O., in Buchanan (Petrograd) to F.O., 16 and 18 March 1916, tel. no. 377, Urgent, Private and Secret; F.O. 371/2768/938, Sykes to D.M.I., encl. in Buchanan to F.O., 1 April 1916. At this stage Sykes was still ignorant of Zionism. He learned about it first from Herbert Samuel's memorandum of January 1915 which he read shortly before his departure for Petrograd (Friedman, *The Question of Palestine*, p. 112).

6.   F.O. 371/2767/938, Weakley's observation, dated 17 March 1916, and Grey's initials.

7.   *Ibid.*, Buchanan to F.O., 17 March 1916, tel. no. 382.

8.   Above, Chap. 1, pp. 29-30, and Chap. 2, pp. 58-59.

9.   F.O. 371/2486/34982, McMahon to F.O., 20 October 1915, tel. no. 626.

10.   F.O. 882/16, fos. 53-56, "The Status and Functions of the Chief Political Officer and French Commissioner," February 1917; copy in Wingate Papers.

11.   Friedman, *The Question of Palestine* , pp. 116-117.

12.   F.O. 371/3045/2087, Wingate to F.O., 12 March 1917, tel. no.

257; F.O. (Graham), to Wingate, 14 March 1917, tel. no. 257; F.O. (Sykes) to Wingate, 2 April 1917, tel. no. 338.

13. Friedman, *The Question of Palestine*, pp. 123-129; 164-175, where also the divergence between the Prime Minister's policy and that of the Foreign Office is illuminated.

14. *Ibid.*, pp. 141-142.

15. E. A. Adamov, *Die Europäischen Mächte und die Türkei wärend des Weltkrieges.* . . . (Dresden, l932), no. 282. "Instructions . . . ," Paris, 2 April 1917, pp. 232-236; the original document in MAE, Archives Politique, Guerre 1914-1918, Syrie-Palestine, X, pp. 137-142, 2 April 1917; Friedman, *The Question of Palestine*, p. 144, where the document is cited in full.

16. MAE, Arabie, vol. 1694, Memorandum by J. Gout, 5 April 1917.

17. The whole of this episode is dealt with in the file F.O. 371/2782/217652.

18. F.O. 371/3057/108112, Memorandum on Arabia, 29 May 1917, Intelligence Bureau, Department of Information.

19. F.O. 882/6, fos. 182-185, "Future of Arab Movement" by D. G. Hogarth, Cairo, 12 February 1917.

20. Prof. Kedourie thinks that "in betraying no knowledge of the Sykes-Picot Agreement in his conversation with Hogarth, Fuad al-Khatib was showing no more than a prudent discretion," and that it was "highly unlikely that knowledge which was widespread in the Syrian community in Cairo would have remained hidden from [him]." Kedourie, *In the Anglo-Arab Labyrinth*, p. 155. This, however, is speculation.

21. Durham, Clayton Papers 145/3/33, Note by Clayton 10 March 1917, on the Foreign Office telegram no. 219. dated 6 March 1917 to the High Commissioner.

22. Friedman, *The Question of Palestine*, pp. 116-118.

23. *Ibid.*, pp. 116-117. For deliberations at the Foreign Office on this issue, see above, Chap. 2, pp. 56-59.

24. Above, Chap. 3, p. 92-93, and Friedman, *Palestine: A Twice-Promised Land?*, vol. 2, forthcoming.

25. Wingate Archive, Durham, SAD/145/4/37-41, Memorandum by Clayton dated 3 April 1917; F.O. 882/16, fos. 227-231, Clayton to Wilson, same date.

26. F.O. 882/12, fo. 212, Wilson (Jeddah) to Arbur (Cairo), tel., 9 April 1917; same to Clayton, 11 April 1917.

27. F.O. 882/19, fos. 44-45, Note by Storrs, 12 November 1915; a copy in Wingate Archive. For the British response to the letter of 14 July 1915, see Friedman, *The Question of Palestine*, pp. 68-69, and above, "Preamble."

28. F.O. 371/2767/938, Hussein to al-Mirghani, 28 December 1915, encl. in McMahon to F.O., 7 February 1916, dis. no. 26; a copy in F.O. 141/461/1198 and in F.O. 882/5.

29. F.O. 141/461/1198, fos. 119-126; a copy in F.O. 882/18.

30. Above, Chap. 1, pp. 17, 34-35.

31. As note 28.

32. The Israel State Archives, Jerusalem (hereafter ISA), The George Antonius Archive, P 383/2784, "Notes collected in several interviews with Nassib Bey al-Bakri" (noted); also Antonius, *The Arab Awakening* , pp. 149-150.

33. Above, Chap. 1, p. 18.

34. Other parts of this letter were quoted above, Chap. 1, p. 19.

35. F.O. 141/461/1198, Hussein to McMahon, January 1916 and a "verbal message"; F.O. 371/2767/938, same, encl. in McMahon to Grey, 24 January 1916.

36. F.O. 882/19, fo. 107, Hussein to H.C., June 1916; F.O. 141/461/1198, McMahon to Hogarth, 30 June 1916.

37. F.O. 141/461/1198, al-Faruqi to Clayton (noted), encl. in Cornwallis's report, 8 July 1916.

38. F.O. 371/2776/42233, Grey to Bertie, 22 November 1916, dis. no. 779.

39. F.O. 371/2773/42233, McMahon to F.O., 1 July 1916.

40. Below, Chap. 8, p. 202.

41. F.O. 141/736/2475, Wingate (Erkowit) to Bolland (Cairo), 1 July 1916; F.O. 141/461/1198, Cornwallis (Jeddah) to Arab Bureau, 8 July 1915, encl. in McMahon to Grey, 15 July 1916.

42. F.O. 1411/461/1198, Note by Ruhi, 21 June 1916; F.O. 882/4, fo. 267, R[uhi] to R. S[torrs], Jeddah, 17 July 1916. A copy was sent to McMahon, Clayton, and Wingate (Aug. 1916).

43. F.O. 141/679/4088, McMahon to Wingate, 14 November 1916; F.O. 686/9 contains a number of cables from al-Faruqi which were intercepted by British Intelligence.

44. F.O. 371/2782/342008, Wilson to McMahon, 5 November 1916; F.O. 141/679/4088, F.O. to McMahon, 6 November 1916; F.O. 371/2776/42233, Wingate to F.O., 10 November 1916; McMahon to F.O., 13 November 1916. For Kitchener's letter of 31 October

1914 (approved by Grey), see F.O. 371/2139/2139.

45. F.O. 371/2782/342008, McMahon to Grey, 21 November 1916, dis. no. 334, encl. Wilson to McMahon, 11 November, 1916.

46. As note 45.

47. F.O. 882/6, fos. 33-36, "Visit to Grand Sherif," extract from R. Storrs, diary, 13 December 1916; copy in F.O. 371/3043/893; *Arab Bulletin*, no. 36, 26 December 1916; Storrs, *Orientations*, p. 193.

48. Albert Hourani, *Arabic Thought in the Liberal Age 1798-1939* (Oxford, 1967), chap. ix; also pp. 282-285, 299, 302-303, 344. On Ridā, see also Eliezer Tauber, "Rashid Ridā as Pan-Arabist before World War I," *The Muslim World*, vol. LXXIX, no. 2 (April 1989), pp. 102-112; Emad Eldin Shahin, "Muhammad Rashid Ridā's Perspectives on the West as reflected in al-Manār," in the same issue, pp. 123-132.

49. F.O. 371/2490/108255, Sykes (Cairo) to Calwell (D.M.I.), 14 July 1915, Secret, encl. in W.O. to F.O. , 6 August 1915.

50. Wingate Archive, SAD 135/7/101. Note by Storrs dated 5 December 1915. Ridā met al-Faruqi in October 1915 soon after the latter's arrival in Cairo.

51. Hourani, *Arabic Thought* . . . , pp. 235-236, 243, 304.

52. Wingate Archive, SAD 143/6, Clayton to Wingate, 20 November 1916; F.O. 686/30, Wilson to Arbur, 11 October 1917; F.O. 686/36, Wilson to Arbur, 12 October 1917; MAE, Guerre 1914-1918, Defrance (Cairo) to Ribot, 18 July 1917; Defrance to MAE, 17 September 1917.

53. F.O. 882/7, fo. 82, Wilson to Hussein, 27 August 1917, Private.

54. Archives du Ministère de la Guerre, Service Historique de l'Armée de Terre (Vincennes), 7N214, Jeddah, 17 September 1917, encl. in Defrance to MAE, 17 September 1917; Note 72 by St. Quentin (Cairo), 26 September 1917.

55. Above, Chap. 1, p. 28.

56. Above, p. 131.

57. F.O. 882/12, fo. 215, Clayton to Wilson, 18 April 1917.

58. F.O. 141/825/1198, Wingate (Cairo) to Storrs (Basra), 19 April and Storrs to Wingate, 2 May 1917

59. Above, Chap. 1, pp. 43-45 , and Friedman, *Palestine: A Twice-Promised Land?*, vol. 2, forthcoming.

60. F.O. 882/16, fos. 233-34, "Note on a conversation . . ." by Wilson, 1 May 1917.

61. Friedman, *Palestine: A Twice-Promised Land?*, vol. 2, forthcoming.
62. F.O. 371/2767/936, McMahon to Grey, 29 February 1916, dis. no. 42, encl. Hussein's letter to McMahon dated 18 February 1916; Hussein to McMahon, 1 March 1916, tel. no. 152[?].
63. F.O. 371/2768/938, Hussein to McMahon, 4 March 1916, encl. in McMahon to Grey, 5 April 1916, dis. no. 73.
64. F.O. 371/2768/938, encl. in McMahon to Grey, 13 March 1916, dis. no. 54.
65. F.O. 141/461/198, fo. 298, undated note.
66. F.O. 141/461/198, fo. 269, Hussein to McMahon, 25 Jamad Awal 1334 (29 March 1916). Hussein sent a similar letter with the same contents to Wingate in the Sudan (F.O. 141/461/1198, fo. 249). The messenger brought with him a verbal message, stating, among other things, that "Syria cannot engineer revolution or seize [the Hedjaz] railway owing to dispersal of their chiefs"; a copy in F.O. 371/2768/938, no. 255.
67. F.O. 141/461/1198, fos. 315-316, F.O. to McMahon, 23 May 1916, tel. no. 411 (and marginalia); Parker to Residency, 25 May 1916.

Chapter 6   A Fatal Misunderstanding

1. F.O. 882/12, fos. 241-242, Clayton to Wilson, 28 April 1917.
2. Wingate Archive, SAD 145/3/97/99, Clayton to Symes, 22 March 1917. On the Syrian colony in Cairo, see Lord Cromer, *Modern Egypt* (London, 1908), pp. 214-219.
3. F.O. 371/3053/84173, Sykes to F.O., 30 April 1917, tel. no. 80; the William Yale Papers 1917-1919 (in microfilm), St. Antony's College, Oxford, rep. no. 3, 12 November 1917.
4 F.O. 371/3381/146, Sykes's Note, 2 August 1918; Friedman, *The Question of Palestine* , p. 206.
5. F.O. 371/3054/86526, Wingate to F.O., 27 April 1917 , tel. no. 464, Urgent; F.O. to Wingate 28 April 1917, tel. no. 442.
6. *Ibid.*, Wingate to F.O., 28 April 1917, tel. no. 464.
7. F.O. 371/3054/86526, Wingate to F.O., 7 May 1917, tel. no. 496, citing Sykes's cable from Jeddah, dated 6 May.
8. Durham, Clayton Papers SAD 693/12/13-16, Clayton to Storrs

(Basra), 7 May 1917.

9.   F.O. 371/3044/1173, fos. 280-84, "Recommendations" [prepared by Sykes and Picot], 17 May 1917.

10.   F.O. 371/3054/86526, Sykes (Aden) to F.O., 24 May 1917; a summary in Wingate to F.O., 25 May 1917, tel. no. 552.

11.   F.O. 882/16 fos. 131-132, Note by Fuad al-Khatib taken down by Lt. Col. Newcombe, June 1917.

12.   See notes 10 and 11.

13.   Picot's formula reads:

> . . . mon Gouvernement est résolu quand les circonstances de la guerre le permettraient, à apporter au souverain en Syrie la méme aide efficace que les Anglais lui ont donné dans l'Irak à Baghdad et à faciliter ainsi éventuellement, par l'occupation de la côté pour les voeux de la population appellant la France, le libération de la race arabe, but commun de nos efforts.

(MAE, Guerre 1914-1918, Turquie. Syrie-Palestine, vol. 877. G. Picot to MAE, Aden, 24 May 1917, pp. 122-123).

14.   See note 10. As a gesture of good will, Sykes put out some feelers to test whether fulfillment of Hussein's wishes was at all feasible, but, as it turned out, any move by the British to promote his status was bound to be counter-productive. It would have made Ibn Saud suspicious of British *bona fides*; nor would Mustapha al-Idrissi have tolerated Hussein's aggrandizement. The suggestion had to be finally written off as "inopportune" and "inadvisable." As in note 10, Shuckburgh (I.O.) to F.O., 12 and 15 June 1917; Oliphant's Minute on a conversation with Col. Jacob, p. l08249; Cox to I.O., 2 June 1917; Wingate to F.O., 12 July 1917, tel. no. 7300.

15.   Wingate Archive, SAD 145/7/86-90, "To All our Brethren— the Syrian Arabs of all Creeds," translated by F. N., 28 May 1917.

16.   Before leaving Jeddah, Picot conferred with Hussein separately (Levant, Arabie, doss. 18, Picot to Cherchali (Djeddah), 15 June 1917, p. 89.

17.   MAE, Guerre 1914-1918, Turquie, Syrie-Palestine, vol. 877, Picot (Aden) to MAE., 24 May 1917, p. 127.

18.   Above, pp. 147-148.

19.   See note 17. Jules Cambon (Paris) to Picot (Cairo), 29 May 1917.

For a discussion about this term, see below, pp. 160-161.

20.   F.O. 882/16, fos. 102-112, Wilson to Clayton, 24 May 1917.

21.   See note 1, above.

22.   See note 20.

23.   F.O. 882/16, fos. 115-119, Note by Lt. Col. Newcombe, 20 May 1917.

24.   F.O. 882/16, fos. 141-142, "Jeddah," Memo by Capt. George Lloyd, June 1917; the original is found in F.O. 371/6259, fos. 123-124.

25.   F.O. 882/16, fos. 129-130, Clayton to Wilson, 26 June 1917. Professor Kedourie glosses over these documents and maintains that Sykes concealed from Hussein the nature of British policy in Baghdad. Kedourie accuses Sykes of putting into practice his own views in contravention of instructions he had received. Moreover, he claims that Sykes involved Picot in the "elaborate game of mutual deception" and that, far from dispelling Hussein's misapprehensions, his diplomacy "produced new misunderstandings" (Kedourie, *In the Anglo-Arab Labyrinth*, Chap. 5, particularly pp. 181-182). This view is untenable. For a discussion, see Friedman, *Palestine: A Twice-Promised Land?*, vol. 2, forthcoming.

26.   F.O. 882/16, fos. 131-137, "Note by Sheikh Fuad el-Khatib taken down by Lt. Col. Newcombe," Secret, June 1917.

27.   Kedourie, *In the Anglo-Arab Labyrinth*, p. 177. In this case, too, Kedourie is at fault. No such promises as he assumes were ever given by Sykes to Hussein.

28.   See note 26.

29.   See above, pp. 151-152, note 20, fos. 106, 109.

30.   Kedourie relies heavily on the first part of Wilson's letter, but ignores the second part.

31.   F.O. 882/16, fos. 122-123, Clayton to Sykes, 27 May 1917.

32.   F.O. 882/6, fo. 360, Wingate to Robertson, 14 May 1917.

33.   *Ibid.*, fos. 127-128, Wilson to Sykes, 20 June 1917.

34.   *Ibid.*, fos. 143-144, Clayton to Sykes, 22 July 1917; a copy in Clayton Papers.

35.   F.O. 371/3054/87288, "Note on Anglo-French-Russian Agreement, 1916," by Hogarth, 9 July 1917; copy in F.O. 882/3.

36.   F.O. 882/16, fos. 148-150, Albina (Cairo) to Sykes (London), 30 July 1917 (drafted on 27 inst.); encl. in Clayton to Sykes, 31 July 1917.

37. CAB 27/22, fos. 67-68. "Mesopotamia Administration Committee."

38. F.O. 371/3054/86526, Note by T. E. Lawrence, 29 July 1917, encl. in Wingate to Balfour, 16 August 1917, dis. no. 179.

39. *Ibid.*, Wingate to Balfour, 16 August 1917, dis. no. 179.

40. *Ibid.*, Minutes dated 11 and 15 September 1917.

41. Durham, Clayton Papers, SAD 693/12/13-16, Clayton to Storrs, 7 May 1917.

42. *Ibid.*, SAD 693/12/28-32, Clayton to Sykes, 30 July 1917.

43. F.O. 141/654, file 356/144, Wilson to Cairo, tel. 26 November 1917.

44. F.O. 371/3054/86526, Wingate to F.O., 29 November 1917, tel. no. 1286.

45. Guerre 1914-18, Turquie, Syrie-Palestine, vol. 877, Jules Cambon to Picot, 29 May 1917, p. 150; same to same, 11 June 1917, p. 208.

46. *Ibid.*, vol. 1695, instructions to Cherchali, 1 May 1917.

47. See note 45, p. 187, Picot (Cairo) to Cambon, 18 June 1917.

48. *Ibid.*, p. 208, Cambon to Picot, 11 June 1917.

49. *Ibid.*, p. 258, Picot to Cherchali, 13 June 1917.

50. Levant, Arabie, doss. 18, Cherchali to Bremond, Mecca, 11 July 1917.

51. Above, p. 158.

52. On which, see below, Chap. 7, pp. 169-171.

53. For the text of this speech, see W.O. 106/1420, fos. 196-198; Antonius, *The Arab Awakening*, pp. 255-256. Early in June 1918, the 1916 Agreement was published in the Arabic paper *Mustakbel*, which appeared in Paris. The article annoyed King Hussein, and he complained that it should not have been allowed to be published (F.O. 371/3381/146, Hussein to Wingate, 5 June 1918, encl. in Wingate to Balfour, 25 June 1918, dis. no. 129).

54. F.O. 371/3381/146, p. 123868, Minute by Sykes, undated (end of June?) 1918.

55. Above, Chap. 2, pp. 49-50.

56. Elie Kedourie, *The Chatham House Version and other Middle-Eastern Studies* (London, 1970), p. 27, citing *al-Manār* xxxiii (1933), p. 797.

57. Friedman, *Palestine: A Twice-Promised Land?*, vol. 2, forthcoming.

Chapter 7   The Sharifians, the Palestinians, and the
                 Zionists

1.   Above, Chap. 5, pp. 141-143.
2.   Above, Chap. 1, pp. 40-45.
3.   Wingate Papers, The Sudan Archive, 135/5/21, Wingate to
      Clayton, 1 November 1915; above, Chap. 1, pp. 34-35, 42.
4.   F.O. 882/13, fos. 349-351, Mirghani to Wingate, 6 May 1915,
      encl. Wingate to McMahon, 15 May 1915; F.O. 141/461/1198,
      Mirghani to Hussein, 17 November 1915.
5.   F.O. 141/461/1198, Clayton (Cairo) to Maxwell (Mudros), 12
      November 1915, cable E.R. 195.
6.   CAB 27/23. Minutes of the meeting of the Eastern Committee, 2
      February 1918.
7.   General Records of the Department of State. Record Group 59,
      File 763, 72/13450: National Archives, Washington, DC, Wil-
      liam Yale Papers, rep. nos. 3, 7, 12 November, 10 December
      1917. The Yale Papers are deposited at the Yale University
      Library, New Haven, CT, USA, and a microfilm at St.
      Antony's College, Oxford. In 1917-1918, Captain Yale served
      as an American Intelligence Agent in Cairo. See also Lloyd
      George, *The Truth . . .*, vol. II, p. 1142.
8.   Antonius, *The Arab Awakening* p. 269.
9.   Yale Papers, rep. nos. 3, 10, 12 November, 31 December 1917.
10.   Yale Papers, rep. no. 4, 19 November 1917.
11.   F.O. 141/154, fo. 365, where the English translation is pro-
      vided. The Arabic original is missing.
12.   F.O. 686/39, Note on an interview with Hussein by C. E.
      Wilson, Jeddah, 21 July 1918.
13.   *Der neue Orient* (December 1917), cited in Yale Papers, rep. no.
      17.
14.   *Ibid.*, rep. no. 13, 4 February 1917.
15.   F.O. 371/3055/243033, Wingate to F.O., 24 December 1917, tel.
      no. 1394; a copy in F.O. 371/3380/146.
16.   F.O. 371/3048/2087, Wingate to F.O., 2 November 1917, tel. no.
      1153, circulated to the King and to the War Cabinet. Hussein
      thought that the easiest and most affective remedy to the
      situation was "an increase on subsidy which will enable him to
      placate discontented elements" (*ibid.*).
17.   F.O. 882/9, fos. 20-22, Arabian Affairs, Note on a meeting held

at the Residency, Cairo, on 21 January 1918.

18.   Yale Papers, rep. no. 17; Djemal Pasha, *Memoirs of a Turkish Statesman, 1913-1919* (London, 1922), p. 133.

19.   F.O. 371/3394/11053, War Cabinet, Middle East Committee held on 19 January 1918, statement of Sir Mark Sykes.

20.   As note 17, above.

21.   F.O. 371/3054/86526, draft telegram to Wingate, no. 24, 4 January 1918, signed by Sykes, amended by Hardinge and Graham. The "formulae," later known as "The Hogarth Message," have been printed in Cmd. 5964, *Statements made on behalf of His Majesty's Government during the year 1918 in regard to the Future Status of certain parts of the Ottoman Empire, 1939 . . . Vol. XXII*, 1938-1939.

22.   F.O. 882/7, fo. 240, Hogarth's diary on "Interviews with King Hussein," 8-14 January 1918.

23.   F.O. 371/3383/675, fos. 283-285. Hogarth's Report on his Mission to Jeddah, 15 January 1918, encl. with Wingate's dis. no. 15, Cairo, 27 January 1918. Sections of this report, as well as notes or conversations with Hussein, were printed in Cmd. 5964 (1939), cited above (note 21). *See also Arab Bulletin*, no. 77, 27 January, 1918, *Mission to King Hussein*, signed by D. G. H[ogarth].

24.   As note 22, above.

25.   As note 23, above.

26.   As note 22, above.

27.   As note 22 and 23, above.

28.   Friedman, *The Question of Palestine*, pp. 311-316.

29.   Antonius, *The Arab Awakening*, p. 333.

30.   Quoted in Jewish Agency for Palestine, *Documents Relating to the McMahon Letters* (London, 1939), p. 6, and *Documents Relating to the Palestine Problem*, Jewish Agency for Palestine (JAP) (London, 1945), pp. 16-17; see also Kemal H. Karrpat, "The Syrian Emigration from Ottoman State 1870-1914," in A. Temimi, ed., *Les Provinces Arabes et leur sources documentaires a l'epoque Ottomane* (Tunis, Tunisia, 1984), pp. 285-300.

31.   The Sudan Archive, SAD 693/13/18-22, Clayton Papers, Clayton to C. E. Wilson (Jeddah), 17 December 1917; a copy in the Antonius Archive, Box 382, file 2748.

32.   Antonius, *The Arab Awakening*, p. 219. For a discussion, see Friedman, *Palestine: A Twice-Promised Land?*, vol. 2, forth-

coming.

33.   F.O. 371/3403/1142, Wingate to Balfour, 8 April 1918, dis. no. 70, encl. in Hussein's letter to Feisal, undated, translated. On the same day, Wingate cabled to the Foreign Office (*ibid.*, tel. no. 655): "He [i.e., Hussein] enjoins Feisal in his dealings with Zionists to preserve their rights and defend them in every way."

34.   Sir Mark Sykes Papers, F.O. 800/221, Sykes to Feisal, 3 March 1918; a draft is found in F.O. 882/3, fos. 161-169.

35.   *Ibid.*, Feisal to Sykes, dated 18.7.1918. The figure "7" is in all probability a misprint for "4"; i.e., April 1918. Both the contents and the tenor of the letter indicate that it had been written some time before Feisal's meeting with Weizmann in Akaba on 3 June 1918. It is inconceivable that Feisal would have replied to Sykes after such a long lapse of time.

36.   F.O. 371/3398/27647, fo. 620, Clayton to Sykes, 4 February 1918; a copy is in Clayton Papers.

37.   F.O. 882/7, fo. 267-270, T. E. Lawrence to Clayton, 12 February 1918.

38.   Clayton Papers, SAD 693/13/47-52, Clayton to Sykes, 4 April 1918.

39.   As note 37 above.

40.   Yale Papers, rep. no. 9, 24 December 1917. So widespread was this belief, that even Jack Mosseri, President of the Zionist Organization in Alexandria, told Yale that he anticipated that Palestine would become "a purely Jewish state" (*Ibid.*, rep. no. 5, 26 November 1917).

41.   Sir Mark Sykes Papers, MSS Library, Hull University, Hull (formerly Sledmere Papers), Clayton to Sykes, 28 November 1917, DDSY(2) 11; a copy in Clayton Papers.

42.   F.O. 371/3394/11053, fos. 13-15, first meeting of the Middle East Committee, 19 January 1918.

43.   Sir Mark Sykes Papers, Sykes to Clayton, 16 November 1917, for the Syrian Committee.

44.   As note 40, above.

45.   F.O. 882/17, fos. 4-8, MacKintosh to Clayton, 27 December 1917 and encls.

46.   F.O. 371/3398/27647, pp. 449-500, Nasif to Sykes, 17 January 1918, where he lists the members of the Syrian Committee. They were: K. Ayoub, Hakki Bey al-Azm, Rafik Bey al-Azm,

Fauzi Bey al-Bakri, Muktar Bey al-Sulh, Dr. Faris Nimr, Khalil Zeinid, and Nasif , who acted as Chairman.

47.   *Ibid.*, pp. 510-511, Sykes to the Syrian Welfare Committee, 15 February 1918.

48.   *The Letters and Papers of Chaim Weizmann* (New Brunswick, NJ, 1977), vol. VIII (cited hereafter as *L.Ch.W.*), Weizmann to Vera W., Cairo, 24 March 1918. General Allenby, whom Weizmann met on 3 April 1918, also thought that "the Zionists were misunderstood by the Arabs, who were ignorant of the principles of Zionism" (C.Z.A. Z4/170, meeting between Weizmann and General Sir Edmund Allenby, 3 April 1918).

49.   F.O. 371/3383/747, Ormsby-Gore (Cairo) to Sykes, 31 March 1918, Personal and Confidential. Seen by Lord Hardinge, Sir Ronald Graham, and the War Department. On Ormsby-Gore, see Friedman, *The Question of Palestine*, pp. 126-128, 175-176, and *passim*.

50.   *Ibid.*; C.Z.A., L3/285, App. no. 10 to Minutes of the meeting of the Zionist Commission, 27 March 1918. A copy in C.Z.A. Z4/483, reproduced in Isaiah Friedman, ed., *The Rise of Israel. A Documentary Record from Nineteenth Century to 1948* (New York and London, 1987), vol. 9, doc. 67, pp. 180-181 (cited hereafter as Friedman, *The Rise of Israel*). Ormsby-Gore erroneously attributed Shuckair's statement to Nasif. Shuckair held a senior administrative post in Emir Feisal's administration in Damascus.

51.   C.Z.A., Z4/538, meeting of the Zionist Commission with Palestine Committee of Moslems and Christians and members of the Syrian Welfare Committee, Minutes, dates 1 April 1918; *L.Ch.W.*, vol. VIII, Weizmann to Sokolow, 18 April 1918, p. 137.

52.   F.O. 371/3394/1053, Memorandum by Major Kinahan Cornwallis, 20 April 1918, reproduced in Friedman, *The Rise of Israel*, vol. 9, doc. 77, pp. 238-240.

53.   Clayton Papers, SAD/693/13/47-52, Clayton to Sykes, 4 April 1918.

54.   *L.Ch.W.*, vol. VIII, no. 175, Weizmann to Brandeis, Tel-Aviv, Jaffa, 25 April 1918; F.O. 371/3391/4019, Clayton, in Wingate to F.O, 14 January 1918, tel. no. 93; *ibid.*, Clayton to F.O., 9 March 1918; F.O. 371/3398/747, Ormsby-Gore to Sykes, 31 March 1918; F.O. 371/3395/11053, rep. no. 2 by Ormsby-Gore, 19

April 1918, encl. Clayton to Balfour, 21 April 1918.

55.   Ormsby-Gore's rep. no. 2, 19 April 1918 as in note 54; fully reproduced in Friedman, *The Rise of Israel,* vol. 9, doc. 78, pp. 243-249; see also W.A., Leon Simon diary, 7 April 1918.

56.   F.O. 371/3394/11053, Report by Storrs, dated 30 April 1918, on the dinner party. Weizmann's speech is reproduced fully in Friedman, *The Rise of Israel,* vol. 9, doc. 81, pp. 264-269; a copy is in C.Z.A., L3/285.

57.   *Ibid.*

58.   F.O. 371/3395/11053, "Future of Palestine," Note, dated 8 May 1918.

59.   *L.Ch.W.,* VIII, to Vera, Tel-Aviv, 30 April 1918, pp. 170-171.

60.   *Ibid.,* Weizmann to Ormsby-Gore, 16 April 1918.

61.   *Ibid.,* Weizmann to Balfour, 30 May 1918, pp. 197-199.

62.   Sir Mark Sykes Papers, P.R.O., F.O. 800/221, pp. 62-72, A. P. Albina to Sykes, 15 June 1918; rep. no. 15, Secret.

63.   I.S.A., M5/163, "The effect of the Sharifian movement on the military situation in Palestine," Memorandum by Captain M. D. Brunton to the General Staff Intelligence, G.H.Q. Jerusalem, 28 February 1921.

64.   James Finn, *Stirring Times or Records from Jerusalem Consular Chronicles* (London 1978), vol. I, p. 215.

65.   Muhammad Y. Muslih, *The Origins of Palestinian Nationalism* (The Institute for Palestine Studies Series, Columbia University Press 1988), Preface, pp. 44-45, 54, 86-87, 212; also Friedman, *The Question of Palestine,* p. 99.

66.   *Ibid.,* pp. 89-90. It was Asad al-Shuqayri who was one of the first people to report to Djemal Pasha that the secret societies were conspiring a rebellion (*Ibid.,* p. 91). On Muzaffar, see Friedman, *Palestine: A Twice-Promised Land?,* vol. 2, forthcoming.

67.   The Ha'agana Archives, Tel-Aviv, Intelligence files of L. She'ersohn, no. 80/145/19, 1918.

68.   C.Z.A., L3/440, Note dated 18 June 1919. After the conquest of Jerusalem by General Allenby, the Beduin changed their attitude toward Emir Feisal.

69.   Muslih, *The Origins of Palestinian Nationalism,* p. 90. Muslih questions the accepted view that following Djemal Pasha's measures the Moslem Arab leaders made up their minds once and for all to break away completely from the Ottoman

Empire (*ibid.*).

70. F.O. 141/461/1198, fo. 636, Intelligence rep., October 1916. F.O. 882/16, Arab Bureau to Miss Bell (Basra), 8 July 1916.

71. The text in full is cited in R. Gordon-Canning, *Arab or Jew?* (London, noted), p. 15.

72. See above, Chap. 6, pp. 150-151.

73. F.O. 371/3048/22841, November 1917.

74. Djemal Pasha, *Memoirs of a Turkish Statesman*, pp. 167, 213 and *passim*. During the Dardanelles Campaign, Djemal Pasha had to dispatch all the Turkish troops to the Straits. The twelve battalions that remained "consisted exclusively of Arabs from Syria and Palestine" (*ibid.*).

75. Ronald Storrs, *Orientations* (London, 1939), p. 364.

76. F.O. 882/14, *Arab Bulletin, Supplementary Papers*, no. 1, 1 February 1918, "Syrian Cross Currents," by T. E. Lawrence, p. 4.

77. Philip Graves, *Palestine, the Land of Three Faiths* (London, 1923), pp. 40, 112-113.

78. C. S. Jarvis, *Three Deserts* (London, 1936), p. 302.

79. F.O. 371/3391/4019, Clayton to Sykes, 4 April 1918; Clayton to F.O., 15 June 1918; Hansard, 19 June 1936, col. 1379, statement by James de Rothschild, M.P.

80. Colonel R. Meinertzhagen, *Middle East Diary, 1917 to 1958* (London, 1959), p. 6. It is worthwhile to mention that Allenby's forces entered Jerusalem on 9 December 1917.

81. Sir Mark Sykes Papers, DDSY(2), Ormsby-Gore to Sykes, Jaffa, 9 April 1918.

82. CAB 21/8, Ormsby-Gore (Tel-Aviv, Jaffa) to Hankey, 19 April 1918.

83. Clayton Papers, SAD 694/6/10-19, rep. no. 5 by Ormsby-Gore, Tel-Aviv, Jaffa, 19 May 19189, Secret and Confidential, encl. in Ormsby-Gore to Clayton, same date. *Mouktar*, or rather *mukhtar* stands for head of a village; *fellah* (pl. *fellaheen*) means peasant, cultivator. *Effendi* means landlord, master, or a man of standing.

84. F.O. 371/3395/11053, "Report on the existing Political Situation in Palestine . . ." by Ormsby-Gore, Confidential, 10 pages, 22 August 1918. Robert Cecil minuted: "These views should be carefully considered in the Middle East Department. Most of these appear sound and reliable." See also, Lord Hardinge, Sykes and others.

85. *Ibid.*, Clayton to Balfour, 16 June 1918; the dispatch is reproduced fully in Friedman, *The Rise of Israel*, 9, doc. no. 91, pp. 322-337. Muhammad Izzat Darwaza, a Palestinian activist and historian, admitted that urban notables were either reserved toward the Arab revolt or opposed it, and in their own interest continued to serve the Ottoman cause (Muslih, *The Origins of Palestinian Nationalism*, p. 91).

86. Ormsby-Gore paid tribute to the spontaneous volunteer movement to the Jewish Battalions, considering it as a "great historic fact" linking the Zionist ideal with that of the Allied Powers and America in their struggle for human freedom (F.O. 371/3409/116565, Memorandum by Ormsby-Gore, 2 July 1918, encl. in Clayton to Balfour, 10 July 1918). The War Council also noted with pleasure the enthusiastic enlistment of Palestinian Jews for the Jewish Battalions (*ibid.*, W.O. to F.O. June 1918). "I have now got my Jews in the front line facing the Turks and they are doing very well indeed. . . No Turk dares come into 'No Man's-Land' [in the Judean Mountains] for fear of meeting our fighting patrols. Allenby is pleased with us . . ." (Extract from a letter by Colonel J. M. Patterson, noted, probably end of July 1918, Milner Papers, p. 57, Bodleian Library, MS Dept. 137, Oxford.

87. Friedman, *The Question of Palestine*, pp. 221-222; also p. 207.

88. *Ibid.*, pp. 203, 206.

89. Weizmann Archives, Leon Simon diary (unpublished), entry 27 March 1918; Author's interview with Sir Leon, 9 June 1961.

90. *L.Ch.W., VIII*, pp. 150-151, Weizmann to Ormsby-Gore, 21 April 1918.

91. St. Antony's Middle East Library, MSS Dept. Akaba Archive, W. Joyce Papers, DS 244.4, Dawnay to Joyce, 27 May 1918. Colonel Dawnay served as a Liaison Officer between Allenby's forces and those under Emir Feisal.

92. W.O. 95/4370, G.H.Q. Cairo (Clayton) to Commandant Akaba, 24 May 1918, dis. no. 2300.

93. The above is based on: Akaba Archives, Joyce Note, 4 June 1918; F.O. 371/3398/27647, Clayton to F.O., 12 June 1918, tel. no. p. 174; C.Z.A., Z4/483, Weizmann's report at a meeting of the Zionist Commission, 16 June 1918; and F.O. 882/27, P.C. Joyce, "Feisal and Weizmann," *Arab Bulletin*, 18 June 1918, p. 208. Weizmann's account in his memoirs, *Trial and Error*

(London, 1949), is inaccurate.

94. *L.Ch.W.*, *VIII*, p. 210, to Vera, 17 June 1918.

95. C.Z.A., Z4/483, meeting . . . , 16 June 1918.

96. *Ibid.*, JI/8764, Weizmann's speech at the Second Constituent Assembly of the Palestine Jews, Jaffa, 17 June 1918.

97. Sir Mark Sykes Papers, P.R.O., F.O. 822/221, Feisal to Sykes, 18 July 1918; *ibid.*, Husheimi to Hegib [or Negib?] translated from Arabic, probably intercepted by British Intelligence. The date given (29 May, 18) must have been a slip of the translator's pen, since the Weizmann-Feisal meeting took place on June 4.

98. *Ibid.*, F.O. 808/221, Note by George Stewart Symes, dated 13 June 1918. Symes served in the British Residency in Cairo.

99. F.O. 371/3381/146, appendix to a copy of Hogarth's undated memorandum, encl. in Hogarth to Graham, 9 August 1918. See also I. Friedman, *Germany, Turkey and Zionism, 1897-1918* (Oxford, 1977), p. 413.

100. Although eager to detach Feisal from the British, the Porte found his demand for the reorganization of the Empire on a federal basis too far-fetched. However, negotiations continued practically until the end of the War (Friedman, *Germany, Turkey and Zionism, 1897-1918* , as in note 99).

101. F.O. 371/3395/11053, Clayton to Balfour, 16 June 1918. Sykes minuted, "A very good dispatch." Wingate Archives, Clayton Papers, SAD 693/13/55-56, Clayton to Wigram, 17 June 1918.

102. Wingate Archives, Clayton Papers, SAD 693/13/55-56, Clayton to Miss Bell, 17 June 1918.

103. Friedman, *The Question of Palestine*, pp. 172-173.

104. F.O. 371/3395/11053, "Report on the existing Political Situation in Palestine . . ." by Ormsby-Gore, 22 August 1918, *Confidential*; reproduced in full in Friedman, *The Rise of Israel*, vol. 9, pp. 387-395.

105. Sir Stewart Symes, *Tour of Duty* (London, 1946), p. 32. Lawrence statement was dictated and Symes recorded it word for word.

106. Friedman, *The Question of Palestine*, p. 225; Jeremy Wilson, *Lawrence of Arabia* (London, 1989), p. 442-442.

107. Weizmann's Archives, Weizmann's diary, 16 June 1918; C.Z.A., Z4/843, Minutes of the Zionist Commission meeting.

108. Sir Mark Sykes Papers, F.O. 800/221, Clayton to Sykes, 16 June

1918; also Clayton to A. Lloyd, 18 June 1918, Lloyd Papers, G11d 913, Churchill College, Cambridge.

109. Symes, *Tour of Duty*, p. 31.

110. Above, p. 181, note 76, p. 192; and Friedman, *Palestine: A Twice-Promised Land?*, vol. 2, forthcoming.

111. T. E. Lawrence, *Oriental Assembly*, A. J. Lawrence, ed. (London, 1939; New, York 1940). The article "The Changing East" was published first in *The Round Table* (September 1920) anonymously, in accordance with the practice of that journal. However, it was in all likelihood written in 1918 or early 1919.

112. Symes, *Tour of Duty*, pp. 34-35.

113. F.O. 371/3381/146, Wingate to Balfour, 25 June 1918, dis. no. 129, Secret.

114. F.O. 371/3398/27647, Clayton to Balfour, 1 July 1918. Reproduced fully in Friedman, *The Rise of Israel*, vol. 9, doc. 93, pp. 335-339.

115. *L.Ch.W., VIII*, doc. 232, Weizmann to Balfour, 17 July 1918, pp. 228-229.

116. C.Z.A., Z4/843; a copy in W.A.; F.O. 371/3395/11053, Extracts from app. 105 to the Minutes of . . ., encl. in Clayton to Ormsby-Gore, 29 June 1918, encl. in Clayton to Balfour, 11 July 1918. A number of sections regarded as confidential were excised.

117. F.O. 371/3395/11053, Clayton to Balfour, 16 June 1918 and F.O. 371/3398/27647, Clayton to Balfour, 1 July 1918. Reproduced in Friedman, *The Rise of Israel*, vol. 9, doc. nos. 91, 93, pp. 320-331, 335-339.

118. The story is described in Jon Kimche, *The Second Arab Awakening* (London 1970), pp. 179-183. Mr. Kimche, a noted journalist and writer, had access to Aref-el-Aref's papers and interviewed a number of Palestinian Arab personalities. There are a number of biographies on Amin al-Husseini: Joseph B. Schechtman, *The Mufti and the Fuehrer: The Rise and Fall of Haj Amin el-Husseini* (New York, 1965); Tyasir Jbara, *Palestinian Leader Hajj Amin al-Husayni: Mufti of Jerusalem* (Princeton, NJ, 1985); Philip Mattar, *The Mufti of Jerusalem* (New York, 1988), Zvi Elpeleg, *The Grand Mufti — Haj Amin Al-Hussaini, Founder of the Palestinian National Movement* (London, 1993).

119. Nor do any of the above biographies enlighten us on this

episode.

120.   F.O. 371/3381/146, "The Arab Question," Memorandum by David Hogarth (undated), appended to Hogarth's note to Graham, Oxford, 9 August 1918 and Minutes by Sykes and Ormsby-Gore.

Chapter 8   The Declaration to the Seven and Lawrence's "Capture" of Damascus

1.   George Antonius, *The Arab Awakening*, pp. 272-273, and App. D, pp. 433-434, where the Declaration is reproduced. Officially it was published in Cmd. 5964, *Statements made on behalf of His Majesty's Government during the year 1918 in regard to the Future Status of certain parts of the Ottoman Empire, 1939, Accounts and Papers, Vol. XXVII*, 1938-39. For a discussion, see Elie Kedourie, *England and the Middle East*, 2nd ed. (London, 1987), pp. 113-117; also his *In the Anglo-Arab Labyrinth*, pp. 291-297.

2.   Antonius gives their names in *The Arab Awakening*, App. D, note 1.

3.   *Ibid.*, Antonius merely mentions it in a note preceding App. D. For the sources that Antonius used when preparing his book, see Friedman, *Palestine: A Twice Promised Land?*, vol. 2 — *The Creation of the Historical Myth, 1920-1939*, forthcoming.

4.   F.O. 371/3380/146, Wingate to Balfour, 7 May 1918, dis. no. 90, Confidential, enclosing the memorandum of the Seven Syrians, translated by Dr. Abd al-Rahman [Shabandar] and O[sward] W[alrond].

5.   Clayton Papers, SAD 693/13/47-52, Clayton to Sykes, 4 April 1918.

6.   For a discussion see Friedman, *Palestine: A Twice-Promised Land?*, vol. 2, forthcoming.

7.   Antonius, *The Arab Awakening*, p. 273.

8.   C. S. Jarvis, *Three Deserts* (London, 1936), p. 302.

9.   *Arab Bulletin*, no. 97, 16 July 1918, "Arab Recruiting in

Jerusalem," pp. 249-251.

10. F.O. 371/3391/4079, Clayton to F.O., 4 August, 15 September 1918, tel. nos. 29, 59.

11. Clayton Papers, Feisal to Clayton, no. 863, 24 Shawal 1336. The date of the Field Post Office on the envelope is 11 August 1918. The letter is in Arabic. In this letter, Feisal also mentioned his meeting with Weizmann and described him as an "esteemed and learned man."

12. F.O. 882/17, Hogarth to the Chief Political Officer (Clayton), 18 December 1918, pp. 147-151, para. 13. Copies to C.G.S., the High Commissioner, Col. Cornwallis and Col. Dawnay.

13. Cited in Kedourie, *England and the Middle East*, p. 113.

14. F.O. 882/17, fos. 16-17, MacKintosh to Clayton, 25 February 1918; see also F.O. 371/3381/146, Wingate to Balfour, 25 June 1918, dis. no. 129, *Secret*, p. 5.

15. F.O. 371/3384/747, Clayton to Balfour, 21 September 1918.

16. Kedourie, *England and the Middle East*, p. 115.

17. Antonius states that "copies of . . . the Foreign Office statement . . . were received by the Amir Feisal at his camp in Aqaba" (*The Arab Awakening*, p. 273).

18. T. E. Lawrence, *The Seven Pillars of Wisdom* (Garden City, NY, 1935), p. 555.

19. See Chap. 3, above, pp. 61-62.

20. See Chap. 7, above, pp. 165-174, 183-186, and below. Chap. 9, pp. 218-225, 227-231.

21. That Lawrence was aware it was the work of Sykes is evident from his letter to *The Times* of 8 September 1919; Letters, p. 281.

22. St. Antony's College, Akaba Archives, D.S. 244.4, note by Col. Joyce, 14 July 1941.

23. F.O. 882/14, *Arab Bulletin, Supplementary Papers,* no. 1, 1 February 1981, "Syrian Crosscurrents," by Major T. E. Lawrence, pp. 4-5.

24. D. Garnett, ed., *The Letters of T. E. Lawrence* (London, 1938), pp. 224, 226.

25. Hanna Batatu, *The Old Social Classes and the Revolutionary Movements of Iraq* (Princeton, NJ, 1978), p. 196.

26. On which see H. S. Gullet, *Official History of Australia in*

the War 1914-1918, Vol. VII, *Sinai and Palestine* (Sydney 1935), Chap. XXXV, pp. 599-637.

27. See Chap. 1, above, p. 19.
28. I.S.A., Antonius Archive, Box F330, file 867, Lecture on "Arab Nationalism" by Antonius at Princeton University (no date, probably 1935). *cf The Arab Awakening*, pp. 158-159.
29. Garnett, *Letters . . .*, p. 266.
30. Hubert Young, *The Independent Arab* (London, 1933), p. 276.
31. Lt.-Col. W. F. Stirling, *Safety Last* (London, 1953), p. 90.
32. F.O. 371/3413/179133, The German Liaison Officer to the 8th Ottoman Army, 29 August 1918, translation of a captured document by Australian Mounted Corps.
33. Sir Mark Sykes Papers, F.O. 800/221, Albina to Sykes, 15 June 1918.
34. Gullet, *Official History . . .*, p. 769.
35. Stirling, *Safety Last*, pp. 93-94. In his *Seven Pillars of Wisdom* (London, 1935, Penguin Books, 1962), Lawrence recalled: "I wanted to sleep . . . but I could not. Damascus was the climax of our two years' uncertainty" (p. 665).
36. Akaba Archive, Joyce Papers, DS. 244.4, Note by Col. Joyce, 14 July 1941.
37. St. Antony's College, MSS Dep., Allenby Papers, copies at Kings College University of London, Liddle Hart Centre for Military Archives. Harry Chauvel to Field Marshall Goodwin, Director of Australian War Memorial, Melbourne, 22 October 1929.
38. *Ibid.*, Harry Chauvel to Field Marshall Goodwin, 1 January 1936.
39. *Idem.*
40. Gullet, *Official History . . .*, p. 769.
41. See notes 37 and 38, above.
42. *Ibid.* In his report, dated 2 October 1918, i.e., the day after meeting Lawrence, General Chauvel stated categorically that his troops had entered Damascus on the evening of September 30th, before any Arab irregulars put in an appearance. It is also clear from this report that Shukri al-Ayyubi was Lawrence's appointee (W.O. 95/4371, file 2 96, Chauvel to G.H.Q., E.E.F. "Report on the Capture of Damascus . . .").
43. See notes 37 and 38, above; also, Chauvel to Allenby, 1 January 1936, "Meeting of Sir Edmund Allenby and the Emir Feisal at

Hotel Victoria, Damascus, on October 3rd, 1918"; reproduced also in A. J. Hill, *Chauvel of the Light Horse* (Melbourne, 1978), pp. 242-243. General Chauvel took notes of the meeting word for word at the time. Allenby did not seem to dispute Chauvel's account. Present during the meeting were also Major-General Sir Louis Bols, Chief of the General Staff, E.E.F., Brigadier-General C. A. C. Godwin, Chauvel's Chief of Staff, Nuri Bey al-Said, acting Chief of Staff to the Emir Feisal, Sharif Nasir, second in command of the Hedjazi Forces, Lt.-Col. P. C. Joyce, Major W. F. Stirling, and Capt. H. W. Young of the British Mission to the Hedjaz, and Lt.-Col. Kinahan Cornwallis of the Arab Bureau, Cairo. Lawrence acted as interpreter. In his *Seven Pillars*, Lawrence passed over this episode in silence. See also, Hubert Young, *The Independent Arab*, pp. 255-257. Feisal overplayed his hand when he dispatched Shukri al-Ayyubi to take over Beirut in order to forestall the French. When Capt. Coulondre, who was attached to the Sharifians in Damascus, protested, Feisal was ordered by Allenby to withdraw from Beirut.

44.   Allenby Papers, Allenby (Beirut) to Lady Allenby (Haifa), 17 October 1918.

45.   *Ibid.*, Allenby to W.O., 11 October 1918; a copy in P.R.O., W.O. 33/960.

46.   Kedourie, *England and the Middle East*, 2nd ed., pp. 119-128; "The Capture of Damascus 1 October 1918," *The Chatham House Version and other Middle-Eastern Studies*, new ed. (Hanover and London, 1984), pp. 33-51.

47.   Had the late Professor Kedourie consulted the Allenby Papers, he might have reached a different conclusion than he did.

48.   F.O. 371/3383/747, pp. 498-499, C.I.G.S. to Allenby, 25 September 1918, encl. in W.O. to F.O. 26 inst.

49.   W.O. 37/960, W.O. to Allenby, 1 October 1918, tel. no. 67558.

50.   The article was written on 8 October, the day Lawrence arrived in Cairo. This article, too, was anonymous, but internal evidence leaves no one in doubt that it was penned by Lawrence.

51.   St. Antony's College, MSS Dep., Sir Hubert W. Young Papers, "Notes for the lecture at Staff College" (no date), pp. 28-29. In his book, *The Independent Arab*, which appeared in 1933, Young cited the figure of 600 (p. 277).

52. W.O. 95/4371, Chauvel to Allenby, 23 October 1918. When the *Seven Pillars* appeared, Chauvel wrote to Allenby: "There is the same old lie that Feisal's Arab Forces penetrated Damascus on the night of September 30-October 1st." He made a great number of comments (Allenby Papers, Chauvel to Lord Allenby, 1 January 1936). General A. P. Wavell declared that "Lawrence's story of the events in Damascus . . . is not the whole truth, and is unjust to Chauvel" (*Allenby — A Study in Greatness* (London, 1940) p. 285*ff*. Earlier, Lawrence himself admitted that he was on "thin ice" when writing his Damascus chapter and warned that anyone copying from it "will be through it, if he is not careful. *S.P.* [*Seven Pillars*] is full of half-truths . . ."; see Robert Graves, *T. E. Lawrence to his Biographer* (London, 1938), p. 104.

    The Lawrence myth was exploded by Richard Aldington in his *A Biographical Enquiry* . . . (Chicago, 1955), while Kedourie deserves much credit for his brilliant study of the subject under discussion. Jeremy Wilson is partial to Lawrence and accepts his version uncritically, but seems to be unable to resolve the contradiction between Lawrence's frank admission to Robert Graves — which he quotes — and his own thesis. He considers Chauvel's evidence to be unreliable and makes a disparaging remark about Kedourie, calling him Lawrence's "detractor" (*Lawrence of Arabia. The Authorised Biography* [London, 1989], pp. 1105-1109*ff*).

53. F.O. 371/3413/173356, Sokolow to Hussein, 3 October 1918 (cable); Hussein to Sokolow, 16 October 1918, encl. in Wingate to Balfour, same date, tel. no. 248.

54. F.O. 371/3384/747, Memorandum by R[obert] C[ecil], 28 October 1918. Shortly after, Cecil told Weizmann that it would be most desirable for him to see Feisal again when in London and discuss the whole situation with him (*L.Ch.W.*, vol. IX, doc. no. 7, Weizmann to Clayton, 5 November 1918, p. 13).

55. CAB 27/24, fos. 150-151, Minutes of the 37th meeting of the Eastern Committee of the War Cabinet, 29 October 1918.

56. *L.Ch.W.*, vol. IX, doc. no. 4, Weizmann to Brandeis, 29 October 1918, pp. 2-5; reproduced also in Friedman, *The Rise of Israel*, 10, doc. no. 3, pp. 11-12.

57. *L.Ch.W.*, vol. IX, docs. 7 and 38, Weizmann to Clayton, 5 and 27 November 1918, pp. 9-11, 40-43, respectively.

58. See Chap. 1, above, pp. 4-10, 44-45, and Map 3.

59. See Chap 3, above, pp. 93-94.

60. As note 48, above.

61. F.O. 371/3383/747, pp. 505-506, Foreign Office Memorandum and Conference, 30 September 1918. The British were represented by Lord Robert Cecil (Chairman), Sir Eyre Crowe, Major-General Thwaites (D.M.I.), Sir Mark Sykes, and Lt.-Col. Gribbon, and the French by Ambassador Cambon, M. de Fleurian, and George Picot. The provisions of the convention are described in R. de Gotaut-Biron, *Comment la France s'est installée en Syrie, 1918-19* (Paris, 1923), pp. 65-66.

62. *D.B.F.P.*, First Series, vol. IV, p. 251.

63. F.O. 371/4178/2167, F.O. to Clayton, 9 January 1919, tel. no. 10.

64. Arthur Ruppin, *Syrien als Wirtschaftsgebiet*, 2nd ed. (Berlin, 1920).

65. Gullet, *Official History . . .*, p. 768.

66. *Idem.*

67. On Lawrence's conduct, see: Kedourie, *England and the Middle East*, pp. 122-125, and his "The Capture of Damascus," *The Chatham House Version*, pp. 43-44.

68. Khoury, *Urban Notables ...*, pp. 79-89; Gullet, *Official History . . .*, pp. 768-769.

69. I.S.A., Pol./2223, note by Captain C. D. Brunton, General Staff Intelligence, 13 August 1921.

70. F.O. 371/4152/144, "Syria in October 1919," by G[ertrude] L. B[ell], 15 November 1919, pp. 6-7, encl. in Wilson to Secretary of State for India Office, 15 November 1919. On this memorandum, see also Chap. 10, below, pp. 253, 278-279.

71. Shortly before the fall of Damascus, he came to General Barrow's headquarters at Dera'a asking to see Feisal. He pretended to turn his back on his Turkish masters, but Barrow suspected that he might be a spy; see General Sir George Barrow, *The Fire of Life* (London, 1942), pp. 212-214.

72. F.O. 371/4178/2117, pp. 264-268, Hogarth to the Chief Political Officer, E.E.F. (Clayton), 18 December 1918; a copy in F.O. 882/17, fos. 147-151.

73. F.O. 608/105, pp. 106-116, "Appreciation of the Situation in Syria, Palestine, and lesser Armenia," by Colonel Sir Mark Sykes, 22 January 1919. For the other part of this memorandum, see Chap. 10, below, pp. 240-243.

74.   Yale, rep. no. 112, "The Political Situation in Syria," 9 November 1918.

75.   Khoury, *Urban Notables* . . ., pp. 78-81.

76.   Yale rep. nos. 34, 112, 8 July and 9 November 1918, respectively.

77.   F.O. 371/6344, E 8790/8790/65, undated memorandum by Alois Musil, encl. in Sir George Clerk dis. no. 172, British Legation Prague, 18 July 1921. It seems that Musil's memorandum was prepared in mid-January 1920, before Feisal's expulsion from Damascus by the French. For the other sections from this memorandum, see Friedman, *Palestine: A Twice-Promised Land?*, vol. 2, forthcoming.

In his *Memories of a Turkish Statesman*, Djemal Pasha recalled that, before leaving Jerusalem for the Hedjaz, Emir Feisal made a long speech at his Army Headquarters "in which he swore by the glorious soul of the Prophet to return at an early date at the head of his warriors [fifteen hundred cavalrymen] and help them to fight the foes of the Faith [the British] to the death" (p. 213). On another occasion, animated, Feisal exclaimed, "How could you accuse us? How could we be traitors, members of a family descended from the Prophet, a family whose greatest honour it is to be most devoted and loyal followers of the Khalif. . . . We are the faithful servants of the illustrious sovereign, who has always heaped favours upon us" (p. 221). Djemal Pasha pleaded that he was ignorant of the fact that at the same time Hussein was negotiating with the British and preparing his "treacherous blow at the Khalifate" (p. 214).

78.   The date of this report by Yale is blurred. The meeting most probably took place sometime in mid-October, after the capture of Damascus. The date cited in Kedourie's *England and the Middle East* (p. 161, note 1), that is, "September 12, 1918," is mistaken. Such a meeting could not have taken place "during the War." In September, Ja'afar al-Askari was still in Dera'a.

79.   Report by Miss Bell of November 1919, on which see above, note 70.

80.   Khoury, *Urban Notables* . . ., p. 80; Kedourie, *England and the Middle East*, pp. 157-161.

81.   Memorandum by Musil, on which see above, note 77.

82.   Rep. no. 112, 9 November 1918.

83.   Statement by Colonel Richard Meinertzhagen, 7 January 1960.

84.   Khoury, *Urban Notables . . .*, p. 81.

Chapter 9   The Weizmann-Feisal Agreement and After

1.   F.O. 371/3386/856, p. 57, Memorandum by Balfour, 11 December 1918; *Ibid.*, p. 26, *The Times*, 11 December 1918, quoting *Le Matin*.

2.   CAB 27/44, fo. 186, 41st meeting of the Eastern Committee of the War Cabinet, 5 December 1918.

3.   F.O. 371/3418/194681, fos. 406-407, Minutes by Sir E. Crowe and Lord Hardinge, 5 December 1918.

4.   F.O. 371/4162/521, "Interview with Sherif Feisal," 27 December 1918. Present were also Sir Arthur Hirtzel, Sir Hamilton Grant, Sir John Shuckburgh, and others.

5.   For Montagu's views, see Friedman, *The Question of Palestine*, pp. 22-25, 136-137, 257-263, 266-229.

6.   *L.Ch.W.*, vol. IX, doc. no. 70, pp. 68-71, Weizmann's Memorandum on his interview with Emir Feisal at the Carlton Hotel on 11 December 1918; sent to Sir Eyre Crowe. The original document may be found in F.O. 371/3420/207372.

7.   *Ibid.*, doc. no. 71, pp. 71-72, Weizmann to Eder, 17 December 1918; a copy in F.O. 608/98 and F.O. 371/4170/105.

8.   *The Times*, 12 December 1918, reproduced in M. Perlmann, "Chapters of Arab-Jewish Diplomacy, 1918-22," *Jewish Social Studies* (New York, 1944), p. 132, whose work is a pioneering one on this subject. Documents are reproduced also in Neil Caplan, "Faisal Ibn Husain and the Zionists," *International History Review* (1983), vol. V, no. 4, pp. 570-614; Friedman, *The Rise of Israel*, vols. 10 and 11.

9.   C.Z.A., Z4/56, English text in Lawrence's handwriting.

10.   F.O. 608/97, file 375/1/3, no. 872, Hussein to Wilson (Jeddah), 29 January 1919, encl. in Wilson to Cheetham (Cairo), 31 January 1919, encl. in Cheetham to Curzon, 9 February 1919. See also above, Chap. 7, pp. 163-173; and Friedman, *Palestine: A Twice-Promised Land?*, vol. 2, forthcoming.

11.   David Hunter Miller, *My Diary at the Conference of Paris,*

1918-1919 (New York, 1924), doc. no. 250, vol. 1V, pp. 297-299.

12.   *Ibid.,* vol. XIV, p. 230; *Papers Relating to the Foreign Relations of the United States, The Paris Peace Conference, 1919* (Washington, DC, 1943), vol. III, p. 891; Lloyd George, *The Truth . . .,* vol. II, p. 1040. Feisal made these points earlier in his second memorandum of January 1919 (Miller, *My Diary. . . ,* vol. IV, p. 300, doc. no. 251).

13.   F.O. 371/3386/376, pp. 94-95, "Resolution of. . . ," encl. in Derby (Paris) to Balfour, 13 December 1918.

14.   Yehoshua Porath, *The Emergence of the Palestinian-Arab National Movement, 1918-1929* (London, 1974), p. 80; Muslih, *The Origins of Palestinian Nationalism,* p. 177.

15.   F.O. 371/4179/2117, Clayton to F.O., 14 March 1919, tel. no. 65.

16.   F.O. 608/98, Peace Congress, 1919, Pol. no. 227, file 375/2/1, Minute by A. J. Toynbee, dated 18 January 1919. A carbon copy of the Agreement is found in *ibid.,* no. 159, file 375/2/2.

17.   A photocopy in C.Z.A. Z4/2989 and in W.A.; reproduced in Friedman, *The Rise of Israel,* vol. 10, doc. no. 43, pp. 157-167.

18.   See note 16 above.

19.   Miller, *My Diary . . .,* vol. III, pp. 188-189.

20.   F.O. 371/4178/2117, Clayton to G.H.Q. (Cairo), 9 January 1919.

21.   Antonius, *The Arab Awakening,* p. 439.

22.   H. W. V. Temperley, ed., *A History of the Peace Conference of Paris* (London, 1920, 1924), vol. VI, p. 142.

23.   Jukka Nevakivi, *Britain, France and the Arab Middle East, 1914-1920* (London, 1969), p. 134, note 5, citing the Wilson Papers.

24.   Stephen Bonsal, *Suitors and Suppliants. The Little Nations at Versailles* (New York, 1946), p. 40.

25.   Yale's report, 13 February 1919.

26.   See below, Chap. 10, note 87 and pp. 258, and pp. 87, 265-266, 276-278.

27.   Miller, *My Diary . . . ,* vol. IV, p. 262, doc. no. 246.

28.   Charles Seymour, ed., *The Intimate Papers of Colonel House* (New York, 1928), vol. IV, pp. 283-284.

29.   Statement at the Council of Ten, 27 January 1919, *Foreign Relations, 1919, Paris Peace Conference* (Washington, DC, 1943), vol. III, pp. 741-743; Stannard R. Baker, *Woodrow Wilson and World Settlement* (London, 1923), vol. I, pp. 261-262.

30.   *Foreign Relations,* III, pp. 795-796; Lloyd George, *The Truth*

..., vol. II, pp. 538-541; David Hunter Miller, *The Drafting of the Covenant* (New York, 1928), vol. I, pp. 109-110.

31. Ernest B. Haas, "The Reconciliation of Conflicting Colonial Policy Aims: Acceptance of the League of Nations Mandate System," *International Organization*, vol. 6, no. 4 (1952), pp. 521-536, where the author offers an illuminating discussion.

32. Above, p. 225.

33. Interview by Mr. Michael Almaz early in 1977 for the Television of Israel in connection with the program "The Pillar of Fire," which was broadcast in January 1981. I am grateful to the Israel Television Authority for permitting me to quote from the transcript.

34. Translated version in the *Jewish Chronicle*, 7 March 1919.

35. *L.Ch.W.*, IX, doc. 123, p. 119, Weizmann to Vera, 28 February 1919.

36. C.Z.A., Z4/241, II, Weizmann's statement at the Zionist Council, 5 March 1919; printed in Y. Freudlich and G. Yogev, eds., *The Minutes of the Zionist General Council*, vol. I (Jerusalem, 1975), p. 55 [Hebrew]; *Reports of the Executive of the Zionist Organization to the Twelfth Zionist Congress, Part I, Political Report* (London, 1921), p. 23 *et seq.*

37. See also below, Chap. 10, p. 240.

38. C.Z.A. Z4/25001; a copy *ibid.*, Z4/56, and W. A.; reproduced in full (in Lawrence's handwriting with Feisal's signature) in Friedman, *The Rise of Israel*, vol. 10, doc. no. 62, pp. 240-241 and pp. 242-244 (extract from the *Jewish Chronicle*, 7 March 1919); Caplan, "Faisal Ibn Husain and the Zionists," pp. 581-582. See also Simha Berkowitz, "The Faisal-Frankfurter Letters: An Unending Story," *Community and Culture Essays in Jewish Studies*, Gratz College (Philadelphia, PA, 1987), pp. 1-18.

39. For the Zionist Proposals submitted to the Peace Conference, see F.O. 371/4170/1051, encl. in S. Graham, 3 February 1918; *Reports of the Executive to the XII Zionist Congress at Carlsbad*, the Z.O. (London, 1921), pp. 74-83; *L.Ch.W.*, vol. IX, App. II, pp. 391-402. For Sokolow's and Weizmann's presentation, see Miller, *My Diary . . .*, vol. XV, pp. 104-110.

40. C.Z.A., S/25/3142, Frankfurter to Feisal, 5 March 1919.

41. C.Z.A., A/264/30. See also *Felix Frankfurter Reminisces* (New York, 1960), p. 155.

42. F.O. 371/4183/2117, Zionist Organization, London Bureau, Communiqué no. 44, pp. 23-24, reproduced in full in Friedman, *The Rise of Israel*, vol. 9, pp. 249-250, doc. no. 64.

43. Shmuel Tolkowski, *A Zionist Political Diary, 1915-1919*, Dvora Barzilai-Yaeger, ed. (Jerusalem, 1981), p. 433, entry 4, 5 March 1919 (Hebrew); a copy of the French translation in C.Z.A., A/264/10.

44. C.Z.A., A/264/7; A/264/30; C.Z.A., L/8/193.

45. F.O. 608/99, Weizmann to Balfour, 9 April 1919; a copy in C.Z.A., Z/4/16008, and in *L.Ch.W.*, vol. IX, pp. 128-129, doc. no. 135.

46. C.Z.A., A/264/30, Dear Bob, 7 April 1919.

47. C.Z.A., Z/4/16042, Press Bureau, 24 April 1919.

48. C.Z.A., JI/8791, report by Aaron Eisenberg and David Yellin at a meeting of the Provisional Committee of the Palestine Jewish Community, 25 May 1919; David Yellin, *Letters*, vol. V, to his wife, Paris, 18 April 1919 (Jerusalem 1937), pp. 130-131.

49. See above, Chap. 6, pp. 146-147, Chap. 7, pp. 171-175.

50. C.Z.A., A/153/149. In addition to Dizengoff and Yellin, other delegates who were present during the meeting were: Joseph Mejouchas, Joseph Cheluche, Chaim Kalwaryski, and Commander Biankini. See Appendix 5.

51. Statement by Colonel Richard Meinertzhagen to the present writer, 3 January 1960. Meinertzhagen was also present and received a copy of Feisal's letter to Frankfurter. It is kept among his private papers and reproduced in his *Middle East Diary*, pp. 15-16.

52. Ittamar Ben-Avi, *The Dawn of our Independence* (Tel-Aviv, 1961), pp. 442-447 [Hebrew].

53. C.Z.A., A/264/35, Leonard Stein, Political Secretary of the Z.O. (London) to Frankfurter (USA), 21 September 1923; *Ibid.*, Z4/2019, Louis Lipsky (NY) to Stein, 19 November 1923.

54. Colonial no. 48, *Palestine Commission on the Disturbances of August 1929, vol. I, Evidence Heard during the 1st to 29th Sittings* (London, 1930), pp. 486, 492, 846-847; statement by Auni Abd al-Hadi to Suleiman Mousa in *T. E. Lawrence, An Arab View*, transl. A. Butros (London, 1966), pp. 228-230.

55. C.Z.A., A/264/35, Weisgal to Frankfurter, 2 December 1929.

56. In 1939, Frankfurter was appointed Associate Justice of the U.S. Supreme Court.

57. C.Z.A., A/264/35, a copy, *Ibid.*, S/25/3142, Frankfurter to Weisgal, 3 December 1929. Reproduced in Friedman, *The Rise of Israel*, vol. 10, doc. 66, pp. 252-254.

58. C.Z.A., A/264/30 and A/264/36.

59. Nathan Feinberg, *Some Problems of the Palestine Mandate* (Tel-Aviv, 1936), p. 38, note 2. Interview with the present author, Jerusalem, August 1973.

60. C.Z.A., A/264/39, Yale to Frankfurter, 15 November 1930.

61. e.g., *Jerusalem Post* (16 December 1964); the *Jewish Chronicle* (25 December 1964); interview with the present author, London, January 1965.

62. C.Z.A., A/264/37, Landau (London) to Brandeis, 23 September 1930.

63. See also *L.Ch.W.*, vol. XVII, pp. 263, 273, 281.

64. C.Z.A., S/25/3642, Zionist Intelligence note, 27 December 1937.

65. Bartley Crum, *Behind the Silken Curtain* (New York, 1947), p. 180. For comments by Abdul Hadi in his *Memoirs*, see Caplan, "Faisal Ibn Husain and the Zionists," doc. no. 10, pp. 580-581.

66. Caplan, "Faisal Ibn Husain and the Zionists," doc. no. 41, pp. 613-614, extract of Haidar's letter to the editor, the *Iraq Times* (1 December 1938).

67. Antonius, *The Arab Awakening*, pp. 283-286. In App. F, pp. 437-439, there appears a photostatic reproduction of the original document of the Weizmann-Feisal Agreement.

68. Copies of Miller's *My Diary at the Peace Conference* are kept in the Antonius Archive, ISA, Box 382, files 2743, 2745, 2750. In file 2758, there is a copy of Weizmann's statement on the Feisal-Frankfurter correspondence.

69. Mousa, *T. E. Lawrence: An Arab View*, pp. 228-230.

70. A. L. Tibawi, "T. E. Lawrence, Faisal and Weizmann: The 1919 Attempt to Secure an Arab Balfour Declaration," *Royal Central Asian Journal*, vol. LVI (1969), pp. 156-163; and Tibawi's *Anglo Arab Relations and the Question of Palestine*, pp. 331-333, 348-359.

71. Above, p. 234.

72. Henry Cattan, *Palestine, The Arabs and Israel: The Search for Justice* (London, 1969), p. 259.

73. Bayan N. al-Hout, *Political Leadership and Institutions in Palestine, 1917-1948* (Beirut, 1981), p. 102 [Arabic], cited in Caplan, "Faisal Ibn Husain and the Zionists," p. 563.

74. Above, p. 222.
75. Miller, *My Diary* . . . , IV, p. 297.
76. Antonius, *The Arab Awakening*, p. 252.
77. See also Feisal's statement to the Director of the Jewish Telegraphic Agency in 1930, above, p. 234.

Chapter 10   The King-Crane Commission and the Unmaking of the Weizmann-Feisal Agreement

1. F.O. 371/3398/27647, Clayton to F.O., 17 November 1918.
2. F.O. 371/3386/856, Clayton to Balfour, 6 December 1918.
3. C.Z.A., Z 4/16004, "A Note on the Arab Question," Jerusalem, 8 January 1919; "A Report on Syria, Palestine and Mount Lebanon for the American Commissioners," prepared by William Yale, 26 July 1919; a copy is in Antonius Archive, I.S.A., P384/2841. On this report, see also below, pp. 276-278; F.O. 371/3385/747, Clayton to F.O., 18 November 1918.
4. Yehoshua Porath, *The Emergence of the Palestinian-Arab National Movement, 1918-1929* (London, 1974), pp. 74-77; F.O. 371/4179/2117, Clayton to F.O., 28 February 1919.
5. C.Z.A., Z 4/14437, Biographical Note encl. in Friedenwald to I.A.C., Jerusalem, 29 June 1919.
6. F.O. 371/6262, E3499/3499/91, Major Philips (W.O.) to NOTE Bland (F.O.), 14 March 1921.
7. Yale rep. no. 35(?), Yale to D.M.I., State Dept., 5 November 1918.
8. Muslih, *The Origins of Palestinian Nationalism*, pp. 104, 172.
9. F.O. 371/4153/275, Report by Captain J. NOTE Camp of Military Intelligence, 15 February 1919, reproduced in Friedman, *The Rise of Israel*, vol. XI, doc. 1, pp. 1-8; C.Z.A., Z4/16042, Zionist Press Bureau, Communiqué no. 12, February 1919; Porath, *The Emergence of the Palestinian-Arab National Movement*, pp. 79-85; Muslih, *The Origins of Palestinian Nationalism*, pp. 178-185.
10. Attached to Camp's report (note 9, above), pp. 6-8.
11. F.O. 371/3386/856, "Extract from report rendered by Col. Sir Mark Sykes," dated 15 November 1918.

12. *Ibid*.
13. F.O. 371/3059/159558, "Memorandum on the Asia Minor Agreement," by Sykes, 14 August 1917.
14. F.O. 608/105, "Appreciation of the Situation in Syria, Palestine and Lesser Armenia," by Colonel Sir Mark Sykes Bt. (noted), received 27 January 1919. On this memorandum, see also Chapter 8, above, pp. 213-214.
15. F.O. 608/97, Peace Conference, 1919, file 1503, "Sir Mark Sykes's report on his Mission to Syria and Palestine," 24 February 1919, where the instructions given by the Eastern Committee are quoted.
16. F.O. 371/3384/747, F.O. to Clayton, 12 October 1918, tel. no. 207.
17. See Chapter 8, above, pp. 202-204.
18. See note 15.
19. Captain Young's lecture at the Staff College, on which see Chapter 8, above, note 51. See also memorandum by Young, February 1919 (F.O. 371/4178/2117).
20. W.O. 106/189, fos. 150-157, Pichon to Balfour, 31 January 1919, a translated copy.
21. *Yoman Aaron Aaronsohn, 1916-1919* [Diary of. . .] (Tel-Aviv, 1970), entry of 29 January 1919, pp. 497-498. On Aaronsohn, see Friedman, *The Question of Palestine*, pp. 120-123, 127, 203-207, 272-274.
22. F.O. 371/4153/275, p. 392, Balfour (Paris) to Curzon (London), 19 March 1919; F.O. to Clayton, 23 March 1919.
23. See Chap. 9, above, pp. 225-226; F.O. 371/4144/275, Balfour to War Cabinet, 6 February 1919.
24. F.O. 371/3384/747, Allenby to W.O., 3, 26, 31 October 1918.
25. Harry W. Howard, "An American Experiment in Peace-Making: The King-Crane Commission," *The Moslem World* (April 1942); and his *The King-Crane Commission* (Beirut/London, 1963), pp. 25-26.
26. For Bliss's statement before the "Big Ten" at the Peace Conference on 13 February 1919, see *Papers Relating to the Foreign Relations of the United States, The Paris Peace Conference, 1919* (Washington, DC, 1943), vol. III, pp. 1015-1018 (hereafter, *F.R.U.S.*). Zeine N. Zeine, *The Struggle for Arab Independence* (Beirut, 1960), App. F, pp. 255-259, from the private papers of Dr. Howard Bliss.

27. *F.R.U.S.*, *Peace Conference*, vol. V, pp. 1-14; R. S. Baker, *Woodrow Wilson and World Settlement* (Washington, DC, 1923), vol. III, pp. 1-19.

28. For the terms of reference, see Miller, *My Diary* . . ., vol. XV, pp. 505-508.

29. Henry Wickham-Steed, *Through Thirty Years* (London, 1932), vol. II, p. 323. A record of this meeting by Miss Bell is found in Elizabeth Burgoyne, *Gertrude Bell from her Personal Papers, 1914-1926* (London, 1961), p. 110. A "Memorandum on Syria," 26 March 1919, compiled by the above experts (not signed) appears in Miller, *My Diary*. . ., vol. VII, p. 169 and a copy in Yale Papers, "Confidential Syrian Documents."

30. Comments by Yale on the "Memorandum on Syria."

31. Bonsal, *Suitors and Suppliants*, p. 47, entry 17 February 1919.

32. *Ibid.*, p. 48, 28 February 1919.

33. F.O. 371/4180/2117, Memorandum by Curzon, 18 April 1919.

34. See pp. 343, 345 of "Memorandum by Balfour (Paris) respecting Syria, Palestine and Mesopotamia," 11 August 1919, in *D.B.F.P.*, First Series, vol. IV. See also F.O. 371/4171/1051, pp. 44-45, a note by Balfour, 23 March 1919.

35. F.O. 371/4179/4179, pp. 309-310, Secretary of State to the Prime Minister, February 1919.

36. Quincy Wright, "The Future of the Near East," in Philip W. Ireland, ed., *The Near East, Problems and Prospects* (Chicago, 1942), p. 214.

37. CAB 27/24, E.C. 41 Meeting; a copy in Milner Papers, Bodleian Library, MSS Dept., Oxford.

38. Robert Lansing, *The Peace Negotiations* (Boston, MA, 1921), p. 97. On this subject, Walter Lippmann, the celebrated journalist and writer, made a scathing remark: "To invoke the general principle of self-determination and to make it a supreme law of international life, was to invite sheer anarchy"; Walter Lippmann, *United States War Aims* (Boston, MA, 1944), p. 173.

39. Friedman, *The Question of Palestine*, pp. 186-189, 195-198, 282.

40. On this appointment and on the King-Crane Commission in general, see Howard, "An American Experiment . . . ," pp. 36-41, 55; F. Manuel, *The Realities of American Palestine Relations* (Washington, DC, 1949), Chap. VI and *passim*; S. G. Haim, "The Arab Awakening: A Source for the Historian?" in *Die Welt des Islams* (Leiden, 1953), vol. II, no. 4, pp. 237-250.

41. I.S.A., *Antonius Archive*, F330/869. Present during the meeting was also Said Rashid Ridā, the celebrated theologian and the editor of the monthly periodical *al-Manar*.
42. *F.R.U.S., Peace Conference*, vol. XII, p. 750, Crane and King to the Commission to Negotiate Peace, 10 July 1919.
43. I.S.A., *Antonius Archive*, F 336/860, Crane to Fish, May 1933.
44. *Ibid.*, Crane to Young, 5 May 1933.
45. "Minutes of the Daily Meeting . . . 27 March 1919," *F.R.U.S., Paris Peace Conference*, vol. XI, p. 133; *Editor and Publisher*, vol. 55, no. 27, 2nd Sec. (New York, 2 December 1922), p. 4. A copy is found in the *Antonius Archive*.
46. F.O. 371/4179/2117, pp. 392-394; Howard, "An American Experiment . . . ," pp. 32-34.
47. *L.Ch.W.*, vol. IX, p. 125, doc. no. 132, Weizmann to Simon, Paris, 27 March 1919.
48. C.Z.A., A 264/30, Frankfurter to Brandeis, 28 March 1919.
49. *Ibid.*, Frankfurter to Szold, 7 April 1919; also Frankfurter to Westermann, 23 March 1919 (*ibid.*).
50. *Ibid.*, Frankfurter to House, 14 and 30 April 1919. Weizmann wrote to House separately on this matter (*L.Ch.W.*, vol. IX, doc. 139, 14 April 1919, p. 137).
51. *D.B.F.P.*, First Series, vol. IV, pp. 260-262, doc. no. 180; a copy in C.Z.A., A 226/31. On Wilson's attitude toward Zionism, see Friedman, *The Question of Palestine*, pp. 63-64, 263-264, 267, 269.
52. Friedman, *The Question of Palestine*, pp. 301-302; *Jewish Chronicle*, 17 January 1919; *The Times*, 18 January 1919; Lloyd George, *The Truth . . .*, vol. II, p. 1140.
53. Yale Reports, "Records of the American Commission to Negotiate Peace," Record Group 256, Westermann to Bullitt, 11 April 1919; Note by the Secretary to the Commissioners, April 1919, no. 230; Wilson to (?), 13 April; Lansing to Bliss, 18 April 1919. Wilson's statement to the leaders of the A.J.C. was published in the *New York Times*, 3 March 1919, and in the Egyptian press on the following day.
54. Miller, *My Diary . . .*, vol. IV, doc. no. 246, pp. 262-264.
55. *F.R.U.S.*, Paris Peace Conference, vol. V, pp. 763, 766, 808-812; Yale Reports, "Confidential Syrian Documents," Yale's interview with Robert de Caix and de Caix's memorandum, 12 April 1919.

56. Howard, "An American Experiment . . . ," p. 145; Howard, *The King-Crane Commission*, p. 51.

57. On which see Chap. 8, above, p. 212, note 70, and below, p. 266

58. F.O. 371/4180/2117, "Review of the Situation in the Middle East . . . ," Memorandum by Curzon, 22 April 1919, encl. 2 to no. 1, p. 5.

59. *D.B.F.P.*, First Series, vol. IV, pp. 267-272, App. A, encl. 2 in no. 182. According to Husri, an Arab historian, the meeting took place on May 5 (Zeine, *The Struggle for Arab Independence*, p. 83, notes 1-2).

60. F.O. 371/4180/2117, p. 232; a copy in F.O. 608/99, Peace Conference, p. 393, and in C.Z.A., A 264/32, Frankfurter to Brandeis, 19 May 1919.

61. C.Z.A., L 4/688, Clayton to Friedenwald, 12 May 1919; also Friedenwald to Z.O. (Paris), 16 May 1919, in F.O. 371/4180/2117, p. 377, Clayton to D.M.I.

62. *L.Ch.W.*, vol. IX, p. 142, doc. no. 148, Weizmann and Frankfurter to Feisal, Paris, 19 May 1919; C.Z.A., A 264/7. Brandeis was duly informed (C.Z.A., A 264/32, Frankfurter to Brandeis, 19 May 1919).

63. *D.B.F.P.*, First Series, vol. IV, pp. 265-266, Report . . . dated 16 May 1919, encl. 1 in no. 182.

64. *Idem.*

65. Khoury, *Urban Notables . . .* , pp. 84-85.

66. See Chap. 1, above, p. 19.

67. *Ibid.*, pp. 27-28.

68. Bell's report, "Syria in October," dated 15 November 1919; see Chap. 8, above, p. 212 and note 72; below, p. 256; *cf.* Batatu, *The Old Social Classes and the Revolutionary Movements of Iraq*, p. 197.

69. F.O. 371/4181/2117, Political Officer to I.O., Baghdad, two cables dated 5 June 1919.

70. F.O. 371/4146/275, p. 162, Political Officer to I.O., Baghdad, 14 June 1919.

71. Muslih, *The Origins of Palestinian Nationalism*, p. 134.

72. See note 68, above.

73. Kedourie, *England and the Middle East*, p. 160, note 2.

74. Porath, *The Emergence of the Palestinian-Arab National Movement*, pp. 87-88; Khoury, *Urban Notables . . .* , p. 84.

75. Muslih, *The Origins of Palestinian Nationalism*, p. 122. In

note 20, p. 238, Muslih lists the names of its leaders.

76. C.Z.A., Z 4/16042; copies in L 3/8 L4/245.

77. Above, pp. 253-254.

78. C.Z.A., L 4/688; Clayton to Eder, 11 May 1919.

79. *Idem*; Eder to Feisal, 15 May 1919; copy in L 4/245.

80. *Idem*; Friedenwald to Clayton, 16, 20 May 1919.

81. *Idem*; Waley to Friedenwald, 3 June 1919.

82. *Idem*; Friedenwald to Feisal, 23 June 1919; Feisal to Zionist Commission, 7 July 1919.

83. C.Z.A., Z 4/16044, Eder to Weizmann, 2 July 1919.

84. *Ibid.*, Z 4/16004, Eder to Weizmann (Dear Chaim . . .), 7 May 1919. On the anti-Zionist policy by the Military Administration, see *D.B.F.P.*, First Series, vol. IV, pp. 283-285, encl. 3 in note 197, Samuel to Tyrrell, Paris, 5 June 1919; and pp. 307-308, note 213, "Note by Sir R. Graham of conversations with Mr. Samuel and Dr. Weizmann," 2 July 1919.

85. The relevant files were removed and could not be found. (Statement by the P.R.O. official to the present writer, December 1989.)

86. C.Z.A., as note 83, above; Z 4/25037, memorandum by Szold, July 1919; L 3/8, Szold to the Zionist Executive, 29 June 1919; Z 4/25037, Intelligence Report on the American Commission, July 1919. It seems that the Zionist Intelligence failed to distinguish the discrepancy that had existed between official British policy and that pursued by the British officers in the East.

87. U.S.A., *The National Archives*, General Records of the Department of State, Record Group 59, "A Report on Syria, Palestine, and Mount Lebanon for the American Commissioners, prepared by Captain William Yale, Technical Advisor to the American Section of the International Commission on Mandates in Turkey," dated 26 July 1919, pp. 14-15. A copy in I.S.A. *Antonius Archive*, P 384/2841.

88. F.O. 371/4178/2117, pp. 262-268, Allenby to Wilson ("My dear Henry"), 22 December 1918, and encl. Memorandum by Hogarth. For an analysis of this memorandum, see Chap. 8, above, p. 213.

89. *Ibid.*, p. 526, Allenby to D.M.I., 4 February 1919.

90. F.O. 371/4179/2117, p. 109, Allenby to W.O., 6 March 1919.

91. F.O. 371/4180/2117, p. 247, Allenby to W.O., 14 May 1919. See also Minutes by the Foreign Office officials on Allenby's

statement.

92. *Ibid.*, p. 323, Allenby to W.O., 21 May 1919. For Feisal's correspondence with Clemenceau on this matter, see *D.B.F.P.*, First Series, vol. IV, pp. 251-253.

93. Mayir Vereté, in his essay "The Inter-Allied Peace Commission and 'The Men of Cairo': A Chapter in British-Zionist-Arab Relations," attributes Allenby's objection to his suspicion of a French inspired collusion between Feisal and the Zionists in favor of a French mandate for Syria to the detriment of British supremacy in the area.

     Vereté maintains that, in the spring of 1919, Allenby and Clayton "suspected that their protégés were slipping through their fingers" and that the Feisal-Clemenceau accord "caused them great anxiety." They feared that it would strengthen pro-French tendencies among the Arabs and induce them "to express a clear preference for a French mandate, paving the way for a greater Syria, united and undivided." Moreover, Allenby and Clayton suspected that the Zionists, who were aggrieved with the attitude of the British officers, might turn to France as well. "The conclusion," Vereté goes on, "was obvious: to keep Feisal and the Zionist Commission at a long arm's length from each other. Keeping them separated would considerably smooth the path of Allenby and Clayton in their attempts to influence both sides to continue their support for a British mandate." See, *From Palmerston to Balfour. Collected Essays of Mayir Vereté*, Norman Rose, ed. (London, 1992), pp. 181, 185, 189-190, 193-194. The essay appeared first in Hebrew in the quarterly, *Zion*, vol. 32, 1967, pp. 76-115.

     This reasoning is absurd, and Vereté's argument does not hold much water. Nor is it consistent with the facts. Weizmann and his followers would not entertain for a moment the idea of substituting a French for a British mandate, while Feisal was violently anti-French. Moreover, in mid-May, Feisal revealed to Clayton that he "had never any intention of carrying out his arrangement" with Clemenceau (see above, p. 260; cited also in Vereté, p. 187). Most of Vereté's hypotheses, as he had himself admitted, are "mere speculations" (p. 180).

94. Below, p. 280; and Friedman, *Palestine: A Twice-Promised Land?*, vol. 2, forthcoming.

95. Friedman, *The Question of Palestine*, pp. 97-101, 104.
96. Lloyd George, *The Truth* . . ., vol. II, p. 1045.
97. *Passim*. Ormsby-Gore and Arnold Toynbee, in their joint memorandum dated February 1919, which was prepared at the request of the Prime Minister, stated that the British Government "is quite disinterested [in Syria] and desires an amicable arrangement between conflicting points of view" (F.O. 608/93, file 360/1/7, p. 126).
98. Baker, *Woodrow Wilson and World Settlement*, vol. III, pp. 1-19; *F.R.U.S.*, *The Paris Peace Conference, 1919*, vol. V, pp. 1-14.
99. F.O. 371/4180/2117, p. 358, Allenby to W.O., 21 May 1919.
100. *D.B.F.P.*, First Series, vol. IV, p. 251, note 174, Allenby to Balfour, 30 May 1919.
101. F.O. 608/107, Peace Conference, p. 235, Allenby to W.O., 29 May 1919.
102. *D.B.F.P.*, First Series, vol. IV, pp. 298-299, note 206, Balfour to Allenby, Paris, 26 June 1919; also *ibid.*, p. 484.
103. *Ibid.*, pp. 341-342, note 242, Memorandum by Balfour, 11 August 1919, on which see also above, p. 246.
104. *Ibid.*, p. 259, note 178, Balfour to Allenby, 31 May 1919.
105. C.Z.A., A 264/7, Friedenwald (Tel-Aviv) to the Zionist Bureau (London), 2 May 1919.
106. C.Z.A., Z 4/25037, Zionist Intelligence Report on "the American Section of the International Commission . . . ," no date.
107. Above, pp. 250-252.
108. C.Z.A., A 264/7, Frankfurter to Friedenwald, 28 May 1919.
109. Howard, "An American Experiment . . . ," p. 133. *cf.* Clayton's argument in *D.B.F.P.*, First Series, vol. IV, p. 272, note 1, and that of Money, *ibid.*, p. 273, note 2.
110. C.Z.A., L 3/8, Szold to the Zionist Executive (Paris), 29 June 1919, Secret and Confidential; *ibid.*, Z 4/25037, Memorandum by Robert Szold, July 1919.
111. *Ibid.*, Z 4/16004, memorandum on the Arab situation, an unsigned copy, March 1919.
112. Below, pp. 275-276.
113. Undated report by Montgomery, probably July 1919; for reference, see note 87 above, a copy in I.S.A., *Antonius Archive*, P 384/2841.
114. Report by Yale, 26 July 1919, on which see above, note 87.
115. Khoury, *Urban Notables* . . . , p. 80.

116. Memorandum by Gertrude Bell, on which see Chap. 8, above, p. 212, and note 70.

117. F.O. 371/4182/2117, Acting Chief Political Officer to Balfour, 7 August 1919.

118. See note 115. For Lawrence's description of the relations among the four cities, see Chap. 1, above, pp. 24.

119. Report by Yale, 26 July 1917, on which see above, note 87.

120. F.O. 371/4182/2117, pp. 330-333, "Report on a conversation with Michel Bey Lotfullah . . . August 5, 1919," encl. in French to Curzon, 14 August 1919.

121. Muslih, *The Origins of Palestinian Nationalism*, pp. 193-198.

122. Khoury, *Urban Notables* . . . , p. 88.

123. Cited in Kedourie, *England and the Middle East*, p. 160. For Kurd Ali's complaints against the adverse influence of the Palestinians on Syrian affairs, see Muslih, *The Origins of Palestinian Nationalism*, p. 138.

124. See note 120.

125. Muslih, *The Origins of Palestinian Nationalism*, p. 240, note 18.

126. F.O. 371/4182/2117, pp. 205-209, encl. in C.P.O. to Balfour, 7 August 1919; also in "Report of the American Section of the Inter-Allied Commission on Mandates in Turkey," *Editor and Publisher* (Dec. 2, 1922), Section II, p. VII-VIII. Reproduced also in Yale's report of 26 July 1919, on which see above, note 87. An edited version is given in Antonius, *The Arab Awakening*, App. G, pp. 440-442.

127. *Idem.*

128. F.O. 371/4181/2117, French (Cairo) to F.O., July 10, 1919, tel. no. 378, p. 312; also Howard, *The King-Crane Commission*, pp. 120-123.

129. C.Z.A., A 153/162, Abbadi (Damascus) to David Yellin (Jerusalem), 27 July 1919 (Hebrew); a translated version in English and amplified, *ibid.*, A 18/38/1, 12 August 1919, and a copy in L 3/340.

130. *D.B.F.P.*, First Series, vol. IV, p. 368, doc. no. 257, French to Curzon, 30 August 1919.

131. *Ibid.*, pp. 364-365, encl. no. 253, Report by Major J. N. Camp in "Arab Movement and Zionism," Jerusalem, 12 August 1919, French to Curzon, 26 August 1919.

132. *L.Ch.W.*, vol. IX, pp. 199-200, Weizmann to Eder, doc. no. 201,

17 August 1919.

133.   As note 128, above.

134.   Ronald Storrs, *Orientations* (London, 1939), p. 369.

135.   Above, p. 249.

136.   C.Z.A., Z 4/14437, Zionist Intelligence Report, 26 June 1919.

137.   *Ibid.*, L 3/13(a&b), "Report on a Tour in Syria," Abraham Elmaliyach (July 1919). Elmaliyach was a Sephardi Jewish notable and an historian who had numerous Arab friends.

138.   John de Vere Loder, *The Truth about Mesopotamia, Palestine and Syria* (London, 1923), p. 36.

139.   Report by Yale, 26 July 1919, on which see above, note 87.

140.   Cited in Howard, "An American Experiment . . . ," pp. 132-133. This supplement is omitted from the version of the King-Crane Commission's Report reprinted by Antonius in *The Arab Awakening*, App. H, pp. 443-458.

141.   See note 137.

142.   *F.R.U.S., Paris Peace Conference*, vol. XII, pp. 745-747; see also Balfour's instruction to Allenby, above, p. 262.

143.   Above, pp. 250-251.

144.   *F.R.U.S., Paris Peace Conference*, vol. XI, pp. 432-433.

145.   The *Editor and Publisher*, New York, 2 December 1922; see also Howard, "An American Experiment . . . ," pp. 258-260.

146.   Cited in Esco Foundation for Palestine, *Palestine. A Study of Jewish, Arab and British Policies*, vol. I (New Haven, CT, 1947), p. 222.

147.   I. B. Berkson, "The Abortive King-Crane Recommendations— Science or Propaganda?" cited in Esco Foundation, *Palestine, A Study . . .* , pp. 213, note 74, 220.

148.   Antonius, *The Arab Awakening*, p. 296.

149.   Found in I.S.A., *Antonius Archive*, P 384, file 2841. See above, note 87.

150.   Above, p. 244-247, 252-253.

151.   Howard, "An American Experiment . . . ," p. 78.

152.   Report on Syria by Gertrude Bell, on which see Chap. 8, above, pp. 212. and note 70.

153.   F.O. 371/4152/144, report by A. T. Wilson, Acting Civil Commissioner in Mesopotamia, to Secretary of State, India Office, 15 November 1919.

154.   See note 152, above.

155.   F.O. 371/4182/2117, pp. 370-374., W.O. to F.O., 5 September

1919 and Appendix on "Turkish-Arab Pan-Islamic Activities."

156. The subject matter lies outside the scope of the present study.

157. See note 152.

158. F.O. 371/3403/52131, Draft of telegram by Graham to Clayton, 2 April 1918, Secret. Confirmed by Lord Hardinge.

159. See Chap. 7, above, p. 183-185.

160. *D.B.F.P.*, First Series, vol. IV, p. 366, note 255, French to Curzon, 29 August 1919.

161. *Ibid.*, p. 370, no. 258, Meinertzhagen to Curzon, 3 September 1919.

162. F.O. 371/4182/2117, Minutes dated 8 September 1919 on Meinertzhagen's report of 3 September 1919.

163. *D.B.F.P.*, First Series, vol. IV, p. 381, note 272, Meinertzhagen to Curzon, 11 September 1919.

164. *Ibid.*, pp. 382-383, note 276, Meinertzhagen to Curzon, 12 September 1919.

165. See Friedman, *Palestine: A Twice-Promised Land?*, vol. 2, forthcoming.

Appendices

Appendix I
Arabic version of McMahon's letter to the Sharif Hussein, dated 24 October 1915.

Appendix II
Arabic version of McMahon's letter to Hussein, dated 14 December 1915.

Appendix III
Arabic version of McMahon's letter to Hussein, dated 10 March 1916.

Appendix IV
Literal translation (by Keown-Boyd, Cairo?) of the original Arabic version of McMahon's letter to Hussein, dated 24 October 1915.

Appendix V
An Agreement between the Hedjazi Delegation to the Peace Conference and the representatives of the Jewish Community in Palestine on rapprochement and cooperation between the Arab and Jewish communities in Palestine, Paris, 20 April 1919 (a draft).

Reference :—

F.O. 371/20807

CERTIFIED TRUE COPY.

[signature]

Assistant Oriental Secretary.
19.6.37.

Arabic version of [letter from] Sir Arthur McMahon to King Hussein dated 26.10.15 (dispatch No. 13 of 26.10.15)

بسم الله الرحمن الرحيم

الى فرع المجد وحمة المحتديه وسلالة النسل النبوى الكريم النسيب دولة صاحب المقام الرفيع الامير المعظم السيد الشريف بن الشريف بن الشريف امير مكة المكرمة صاحب السترة العليا جعله الله عزا منيعا للاسلام والمسلمين بعونه تعالى امين وهو دولة الامير الجليل الشريف حسين بن على اعلى مقامه

تلقيت بيد الاحتفاء والسرور رقيمكم الكريم المؤرخ بتاريخ ٢٩ شوال ١٣٣٢ وبه من عباراتكم الودية المحضة واجدكم ما اورثني رضاءاً وسرورا

الى منتهاه فانكم استنتجتم من عبارة كتابي السابق اني تحامَلت مسالة الحدود والتخوم بالارتياد والفتور فان ذلك لم يكن القصد من كتابي قط ولكن رأيت حينئذ ان الفرصة لم تكن قد حانت بعد للبحث في ذلك الموضوع بصورة نهائية

ومع ذلك فقد ادركت من كتابكم الاخير انكم تعتبرون هذه المسأله من المسائل الراهنة الحيوية المستعجلة فلذلك فاني قد سرعت في ابلاغ حكومة بريطانيا العظمى بمضمون كتابكم وان يجمال السرور ابلغكم بالنيابة عنها التصريحات الآتية التي لا اشك في انكم تتلقونها منزلة الرضى والقبول

ان ولايتي مرسين واسكندرونه واجزاء من بلاد الشام الواقعة في جهة الغربية لولايات دمشق الشام وحمص وحماة وحلب لا يمكن ان يقال انها عربية محضة وعليه يجب ان تستثنى من الحدود المطلوبة

ومع هذا التعديل وبدون تعرض للمعاهدات المعقودة بيننا وبين بعض رؤساء العرب نجن نقبل تلك الحدود

واما من خصوص الدخالي التي تقرها تلك الحدود حيث بريطانيا العظمى مطلقة التصرف بدون ان تمس مصالح حليفتها فرنسا فاني مفوض من قبل حكومة بريطانيا العظمى ان اقدم المواليف الآتية واجيب على كتابكم بما يأتي

(١) انه مع مراعاة التعديلات المذكورة اعلاه فبريطانيا العظمى

مستعدة لأن تعترف باستقلال العرب وتؤيد ذلك الاستقلال
في جميع الأقاليم الداخلة في الحدود التي يطلبها دولة شريف
مكة .

(٢) أن بريطانيا العظمى تضمن الأماكن المقدسة من كل اعتداء
خارجي وتعترف بوجوب منع التعدي عليها .

(٣) وعندما تسمح الظروف تقدم بريطانيا العظمى العرب
بما تجد وتساعدهم على إيجاد هيئات حاكمة ملائمة لتلك
الأقاليم المختلفة .

(٤) هذا وأن المفروض أن العرب قد قرروا طلب نصائح وإرشادات
بريطانيا العظمى وحدها وأن المستشارين والموظفين الأوروبيين
اللازمين لتشكيل هيئة إدارية قويمة يكونون من الأنكليز .

(٥) أما من خصوص ولايتي بغداد والبصرة فأن العرب
تعترف أن مركز ومصالح بريطانيا العظمى الموطدة هناك تستلزم
اتخاذ تدابير إدارية مخصوصة لوقاية هذه الأقاليم من الاعتداء
الأجنبي وزيادة خير سكانها وحماية مصالحنا الاقتصادية المتبادلة .

وإني مثيق أن هذا التصريح يؤكد لدولتكم بدون أقل
ارتياب ميل بريطانيا العظمى نحو غالب أصهار العرب وتشريح
بعقد حلفة دائمة ثابتة معهم ويكون من نتائجها المستعجلة
طرد الأتراك من بلاد العرب وتحرير الشعوب العربية من نير
الأتراك الذي أثقل كاهلهم السنين الطوال .

ولقد اقتصرت في كتابي هذا على المسائل الحيوية ذات
الأهمية الكبرى وأن كان هناك مسائل في خطاباتكم
لم تذكر هنا فسنعود الى البحث فيها في وقت مناسب
في المستقبل .

ولقد تلقيت بمزيد السرور والرضى خبر وصول الكسوة
الشريفة وما جرى من الصدقات بالسلامة وانزا بفضل
ارشاداتكم السامية وتدابيركم الحكمة قد انزلت الى البر بلد
تعب   ولأصدر نجاً عن الأخطار والمصاعب التي ستنشرها
هذه الحرب المحزنة   ونرجو الحق سبحانه وتعالى أن يعجل
بالصلح الدائم والحرية لأهل العالم

اني ارسل   خطابي هذا مع رسولكم النبيل الأمين الشيخ
حمود بن عارف بن   حريفان وسيعرض على سماعكم

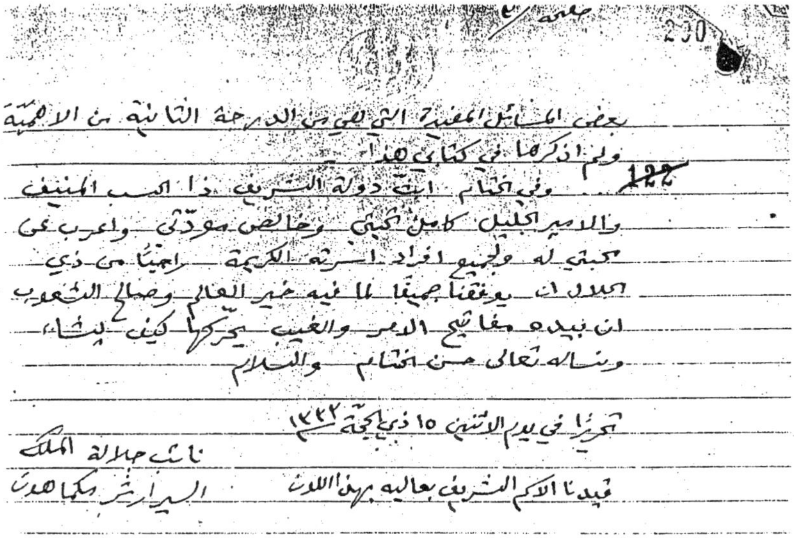

بعض المسائل المفيدة التي هي من الدرجة الثانية من الاهمية
ولم اذكرها في كتابي هذا
وفي الختام ابث دولة الشريف ذا الحسب المنيف
والامير الجليل كامل حبي وخالص مودتي واعرب عن
حبي له ولجميع افراد اسرته الكريمة راجيا من ذي
الجلال ان يوفقنا جميعا لما فيه خير العالم وصالح الشعوب
ان بيده مفاتيح الامر والغيب يحركها كيف يشاء
ونسأله تعالى حسن الختام والسلام

تحريرا في يوم الاثنين ١٥ ذي الحجة ١٣٣٣

نائب جلالة الملك
السير ارثر مكماهون

قيدنا الاكرم الشريف بعالية بهين اللاث

لنا والذين هم يعملون على ضرر مصالحنا الحربية البحرية في
البحر الاحمر وعليه نرى انه من الضروري ان ناخذ التدابير
الفعالة ضدهم ولكننا قد اصدرنا الاوامر القطعيه
انه يجب على جميع بوارجنا ان تفرق بين عساكر
الاتراك الذين يبدون بالعداء وبين العرب الابرياء الذين
يسكنون تلك الجزائر لاننا لا نقابل العرب اجمع الا
بكل عاطفة ودية
وقد ابلغنا دولتكم ذلك حتى تكونوا على بينة من الامر اذا
بلغكم خبرا مكذوبا عن الاسباب التي تضطرنا الى اي عمل من
هذا القبيل وقد بلغنا اشاعات مؤداها ان اعدائنا
الالداء باذلون جهدهم في اكمال السفن ليبثوا بها الالغام
في البحر الاحمر ولالحاق الاضرار بمصالحنا في ذلك البحر وانا
نرجوكم سرعة اخبارنا اذا تحقق ذلك لديكم
وقد بلغنا ان ابن الرشيد قد باع للاتراك عددا عظيما
من الجمال وقد ارسلت الى دمشق الشام ونؤمل ان تستعملوا
كلما لكم من التاثير عليه حتى يكف عن ذلك واذا ما صمم على
ما هو عليه امكنكم عمل الترتيب مع العربان الساكنين بينه وبين
سوريا ان يقبضوا على الجمال حال سيرها ولا شك ان في
ذلك صالح لمصلحتنا المتبادلة
وقد يسرني ان ابلغ دولتكم ان العربان الذين ضلوا السبيل
تحت قيادة السيد احمد السنوسي وهم الذين اصبحوا ضحية
دسائس الالمان والاتراك قد ابتدأوا يعرفون خطاهم
ولهم ياتون الينا وحدانا وجماعات يطلبون العفو عنهم والتودد
اليهم وقد والحمد لله هزمنا القوات التي جمعها هؤلاء
الدساسون ضدنا وقد اخذت العرب تبصر الغش والخديعه
التي حاقت بهم
وان لسقوط ارضروم من يد الاتراك وكثرة انهزاماتهم
في بلاد القوقاس تاثير عظيم وهو في مصلحتنا المتبادلة
وخطوة عظيمة في سبيل الامر الذي نعمل له واياكم . ونسال الله عز
وجل ان يكلل مساعيكم بتاج النجاح والفلاح وان يمهد لكم في
كامل اعمالكم احسن السبل والمناهج . وفي الختام اقدم لدولتكم
ولكامل افراد اسرتكم الشريفه عظيم الاحترامات وكامل ضروب
المودة والاخلاص مع المحبة التي لا يزعزعها كر العصور ومرور الايام

كتبه المخلص
السر ارثر هنري مكماهون
نائب جلالة الملك بمصر

تحريرا في ٦ جمادى الاولى ١٣٣٤
الموافق ١٠ مارث ١٩١٦

Appendix 2

F.O. 371/20807
CERTIFIED TRUE COPY.
[signature]
Assistant Oriental Secretary
19.6.37.

204

(14)

10.

*Arabic [...] letter from Sir Arthur
McMahon to King Hussein dated 10.3.16
(Despatch No. 54 of 13.3.16)*

بسم الله الرحمن الرحيم

الى ساحة ذلك المقام الرفيع ذي اسمى الطاهر والنسب
الفاخر قبلة الاسلام والمسلمين معدن الشرف وطيب
المحتد سلالة مهبط الوحي المجيد الشريف بن الشريف
صاحب الدولة السيد الشريف حسين بن علي امير مكة
المعظم زاده الله رفعة وعلوا امين

بعد ما يليق بمقام الامير العظيم من التبجيل والاحترام
وتقديم خالص التحية والسلام وشرح عوامل الالفة
وحسن النظام والمودة الممزوجة بالمحبة القلبية ــ ارفع
الى دولة الامير المعظم اننا تلقينا رقيمكم المؤرخ ١٤ ربيع
الآخر ١٣٣٤ من يد رسولكم الامين وقد سرنا الوقوف منه على
التدابير الفعلية التي تنوونها وانا لموافقة في الاحوال
كافة . وان حكومة جلالة ملك بريطانيا العظمى تصادق
عليها وقد يسرني ان اخبركم بان حكومة جلالة الملك
صادقت على جميع مطالبكم وان كل شيء رغبتم الاسراع فيه
وفي ارساله فهو مرسل مع رسولكم حامل هذا والاشياء
الباقية تتحضر بكل سرعة ممكنة وتبقى في بورتسودان فمتى
اتاكم الجس ابتداء الحركة وابلغنا اياها بصورة رسمية (كما
ذكرتم) وبالمواقع التي يقتضى عقبل البر والوسائط التي
تكونوا حاملين الوثائق بتسليمها اياها

ان كل التعليمات التي وردت في مذكرتكم قد اعطيناها معاونا
ببورتسودان وهو سيرعل حسب رغبتكم ـ وقد عملت بجميع
والتجربة بلدت الادرية لادسال رسولكم حامل خطابكم الاخير الى
جدة حتى يؤدي مأموريته التي نسأل الله ان يكللها بالنجاح
وحسن النتائج وسيعود الى بورتسودان وبعدها يبلغكم
بحراسة الله ليقف على مساعي دولتكم نشيطة تحله
وننتهز الفرصة لنوضح لدولتكم في خطابنا هذا ما بقيا
لم يكن واضحا لديكم او ما عساه ينتج سوء تفاهم الا وهو
انه يوجد بعض المراكز او النقط العسكرية فيها بعض العساكر
التركية على سواحل بلاد العرب يقال انهم يجاهرون بالعداء

في الوقت نفسه نرى من الضروري جدًا ان تبذلوا جهودكم دائما

في جمع كلمة الشعوب العربيه الى غايتنا المشتركة وان تقنعوهم

على ان لا يمتازوا بين المساعدة الى اعدائنا باي وجه كان ، فانه

على نجاح هذه المجهودات وعلى التدابير الفعليه التي يمكن للعرب

ان ينفذوها لاسعاف غرضنا عندما يجيئ وقت العمل تتوقف

قوة الاتفاق بيننا وثباته .

وفي هذه الاحوال فان حكمة بريطانيا العظمى تدعوني

لي ان ابلّغ دولتكم ان تكونوا على ثقة من ان بريطانيا

العظمى لا تنوي ابرام اي صلح كان الا اذا كان من ضمن

شروطه الاساسية حرية الشعوب العربية وخلاصها من

سلطة الالمان والاتراك .

هذا وعربون على صدق نيتنا ولاجل مساعدتكم في

مجهوداتكم في غايتنا المشتركة فاني مرسل مع رسولكم مبلغ

عشرين الف جنيه .

واقدم في اختام عاطر القلبات القلبية وخالص التسليمات

الودية مع مراسم الاجلال والتعظيم المشمولين بروابط

الالفة والمحبة الصرفة لمقام دولتكم السامي ورجائي ان

استرّكم المكرمة مع فائق الاحترام .

المخلص   حررًا في ٨ صفر ١٣٣٣

نائب جلالة الملك حسن

السيد عبد الحميد مكماهون

FO 686/42

Literal Translation of original Arabic letter sent by

Sir H. McMahon to King Husein. ndu copy

at ... by C.P. ...

In the name of God, the Merciful, the Compassionate.

To the branch of Mohamed's tree, the descendent of
Prophetic origin, His Highness owner of the Sublime Post; the
illustrious Emir; Es-Sayed El Sherif son of a Sherif, Emir
of Holy Mecca, owner of the high throne; May God make him a
strong amulet to Islam and Moslems by the help of God Amen !
His Excellency the revered Emir, El-Sherif Husein ibn Ali;
may Allah make his post still higher.

With the hand of joy and pleasure I received your
esteemed letter dated the (26th Shawal 1333 - 6th September
1915) in which your pure, friendly expressions and your
loyalty gave me satisfaction and gladness.

I regret that you have concluded from the expressions in my former letter that I faced the question of boundaries and limits with hesitation and coldness.   That was not
the object of my letter at all.   But I considered then that
the opportunity had not yet arrived for discussion on that
subject in a definite manner.   However I understand from
your last letter that you consider that this is one of the
questions which are important, vital and urgent.   Therefore
I hastened to communicate to the Government of Great Britain
the contents of your letter, and with great pleasure I convey to you on their behalf the following declarations which
I do not doubt you will receive with satisfaction and
acceptance.

The two "vilayets" of Mersina and Alexandretta
and the parts of the country of "Esh-Sham" (Damascus) situat-
ed in the Western directions of the "Vilayets" of Damascus,
Homs, Hamah and Aleppo cannot be said to be purely Arab.
Therefore they must be excluded from the claimed boundaries.

/With

Appendix 4

No. 2.

(2).

With this modification and without interfering with
treaties concluded between us and some Arab Chiefs, we accept
those boundaries.

As for the districts which are included within those
boundaries, where Great Britain gave freedom of action without touching the interests of her Ally, France, I am authorized by the Government of Great Britain to offer the following covenants and to answer your letter with what follows:-

(1).   Taking into consideration the modifications above
mentioned, Great Britain is prepared to acknowledge the
independence of the Arabs and to support that independence
in all the districts entering within the boundaries which
His Highness the Sherif of Mecca will ask for.

(2).   Great Britain will guarantee the holy places against
any outside aggression and admits the necessity of preventing
any aggression against them.

(3).   When circumstances admit Great Britain will support
the Arabs with her counsels, and help them to organize
governing administrations to suit those various districts.

(4).   It is understood that the Arabs have decided upon
asking for the counsels and guidings of Great Britain alone,
and that the advisers and European officials required to
organize a strong and honest government will be British.

(5).   With regard to the two vilayets of Baghdad and Bass-
orah, the Arabs admit that the strong situation and interests
of Great Britain there, necessitate the adoption of special
administrative arrangements to protect these districts
against the aggression of Foreigners, and to increase the
welfare of the inhabitants and to defend their mutual econom-
ical interests; and I am confident that this declaration will

/assure

Appendix 4

No.2.

(3).

assure Your Excellency without the least doubt, of the
sympathy of Great Britain towards the wishes of her friends
the Arabs, and we will finish by concluding with them a
permanent and fixed treaty, the immediate results of which
will be to drive the Turks out of the country of the Arabs,
and to liberate the Arab peoples from the yoke of the Turks
which has been heavy on their shoulders for long years.

I have confined this letter to the vital questions
of great importance.   If there were other questions in your
letters, not mentioned here, we will return to discuss them
at a suitable date in future.

15th Zil Hijjah, 1333.
24th October, 1915.

McQ.

Appendix 4

A153/149 (1)

Le 20 avril 1919 se sont réuni 72 Avenue du bois de Boulogne, à la résidence de Son Altesse l'Emir Faiçal MM. David Yellin, M. Dizengoff et Aouni Abdul Hadi effendi pour délibérer sur les relations entre la population arabe et juive en Palestine. Après un échange de vues il a été décidé à l'unanimité de fonder en Palestine un comité arabo-juif qui aura pour but:

1° Rapprochement et entente entre les deux éléments de la population, en vue du développement futur du pays au point de vue politique et économique.

2° Empêcher toute manifestation hostile de la part d'un élément de la population envers l'autre.

3° Élaborer un Status définitif établissant les droits et les devoirs de tous les groupes ethniques habitant la Palestine en ce qui concerne l'organisation administrative future du pays et tous les autres côtés de la vie sociale commune.

Le comité central aura à instituer des comités régionaux dans tous les centres de la Palestine: dans le but mentionné plus haut.

Le comité central aura son siège à Jérusalem et sera composé de douze membres dont six arabes et six juifs. Les premiers seront nommé par Abdul Hadi effendi et ses amis; les seconds seront les suivants:

A153/149

Appendix 5

Index

on the Jewish National
Home, lxvii
Frankfurter, Professor Felix, 227,
254, 263
    and the King-Crane
    Commission
        and Crane, 250
        and Colonel House, 250
        cable to Brandeis on
        instructions given to
        King and Crane to
        exclude Palestine from
        their inquiry (28 March
        1919), 250
    on Feisal letter of 3 March
    1919, 229
        distribution of letter,
        229, 233
        statement to Shaw
        Commission on the
        signing of the letter, 233
        wrote to Brandeis on
        Feisal letter of 3 March,
        229
French Apostolic Missionary, 9
French, Colonel C.
    Feisal's dilemma described,
    270
    report of Feisal's appearance
    before the King-Crane
    Commission (3 July 1919), 269
Friedenwald, Harry, 263
Friedman, Isaiah, 1

Gabriel, Sir Vivian
    claimed that Kitchener
    "would not have admitted the
    exclusion of Palestine," xliii
    no foundation for Gabriel's
    contention, xliii

Ganem, Chekri
    editor of the Arabic
    newspaper *Al-Mustakbal*, 55
Garland, Major H. G.,
    Acting Director of the Arab
    Bureau, 43
Gaza, 16
German Consul in Beirut *(see
Mutius)*
German records
    belie al-Faruqi's claim of
    Young Arab influence and
    revolutionary fervor among
    the population, xxv
Gibb, H. A. R., 3, 6
Gout, Jean
    with the *sous-direction
    d'Asie*, Quai d'Orsay
    and the Inter-Allied
    Agreement of 1916, 127
Gowers, E. A., 110
Grafftey-Smith, Sir Laurence, 43,
45
    Acting Consul-General,
    Alexandria, 42
Graham, Sir Ronald, 88, 159
    on Feisal's negotiations with
    the Turks, 280
Graves, Philip, 13
    on Arabs, xxxiv
        Arab support during the
        War, 181
Grey, Sir Edward, xx, xxiv, xxvii,
xxx, xlii, lxv, lxvi, 14, 15, 16, 24,
33, 51, 56, 57, 59, 92, 99, 125, 141
    and Zionism , 98-100
    cable to McMahon (20
    October 1915), 35
    dismissed McMahon, 51
    proposition to Paul Cambon